THE ALTERNATIVE
CULTURE

THE ALTERNATIVE CULTURE

Socialist Labor in Imperial Germany

Vernon L. Lidtke

New York   Oxford
OXFORD UNIVERSITY PRESS
1985

OXFORD UNIVERSITY PRESS
Oxford   London   New York   Toronto
Delhi Bombay   Calcutta   Madras   Karachi
Kuala Lumpur   Singapore   Hong Kong   Tokyo
Nairobi   Dar es Salaam   Cape Town
Melbourne   Auckland

and associated companies in
Beirut   Berlin   Ibadan   Mexico City   Nicosia

Published by OXFORD UNIVERSITY PRESS, Inc., 200 MADISON AVENUE
NEW YORK, NEW YORK 10016

Library of Congress Cataloging in Publication Data

Lidtke, Vernon L.
The alternative culture.

Bibliography: p.
Includes index.
1.   Socialism—Germany—History.   2.   Labor and laboring
classes—Germany—Political activity—History.   I.   Title.
HX279.L64   1985   322'.2'0943   84-7154
ISBN 0-19-503507-0

Printing (last digit):   9 8 7 6 5 4 3 2 1

Printed in the United States of America

To My Mother
Aganeta Lidtke

Contents

Acknowledgments

This book is the outcome of a sustained endeavor to penetrate the inner nature of the social-cultural milieu of the Social Democratic labor movement and to comprehend that milieu in its relationship to other segments of German society. In pursuit of these goals I have been led to investigations in a wide variety of subject areas, all made possible by the generous support of numerous institutions and colleagues. I take great pleasure in expressing my gratitude at this time. The research has been supported by grants from the National Endowment for the Humanities, the Social Science Research Council, the Historische Kommission zu Berlin, and the Davis Center for Historical Studies at Princeton University. The Johns Hopkins University has supported my research with both funds and sabbatical leave, while colleagues and students in the Department of History have created the kind of critical and stimulating environment that is always of benefit to scholarly inquiry. To Betty Whildin and the departmental secretaries I express my thanks for typing the manuscript.

Finding the diverse and widely scattered source material for this book has been facilitated not only by the use of large libraries, notably the Library of Congress and the Bayerische Staatsbibliothek in Munich, but also by several specialized collections with both published and archival materials. In particular, my thanks go to the following: the Institut für deutsche und ausländische Arbeiterliteratur, Dortmund, and to its founder, the late Fritz Hüser; the Arbeiterliedarchiv of the Deutsche Akademie der Künste zu Berlin (DDR), and in particular to Inge Lammel, who assisted my research on political songs; the Archiv der sozialen Demokratie, Bonn, and to its director, Werner Krause, who has helped on numerous occasions; the Stadtbibliothek in Mönchengladbach (with the holdings of the former Volksverein für das katholische Deutschland); the Stein Sammlung in the Universitätsbibliothek der Freien Universität in Berlin; the Archiv und Bibliothek of the Deutscher Gewerkschaftsbund, Düsseldorf; the Zentralbibliothek der Gewerkschaften, Berlin (DDR); and, finally, one of the most important, the Internationaal Instituut voor Sociale Geschiedenis, Amsterdam.

To the many colleagues, students, and friends who offered assistance and counsel I express my deep gratitude: to Mack Walker, Peter Gay, Michael Neufeld, and Gary Steenson, who read parts or all of the manuscript in various stages of preparation; to Dieter Dowe of the Institut für Sozialgeschichte, Bonn, for always sharing with me his considerable knowledge of sources; to Stanley Pierson, Roger Chickering, Robert Berdahl, and Thomas Brady for critical comments and discussions during a fruitful year at the University of Oregon; to Nancy Lane and Henry Krawitz of Oxford University Press for being imaginative and skillful editors; and to William Bowman for his scrupulous attention to the manuscript in its final stages. The fifth chapter of this book initially appeared in German in a slightly different version ("Lieder der deutschen Arbeiterbewegung, 1864–1914," *Geschichte und Gesellschaft* 5 [1979]) and is included here with permission of the publishers. Finally, to my wife, Doris, a word of special appreciation.

Baltimore, Md.   V.L.L.
September 1984

THE ALTERNATIVE
CULTURE

I

Introduction: The Social-Cultural Milieu of the German Labor Movement

This is a study of the social-cultural milieu of the Social Democratic labor movement in the era between the 1860s and the outbreak of the First World War. It is an attempt to describe and interpret those aspects that tended to create within the Social Democratic labor movement an alternative culture in which organized workers could fulfill their needs for companionship, sociability, recreation, learning, and aesthetic satisfaction. Although the book does not focus on the organizations of the Social Democratic party and free trade unions themselves, they constitute the larger and vital framework for the endeavors discussed in the following chapters. The role of Social Democracy as a political party within the Imperial, state, and municipal systems has been the subject of innumerable inquiries, and that history is included here only insofar as it is essential for explicating the other activities in the world of the socialist labor movement. The same is true of the free trade unions whose growth after 1891 and predilection for amalgamation and centralization created a reasonably stable organizational core around which organized workers could establish other types of voluntary associations. A special social-cultural milieu emerged, first chiefly around the socialist-oriented political organizations of the 1860s and 1870s. Trade unions, small and struggling, played a minor role in shaping that environment until the mid-1890s, when they became increasingly important. In the first decade after the turn of the century unions influenced to a large degree the quality of the labor-movement milieu; and, moreover, it was often their members who furthered the activities of the affiliated associations and made up a large part of their followers.

How the Social Democratic labor movement and its social-cultural milieu is to be interpreted is an issue of considerable complexity. Since the publication in 1963 of Guenther Roth's work, it has become almost commonplace for scholars in the West to conceive of the Social Democratic movement as a "subculture," distinct from the dominant culture of Imperial Germany.[1] This interpretation has become so widespread that it is often assumed without question that it explains nearly every aspect of the German labor movement. But this needs to be brought under scrutiny.[2] Misconceptions and even distortions have resulted from the widespread application of the subculture concept to the labor movement. The advantage of this concept—its stress on separation, on deviations from dominant cultural norms—has also been the cause of some misleading implications. The uncritical use creates the impression that the cleavage between the Social Democratic labor movement and the "dominant culture" was all-pervasive and affected everything undertaken by the constituency of the labor movement. In reality, the relationship was very complex and the border lines between the two realms were at some points scarcely discernible. To avoid what seems to me to be serious misconceptions and untested assumptions, I have used terms that suggest more readily the complexities and the positive as well as the negative aspects in the relationship between the labor movement and the rest of German society.[3]

One of the confusions in the literature revolves around the question of what groups are thought to have made up the constituency of the "Social Democratic subculture." This difficulty appears in Roth's book itself. He explicitly argues that the trade unions were not an integral part of the subculture. He does not explain precisely where the subculture border is to be drawn, but asserts that the free trade unions were an "intermediate" group between the Social Democratic party and the "dominant system."[4] If the language throughout the book were consistent with this position, the confusion would be held to a minimum. But that is not the case. He frequently interchanges "labor movement" and "Social Democracy" or "Social Democratic party" without explaining precisely what he includes under "labor movement." He appears, nonetheless, to use "labor movement" in its conventional meaning, namely, as a term that includes both the Social Democratic party and the free trade unions. With this usage he blurs what he initially intended to separate—the realms of the party and the unions.[5] The shift in language is crucial because it gives rise to a serious self-contradiction within Roth's book. His conscious intention was to exclude the trade unions from the Social Democratic subculture because he recognized that he could not simultaneously include them and also make an argument for the internal ideological cohesion of the subculture. That is, the emphasis he places on Marxism and its role in the subculture is tenable only if the focus is on the party and not also on the trade unions. But when Roth refers frequently to the "labor movement," he implicitly includes the trade unions and their whole constituency within the subculture. It is not surprising therefore that subsequent writers have assumed that Roth intended to include the trade unions in his conception of the subculture.[6]

The decision to exclude the trade unions from the definition of the subculture served the analytical needs of a sociological theory, but distorted historical reality. By the end of the nineteenth century, in nearly every locality with an organized labor movement, the Social Democratic party and the free trade unions collaborated closely in many activities. Each had its own realm, to be sure, but their common undertakings were substantial.[7] In instances of close cooperation it is difficult, if not impossible, to differentiate party tendencies from those of the unions. It should be stressed as well that there was considerable overlap in the membership of the two organizations. If the two constituencies had been clearly separate, isolating the unions from the Social Democratic subculture would be more convincing. The contrary is more the case. It has been argued persuasively that the trade unions came to dominate the party after about 1906.[8] In view of this, and the fact that by the same time the ratio of trade union to party members was four to one, it is even more difficult to see how unionists can legitimately be excluded from a treatment of what is called a Social Democratic subculture. One can more justifiably argue that in the decade immediately preceding the First World War that it was the free trade unions, more than the Social Democratic party, that influenced the life of the labor movement. To exclude the trade unions is an arbitrary separation that cannot be demonstrated empirically.

The analytical advantages of the concept of subculture seem to me to be outweighed by the erroneous and misleading assumptions associated with its application to the socialist labor movement. A broader language seems to be more suitable, and for that reason the terms *social-cultural milieu* and *labor movement culture* have been employed in this study. They do not imply a tightly knit system or a cohesive, self-consistent ideological posture. They are broader and allow more easily for the blurred and fluctuating borders between the labor movement and the rest of German society.[9] This book attempts to analyze in some detail the various currents that can be found in the social-cultural milieu of the socialist labor movement. It argues, implicitly, that the milieu was held together by a number of interacting elements—occupational identification, class awareness, secular rituals, symbolisms, the hostility of nonsocialist German society, a broad and diffuse sense of ideology, to name only the most important—no one of which in itself would have achieved that end.

One other important aspect of Roth's interpretation, the idea of negative integration, must be discussed critically. As applied to Social Democracy in Imperial Germany the concept of negative integration is guilty, paradoxically, of two contrary distortions: It underestimates the degree to which various elements of the socialist labor movement were in fact positively integrated into the larger society and, on the other hand, it dismisses too easily the seriousness of the labor movement as a destabilizing force. The first error resulted essentially from a definitional preference that disregards historical reality. Roth simply cut out of his definition of the Social Democratic subculture the largest organizational foundation for reformist and non-Marxist elements. The second error resulted from certain presuppositions inherent in integrationist sociological theory and a willingness to overlook the implications of the upheaval at the end of the First World War. This requires closer scrutiny.

The integrationist model of society assumes a functional interworking of the major social elements even when a measure of conflict is evident.[10] This approach looks for the mechanisms that guide this interworking. Since its emphasis is on the functional role of segments of society in relation to the whole, it is inclined to view conflict as minimal as long as the system appears to work and hold together. When applied to the labor movement in Imperial Germany the integrationist model directs attention to the system—political, economic, and social—as a functioning whole and encourages the investigator to conclude that the parts were not in fundamental conflict. This tendency meshed with the inclination of various historians to look back on the socialist labor movement in Imperial Germany and to argue that since no revolutionary action took place prior to the First World War, none was intended.

Sweeping conclusions of this kind were encouraged, moreover, by the general disenchantment that had been widespread among radicals of many kinds, not the least of whom were the Leninists. In actuality the socialist labor movement was a genuine threat to the Imperial system, though not necessarily through overt revolutionary political action. The assumption that the kaiser's government could be undermined or destroyed only by means of "revolutionary" action overlooks the fact that movements can threaten existing systems without calling their followers into the streets. If contemporaries in Imperial Germany were sometimes misled and took Social Democratic rhetoric at face value, historians have made the opposite error by overlooking the extent to which the socialist movement embodied dimensions that were truly subversive. The question of whether or not the labor movement undermined or helped stabilize the Imperial system cannot be answered simply by noting that the empire coped successfully with threats to its existence, at least until 1918. Seldom, if ever, has it been the case that a revolutionary movement has created serious upheaval by its own power. German Social Democracy was no exception, but the labor movement as a whole frequently disrupted existing arrangements and always bore within itself the potential to create havoc, if not actually to overthrow the *Kaiserreich*. To be sure, the tradition of intransigent parliamentary opposition, combined with the frequent use of a revolutionary vocabulary, created an image of a party that could at any time mobilize its cadres for a decisive onslaught against the whole order. By its repeated discussions of revolution and its vigorous propaganda against capitalism and the *Kaiserreich,* the German socialist movement set high standards of radical behavior for itself. Since these standards were drawn in large part from Marxist as well as other socialist theories and less from practical experience in rebellious activity, Social Democrats did not bother to draft insurrectionist strategies or try to instigate popular uprisings. In the insurrectionist sense, they were not a direct threat to the system, but to insist that only a direct physical assault on the ruling system would constitute a genuine danger is too narrow.

The threat of the socialist movement to the social-political order of Imperial Germany came in other ways. These were not as spectacular as conspiracies and insurrections, but they were no less real. The socialist labor movement presented German society with a radical alternative to existing norms and arrangements. This alternative may be called radical not because it proposed to overturn the *Kaiserreich* in one bold stroke, but because it embodied in its principles a conception of production, social relations, and political institutions that rejected existing structures, practices, and values at almost every point. It has been popular among historians, almost regardless of their other differences, to stress the fact that the party failed to implement its principles. But this too is an oversimplification. The movement's behavior did in fact approximate many of its principles, so much so that the conservative elements of German society were not mistaken when they perceived Social Democracy as a threat to their way of life and to their social control. To be sure, the Social Democratic alternative, despite a strong Marxist theoretical strand, did not present a conception of society that was complete in all details. It still had many loose ends. But if it seemed to be lacking in certain respects, it was still a credible alternative and, no matter how it might be interpreted, it stood opposed to the basic assumptions of the existing order and to the controlling elites. Even in its most moderate form, as embodied in the vision of reformists and revisionists, the socialist alternative would have required substantial political and economic modifications in Germany before it could be realized. The centers of power would have been shifted markedly. A wide gulf lay between the established political, economic, and cultural institutions of Imperial Germany and all versions of the alternate socialist model. This point is often overlooked by historians of Social Democracy because in intramovement debates radicals frequently claimed, for polemical and tactical reasons, that those who disagreed with them—moderates, centrists, reformists—were implicitly lending full support to the capitalist, imperialist order. Such charges need to be recognized as polemical and we are under no obligation to accept at face value the claims of the left, center, or right of the party as reliable statements about the true condition of the movement.

The danger lay not only in the principles of the radical alternative but in the additional fact that support for that alternative grew dramatically from the 1870s to 1914. The party's electoral constituency, as measured in Reichstag elections, expanded from 311,961 votes in 1881 to 4,250,399 in 1912, or from 6.1 to 34.7 percent of the total. Membership in the party rose from 384,327 in 1905 to 1,085,905 in 1914. The free trade unions, with no more than 223,530 members in 1893 (227,659 in 1891), could boast of 2,548,763 by 1913.[11] There was reason to believe that both figures would continue to grow, though that depended on a number of unpredictable factors. But it was clear that neither the party nor the unions had yet succeeded in attracting all workers, though the party had drawn increasing numbers of nonworkers to the polls. On the assumption that the party and the trade unions would continue to expand, even if at a slower rate, it seemed likely, to friend and foe alike, that at some time in the future the socialist alternative would become the German reality. While the threat of socialist insurrectionary violence might be more frightening to middle-class Germans than the prospect of a gradual and peaceful socialist takeover, even the slightest possibility of the latter was intensely repugnant to them.

The danger of the socialist labor movement as perceived by non-socialist Germans was also heightened by the fact that the Social Democratic alternative could be seen to affect every aspect of life—work, marriage, family, education, religion, recreation, etc.—as indeed it did in the minds of its most vigorous advocates. In one sense the labor movement's alternative was moving gradually from the realm of ideas to take on concrete form as the nineteenth century closed. A process was under way whereby the socialist labor movement was creating a world of its own within the larger context of Imperial German society. The term *process* must be stressed here because it would be enormously misleading to imply that the world of the Social Democratic labor movement was a fixed entity or that it ever reached a static stage. It is nonetheless possible to try to discern salient features, trends, and directions embedded in the social-cultural milieu of the movement, some of which, to be sure, closely resembled the characteristics and institutions of the rest of German society. But even when they did so, the socialist movement's organizations were understood to stand for a different kind of society. The fact that nonsocialist Germans were very much aware that the labor movement was creating a world of its own, that it had a special social-cultural milieu, lent credence to the fear that Social Democracy represented a profound danger to nearly every aspect of life in Imperial Germany.[12] All of these threatening realities tend to be discounted by interpretations that rest on integrationist sociology or use the "negative integration" formula.

As a second critical task, the nature of Imperial German society needs to be analyzed more closely because the role of the labor movement and the meaning of its social-cultural milieu were affected, positively and negatively, by their location within the authoritarian social and political system. The acceptance by historians of the labor movement of an integrationist model of society has built into the literature a set of assumptions about Imperial Germany that are only partially justified. The scholarship itself has often been of high quality, but reliance on the integrationist model has done as much to confuse as to clarify the many dimensions of the labor movement in Imperial German society. If one begins with an integrationist model, explicitly or implicitly, then one ought to define the nature of the larger society into which the integration is to take place. On this matter the historical literature falters, and this is not surprising. At the heart of the matter is the untested assumption, frequently only implicit in the use of the integrationist model, that German society between 1871 and 1914 was characterized by features that were fundamentally, if not perfectly, coherent.

This assumption about the fundamental coherence of Imperial society is highly questionable[13] and has led at times to an oversimplified view of the various relationships of the social-cultural milieu of the labor movement within the larger environment. It distorts historical reality by reducing the numerous social and cultural divisions of Imperial Germany to a simple polarity between an essentially coherent "dominant culture" on the one side and an excluded Social Democratic "subculture" on the other. Perhaps most oversimplifications contain a kernel of truth, and this one is no exception. It is true and beyond dispute that a fundamental conflict took place between the Social Democratic movement and the ruling political system of Imperial Germany. It is also true that this political conflict coincided to a considerable degree with tension in the economic sphere between dependent wage earners and employers and other propertied groups in the society. These conflicts were real and deep, but this does not justify the implication that conflict between wage earners and employers in the economic realm overlapped perfectly with the conflict between the Social Democratic party and the Imperial political system. Nor does it warrant the assumption that the opponents of Social Democracy constituted a unified amalgamation of intellectual, political, social, and economic groups and forces that can be identified as a coherent dominant culture.[14] It is not my contention that all scholars who use an integrationist model consciously hold these misconceptions about Imperial Germany, but that such oversimplifications are embedded in the conceptualization and have led historians to overlook significant complexities and contradictions within what has been called the dominant culture. An alternative conception of Imperial German society is needed.

An interpretive conception of Imperial German society can be persuasive and usable only if it offers a way of encompassing multiple levels of both cultural diversity and social conflict. Such a conception must also recognize that there were some striking weaknesses in the political and social system, weaknesses that raise questions about any assumption of a strong and confident dominant culture.[15] This is not to say that the machinery of control—primarily police and military—was unsteady, though it should be stressed that politically the strongest parts of the machinery were the long-standing institutions of the individual states, especially Prussia, and not of the Reich as a whole. The continued significance of local and state political institutions highlights the fact that at the founding of the Reich Germany had little of what can be called a national political culture. The weakness of a German national political culture thus went hand in hand with the reality and strength of numerous local and regional cultures, which only gradually gave ground to the nationalizing impulses that grew increasingly powerful after the turn of the century.

In place of a language that implies social cohesion, integration, and the existence of a strong national political culture in Imperial Germany, the conception used here seeks to find a more balanced and historically accurate approach. This view may be summarized in its three basic notions: segmentation, conflict, and coercion.[16] It emphasizes that Imperial German society was far more of an agglomeration of separate segments than an integrated system with a clearly defined dominant culture. The segments of German society may be differentiated and defined along lines that are essentially horizontal (for example, classes and strata) or vertical (for example, confessional and regional differences). It is also important to note that the segments were not equal in size, political power, economic resources, or in general cultural and educational attainments.

Antagonism, real or potential, more than harmony characterized the relationships between most of the segments, although such relationships were not static but fluctuating. This can be illustrated briefly by reference to the social groups in the industrializing Ruhr after the 1870s. Native German Catholics in the Ruhr were in constant conflict with Social Democracy, but that did not alter the fact that they also lived in a condition of variable tensions with the Protestant-dominated Prussian state. The influx into the Ruhr of Polish Catholic workers from the eastern areas, especially after the 1880s, added another social-cultural segment that found itself in antagonistic relationships not only with officials of the Prussian state, but also with socialist-oriented labor organizations and, more interesting, with most of the institutions of the native German Catholic population.[17]

The most powerful segment of German society was constituted of those groups closest in outlook and social standing to the Prussian monarchy and the institutions it controlled directly. These groups were dominant politically, to a large extent economically, and, whether aristocratic estate owners, military officers, civil servants, or successful entrepreneurs, they shared many of the same values, practices, and aspirations. In that sense they represented a dominant political culture in Prussia—Protestant, authoritarian, militarist, and loyal to Prussia and Germany—but not necessarily for all of Germany. Because of Prussia's overwhelming political and economic position within the Reich, they too exercised a certain influence throughout the national state, but that influence should not be overestimated. For example, their counterparts around the ruling Wittelsbachs in Bavaria may have exerted less political and economic influence throughout the Reich, but at the same time Prussian elites could not assume to prescribe a complete value system for Catholic Bavarians. The tension between Bavarian and Prussian ruling circles remained muted, for the most part, but that did not mean that it was any less significant as an obstacle to the formation of a dominant culture on the national level.

The segmentation of German society could be explored at great length. This discussion is designed only to illustrate some basic characteristics of segmentation and conflict that are incompatible with the assumptions and implications of an integrationist model of society. Although it should not be denied that large numbers of Germans shared many of the same values and modes of behavior, it is also important to stress that the degree of commonality was insufficient to hold all of the pieces together. Coercion and the threat of coercion, whether physical or legal, played an essential role in maintaining stability on the surface. The possibility of coercion so pervaded Germany, especially in the North, that the threat alone was sufficient to instill cautiousness in those who might wish to rebel against the system. In part this pattern accounts for the general reluctance of most Social Democrats to take risks that would arouse the fury of those in control of the authoritarian institutions and possibly endanger the life of the labor movement. Adapting to coercion, that is, finding ways to achieve limited goals without inciting an open physical confrontation with the administrators of legal compulsion, became a way of life for every group or movement that at one time or another believed in ideas or behaved in ways unacceptable to officials of the authoritarian state. Early in the century liberals confronted the challenge of finding ways to respond to coercion, while Catholics ran the coercive gauntlet after the founding of the Reich. Social Democrats and workers responded in various ways to coercion not only by adapting peacefully, but at times with physical violence and almost always with political intransigence. The experience of every dissident group showed repeatedly how much Imperial Germany depended on coercion to hold in place the disparate elements of the society.

This view of society—involving the three central notions of segmentation, conflict, and coercion—provides a much more flexible framework for understanding the seemingly ambiguous behavior of organizations in the social milieu of the labor movement than is possible if we try to interpret their actions within the confines of an all-inclusive polarity that envisages a Social Democratic movement standing alone against a coherent dominant culture. The organizations of the labor movement were not completely on the outside in the sense of being both socially and intellectually isolated from all other groups and traditions of German society. As will become clear in the following pages, various organizations within the social-cultural milieu of the labor movement could on occasion and for different reasons relate positively to other segments of German society, but not to all. The same was true for almost every segment of German society: They had positive links to some segments and antagonisms to others. Throughout much of the Imperial era the Social Democratic labor movement had serious reservations about forging links to other nonsocialist and non-working-class segments and, for the most part, the other segments reciprocated with equal reluctance. Nonetheless, it is essential to see that such linkages were possible because segmentation and conflict in the Reich were multidimensional, not unidimensional. That gave the labor movement a chance for a limited degree of flexibility in defining its relationship to the constituent parts of the larger society. Regional differences were also significant. What was a possible linkage between the labor movement and another segment in one region did not necessarily hold for all areas of Germany. The linkages between the labor movement's recreational and cultural organizations and other segments of German society thus remained tenuous and uncertain before the First World War.

The generality of social tension in Imperial Germany should not of course be taken to imply that conflicts did not vary in number, intensity, and duration. In these respects the conflict between organized workers and the socialist movement on one side and employers and government officials on the other reached a magnitude greater than was characteristic of other major conflicts.[18] For example, the struggle between the Catholic church and the Prussian state went through nearly a decade of extreme vehemence before passions cooled a bit on both sides. Mutual suspicion and hostility lingered and Catholics in Prussia continued, with justification, to view themselves as victims of popular as well as official discrimination. However uncomfortable Catholics continued to feel in Prussia, their situation differed considerably from that of organized socialist workers. Not only had the conflict with Prussia diminished by the final decade of the century, but viewed from the context of the Reich as a whole, Prussia's hostility to the Papacy and Catholic orders was balanced to some degree by the vigorous pro-Catholic principles and policies of Bavaria. Confronted by Prussian legal coercion, members of Catholic orders could anticipate encouragement from or take refuge in another German state. Socialists and their working-class disciples had no comparable refuge. The most important discriminatory legislation against them was passed on the national level and no German state or municipal government welcomed them during the years of their most intense legal persecution. Even later, when increasing numbers of Social Democrats won seats on city councils, they still were too weak politically to shape general municipal policies.

Despite the strength of reformist and revisionist currents within Social Democracy, especially after the turn of the century, Imperial ministries and high Prussian officials did not alter their conviction that the socialist labor movement constituted a dangerous and evil force and that if it could not be rooted out, it had at least to be restrained and frustrated by every available legal means. Recent research has established that far from ameliorating their hostility to Social Democracy in the years after 1900, the Imperial and Prussian governments stepped up their campaigns of bureaucratic obstructionism, police harassment, and legal constraints.[19] These campaigns were directed not only against the party and the trade unions but against all associations affiliated with the labor movement. Prussian officials endorsed every kind of effort that would hamper the work of socialist labor. In the 1890s they worked with mayors, *Landräte,* pastors, teachers, employers, and organizations such as the Central Committee for the Promotion of Youth Games in Germany to combat socialist recreational clubs.[20] The Ministry of Trade required that every town with a population in excess of ten thousand should found Continuation Schools (*Fortbildungsschule*) for teenagers between fourteen and eighteen years of age. Even at that the minister feared failure unless organized forms of entertainment and recreation (gymnastics, excursions, evening programs) could be added. Once the new Imperial association law went into effect in 1908, the Prussian Ministry of the Interior began to exploit the provision that made it possible to classify organizations as political and thereby to make them off-limits to people under twenty-one. In 1910 the Ministry of War encouraged army officers to join the German Gymnastic League (Deutsche Turnerschaft) as a way of increasing military influence among young people and of making sure that the *bürgerlich* gymnasts themselves remained intensely hostile to their counterparts in the Workers' Gymnastic Federation (Arbeiter-Turnerbund). Early in 1911 the Prussian Ministry of Culture undertook measures to coordinate or amalgamate nonsocialist youth organizations into one gigantic anti-labor-movement association, but without too much success. And on the eve of the war, on July 2, 1914, the Kaiser approved a measure to establish a cumpulsory national youth organization for all boys between the ages of thirteen and seventeen. Though it was never implemented, the plan specified that the organization would be devoted to organized sports (gymnastics, games, hiking), that it would receive a large subsidy (6,699,320 German marks during the first year alone!), and that retired army officers were to be used as organizers and leaders wherever feasible.[21] These plans and policies were part of a concerted, though not very effective, effort to push nonsocialists into vigorous action against the growth and increasing viability of the labor movement's programs of recreation and education. They give ample evidence that government officials viewed all endeavors of the labor movement, family entertainment as well as party congresses and union strikes, as serious threats to the existing order.[22]

Their alarm may be comprehensible because the social-cultural milieu was a substantial part of the emancipatory thrust of the socialist labor movement.[23] In some historical situations the work of emancipation may go forward in great leaps and bounds, but just as often it is a slow and piecemeal process in which the oppressed and disadvantaged learn only gradually and haltingly how to use even the smallest opportunity to enlarge the degree of control they can exercise over their own lives. The major organizations of the socialist labor movement, the party and the trade unions, rightly assumed that they offered the most concrete and efficient instruments through which German workers could improve their political and economic condition. From the perspective of a disadvantaged group learning to exploit opportunities for emancipation, participation in organizations can be particularly significant. Even in organizations that are not of great political consequence, attending meetings, voting, and holding offices can be significant for the inexperienced participant. Although many of these activities may appear inconsequential in comparison to the public roles played by Social Democratic Reichstag deputies, even the most modest responsibility could be a personal breakthrough for a worker whose life had accustomed him to accept as inevitable whatever fate befell him. It is no doubt true, as a number of labor historians have argued, that even apart from involvement in the labor movement workers were not mere passive recipients, that they often enhanced their sense of worth by holding firmly to "disrespectful" customs or resisting "improvements" that others wished to introduce.[24] But preserving custom was seldom in itself a further step toward emancipation. An hour or two of trade union or party involvement each week could give workers a heightened awareness of how to combine and sharpen the skills needed to promote their own cause. Through such participation they could learn to go beyond resistance to external encroachments on their accustomed behavior, to the advocacy of an entirely different set of social relationships.

The same expectations could be aroused and similar skills learned through participation in the other voluntary associations of the labor movement. Clubs within the social-cultural milieu of the labor movement did not have to emblazon provocative political slogans on their banners in order to contribute to the emancipatory learning process of organized German workers. A miniscule symbol, an insignia or a phrase, could indicate that a club belonged to the world of the labor movement, and this sufficed to give it a special dissident political meaning within Imperial Germany. To affiliate with such a club, even sporadically, could quickly label a worker as a malcontent and a troublemaker. Some workers took such steps timidly, others with more assurance. Even the timid ones were gaining emancipatory experience by affiliating in some way with the labor movement. With that simple step they were defying the wishes of the kaiser and his ministers, rejecting the admonitions of clergymen and teachers, and bringing on themselves the hostile and often capricious supervision of the police and military. They moved into an environment of clubs, activities, and relationships permeated with socialist political assumptions and implications, and this applied even to labor movement associations that officially denied all political purposes. To enroll in a club known to have labor movement connections, whether singing society, gymnastic club, or hiking association, was tantamount to taking a political stand because it implied a set of preferences—political, ideological, social—that were unacceptable to most other segments of German society. To go further, to participate openly and actively in such organizations was not only a personal emancipatory move, it also provided a favorable environment for gaining organizational experience, absorbing liberationist ideals, and nurturing undeveloped talents. The encouragement of personal talents was an important aspect of emancipation for workers in ways that may not be immediately self-evident. Even highly skilled workers had had very little time during their early years to take up hobbies or to participate in organized sports. They knew, perhaps, that they possessed some ability—to produce by the application of muscle power and the use of skills—but they had only a limited training, if any, in other kinds of activity.

The ability to speak in public is a fitting example to illustrate the above point. Pupils in German *Volksschulen* learned to memorize, recite, and give answers to direct questions, but they were not trained to speak in public, not even to small groups of their peers. This is not at all surprising, for even the well-educated received no special training in speaking. One was either an orator or one was not, and certainly teachers at elementary schools could not have imagined that working-class children would ever have much reason to engage in public speaking. But some leaders in the socialist labor movement recognized that young workers, still in their teens, could benefit from speaking experience, and that the movement would benefit as well by having more trained speakers. Participation in voluntary associations, though it seldom provided formal guidance in speech, nonetheless offered opportunities for acquiring such experience. The opportunities varied from club to club, to be sure, but even the rather uninspired business meetings of sports organizations, for example, gave a handful of members a chance to speak extemporaneously to their fellow members. Practice was important for members, individually and collectively. Individually it could give them personal confidence and improved skill in the use of language. Collectively it had considerable significance because the importance of the spoken word for emancipatory movements of all kinds can scarcely be exaggerated. The rank-and-file member who could spontaneously address a small meeting or an informal gathering of fellow workers had achieved a degree of proficiency that made him immensely valuable to the movement as a whole. Local labor organizations seldom had more than a few members who could address an audience, and for that reason the same names appear repeatedly in reports of meetings and public gatherings. On the national level Social Democracy seems to have had as many able speakers as any other political party in the Reich, but local organizations had less need for a stunning orator than for a large number of speakers of moderate or even mediocre ability. The more people with speaking ability in any one area, the more effective the whole movement would be in arousing the consciousness of workers who were not yet part of the socialist milieu.

Political, union, and educational leaders in the labor movement, despite years of experience in organizing and mobilizing workers by speaking and by word of mouth, were still more enthralled by the written than the spoken word. That speech was more important than printed texts for the politicization process of German workers has been argued and documented very persuasively. Talking to colleagues, attending meetings, and listening to speeches could make an immediate impact, whereas the printed word could be influential only if the potential follower made the effort to read.[25] Whatever the weakness of formal labor-movement training in speaking, the opportunity to gain experience always existed in the vast number of affiliated associations. Gaining that experience constituted but one part of the emancipatory contribution of the social-cultural milieu of the labor movement.

Social Democratic assumptions about what means to use to achieve their emancipatory goals directly influenced the social-cultural milieu of the labor movement. Economic emancipation meant freedom from wage slavery and, whatever theories were discussed in the party, in practice it had accepted trade union organization and activity as the most appropriate means. Political emancipation meant gaining ultimate control over state machinery and transforming it; again, whatever theories were debated by Social Democrats, in practice they had settled chiefly on elections and parliamentary activity. In the broad realm of education, entertainment, the arts, recreation, and cultural values, the answers were not as clear-cut, because for most Social Democratic thinkers these were not areas of high priority. Nonetheless, they generally assumed that in this realm emancipation meant that workers first had to learn, understand, and absorb what was of value in *bürgerlich* culture and then, at some time in the distant future, to go beyond that to build a socialist culture. The immediate task for workers was to raise themselves through studying, attending lectures, reading books, and participating in party and union activities.[26]

Social Democrats did not believe, for the most part, that there was much of value in what workers already had. Socialists glorified the proletariat unceasingly, but in practice they did not recommend that a future socialist culture should take over the mores, customs, behavior, and cultural values as they existed in the way of life of contemporary workers. This was not hypocrisy but resulted from focusing attention almost exclusively on the deprivations, misery, and insecurity of working-class life. It meant, nonetheless, that Social Democrats did not seek to draw on the existing working-class culture, on the workers' total way of life, as a source for the cultural endeavors of the labor movement. Despite such attitudes workers in fact made up the world of the labor movement, and they did not set aside normal ways of behaving and thinking when they entered the socialist milieu. In that sense they brought their working-class culture with them and, if it did not determine directly the programmatic substance of a socialist festival, for example, it did influence the way people behaved and the general atmosphere. The social-cultural milieu of the labor movement inevitably reflected many features of working-class culture, but Social Democrats seldom sought to incorporate such features intentionally. That is, working-class culture, understood as the totality of a way of life, manifested itself continuously, but was not the guiding force in the development of the social-cultural milieu of the labor movement.

On the other hand, one should not dismiss casually the fact that the Social Democratic labor movement had touched the lives of many workers for decades. Because of its early and visible growth in Germany, Social Democracy could affect the lives of working people in various ways, and it is evident that by the 1890s sentiments and ideas associated with the labor movement were commonplace among a segment of the working class. The problem is, admittedly, that it is nearly impossible to gauge the degree and quality of that influence. If researchers look chiefly for indications of well-understood Marxist ideas, they will surely miss the actual evidence of the labor movement's diffuse influence. The impact

was seldom clear-cut. Rather, it could manifest itself in a slightly
altered vocabulary, in sharpened social (and political) preferences,
and in vague notions about how to reform society, all extremely
difficult phenomena for historians to discern and present systematically. Nonetheless, it is clear that the lives of many German
workers were affected by contact with Social Democracy, that is,
that worker culture and labor movement culture were not mutually
exclusive but partook of each other in varying degress. But social
reality, far more than the socialist labor movement, lay at the root
of working-class culture. For that reason this book makes no claim
to be an account of German working-class culture. The chapters
that follow describe and analyze the efforts of Social Democrats
and trade unionists to create an environment in which workers
could remedy the most odious aspects of working-class life and
through which they could contribute to their own emancipation.

2

Labor Movement Associations: Growth, Structure, and Composition

Life in the social-cultural milieu of the labor movement took place in a number of settings. The most visible were local and national gatherings of the Social Democratic party and the free trade unions. Here participants were at the center of the political and economic work of the movement. But other settings, though less prominent, were no less significant for rank-and-file members who seldom, if ever, were delegates to national or district meetings of the party and trade unions. Neighborhood taverns, with links to the movement or with substantial laboring clienteles, were particularly important as informal gathering places where organized workers could mix beer drinking and lighthearted banter with more serious talk about family, work, and the labor movement. During the era of the antisocialist legislation (1878–90), certain taverns were especially significant as being among the few places where, though not without interruptions, the life of the movement could go on. Indeed, the connection between Social Democracy and taverns was so close at that time that they seemed bound together intrinsically in the minds of some people.[1] The shop floor itself was a natural place for talking to fellow workers about what was happening in the movement as a whole. If an extremely hostile owner sought to forbid pro-labor-movement discussion in the shop, workers had to wait for a free exchange of opinions until they were outside, perhaps in the immediate vicinity of the plant. In either case, these settings too were essential parts of the total milieu of the labor movement. The list of settings can be expanded to the labor movement may be analyzed within the context of the expressive/instrumental typology, there is another typology that is even more appropriate and helpful. This typology differentiates voluntary associations on the basis of the functional value that the club's activities are assumed to have for the members as a collectivity. Five types can be distinguished according to their leading functions. The first is a type in which the chief value is in taking "pleasure in performance," that is, clubs that specialize in activities, such as games, dancing, or singing, that require some skill for participation. The second is a category in which the greatest value is placed on sociability and in which other "activities are solely a vehicle for communion among the members. . . ." In the third type the value is in the organization's significance for symbolizing beliefs or ideologies, designated in short as "ideological symbolism." Then, there are, fourthly, those associations designed primarily to provide services, and, the fifth type, those in which the salient function is educational, where value is placed on the opportunity the organization offers its members for learning. The latter is closely related to the fourth type but is distinguished from it because in the educational societies only a few leaders provided the service and members as a whole were learners.[5]

This typology is not sufficient in itself to provide a comprehensive interpretation of all aspects of labor movement associations, because functional analytical schemes have limitations and are not well suited to deal with substantive issues of belief and ideology. The typology is helpful nonetheless for differentiating and clarifying the variety of meanings club life could hold for participants. It offers an approach, for example, for dealing with the obvious fact that people can see several value functions in one particular organization. This was especially true of clubs in the socialist labor movement. Many of them had at least three value functions that appeared to be of comparable significance. Indeed, the regularity with which labor movement clubs manifested overlapping and seemingly balanced value functions is very striking. Symbolizing ideology played a role in all of the clubs, although it should be pointed out immediately that what was symbolized ideologically was not as uniform as some historians of the labor movement might assume. Sociability was also a prevalent function of nearly all clubs, but very few workers' associations were founded exclusively for that purpose. An overwhelming majority of the ancillary associations were designed chiefly, if one takes their statutes literally, to provide an opportunity to take pleasure in performance.

The importance that members ascribed to one function or another revealed something about their other preferences within the larger context of the socialist labor movement. Within the life of the clubs one can frequently discern tensions between several functions, tensions that reveal much about the precise nature of the ambiguities embedded in the movement's social-cultural milieu.

The multitude of workers' clubs constituted one part of a much longer and larger development of voluntary associations in Germany. The process began in the eighteenth century as the corporate organization of society weakened. As the old order declined, first in towns, urban middle classes took the initiative in founding voluntary associations as a way of restructuring their social existence. Urbanites could reach out beyond the limits of traditional institutions, such as family, church, and guild, to form social bonds with people of their own choosing. The hallmarks of the *Verein* were that membership was individual and voluntary, two features that differentiated them from much of the corporate organization of the Old Regime. Voluntary associations were flexible; they could be formed to gain a particular goal and then dissolved; they could be expanded to include numerous functions; and they could be structured to be socially exclusive (membership was voluntary but not automatic) and to become institutions of social distinction. Numerous voluntary associations were formed in the first half of the nineteenth century, all as part of the life of the expanding middle classes in towns and cities.[6] The most rapid growth in voluntary associations came after the founding of the Reich in 1871, as illustrated in numerous urban communities. In Nuremberg, for example, there were 455 *Vereine* in 1880, 912 in 1890, and 1,811 by 1900. In the very small town of Weinheim an der Bergstrasse, the first association, the Singverein, was founded in 1842; some eighty years later, on the eve of the First World War, the town had no less than 100 voluntary associations.[7]

The massive expansion in the number of voluntary associations was accompanied by a number of general trends and features. The earliest *Vereine* were founded by and composed of burghers from the wealthiest and most prestigious strata of urban society. In the course of the century other social groups became active. Lower-middle-class elements were amply evident by midcentury, but it was only toward the end of the century, with the formation of labor movement clubs, that unpropertied wage earners began to participate in *Vereine*.[8]

The general trend went from exclusivity to greater inclusiveness,

but membership rolls of particular clubs continued to reflect the
social stratification of German society. Membership in certain
clubs reflected high rank and carried prestige in the local society.[9]
In Weinheim an der Bergstrasse, for example, no well-educated
person, entrepreneur, or high-ranking official would have overlooked membership in the Casinogesellschaft. In the same town
there were five singing societies, each composed largely of members from identifiable social groups. The most prestigious of the
choral societies was also the oldest, the Singverein. Differentiation
could be vertical as well as horizontal, especially in areas of mixed
confessional populations. But no voluntary association included a
complete cross section of the population.[10]

Strong tendencies toward specialization and centralization accompanied the massive growth of German voluntary associations.
At one time, for example, gymnastic clubs (*Turnvereine*) were the
only athletic organizations, but that had changed radically by the
end of the nineteenth century. In nearly every town, for example,
clubs for cycling, football, and hiking had emerged and were growing rapidly. Concomitantly, participants felt a need to affiliate
regionally and nationally with other clubs engaged in the same
activity, and these leagues and federations sprang up throughout
Germany.

The development of voluntary associations within the labor
movement reflected these tendencies toward specialization and
centralization. Throughout most of the 1860s there were as yet few
labor movement clubs for special activities. Members who wished
to devote time to singing or acting formed subsections for those
purposes within the larger organization. Special sections for singing
appeared in many Lassallean organizations shortly after they were
founded. Singers in the Lassallean organization in Frankfurt am
Main formed a special division as early as 1863. The following year
a singing division of the Lassalleans in Duisburg was founded and
named itself Teutonia.[11] At the same time, those workers' educational societies that had not joined the Lassallean movement also
formed committees or subgroups for various activities. The Leipzig
Workers' Educational Society, for example, set up an "amusement
division" (*Vergnügungsabteilung*) and charged it with arranging entertainment for special occasions. Other workers' educational societies appointed standing "festival committees" to serve the same
purpose.[12]

The trend toward specialized labor movement associations became evident at the end of the 1860s. Socialist singers, especially

among the Lassalleans, were the first to form their own organizations. By 1870 Lassalleans in Hamburg had already founded five singing societies, all strictly male choirs, named appropriately Ferdinand, Lassalle, Freiheit (Freedom) Unter Uns (Among Ourselves), and Vorwärts (Forward). By 1873 there were in Hamburg, if the reports are correct, no less than twenty-six Lassallean singing societies with a total membership of five hundred. At about the same time Lassalleans in Frankfurt am Main founded several male choirs and joined them together in an urban federation, the Workers' Singing League Lassallia (Arbeiter Sängerbund Lassallia). Following the unification of Lassalleans and Eisenachers in 1875 there was a continuous growth of singing societies until 1878, when nearly all socialist organizations were abolished. By the latter date labor movement adherents had established singing societies in many other places, including Osnabrück, Cologne, Kalk, Vingst, Hanover, Limmer (near Hanover), Stuttgart, Heilbronn, Reutlingen, and Chemnitz (and four of its surrounding towns).[13]

Singing clearly stimulated the initial trend toward specialized voluntary associations within the labor movement. If structured, other activities such as acting remained within the major political organization until the 1890s. In a few scattered places one might find the exceptional specialized club affiliated with the labor movement, but as of 1878 singing was the only activity for which a network of clubs had developed. Gymnastics had not yet been promoted as an organized recreation within the labor movement. Singing had immediate benefits for the movement not easily matched by most other recreational or artistic activities. Through song lyrics, slogans, and phrases—ideology simplified—could be communicated and brought to the consciousness of large masses of people. Melodies also contributed to the cause. If they aroused emotions, listeners were drawn more quickly to the sentiments expressed in a text; if they were aesthetically pleasing, singers gained an added measure of satisfaction. Just as songs can communicate, so singing frequently accompanied and promoted socializing. For that reason the early singing clubs often served as the labor movement's social and entertainment clubs. Mass singing drew all participants into an experience that could integrate ideological communication, aesthetic expression, and communal sociability.[14] In addition, practical considerations also gave singing societies precedence over other kinds of organized leisure activity in the movement. Singing and the formation of choral societies required only a limited investment of both money and time. Special clothing or equipment, such as stage props for drama, were not necessary. A pitch pipe helped since much singing was a cappella. The only substantial expense was in music scores, but because of the market created by the widespread popularity of German male singing societies Germany had an abundance of moderately priced publications.[15]

All trends and the expansion of labor movement associations were disrupted and thrown into disarray by the imposition of the antisocialist legislation in 1878. Most existing labor movement voluntary associations were dissolved by order of local authorities or seriously threatened with dissolution. Although some of the associations reappeared under different names and a handful even survived more or less intact, they were the exceptions. The antisocialist law thwarted the associational life of the movement and forcibly diverted it from its dominant tendencies. It seems certain that except for the antisocialist legislation the trend toward specialization would have continued during the 1880s and would have been accompanied by the formation of municipal, regional, and even national federations.[16] (After the expiration of the discriminatory legislation in 1890, voluntary associations in several activities quickly formed regional and then national federations.) The pattern of associational life had special features during the era from 1878 to 1890 and needs to be explored briefly in order to see the elements of both continuity and discontinuity.

Since socialist trade unions as well as party organizations were almost immediately abolished under the provisions of the antisocialist legislation, the labor movement faced an urgent need to establish ways by which party members could remain in contact. One obvious means was to use the ostensibly nonpolitical clubs of the movement as camouflage organizations (*Tarnvereine*), or fronts, in modern parlance. Since those singing societies which were not actually subsections of a party organization were not defined, by their statutes, as legal appendages of the Social Democratic party, or even as political associations, they had some faint hope of avoiding dissolution. To be sure, singing clubs affiliated with the labor movement, despite the nonpolitical declarations in their statutes, had always been and would always be implicitly political. Conditions under the antisocialist legislation made manifest their underlying political nature as a number of them became organizational linchpins for local party members. Such a system was fragmented and easily disrupted, however. Watchful policemen, once suspicious, would quickly establish that a certain singing society had an overwhelmingly Social Democratic membership, and that would be taken as sufficient grounds to dissolve the club.[17] Once a club had been dissolved, the members could try a number of tactics. They could establish a new club, pursuing the same activity, with slightly altered statutes and under a different and more innocent-sounding name. That done, there was still no guarantee that the police would not soon discover the deception and once again dissolve the organization. The members could, as a second option, found a club for the purpose of pursuing a different kind of nonpolitical activity. In changing the activity they ran the risk of losing a good portion of the club's constituency. A third tactic, though an infrequent possibility, was for a substantial percentage of the members to infiltrate a *bürgerlich* singing society and to use rehearsal performances and business meetings as occasions for contacting each other.[18]

Whatever tactic they used, the operation was at best cumbersome and fragile. What worked in one place would not in another. Moreover, because some clubs served as camouflage organizations did not mean that all did.[19] Even when it is clear that a singing society served as a front for political activity, it is not known precisely how the members used it. Members avoided written communications if at all possible, and frequently destroyed incriminating letters and notes. Documentation on activities and life within the few labor movement associations that were tolerated is therefore especially sparse and scattered for the years between 1878 and 1890. Toward the end of the 1880s authorities in Germany were less determined to eradicate all Social Democratic associations, and the number of clubs increased gradually. However, they were still hemmed in, forced to be cautious and to appear on the surface to be completely free of any political intent or affiliation.

For labor movement clubs the antisocialist law era meant fragmentation, discontinuity, and uncertainty. The alternative to that was nonexistence. For twelve years the law frustrated the dynamic growth in associational life and, as a consequence, a reserve of energy accumulated during that era. When the legal restrictions were removed, the pressure was released and a frenzy of associational activity erupted during the following decades. Deprived at one time of their right to form associations, labor movement members developed an even deeper appreciation for their clubs when tolerated again. The role played by avowedly nonpolitical clubs during the "heroic era" imbued them with an aura of importance that they would not otherwise have enjoyed. Within the labor

movement the fear lingered, and with justification, that the Imperial government might again succeed in getting legislation passed
that would either abrogate their right to form associations or sharply restrict it. Moreover, after the expiration of the antisocialist
legislation, the laws regulating associations could still be used quite
effectively by local authorities throughout most of Germany to
harass and obstruct the activities of labor movement clubs.

The legal system within which the labor movement existed in
Imperial Germany had a direct impact on the life and development
of the clubs. Until the Imperial law on associations (Reichsvereins-
gesetz) went into effect on May 15, 1908, laws of the individual
states defined the legal status of all organizations. Those laws had
been in effect, for the most part, since the early 1850s, when,
following the revolution of 1848–49, governments throughout Germany revised their legislation on associations and assembly. These
new laws were more liberal than had been known in most German
states before the revolution, but still included some severe restrictions. Associations organized for purposes that concerned public
affairs and politics could be formed only after receiving approval
from local police or higher authority. In most states that meant
that associations had to provide the police not only with a copy of
the statutes, but also with membership lists.[20] Women and minors
(defined variously, but usually those under twenty-one) were prohibited from participating in political associations. The definition
of what constituted politics, or public affairs (*öffentliche Angelegen-
heiten*), could be very broad, as in the case of the Saxon law which
included everything that related to "politics, religion, agencies of
the state, church and school, communal systems, commerce and
production.–. . ."[21] With such a broad definition authorities could
easily place almost all associations under strict police surveillance.
Under provisions calling for the preservation of public order and
security, assemblies, processions, and other gatherings could be
prohibited. Saxon law was particularly harsh with respect to the
formation of federations by associations concerned with public affairs, a provision that interrupted the growth of several regional
federations of singing societies in Saxony after 1890.[22] Labor movement associations had little choice, since they wished to operate
legally, but to adapt to all laws of association. That is one reason
why statutes of Social Democratic clubs stressed their nonpolitical
purposes and claimed not infrequently that all politics were excluded. Whatever their motives, founders of most clubs had no
choice but to disavow political affiliation, a fact that served, ironi-

cally, both to disguise the genuine socialist commitments of many members and to provide an excuse to proclaim strict political neutrality on the part of some who were more interested in a club's specialized activities than in its potential for socialist ideological symbolism. Despite a multitude of constraints—some minor, others harsh—and sporadic harassment, especially in Prussia, labor movement associations learned to cope with a hostile environment and grew steadily after 1890.[23]

A new and somewhat more favorable phase for labor movement clubs began on May 15, 1908, when the Imperial law on associations became effective and individual state laws simultaneously lapsed. The new law clearly guaranteed the unlimited right of every German, without regard to sex, to form associations and to be active in them as long as such associations did not pursue purposes forbidden by the penal code. Certain minor limitations on association remained with the states, but, except for those, no general grounds existed on which police could dissolve an association. That meant, in contrast to the earlier situation, that permission from authorities was no longer necessary in order to form a club. Unlike some of the earlier state laws, the new law had a reasonably narrow definition of political affairs. If an association, in its statutes, openly proposed to engage in political matters, then it was subject to certain restrictions; the names of the executive committee and the statutes had to be deposited with local police authorities. Persons under eighteen were neither permitted to join nor to participate in any but social activities.[24]

The new law allowed for a more lively activity in the party and in the clubs of the labor movement. Women now had a fully recognized right to participate in political organizations. The result was immediately noticeable. In the Düsseldorf area, for example, by the middle of 1909 there were an increased number of meetings, a markedly greater participation of females, and more socialist agitation among youth. There were still measures, however, by which police could hamper the activities of labor movement clubs.[25] Open-air assemblies and processions required police permission, which had to be requested 24 hours in advance. According to the law, the only ground on which a request could be rejected was that the proposed assembly constituted a danger to public safety. This point was open to differing and subjective interpretations, offering police a legal excuse for pursuing a repressive policy that was in fact discriminatory and politically motivated.[26]

A more effective means for restricting the activities of clubs was to get them categorized legally as organizations that pursued "political" rather than "ideal" objectives. To achieve this end required court action, not simply an administrative decision, and a number of Prussian ministries encouraged officials to initiate legal proceedings to stamp self-proclaimed nonpolitical associations as political. By 1913 authorities in many areas of Germany had prosecuted the executive committees of numerous workers' singing societies on grounds that they were in violation of the law for not submitting lists of executive members and the association statutes to police. In April of that year the executive committee of the German Federation of Workers' Singing Societies (Deutscher Arbeiter-Sängerbund) was convicted of violating the law and the whole national federation was declared to be a political association. The courts held that evidence showing that the federation was close to the Social Democratic party was sufficient grounds for declaring it a political association. Athletic clubs were particularly vulnerable. Since the law forbade youth under eighteen from participating in political organizations, police could severely hamper the work of sport clubs if they could be classified as political. In the few years just prior to the First World War authorities went to considerable ends to try to get many of the federations of labor movement associations declared to be political.[27]

That was just one part of a larger campaign, directed from several Prussian ministries, to counteract the growing influence of Social Democracy among lower-class youth. The ministries hoped to succeed by creating new organizations for German youth, encouraging existing confessional and patriotic youth associations to form a solid antisocialist bloc, and giving special support to the patriotic German Gymnastic League in its fight against the Workers' Gymnastic Federation. The campaign threw up all kinds of obstacles to thwart the efforts of labor movement associations, but it was not at all successful in reducing the influence of socialism among the young.[28] Socialist influence with youth, built in good part on the appeal of labor movement recreational clubs, had gained momentum and could not easily be undermined by organizations created by ministerial action.

Once the reservoir of pent-up energy was released in 1890, labor movement associations entered a period of sustained growth that continued to the outbreak of the First World War. The emergence of more specialized clubs went hand in hand with membership expansion. The trend toward centralization followed almost immediately, so that as new types of associations emerged they also, following the overall pattern in the labor movement, banded together in local, regional, and national federations. The early formation of national federations of specialized labor movement clubs meant that local and regional differentiations were increasingly overshadowed by standardized guidelines emanating from central offices. Centralization of the clubs paralleled, and was itself strengthened by, a comparable trend in the Social Democratic party and the free trade unions.[29] An overriding goal of the whole Social Democratic movement—party, trade unions, and national leaders of the voluntary associations—was to transform the consciousness of German workers according to a pattern that stressed common denominators of socialist ideology and class identity and downplayed differentiating tendencies inherent in local traditions and craft loyalties. On the basis of this centralizing development, the social-cultural milieu of the labor movement also became increasingly uniform throughout Germany.

Workers' singing societies moved rapidly toward centralization. In 1892 delegates from 14 regional associations, representing 9,150 members in 319 singing societies, met in Berlin for the first national congress of workers' singing societies. The delegates founded the Liedergemeinschaft der Arbeiter-Sängervereinigungen Deutschlands (literally, Song Community of German Workers' Choral Federations), known popularly as the Liedergemeinschaft. It set to work immediately to establish a common pattern of associational behavior for workers' singing societies throughout Germany. Its statutes spelled out the principles which regional federations, and thereby all individual clubs, had to adhere to in order to affiliate with the national federation. The Liedergemeinschaft established competitions to encourage socialist musicians to compose new choral music that would embody the values of the socialist labor movement. Worthy compositions were then published by the federation in its own series of choral music, *Der freie Sänger*. An organizational newspaper was founded in 1899, the *Liedergemeinschaft*, which every club in the national federation was expected to support. It carried articles on music in the labor movement, on ideological subjects, on technical musical matters, and reports on special events in the singing societies. In this way organizational centralization led directly to standardization of nearly all aspects of the musical culture of the labor movement.[30]

The same pattern can be seen in nearly every organized activity affiliated with the labor movement. Workers' gymnastic clubs had not existed before 1890, but multiplied rapidly in the early 1890s. By the spring of 1893, 39 delegates, representing some 4,000 members in local gymnastic clubs, met in Gera (Reuss) and founded the German Workers' Gymnastic Federation (Deutscher Arbeiter-Turnerbund). With notable administrative precision, federation leaders divided Germany into regions (*Kreise*) and, below that, districts (*Bezirke*), making two intermediate levels in an organizational pyramid of four layers. The statutes of the Workers' Gymnastic Federation set forth the general principles which all affiliated clubs were to follow; to serve the needs of communication, an organizational journal, the *Arbeiter-Turnzeitung*, was founded the same year (1893). Considering the harassment faced by most labor movement associations in the 1890s, the growth of the gymnastic societies was phenomenal: by 1895 there were 10,367 members; by 1900, 35,871; by 1905, 73,551; by 1913, 186,958.[31]

Workers' cycling clubs also appeared in the early 1890s. Authorities abolished the first national federation of workers' cycling clubs (formed in October 1893 at a congress in Leipzig), and after a second attempt also failed, a third succeeded in 1896 at a conference held in Offenbach. Organizationally the cyclists were unique among labor movement associations: A decade later they split into two organizations. The largest, the Workers' Cycling Federation "Solidarity," dominated; by 1902 it had a membership of 10,000; by 1914, of 150,000. The clubs in Berlin and the surrounding region had their own league, known as Freedom (Freiheit), with a membership of about 1,500 in 1914. Despite the split, the main organization, "Solidarity," developed a highly centralized structure, with its own publication, the *Arbeiter-Radfahrer,* and it also fashioned a common pattern of associational life for member clubs.[32] The same was true for the Workers' Swimming Federation, founded in 1897, though it was limited largely to the area around Berlin until 1905. By 1910, however, it had clubs in twenty-three German cities.[33] Other federations were also formed on the national level: the Workers' Athletic Federation in 1907, the Workers' Samaritan Federation in 1909, a union of Workers' Chess Societies in 1912, the Federation of Workers' Theatrical Clubs in 1908, a Workers' Stenographic Federation in 1909, the Proletarian Freethinkers' Federation in 1905, the Friends of Nature in 1905, and the Workers' Temperance Federation in 1903. A further step in centralization among sport clubs was taken in 1912 when the federations of gymnasts, cyclists ("Solidarität"), athletes, and swimmers formed a Central Commission for Workers' Sport and Physical Fitness (Zentralkommission für Arbeiter-Sport– und Körperpflege).[34]

All of that centralization—paralleled by specialization and growth—had both practical and cultural implications for associational developments in the labor movement. On the practical level, large centralized organizations could also provide members with services and benefits well beyond the capabilities of local organizations. The federation of cyclists was particularly active on behalf of its members. It provided accident insurance, death benefits for survivors, legal assistance, and free road maps. In 1905 it founded a bicycle store and repair shop, Frischauf, in Offenbach, which by 1910 had branches in six other cities; by 1914 there were branches in eighteen cities, and no less than two hundred retail outlets. Frischauf worked on the principle of consumer cooperatives and promised its member-customers higher-quality goods at lower cost than they would find in other workers' cycle shops. It did a thriving business. The Workers' Gymnastic Federation also promoted the group purchase of equipment but did not establish its own retail business. Accident insurance was also provided by the federations of gymnasts and athletes.[35]

Expansion meant that the affairs of the organizations, especially on the national level, became too burdensome for officers who freely contributed their time and energy. As far as can be established, except for a number of choir conductors, there were as yet no paid officers of the associations in the 1890s. Volunteers continued to run the associations at all levels, but at the turn of the century the Workers' Cycling Federation "Solidarity" installed a salaried executive secretary (*Geschäftsführer*). At the fifth national conference of cyclists in 1904, the delegates raised the annual salary of the executive secretary to two thousand marks with an assured annual increment of one hundred marks. The Workers' Gymnastics Federation considered the appointment of a salaried executive secretary as early as 1900, and a few years later, in 1904, the position was actually established. By 1910 the gymnastic federation had five full-time functionaries. The Workers' Athletic Federation salaried an editor to put its newsletter in order in 1911, and about the same time the federation of singers provided money for a second salaried functionary.[36] In comparison to the large salaried staffs in the Social Democratic party and the free trade unions, the clubs had only a handful of functionaries prior to the First World War, but their appearance, even in small numbers, reflected the extent to which centralization had succeeded and recreation and entertainment had become serious matters not to be left entirely in the hands of volunteer amateurs.

Organizational expansion, and all that went with it, had significant implications for the nature and development of the social-cultural world of the labor movement. Specialization provided diversity and meant that increasingly larger numbers of people were
able to satisfy recreational and socializing needs within the labor
movement. The formation of clubs with so many diverse interests
also meant that numerous activities in Wilhelmian Germany became more openly and consciously politicized than would otherwise have been the case. The existence of these voluntary associations made it almost inevitable that a young German made an
implicit political decision when he joined, for example, any kind of
cycling club. The political implications of the decision were most
apparent when he joined a workers' cycling club. The high degree
of centralization achieved by the most popular clubs by the middle
of the 1890s meant that by joining one of the workers' clubs, a
young worker, hitherto perhaps familiar only with the affairs of his
immediate environment, would soon be linked with Social Democracy and be confronted by issues of national as well as local im-
port. Throughout Germany, as club members were exposed to the
same values and ideas, centralization made its contribution to the
consolidation of the labor movement's cultural world. But centralization was not imposed from above on a passive mass of local
clubs; centralization was itself possible because local leaders
throughout Germany promoted it. Socialist ideology and class consciousness assured them that theory and social reality prescribed
centralization; practicality alerted them to its advantages for the
preservation and improvement of their local clubs.

Equality among members within a club had always been a principle of German voluntary associations, but labor movement associations carried equality and democracy further. In many German
clubs members had traditionally addressed each other with the
familiar *du;* in labor movement clubs the practice was universal.
Friedrich Jahn had insisted on the familiar form in the gymnastic
clubs. However, late in the nineteenth century that practice began
to fall out of favor in many gymnastic clubs, and in Hamburg the
compulsory *du* was dropped in 1893, interestingly, at the same
time that the more egalitarian gymnastic clubs of the labor movement were rapidly taking shape.[37] Labor movement clubs normally
opened membership to anyone who agreed to the principles and
practices as stated in the statutes. Other German associations were
seldom so open. A candidate usually had to be recommended by
someone within the club; moreover, by means of the blackball veto

system any single member, without explanation, could exclude an aspirant.[38]

Throughout the nineteenth century women had a miniscule part in only a few kinds of German *bürgerlich* voluntary associations, though they were normally invited to attend festivals and other events, which would be called "an evening with ladies" (*Abend mit Damen*). In the early decades labor movement clubs too were overwhelmingly masculine, but that changed markedly after the 1890s. By law German women were still forbidden to join political associations, so under no condition could they enroll in Social Democratic "election clubs" (*Wahlvereine*), as local party organizations were generally known. But tradition and the German social environment, not laws, held them back from joining workers' nonpolitical clubs in large numbers. Although Social Democratic principles clearly rejected that exclusionary tradition, the clubs were slow to put the new ideals into practice. Male leaders often were openly skeptical about the wisdom of admitting females and advised caution and gradualness. As late as 1910, after scores of female divisions had been formed in workers' gymnastic clubs, there were still socialist males who disliked seeing women on the training bars—especially if they were in "gymnastic pants."[39] Despite male skepticism and prejudice, hundreds of women's divisions were established in workers' sport clubs. Singing societies enrolled women to form mixed choirs, although more frequently they would set up an independent women's choir. From the early 1890s, when essentially no women had participated in workers' singing societies, the situation changed so that by 1913, of the 2,818 societies, 2,311 (82 percent) were still all-male choirs, 230 (8 percent) were mixed, and 277 (10 percent) were female choirs.[40] The number of women members was still small, but in other German singing societies women were seldom welcome. In the five years before the outbreak of the war the number of women in Social Democratic organizations expanded rapidly, in part because the new law on associations allowed them to join political organizations and in part because more Social Democrats perceived advantages for the whole movement in female participation.[41]

Nearly all labor movement federations used the term *worker* in their titles, a usage that was not literal but was understood to have ideological connotations that were as significant as its sociological implication. Many members were workers, but that was not normally a precondition for membership in a workers' club. Sympathy with Social Democratic ideals, however understood, was a more important prerequisite. In this context *worker* became a highly symbolic term, charged with diffuse, even fluctuating emotional and ideological meaning. Although some nonsocialist organizations also carried *worker* in their names, they did so most often in conjunction with some restricting adjective, as in "Catholic Workers' Association" (Katholische Arbeiterverein). Used without modifiers, *worker* (as in "workers' club") came to be synonymous not with socialism as such but with the social-cultural milieu of the socialist labor movement. It is important to emphasize this point because the broad symbolic meaning of the term *worker* accurately reflected the breadth of the whole milieu.

On social composition the best general statement is that few if any Germans would have joined workers' clubs unless they were workers, perceived themselves as workers, or belonged to or sympathized strongly with the Social Democratic movement. The stratification of German society, traditions of existing German voluntary associations, and the oppressive hand of hostile authorities all helped to ensure that labor movement clubs would draw their constituencies chiefly from the lower classes. Voluntary associations in Germany generally reflected broadly defined social differentiations. In Weinheim an der Bergstrasse, for example, there were five choral societies and each was loosely associated with a broad social stratum: Concord (Eintracht) had a working-class constituency; Harmony (Harmonie) apparently attracted local peasants; Germania drew on artisans; the Singers' Union (Sängervereinigung) appealed to small shopkeepers; and the most respected burghers belonged to the Singing Society (Singverein), the oldest and the most prestigious of the town's choral groups. The same pattern held for other cities. In Hamborn, "when one was to go singing or bowling, then workers, white-collar workers, and businessmen sang and bowled among themselves."[42] And in Göppingen (near Stuttgart), "virtually all formal and informal associations were divided along class lines. These divisions were most pronounced in the professional organizations such as guild associations and the labor unions. But even in athletic clubs and hobby clubs social and political lines of demarcation were fairly clear-cut." The labor movement in Göppingen, as in other towns, had built an "elaborate associational structure," providing a special social and cultural milieu for its constituency. "It is hardly an exaggeration to note that it [the labor movement's associational network] formed a community within a community. Workers in connection with some members from the petite bourgeoisie supported a wide variety of social, economic, and educational organizations which permitted them to carry on their avocations and activities within their own circles. Social contact with the bourgeoisie was thus kept to an absolute minimum."[43] Although the author of a detailed study of voluntary associations in Hamburg is inclined to argue that club memberships did not reflect social differentiations, the evidence he himself presents suggests the contrary.[44]

Club constituencies thus overlapped substantially with those of the party and trade unions. Of 4,263 members in 97 workers' singing societies in Hamburg in 1896, 74.4 percent belonged to the Social Democratic party, 52.1 percent belonged to a free trade union, and only 9.5 percent did not belong to either.[45] The overlapping percentages were generally lower during the same year in Chemnitz, where of 6,751 members 66.5 percent were in trade unions, 62.2 percent in the party, 54.2 percent in both the party and a trade union, and 79.7 percent subscribed to a labor movement newspaper. As years passed and the free trade unions expanded in size and scope, overlapping memberships also rose. Among singing societies in the Leipzig district in 1910, 90.2 percent belonged to trade unions, 85.4 percent to the party, and 88.3 percent subscribed to a party newspaper.[46] The data on membership in the Workers' Educational School in Berlin shows that the percentage of organized members (in either the party, a trade union, or both) rose from 66.7 percent in 1898–99 to 88.1 percent in 1909–10 (see chapter 7). Overlapping membership was always encouraged, and a considerable number of clubs actually tried to make parallel membership in a party or trade union organization a fixed obligation. The Workers' Cycling Club of Hamburg made it mandatory that members belong to the party or a trade union. In 1906 the Berlin district federation of singing societies passed a regulation that stipulated that it would take in only those choirs that required that their singers also belong to a trade union, the party, or both. As of 1909, of thirteen workers' singing societies in the Mecklenburg district, four required membership in a trade union and four others required it in both a trade union and the party. Out of 142 singing societies in the Chemnitz district in 1913–14, 29 made party membership a precondition for participation in their societies. After the Federation of Workers' Theatrical Clubs was formed in 1909, there was a concerted effort to make party membership an obligation, but the policy was soon dropped because it hampered the work of the clubs.[47] It is noteworthy that the only instances of clubs or federations requiring parallel membership in trade unions or the party come from northern Germany, especially Prussia. The more beleaguered they felt, the more they closed ranks. Whether voluntary or compulsory, such a high degree of overlapping memberships argues strongly for the intense commitment of the participants and, concomitantly, for the view that a comparatively small core of organized workers were the chief bearers of labor movement culture.

Organized craft and skilled workers constituted the vast majority of club members throughout the Wilhelmian era. The number of unskilled factory employees in the clubs increased only gradually after the turn of the century. In the Workers' Educational Society in Leipzig, members were almost exclusively skilled craft workers while the "industrial proletariat" played hardly any role. The data on the Berlin Workers' Educational School (see chapter 7) supports the same conclusion, but with one variation. The number of participants listing themselves simply as "workers" increased gradually after the turn of the century, reflecting the increased unionization of unskilled labor. Among the five founders of a Workers' Cycling Club in Hamburg in 1894, there was one locksmith (twenty-seven years old), one painter (twenty-four), one paperhanger (twenty-five), and two cabinetmakers (one twenty, the other thirty-nine). The same pattern of skilled-worker involvement held true in Göppingen, where, it is estimated, between 10 and 20 percent of the organized workers participated actively in the programs of the movement.[48] Until more local studies estimate the level of participation, we must assume that the activist core probably ranged from 10 to 25 percent of organized workers, varying from place to place. It is clear that in the decade immediately preceding the First World War the free trade unions became more important than the Social Democratic party as the broad organizational base from which the ancillary associations drew their members. Trade unionism increasingly influenced the nature of the social-cultural milieu.

Age distribution of members varied according to the type of club. In the labor movement generally the most active members tended to be in their twenties and thirties.[49] Educational societies had large concentrations of young adults. In the various workers' educational schools at least two-thirds were between twenty and thirty and about one-fifth were between thirty and forty (see chapter 7). From limited evidence it appears that even in singing societies participation dropped off substantially among people over forty. The one systematic survey on age distribution for singing societies, as summarized in Table 1, corresponds to this general pattern.

The youthful element was most marked in sport clubs. Exact reports from surveys are lacking, but 50 percent or more of the members in gymnastic clubs were probably twenty or younger. In the gymnastic club Fichte in Berlin in 1900, 49 percent of the members were between fourteen and twenty. In Cottbus, a report indicates that 90 percent in the local gymnastic club were between fifteen and twenty-one. Schuster thus concludes that for the period before the First World War about one-half of the members in the workers' gymnastic clubs were between fourteen and twenty.[50] In the cycling clubs, owing to the cost of equipment members were probably slightly older than in the gymnastic clubs. The sharp contrast in age distribution was in the number of members under twenty, high in the sport clubs and understandably very low in singing societies. Even with the slightly older age distribution in the singing societies, a youthful element dominated.

Labor movement associations were accustomed, as were trade unions, to fluctuating memberships and high turnover rates.[51] Part of the reason lay in the youthful nature of the clubs' constituencies. Young craft workers often traveled from town to town, joined a club here or there, and then moved on to another job. Late teenage years and early twenties were likely to be unsettled times for workers. Unemployment forced people to look for work beyond their native area or deprived them of the few extra pfennigs needed for membership dues. A new employer might be especially hostile to the labor movement, making it expedient for a worker to avoid contact with labor movement clubs. Given all of the reasons

Table 1
Age Distribution: Workers' Singing Societies
Leipzig District, 1909

Age	Number of Members	Age	Number of Members
to 20	14	41–45	200
21–25	383	46–50	119
26–30	613	51–55	46
31–35	592	56–60	22
36–40	331	61–65	4

Source: Victor Noack, *Der deutsche Arbeiter-Sängerbund* (Berlin, 1911), p. 55. The survey included information on 2,451 members, though there were 2,913 active and about 156 passive members in the whole district. In addition, age information is lacking for 127 of those surveyed.

for fluctuations, it is impressive that the voluntary associations of the labor movement nonetheless achieved both high and steadily growing memberships in the era between 1890 and 1914.

Leaders were constantly seeking new members, trying especially to draw young teenage workers into the orbit of the labor movement. They faced a particularly complicated task if local authorities had succeeded in getting a club officially labeled a political organization, for teenagers were then legally prohibited from membership. After passage in 1908 of the new Imperial law on associations authorities launched a vigorous campaign to get as many labor movement associations as possible legally classified as political. The pressure against the clubs built up very rapidly after March 1911, when the Prussian Oberverwaltungsgericht officially labeled the Freie Turnerschaft (Free Gymnastic Corps) in Königsberg a political association. More cases were brought in the following year against individual workers' gymnastic clubs. At the end of 1912 the Prussian Oberverwaltungsgericht stamped the whole Workers' Cycling Federation "Solidarity" as a political association. By 1913 courts in Prussia had extended the political category to include the Workers' Gymnastic Federation, the Federation of Workers' Singing Societies, the local youth committees (*Jugendausschüsse*), and all other Social Democratic youth organizations.[52] Such harassment required that labor movement associations divert considerable energy to defending their interests in court. The overall impact of the drive to declare labor movement associations political is difficult to assess. Since these legal moves came a short time before the outbreak of the First World War— nearly all associational activity ceased during the war—the force of the decisions was felt at most for only a few years. Nonetheless, the fact that by 1913 officials in Prussia had succeeded in having all youth organizations of the labor movement classified as political created a serious crisis for these groups.

Viewing the auxiliary organizations of the labor movement in terms of how they were founded highlights some special features of their constituencies and their relationships to other German voluntary associations. Four main patterns can be distinguished: (1) as direct satellites of the Social Democratic party or the free trade unions; (2) by a transfer of a club's affiliation from a *bürgerlich* federation to a workers' federation; (3) by the secession of a group of members from a *bürgerlich* association; and (4) as an autonomous creation that remained unaffiliated for some time before affiliating with a workers' federation. The oldest pattern in the

German labor movement was the first, the establishment of satellite organizations. Both the Lassallean and Eisenacher wings of the socialist movement started divisions for special activities within their political organizations and later established special clubs as direct satellites of the party. When the early singing societies were founded in this way, there was no question but that all members were also clearly committed to the socialist movement even if they did not happen to pay party dues. The same pattern was used after 1890 as well, for example, when a craft union would found its own singing society, which in turn would affiliate with the national Federation of Workers' Singing Societies. Founding new clubs by drawing directly on existing labor movement organizations had obvious advantages. As pointed out by Fritz Wildung, prominent leader of the Workers' Gymnastic Federation, this approach assured outside support and thereby increased the chances that the new club would survive and succeed. Founded in this manner the new club almost certainly had an overwhelmingly labor movement constituency; memberships overlapped almost perfectly.[53]

By contrast, clubs that fit the transfer pattern (the second type) were more likely to have mixed constituencies. The transfer pattern was particularly common among gymnasts and singers, in part because voluntary associations for these two activities had flourished for decades. The pattern can be reconstructed from the histories of numerous workers' singing and gymnastic clubs. In such cases a society would have been founded by nonsocialists, usually from middle- or lower-middle-class social groups, and would gradually have come under the influence of members committed to Social Democracy. When there were sufficient votes the socialist-oriented members would persuade the whole society to affiliate with the appropriate federation of workers' societies. Noack has stressed that this pattern was typical for many of the singing societies that joined the workers' federation. The same was true for the gymnastic clubs. The *Arbeiter-Turnzeitung,* the official organ of the Workers' Gymnastic Federation, ran a regular column for several years entitled "Es brökelt," ("It's Crumbling") which reported on clubs that had transferred affiliation from the German Gymnastic League (Deutsche Turnerschaft) to the Workers' Gymnastic Federation.[54]

When clubs transferred, a fundamental transformation was presumed to have taken place. What had been a *bürgerlich* club was assumed to have become a workers' club. The statutes of clubs had to be altered immediately, but other aspects changed only gradually. The old club names were often retained. Singing societies acquired new choral music, but did not immediately or necessarily discard the songbooks and scores that they had been using. Even if old scores were cast aside, traditional forms of associational behavior had a way of holding on.[55]

Adherents of the labor movement were not always successful in persuading the membership of a *bürgerlich* association to transfer its allegiance to a workers' federation. When they failed, they had a choice: to remain and try gradually to move the club in the desired direction, or to secede and found a new organization. A few secessions from patriotic singing societies took place already in the 1870s and the pattern became very common among singers and gymnasts, as well as others, after 1890. The Workers' Samaritan Federation, formally organized on a national level in 1909, came about after labor movement adherents in a number of cities had seceded from the German Red Cross and founded their own first-aid service associations.[56] When workers' clubs were founded following a secession, the initial membership in the new club was certain to be fully committed to the labor movement. In some ways they were making a new start, in others carrying on tradition. Secessionists had no claim to the property or the name of the parent club. They had founded a new enterprise, but on the basis of their experiences in the old club. They built according to the model they knew and took old practices with them. This was amply evident in workers' swimming clubs originally founded largely by secessionist groups. According to one socialist commentator, they retained for a considerable time all of the "errors and foolishness" (*Fehler und Mätzchen*), even the "patriotic humbug" (*vaterländischen Klimbim*), of the *bürgerlich* organizations.[57] Once a secessionist group had founded a new club and affiliated itself with a federation of labor movement clubs, it began to adapt to the norms and expectations of its new associational environment. The change was gradual, not sudden. The fact that numerous workers' clubs were created either by transfer or secession helps to explain why so many of their practices closely resembled those in other German organizations.

What cannot be determined on the basis of available evidence is whether it was primarily social differentiation or ideological inclinations that divided secessionists from others in parent organizations. Both played a role. Ideological matters seem to have been more decisive in a number of instances, but they are too few to allow generalization. There is also the intriguing fact that leaders of labor movement clubs complained throughout the era from the early nineties to 1914 that numerous workers, including organized workers, betrayed their class and political interests by remaining in *bürgerlich* clubs. (Karl Frey, one of the well-known national leaders of the Workers' Gymnastic Federation, complained ruefully that the "great mass" of unorganized workers were strangers to the organization.) To the extent that these complaints were founded in fact, they clearly suggest that some Social Democrats did not feel unwelcome in nonsocialist associations. Those who remained in *bürgerlich* clubs reported that they did so for reasons of performance, explaining, for example, that a local workers' choral society lacked the talent to sing music of outstanding merit or that the workers' gymnastic club used inferior equipment.[58] The explanation is entirely plausible—many people joined clubs primarily for success in performance—but it also suggests that conflict along class and ideological lines was not as pervasive throughout all of German society as leaders of Social Democratic clubs maintained.

A certain percentage—impossible to determine—of organized workers moved both within the world of the labor movement and as part of some other segment of German society. To illustrate this and the ambiguities that could be associated with transferring a society's affiliation from a *bürgerlich* to a workers' federation, the story of what happened in the small town of Heidersbach bei Suhl (Saxony) in 1907–8 is worth recounting. The local gymnastic club belonged by tradition to the German Gymnastic League, but had a strong contingent of labor movement members and sympathizers who proposed that the club's allegiance should be transferred to the Workers' Gymnastic Federation. The motion carried by a vote of thirty-four to twenty-six and the officers prepared to carry out the transfer. Shortly thereafter, however, the membership reversed the action by a vote of forty-two to thirty-four and the club then dutifully returned to the patriotic fold, the German Gymnastic League. The author of the report noted with obvious disappointment that those opposed to joining the Workers' Gymnastic Federation as well as those in support were "without exception organized workers" and among them were also members of the local workers' cycling club.[59]

Relationships between the Social Democratic party, free trade unions, and the voluntary associations were, in most instances, assumed to be close and harmonious. At the same time a certain ambiguity, tension, and even distance was also evident. The degree of closeness varied for different kinds of associations. In part, the ambiguity was intentional. In order to avoid classification as political organizations, the voluntary associations, with only a few exceptions, had no official connection to the Social Democratic party. The major exceptions were clubs which were actually subdivisions of either a party or trade union organization. A number of singing and gymnastic groups fell into that category and, especially after the establishment of the party's Central Educational Commission in 1906, also a large percentage of the educational societies. However, since most clubs were not recognized as official divisions of the party or the trade unions, they were not automatically granted use of the unions' resources and facilities. The societies financed themselves, largely through dues and sometimes through monies raised at festivals. Except for the educational organizations, the party had no regular pattern of material assistance, and even moral support was sometimes given grudgingly.

Opinions in the Social Democratic party varied concerning the value of the clubs for the labor movement. A common complaint, voiced by moderate as well as radical party leaders, was that club activities distracted organized workers from more essential political work. Workers had limited time and energy to contribute to the labor movement, the argument went, and they should not squander their reserves on endeavors of no political or economic consequence. Karl Legien, reformist leader of the free trade unions, expressed disdain for the gymnastic clubs at the Trade Union Congress in 1905, much to the dismay of the gymnastic clubs' leaders.[60] Radical Marxists were likely to be critical of societies that centered on artistic endeavors on the ground that involvement with the arts encouraged workers to absorb bourgeois principles. Despite the criticisms thousands and thousands of ardent party and trade union members also participated in the life of the clubs, and the dominant opinion recognized that both organizations reaped substantial benefits from the work of the clubs.[61].

On the other side, club loyalties prompted leaders of almost all kinds of associations to complain at one time or another that they were inadequately appreciated by the party and trade unions. Singing societies were especially sensitive because they in particular played a visible role at all kinds of labor movement functions. Party congresses, national and regional, opened almost invariably with a presentation by one or more choral societies. Indeed, singers performed on nearly every occasion when substantial numbers gathered—at trade union meetings, May Day programs, party festivals, and of course at festivals or special events of one of the other associations. They felt fully justified in believing that they played a significant role in the work of the Social Democratic movement. Josef Scheu, the Austrian socialist composer of political songs, summarized the contributions of the singing societies, stressing songs as vehicles for broadcasting ideas of "freedom, equality, and brotherhood" and as a means for attracting new followers. Victor Noack, a few years later, asserted even more positively the political value of workers' singing societies. He also granted that strict party discipline and artistic ambitions were not easily harmonized, noting that "party discipline encounters a certain antipathy in artistic personalities." From that he concluded that "proletarian art, especially the workers' choral movement, will be a stepchild of the party for a long time."[62] The stepchild imagery carried a measure of truth, but more significantly it reflected the hurt feelings aroused in club members when their artistic endeavors were not valued highly by party and trade union leaders. That happened repeatedly because Social Democratic politicians and theorists agreed that political and economic actions were the essential instruments for achieving the emancipation of the working class. Even Social Democracy's outstanding cultural commentator, Franz Mehring, did not believe that amateur artistic endeavors could play an important role in the movement's emancipatory work.[63]

The same party skepticism applied to other associations, but with differences. Singing was particularly susceptible to tension with the party, both because artistic ideals could conflict with party directives and because song texts carried messages that could diverge, sometimes sharply, from the ideological assumptions of Social Democracy. Sport clubs too had ideological implications, but not so immediately perceptible as the singing societies. At the turn of the century workers' gymnastic clubs were especially concerned to be endorsed by the Social Democratic party and the free trade unions as a means to boost membership.[64] Gradually the gymnasts made headway in their effort to get approval. Delegates to the Social Democratic party congress in Nuremberg (1908) passed a resolution urging all comrades to leave the German Gymnastic League and to join clubs affiliated with the Workers' Gymnastic Federation. Such support was encouraging, but it also had an undesirable consequence. German authorities used the resolution as evidence when arguing before the courts that workers' gymnastic clubs should be classified as political associations.[65]

Cyclists were never as reluctant as other groups to identify themselves openly with the Social Democratic party. Unlike singing and gymnastics, cycling was a new recreational form and thus almost all of the workers' cycling clubs were entirely new organizations founded in close collaboration with party and trade union members. In cycling there was as yet no accumulation of honored practices and mores that members could bring with them from nonsocialist clubs. Workers' cycling clubs quickly developed their own customs, heavily influenced by the fact that already during the era of the antisocialist legislation cyclists performed significant services for the party as messengers and distributors of newspapers and leaflets. Their services appreciated, cyclists continued to work closely with local party and trade union organizations and won considerable recognition.[66]

The more intellectual substance inherent in a club's endeavors, the more likely that it would be treated indifferently by the party. This is illustrated by the Proletarian Freethinkers' Federation, founded in 1905, which identified itself fully with the socialist labor movement but enjoyed only the barest minimum of reciprocal support. Konrad Beisswanger, the leading spirit in the movement, complained frequently that although most Social Democratic political leaders were freethinkers they did not embrace his organization. He used various tactics and arguments in an effort to obtain full party endorsement, claiming, for example, that three out of every four members in the freethinkers' clubs were workers.[67] He and the proletarian freethinkers honored Wilhelm Liebknecht as one of their forefathers, but still could not persuade many socialist leaders that a special organization was needed to fight establishmentarian Christianity.[68] In the 1860s and 1870s socialists had carried on a vehement campaign against Christianity, but by the 1890s they began to doubt the wisdom of that approach. For purposes of electoral tactics, close adherence to the neutrality declaration that "religion is a private matter"—written into the party program— promised better results at the polls. On the theoretical level the increased influence of Marxism dovetailed neatly with these tactical considerations. Marxists might personally be atheists or agnostics, but they argued that the fight against Christianity was secondary, that a socialist victory in the political and economic struggle would be followed by popular enlightenment and an ensuing decline in the appeal of religion. To give preeminence to anti-Christian propaganda, they concluded, would mean that socialists had confused their priorities.[69]

The recurrent conflicts over beliefs and values within the milieu of the labor movement were a manifestation not of weakness but of vitality. Every segment of the labor movement took its particular function and purpose to be significant and could not understand when other groups did not share that estimate. The free trade unions frequently hurled such complaints at the Social Democratic party, and before the First World War even party leaders fretted about the fact that the unions casually disregarded what they assumed to be the rightful preeminence of the party. The ancillary associations never presumed to lay claim to preeminence in the labor movement as a whole, but their representatives were aware that they contributed substantially to the reality of life in the labor movement. They helped to draw working-class bystanders into the movement; they gave the movement much of its capacity to penetrate many aspects of working-class life; and they reflected the actuality of pluralism and diversity in a movement that believed officially in ideological unity as well as in class solidarity. They rapidly came to constitute an important portion of the organizational base of the alternative culture of the socialist labor movement.

3

Club Life

Club life offered an annual round of meetings and special events, opportunities for practicing skills, expressing values and feelings, being amused, socializing, and serving the labor movement. This associational life took place in two spheres, the inner, when members of a particular club met only among themselves, and an outer sphere, when they joined with other clubs or with many organizations from the whole of the labor movement in festivals and other events. Both spheres were intrinsic to the formation of the culture of the labor movement, the second especially since it involved an active collaboration among the party, trade unions, and auxiliary societies. Jointly and incrementally they formed their own social-cultural milieu, an accumulation of ideological tendencies, values, customs, slogans, and numerous other elements, fitted together gradually into an evolving configuration that was presumed to have an underlying unity. It continued to evolve throughout the Wilhelmian era, acquiring new elements, holding firmly to some but letting others fade into the background. Labor movement clubs were crucial agents for fitting together the diverse pieces, transmitting customs, and symbolizing ideology.

The frequency of events varied according to type of activity and from club to club, but in centers with strong labor movement organizations there was always a vital associational life. As in other matters concerning labor movement associations, the decade of the nineties showed a slower pace in activities than the period from the turn of the century to the outbreak of the war. The Workers' Educational School in Berlin, for example, sponsored but one event during 1898–99, a founders' day festival, but by 1909–10 it sponsored a major festival, an evening devoted to Ferdinand Freiligrath, and six one-day excursions.[1] A survey of the local singing federation in the

Chemnitz district showed that during one year its 142 societies held an average of 44 practice sessions each; 84 of the societies put on 123 concerts; 63 of them participated in "workers' festivals" a total of 163 times; and 124 of the societies had held 223 events devoted exclusively to amusements and sociability.[2] In the course of 1913 a workers' swimming club in Hamburg held 4 general membership meetings, 1 semiannual meeting, 1 children's swimming festival, 2 swimming shows (*Volkstümliches Schauschwimmen*), an autumn festival, and a founders' festival, in addition, of course, to regular weekly swimming sessions.[3]

Cyclists and gymnasts tended to be especially active. In addition to participating in most festivals of the labor movement, they held many of their own special events during the year. Cyclists made club tours (*Vereins-Touren*) and the gymnasts went on gymnast trips (*Turnfahrten*), both activities more and more frequent as clubs increased in number, size, and accumulated more resources. In the Thuringian district (*Kreis*) of the gymnasts, there were, in a period of two years (1908–9), fourteen local gymnastic festivals (*Bezirksturnfeste*) and the 191 clubs in the district had undertaken 650 "gymnastic trips and outings" (*Turnfahrten und Ausmärsche*).[4] The workers' youth clubs (*Arbeiter-Jugendvereine*) sponsored a great variety of activities since they were not specialized but general organizations for youth between fourteen and about twenty. The workers' youth club in Elberfeld-Barmen, for example, held the following events in 1909: eighteen lectures (average attendance 66.32); two literary evenings; seven evenings of light entertainment (attended by 505; 330 males, 123 females, and 52 adults); about eight excursions (average attendance 87.75); twenty-seven general meetings (average attendance 20); and Sunday afternoons normally featured sports and games. During the same year the youth organization in Hanover held more than one hundred general meetings that included lectures; during the summer there were organized excursions almost every Sunday.[5] Clearly, if an organized worker wished to participate in more than one association, he could spend a considerable portion of his nonworking time in activities within the labor movement.

Recreational clubs tried to meet weekly, service-oriented associations less frequently. Discipline and regularity were valued highly in all labor movement organizations. At weekly choral practice in singing societies choir directors were in full command. In gymnastic clubs there was great emphasis on disciplined behavior during weekly exercises. The gymnastic code (*Turnordnung*) spelled out in considerable detail procedures that were to be followed. Exercises were in large part regimented. An elected gymnastic overseer (*Turnwart*) was in charge, while squad leaders (*Vorturner*) were responsible for the performance of their teams (*Riegen*). The code emphasized that "every member must carry out the directions of the *Turnwart* and the *Vorturner*." Absolute subordination and discipline were made preeminent: "Ranks must be strictly held in each *Riege*. No one may move from the *Riege* without special permission."[6] Clubs for other activities, swimming, cycling, weight lifting, and boxing, for example, all insisted that order and strict discipline would prevail during regular practice time.[7]

Weekly meetings, however, were not characterized only by disciplined exercises. In the course of the evening, performance gave way to socializing, to drinking, gossiping, laughing, and singing. Sociability was an especially important function of societies devoted to singing and gymnastics, though in all associations a time of "convivial togetherness" (*gemütliches Beisammensein*) normally followed general meetings and conference sessions. The chance to socialize was a major attraction of club life and made business meetings more appealing. Announcing its quarterly business meeting to be held on a Sunday afternoon in the dance hall Thalia, a newly founded workers' swimming club in Hamburg stressed that "a *gemütliches Beisammensein* with dancing is planned following the meeting. . . ."[8] Sober souls and those devoted exclusively to the serious activity of a club were likely to disapprove of drinking and frivolity. "The gymnastic exercises are hardly finished," wrote one critic, "before one goes to the bar just as fast as possible to pass a few hours as a genuine beer philistine [*Bierphilister*]. In a few minutes the room, normally not very large, is so heavy with smoke from the noble [tobacco] canister that one is no longer able to recognize those who are present."[9] The critic's sarcasm also suggests exaggeration, but his portrayal nonetheless evokes appropriate impressions. Beer drinking, in some measure, often accompanied labor movement socializing. Official reports of the party, trade unions, and clubs frequently overlook the frivolities because they were so common that they appeared to be of no consequence. There were, to be sure, some exceptions. Members of the Workers' Temperance Federation faithfully upheld their principles even when relaxing, and the chess clubs also appear to have been very sober groups.[10]

The special events—outings, amusement programs, festivals—

that supplemented the weekly or monthly routine enhanced club life immensely. Festivals were especially popular, high points in the annual rhythm of activities, but weekend excursions and outings also had appeal. For part or all of one day, usually a Sunday, members would make a communal journey to the country, on foot or by train or bicycle. Sports clubs and the youth organizations were the most energetic sponsors of outings. For gymnasts in Germany it was an old tradition, and workers' clubs too were eager to make excursions as frequently as possible. They often went overnight, starting Saturday evening by marching through the streets with lots of fanfare.[11] The mood on such a *Turnfahrt* can best be recreated by letting a participant describe the event. On June 13 and 14, 1896, the Workers' Gymnastic Club from Pieschen-Dresden made a summer excursion to Sebnitz.

Despite the fact that a small cloudburst hit our Elbtal in the afternoon [of Saturday the thirteenth] 30 *Turngenossen* found their way to the railroad station by 7:50 [P.M.] and steamed away in a fresh-free-happy mood [*frisch-frei-frohen Mutes*] to Sebnitz by way of Schanday. At 11:15 in the evening we arrived and were greeted at the [Sebnitz] station by the local *Turngenossen*. Taken to the gymnastic hall, we were then welcomed by the old and wonderful [*liebenswürdigen*] *Turngenosse,* Herr Factory-Owner Gotthold Strohbach; his speech closed with the poet's words: "The Lord God who created iron, did not want [to create] slaves" ["Der Gott, der Eisen wachsen liess, der wollte keine Knechte"]. Following a short "Thanks" from us we marched to Hertigswalde. We then passed a couple of happy hours with those marvelous Sebnitzers and later sought out our joint overnight camp [*Nachtlager*]. Early in the morning, although it rained furiously the whole night, the sky had a friendly look and, led by several Sebnitz *Turngenossen,* we started out, accompanied by the sounds of two concertinas. The route led us past Saupsdorf at the foot of the Schweizerkrone on to Hinterhermsdorf, [where we took] a breakfast break in the Gasthaus zur Hoffnung (gymnastic locale). Onward then with song and sound through magnificent woods to the Königsplatz (small viewing tower, one of the most magnificent Schweiz panoramas). Further along the valley through the Felsentunnel to the boat landing Obere Schleuse. The boat trip is enchanting, the scenery overwhelming. Then for a stretch up steep forest paths to the viewpoint Hermannseck, through the beautiful Kirnitzschthal to the Kirnitz Pub in Hinterdittersbach. There a midday meal. After a rest of one and one-half hours, strengthened by a good meal and some entertainment, [we went] once again through the Kirnitzschthal, past the Marien springs to the

could get a sense of each other's opinions. A little alcohol encouraged a greater openness than was normal at work, where unfamiliar colleagues and superiors were likely to be listening. News of the day was picked up by patrons, sometimes garbled or colored in transmission. Innkeepers subscribed to at least one newspaper and clients were welcome to peruse it. That also stimulated comments. Patrons who seldom if ever looked at newspapers could still pick up some notion of what they contained. The seriousness of the talk should not be overestimated. Male pub talk, with few exceptions, ran the gamut and was no doubt heavy on swearing, dirty jokes, and gossip. But that too is a form of communication and of a kind that can draw people together as they share a range of feelings from frustration to exhilaration. Whatever the level or the topic, pubs served as crucial focal points for building human contact among people who seemed to belong together and for their exchange of feelings.

Inns and taverns in Germany tended to be differentiated in part by the kind of associational clientele they attracted. The differentiations were not simply matters of class and status, but also reflected vertical lines separating confessional and ideological groups. If some locales made arrangements almost exclusively with associations of prosperous burghers, others made agreements with tradesmen, journeymen, apprentices, and even manual laborers. Inns and taverns came to be identified in the minds of townspeople with particular clubs and their memberships. In Weinheim an der Bergstrasse, for example, each of five singing societies was identified with a particular locale. There, the workers' society had been particularly fortunate because it managed to meet in the same locale, Zum Müllheimer Tal, for many years.[17]

Using beer halls and inns for party and trade union meetings and other activities had a number of significant implications for the labor movement and for life in the affiliated clubs. It was natural for taverns to play a role in the movement because they were so important in the lives of most German workers regardless of ideological orientation. The ease with which German workingmen went to taverns created a natural overlap between a traditional form of relaxation and socialization and attachment to a modern reform movement. During the seventies and the eighties, when the Social Democratic movement faced severe legal repression, the fact that taverns offered places for seemingly innocent and spontaneous gatherings of comrades was crucial for the preservation of the movement in all parts of Germany. The link between the socialist labor movement and taverns did not weaken after the fall of the antisocialist legislation, but in fact became stronger as the movement expanded rapidly. What one author has called the "symbiosis between the tavern and working class politics" made a number of tavernkeepers as prominent in the movement as Reichstag deputies. The German public too recognized a link between tavern life and the labor movement, and antisocialists interpreted that connection negatively, arguing erroneously that it showed the "moral degeneracy" of workers and Social Democrats. For the wider labor movement milieu the tavern environment also went hand in hand with the dominance of men in Social Democracy and in German society generally.[18]

The quality of the locales that cooperated with the labor movement appears to have varied considerably. In Chemnitz Göhre thought that the inn patronized by the Social Democrats was one of the best in the "whole locality." The innkeeper and his wife were both Social Democrats, Göhre believed, and as a young theological student he found much of their behavior repugnant. The wife in particular shocked him with her vulgarity, the equal of which he had never witnessed. Most innkeepers in the district sympathized with Social Democracy, Göhre concluded, or at least they pretended to be sympathizers in order to please their customers. Suspicious of innkeepers' motives, Göhre interpreted their ideological accommodation as mere "business socialism," a widespread phenomenon not particularly appreciated by Social Democrats who looked on such adaptability as pure opportunism.[19] By contrast with Göhre's observation that the Social Democratic locale in Chemnitz was among the best in the industrial district, a description given by a woodworker, Otto Schuchardt, of an inn in Magdeburg that served as headquarters for local trade unions suggests that it was a miserable place. Schuchardt had a room on the second floor of the house. "In the front part of the ground floor," he recounted, "was a restaurant. In the hallway, on the left side, was a large wooden board. On this board, in shiny letters, were the names of the local trade unions, the names of the leaders and the treasurers." One of the rooms was set aside for itinerant workers. "It was a damp room, saturated with the odor of tobacco and alcohol."[20] Despite Göhre's estimate, the dominant impression is that inns and taverns easily accessible to most workers, organized or unorganized, were of mediocre quality and not well equipped to provide the physical resources needed by the clubs of the labor movement.

The "locale question" plagued nearly every labor movement

club, often repeatedly. Gymnastic clubs were especially vulnerable. They needed rooms large enough to hold equipment and to allow for freedom of movement during evening exercises. Owners naturally saw gymnastic clubs as a bigger burden than most other kinds, and they expected, in return for concessions, that club members would consume large quantities of beer. But heavy alcoholic consumption contradicted the primary purpose of gymnastics, and clubs often found themselves homeless. In 1899 Hermann Engst reported with frustration that for two decades the gymnastic division of the well-established Workers' Educational Society in Leipzig still had no secure locale and had moved year after year from one place to another. That was bad, but things did not improve. Twelve years later, in greater frustration, he acknowledged sadly that even then the quest for adequate quarters had not been solved.[21] For six years the workers' gymnastic club in Striessen had enjoyed a satisfactory arrangement with the owner of the restaurant Zur deutschen Eiche. They used a room four hours weekly, with ninety square meters of floor space, for which they paid a rent of forty-two marks annually. In addition, the owner required that they hold their executive and membership meetings and other club affairs in his restaurant. That seemed reasonable, but a new owner raised the rent to ninety marks annually and would hold the room only if it had not been requested by a group that guaranteed him greater sales than the worker gymnasts could promise.[22]

The locale problem could be even worse for associations which, in contrast to singers and gymnasts, were not by tradition accustomed to much drinking. The Berlin Workers' Educational School told of two changes of locale within six months: "In the middle of August [1898], the location had to be moved from Inselstrasse 10 to Buckowerstrasse 9, the 'Luisenhof.' Suddenly the 'Luisenhof' was closed so that on December 23, 1898, we were compelled to move to our present home at Annenstrasse 16."[23] The situation was no better in Hamburg, as a report from 1912 made clear: "The lack of appropriate locales has been a constant calamity. It was not uncommon that on the evening of instruction the students and their teacher had to go looking for a new locale because on the day before the innkeeper had made an arrangement with a club that was sure to do a lot of drinking [*trinkfesten Verein*]."[24] Clubs moved from locale to locale, frequently because owners wanted to maximize profits, but also because, in northern Germany especially, police were likely to harass innkeepers as well as their labor movement clientele.

Over time, but only after the turn of the century, the situation improved for some associations. First, an organization of Social Democratic innkeepers was founded around 1901, reflecting an increasing willingness on the part of owners to identify themselves with the labor movement.[25] With the growth of the party, the trade unions, and the voluntary associations, in certain districts, a labor movement clientele alone could assure an owner of regular sales and a substantial profit. Second, the severity of the locale problem was ameliorated for some associations when trade union cartels in a number of cities acquired their own buildings. Once they existed, the buildings were frequently made available to affiliated associations for special events and sometimes for routine meetings. This improvement did not come about, however, until the decade immediately before the First World War, and then it aided only a small percentage of the organizations. Clubs that needed special equipment had particular problems that could not always be solved in trade union houses.

Worker gymnasts appealed almost everywhere to municipal and higher authorities for permission to use publicly owned gymnastic halls and fields, but only in certain states, notably Baden, Württemberg, and the Rhenish Palatinate, were they likely to be successful after the turn of the century. There municipal authorities often granted workers' gymnastic clubs permission to use the town's facilities.[26] The opposite was the case in Prussia and other middle and northern states where requests were seldom granted. In the Prussian province of Brandenburg there were, as of 1910, fifty-four localities with workers' gymnastic clubs, but in only eight were they permitted to use municipal gymnastic halls. In Düsseldorf the city council rejected a request of the workers' singing societies to use the municipal auditorium. But even in Prussia there were exceptions to the exclusion. In Rostock the gymnasts, who had faced very severe locale problems, were given permission to use the municipally owned hall of the St. Georg-Schule as of 1900.[27]

The ideal solution would have been for local federations of clubs to build or purchase their own quarters. Most clubs or local federations could not even contemplate such an undertaking. Nonetheless, gymnastic clubs and federations in some of the most active centers, especially where public facilities were closed to them, purchased a small piece of property to serve as an athletic field, and a number even built their own halls. As of 1910 there were eighty workers' gymnastic clubs or regional federations with fields, and thirty-one with their own halls.[28] Such self-sufficiency was difficult to attain, and since other associations did not need the kind of equipment required for gymnastics they could more easily forgo the desire to acquire their own buildings.

The uncertainty that so many clubs faced about where to meet was itself a reflection of the insecure and ambiguous place they occupied, as part of the Social Democratic labor movement, in German society. The more comprehensive the network of socialist clubs became, the more it appeared that labor movement culture had created a self-contained world in which organized workers could live without much attention to the rest of the society. But the contrary was also true. As the cultural world of the labor movement encompassed more and more activities—everything from weight lifting to writing poetry—the more vulnerable it became to being a replica of the other segments of German society. Too much imitation threatened to undermine its profile as a clear alternative to what already existed in German society. The emphasis on improving performance, typical of so many clubs, or on socializing, also a prevalent tendency, meant that the socialist ideological thrust was weakened. As the world of the labor movement expanded, quantitatively and thematically, it was continuously enlarging and modifying the cultural configuration that had first taken form in the 1860s.

The contours of that cultural configuration could be discerned from a multitude of symbols. Names, for example, helped give clubs public images and identities. In one or two words a name could symbolize cultural attachments and ideological tendencies. While the national federations of almost all of the clubs used *worker* (*Arbeiter*) in their names, local club names included a more diverse symbolic language. Certain key words signaled the close link to the socialist labor movement.[29] The terms *frei* (free) and *vorwärts* (forward) had become, in German society, almost the exclusive possession of the Social Democratic labor movement. Numerous singing societies used one or the other, and in the gymnastic associations the most popular names were *Freie Turnerschaft* (Free Gymnastic Corps) or some form of *Arbeiter-Turnverein* (Workers' Gymnastic Club). Among the singers a substantial number of societies took the name *Lassalle* (Lassalle), but these were extremely rare among gymnasts. More striking, the names of Marx and Engels were not used, though there may have been one or two exceptions.

A multitude of words or phrases common to German liberal

traditions were absorbed by the labor movement and became an integral part of associational nomenclature. For decades workers' singing societies had been using names—such as *Brüderkette* (Brotherhood Links), *Einigkeit* (Unity), *Eintracht* (Concord), *Freiheit* (Freedom), and *Hoffnung* (Hope). The joy of singing and of sociability comes through in numerous instances: *Freundschaft* (Friendship), *Frohsinn* (Happiness), *Harmonie* (Harmony), *Liederhalle* (Hall of Songs), *Liederkranz* (Wreath of Songs), and *Liederlust* (Love of Song).

There were also names among singers and gymnasts that reflected patriotic sentiment, particularly *Germania* and *Teutonia*. These appear to have been societies that had originally belonged to nationalist federations and had transferred affiliation to a labor movement federation without feeling compelled to change their names. A workers' gymnastic club in Münster (Westphalia) even called itself Turnverein Deutschland. Retention of the patriotic symbolisms reflected that undercurrent of national identity so often noted by historians. Regional loyalties were also evident in a sprinkling of names, such as *Saxonia, Frankonia*, and *Helvetia*. A handful of gymnastic clubs used *Eiche* (Oak) in their names, an old and honorable symbol for strength and greatness.[30] In general, among singers and gymnasts symbolic links to the nonsocialist world remained strong.

Clubs engaged in sports of recent origin—cycling, for example—used names more uniquely identified with the socialist labor movement. *Solidarität* (Solidarity) and *Freiheit* were the names chosen by the two opposing federations of worker cyclists. Due to the special functions for communication and transportation that cyclists quickly acquired in the labor movement, they also picked up colorful nicknames—"Rote Husaren des Klassenkampfes" (Red Hussars of the Class Struggle), "Rote Kavallerie" (The Red Cavalry), and "Pioniere der Partei" (Pioneers of the Party).[31] For local clubs, *Arbeiter* also became a key word as more and more clubs engaged in new activities. Thus, greater uniformity in names became evident as time passed. This corresponded to the trend toward organizational centralization on the national level. And greater symbolic uniformity reflected, in turn, the reality of increasing standardization in the social-cultural milieu of the labor movement.

Labor movement clubs differentiated themselves from others in German society by gradually creating their own "club languages," banners, and emblems. Older, nonsocialist forms were sometimes mixed with new terms. The founder of the German gymnastic movement, Friedrich Ludwig Jahn, had determined from the beginning that *Gut Heil* would be the movement's official greeting. Worker gymnasts used *Gut Heil* both as a greeting and a club name, until the end of the 1890s, when they adopted *Frei Heil* (Hail to Freedom) as a greeting that more accurately symbolized their ideological leanings. (One could also buy *Frei Heil* cigarettes!) In the years following, an increasing number of clubs also used *Frei Heil,* but a handful clung to the old tradition and retained *Gut Heil* as the official name. A delegate to the gymnastic conference in 1899 specifically defended the continued use of *Gut Heil* as a symbolic bridge to quasi-dissident members of the German Gymnastic League who, he implied, would be more likely to join workers' clubs if the old greeting were preserved.[32] The Friends of Nature said hello with *Berg frei,* in contrast to the *Berg Heil* of the German Alpenverein. Cycling clubs in the labor movement used *Frisch auf* as a greeting. The choice is notable because it had no special socialist connotations, although in most other respects the cyclists manifested a high level of political consciousness.

Throughout the labor movement, the key word of "club language" was *Genosse* (comrade). It was used universally and joined with terms designating particular activities. Members addressed each other, for example, as *Turngenosse* (gymnastic comrade), *Schwimmgenosse* (swimming comrade), or *Sangesgenosse* (comrade singer). Members of the workers' stenographic societies were even accustomed to refer to each other as *Schriftgenossen* (writing comrades)! Singers also continued to use *Sangesbruder* (brother singer), a common form in German tradition of male choirs in which, it should be noted, members had also used *Sangesgenosse.*[33]

Banners, flags, and emblems abounded. Throughout European culture flags had acquired sacred meanings for many movements and organizations. They symbolized ideals and hopes and, as such, were to be worshipped in consecration ceremonies and by oaths of allegiance. In patriotic singing societies in Germany the consecration of the flag (*Fahnenweihe*) was a ritual performed in an atmosphere of solemnity and reverence. A cult of the flag permeated German associational life.[34]

Labor movement clubs also honored flags but generally did not attach the same mystical meaning to them that was evident in patriotic societies. Some workers' gymnastic and singing organizations also held flag consecrations at festivals and celebrations, though we do not know how often or precisely how they performed such a ceremony.[35] Preserving a flag when clubs were abolished during the era of the antisocialist law symbolized resistance and the sustaining power of the movement. The singing division of the Social Democratic organization in Lörrach managed, in 1878, to save its flag by taking it across the Swiss border, and the workers' singing society in Duisburg successfully hid its flag until, in 1890, it flew "even more joyously" than before to remind members of their struggle and victory.[36] "Therein perhaps lies the one value of banners and flags," commented Victor Noack, "that they embody a part of history filled with fame and suffering, and in that way arouse feelings of loyalty, pride, and warm devotion in those closely linked by experience to that past and, in young people, feelings of respect and veneration for those who fought and suffered under the flag."[37]

Flags in the labor movement usually carried the name of the club and an appropriate symbolic word, such as *Freiheit, Vorwärts* or *Brüderschaft.* The clasped-hand symbol of brotherhood, solidarity, and internationalism appeared on numerous flags, emblems, and publications. All of this seemingly trivial paraphernalia had a significant function for those within the clubs and the general public. In their diversity flags, emblems, and pieces of clothing (red scarfs, caps, and sashes) represented abstract values and principles in a concrete, perceivable form. As artifacts they could be touched and viewed, giving sensory affirmation to ideals and hopes that otherwise seemed lofty and remote. They could be miniscule, worn discreetly, or barely perceptible and still express effectively the bearer's sense of belonging to a special community. It required only a slight deviation from the dress and emblems of other German associations to symbolize affiliation with workers' clubs. In relating his impression that *Frei Heil* (worker) gymnasts were active in nearly every locality, Heinrich Holek also noted that only one tiny symbol distinguished them from other gymnasts. "Their costume," he observed, "was the same as that of other gymnasts, [except that attached to] the green band on the broad-brimmed gymnastic hat, grey-green in color, they carried a thin, slant-cut [*schräges*], red ribbon."[38]

The club life of labor movement associations was supposed to embody the values and principles embraced by Social Democracy and the free trade unions. That expectation was not always fulfilled. Older members brought along accustomed assumptions and practices from other German associations. Younger members were only becoming familiar with the values and practices of the socialist labor movement. Moreover, each kind of activity implied certain value preferences, not all of which were compatible with or related to fundamental principles of the larger movement. The clubs sought, nonetheless, to fuse their particular value preferences with general labor movement principles.

The Friends of Nature, for example, promoted hiking to improve physical fitness and to stimulate an appreciation for the beauties of nature. Appreciation was easily transformed into a cult of nature to be fused with the emancipation of the working classes. An anonymous author explained the rationale.

> Every human should be able to read in this book [of nature], should understand the language of nature. Only then will it be clear to him what place he has in the cosmos. His eyes will be opened completely when he notices that he belongs to nature and nature belongs to him. For we stand in the center of nature. A thousand threads bind us to its living world. We are but a miniscule part of the matter that has been constantly in motion for millions of years and for which nothing changes but the form. Whoever lives with such thoughts cannot doubt the final victory of enlightenment and truth, he cannot doubt but that freedom and equality will be achieved through great effort by working people on behalf of all producers. A proletarian arrives at such thoughts as a result of wandering in the open air, observing what takes place in nature, [and] of a fruitful and an ennobling exchange of ideas with like-minded people.[39]

That was ingenuous reasoning—the adulation of nature as an instrument for the achievement of working class emancipation! One scholar has recently noted that the "pathos and numerous topoi" found in the theoretical statements promoting "social hiking" by the Friends of Nature hardly differed from ideas of the Wandervogel movement. He adds that in contrast to most other labor movement cultural organizations, the Friends of Nature were not in open conflict with their *bürgerlich* counterparts in the Alpenverein. At the same time it was also true that, unlike the Workers' Temperance Federation and the Proletarian Freethinkers' Federation, the Friends of Nature did not try to get their particular ideological predilections officially endorsed by the Social Democratic party. They were seemingly content to proclaim their allegiance to the socialist labor movement, to play a moderate role in its social-cultural milieu, and to reflect on their *Naturphilosophie,* drawn largely from Goethe and Ernst Haeckel, with genuine conviction, but without the aggressive missionary zeal so typical of Konrad

Beisswanger and the Proletarian Freethinkers Federation. They naively assumed an easy symbiosis between socialism, even Marxism, and *Naturphilosophie.*[40]

Every association took it for granted that its endeavors were compatible with the basic goals and principles of the labor movement, and some sensed an advantage if they could go further and demonstrate that what they did blended intrinsically with Marxist thought. On occasion these efforts could be very inventive, even fantastical, as illustrated in debates that took place in the Workers' Stenographic Federation. Stenography had been important to the labor movement for decades, and by 1911 the federation had 122 societies with 1,916 members. But all was not unity. Stenography had developed to an advanced stage by the early twentieth century, but competing systems were still trying to gain dominance. In Germany, the Workers' Stenographic Federation followed the Arends system; in Vienna a labor movement stenographic association used the Faulmann system. There were still other systems, the Stolze-Schrey and the Tachygraphie, which also had adherents within the labor movement. The leaders of the Workers' Stenographic Federation in Germany were single-minded, however, in their belief that no system but the Arends was appropriate for socialists. In 1912 the president of the federation, Gustav Richter, even maintained that Leopold Arends, who developed his system in the 1860s, had done for stenography what Marx and Engels had done for socialism, namely, laid the systematic and scientific foundations. That being the case, he implied that the Arends system was to be preferred above all others by socialists and workers. Enthusiasm for Arends encouraged Richter to express sympathy for nonsocialist stenographic associations that used the same method and to raise suspicions about the reliability of workers' societies that did not. Class loyalty could be strained even by stenographic commitments![41]

Workers' gymnastic clubs also fused their labor movement ideals with certain customs and values from the German gymnastic heritage, reflected particularly in their continued admiration for the founding father, Friedrich Ludwig Jahn. The memory of Jahn was preserved in many ways, most obviously in the fact that a large number of clubs named themselves after him. This contrasts interestingly with the fact that a complete list of all workers' gymnastic clubs reveals that none used either Lassalle or Marx in its name. The Workers' Gymnastic Federation and the opposing German Gymnastic League each asserted repeatedly that it alone rightfully claimed Jahn's heritage. The nationalist organization maintained that since Jahn had been a great patriot in his own day, it followed that he would also be enthusiastic for nationalist causes—a strong army and navy, and colonial expansion—if he were alive in the Second Reich.[42] By contrast, socialist gymnasts stressed the fact that Jahn had been a critic of the status quo, that he, like many Social Democrats, spent years in fortress confinement, and that the state prohibited him from teaching and had banned him from Berlin and its environs. "Jahn loved his German fatherland," an anonymous worker gymnast wrote. "He strove for the unity and freedom of Germany. That fragmented Germany of many pieces, suppressed by Napoleon, had to be freed from the clutches of the conquerer; that was the goal of every spiritually free human being at the beginning of the nineteenth century."[43] Since each argument included a modicum of historical fact, neither side would concede ground to the other and Jahn enjoyed the ironic honor of being venerated by two opposing camps.

Workers' gymnastic clubs showed both reverence and a measure of inventiveness as they fostered Jahn's legacy. The *Arbeiter-Turn-Zeitung* published special articles on Jahn's life and times and reprinted excerpts from his writings, especially from his classic work on gymnastics, *Die deutsche Turnkunst*.[44] The same paper carried advertisements for "Vater Jahn" cigarettes—also for "Lassalle" cigarettes. The paper defended "Turnvater" Jahn against claims of certain German anti-Semites that he was their "intellectual father" (*Geistesvater*).[45] Although the substance of the article is not very persuasive—except as a forceful rejection of anti-Semitism—it is nonetheless a revealing example of how adherence to Social Democratic principles prompted worker gymnasts to attempt to purge Jahn's legacy of its most unacceptable traits. This is but one instance of frequent efforts to interpret Jahn through labor movement eyes, to create, that is, an historical image of Jahn that would be useful for worker gymnasts. For the regional conference of workers' gymnastic clubs of the Saxon district in 1894, one Friedrich Hermann Bobe composed a "Welcoming Poem," in great part devoted to Jahn. The German Gymnastic League, Bobe wrote, had abandoned the true spirit of Jahn. Workers' clubs were enthusiastically revitalizing the genuine spirit of the old "Turnvater"—the fight for *Freiheit*.[46] At that same conference a delegate, Marx from Dresden, after advocating gymnastic exercises and sociability, concluded with a statement that reflected the deep influence of Jahn's values.

When we strive to develop every gymnast, young or old, regardless of his line of thought [*Richtung*] or religion, into a worthy member of human society, then the noble art of gymnastics [*die edle Turnerei*] will be what it should be according to the spirit of the lively and youthful Jahn and of the venerable Arndt. This first regional gymnastic meet is intended to contribute to that end, so that a free and genuine spirit of the populace [*ein freies, ein wahres Volksthum*] is once again a reality.[47]

Such sentiments were broadly dispersed. In 1905 one club made a pilgrimage (*Pilgerfahrt*) to Jahn's graveside in Freiburg on the Unstrut, the small town in the Prussian province of Saxony where Jahn lived for the last twenty-five years of his life. The emotional appeal exerted by the legendary Jahn is illustrated vividly in the reverential report written by one of the "pilgrims." As they approached the area of the Jahn Museum, the Jahn House, and the Jahn Gymnastic Hall, the labor movement "pilgrims" were overcome by a "kind of holy veneration," conscious that they were standing on "historic ground." Visiting the Jahn Museum, they perused handwritten documents and felt a closeness to the old master. "He [Jahn] wrote words of courage to which we can still subscribe today without reservation." Late that evening, returning home in fourth-class train coaches, they finally met up with a brother club that had made the same pilgrimage. "Oh, and what luck! Our comrades had brought along pipe and drums and just as soon as the train started they let loose with piping and drumming. . . . They drummed the Jahn revelry [*Jahn-Schwelgerei*] completely out of our heads."[48] It took more than pipe and drums to get enchantment with Jahn out of the world of the workers' gymnastic clubs. That only came about during the latter years of the Weimar Republic. His high standing in the milieu of the labor movement was not seriously challenged before the First World War.[49] To some extent, of course, the high standing had been made possible by the attempts of worker gymnasts to interpret Jahn's heritage so that it would fit more easily into a Social Democratic environment. In effect, they tried, though never successfully, to social-democratize "Turnvater" Jahn.

Not all practices of the German gymnastic tradition were taken over uncritically by labor movement clubs. Most German recreational and entertainment associations assumed the value of competitions, awards, prizes, medals, and various forms of distinction. A heated debate on this issue erupted early in the workers' gymnastic and sports clubs and never reached a universally accepted resolution. There were various arguments against competition and prizes, most resting on the assumption that such practices reflected the competitive market system of capitalism and contradicted Social Democratic ideals of solidarity, brotherhood, and equality. The desire for prizes and distinctions diverted attention from the true purpose of sport, physical improvement, and relaxation, and threatened to replace it with ego gratifications and arrogant individualism. As early as 1895 delegates to the national convention of the Workers' Gymnastic Federation, meeting in Magdeburg, passed a resolution forbidding prizes and money awards. Competitive gymnastic exhibitions without prizes were not forbidden, but it was left to regional federations to adopt policies for their member clubs.[50]

That did not settle the matter. On the contrary, the debate became even more vigorous. The supporters of competition and distinctions did not succumb even when their resolutions failed. Toward the end of the decade there was a concerted effort to expunge all competition from the workers' gymnastic clubs. At the national conference of the Workers' Gymnastic Federation in Harburg (near Hamburg) in 1901, the delegates adopted a wide-sweeping resolution, drafted by Karl Frey (Stuttgart), that condemned all competition and distinctions. The purpose of gymnastics, Frey's resolution argued, was to promote the health of the "outer and inner organism." It strengthened the individual worker in the "struggle for existence," and helped ameliorate the harmful effects of the "current, one-sided system of production." These advantages could be undermined, however, if gymnastics was so organized that it overtaxed individual reserves of strength. He called for moderation to preserve health. Individual and group competitions designed to attain a specified level resembled the struggle that went on so "ruthlessly" in economic life. Moreover, prize competitions were costly in money and time, undermined the inner harmony and sociability of clubs, and left dissension and a poisoned atmosphere.[51]

The resolution passed, but it also failed to resolve the issue. The minority in favor of competitions and distinctions grew even more vociferous during the following decade. By 1911 the Workers' Gymnastic Federation had adopted a new position, officially allowing individual competition on condition that it take place within an individual club or at regional meets. Competition between clubs remained forbidden.[52]

What underlay the ongoing debate on awards and distinctions was a tension between two overlapping functions of the gymnastic clubs: symbolizing ideology and deriving pleasure in performance. Advocates of competitions and distinctions wanted to emphasize performance and were prepared to use awards as a means to stimulate motivation. Opponents of awards believed that, regardless of the kind of activity, club practices should manifest the values and principles of the Social Democratic labor movement. They perceived correctly that ideological preferences could be reflected in how recreational activities were structured. On the other hand, advocates of awards were not necessarily indifferent to Social Democratic principles, but they did emphasize performance and its recognition above ideological symbolism. The rationale for their view rested on notions of specialization and compartmentalization, namely, that each organization (whether party, trade union, or recreational club) had to give clear priority to one function and that attempts to balance multiple functions only created confusion. However reasonable that argument may appear, its unlimited acceptance would have undermined the emancipatory role and the significance of the auxiliary associations.

The same underlying tension between symbolizing ideology and stressing performance could manifest itself in all labor movement clubs. Some kinds of clubs favored one function over another. The Workers' Athletic Federation, for example, stated bluntly from its founding in 1906 that it had no place for prizes and distinctions, that its aim was to promote physical fitness (undermined by capitalism) in the working class, and that it intended to ensure that sports would not be a privilege of the propertied class.[53] Workers' swimming clubs banned prize competitions by statute. A member in Hamburg was actually expelled from the local workers' swimming club because he had participated in a prize competition. When it was established that he had been unaware of the statute, he was reinstated. There were conflicting views, however, as to whether the swimming clubs were sufficiently concerned about how their practices symbolized values and principles. In the words of one anonymous commentator, it took years "to free workers' swimming clubs from *bürgerlich* residues, petty clubbishness [*Vereinsmeierei*] and splinterings, obsession with sports [*Sportfexereien*], dizziness over records, distinctions of 'victors,' etc."[54] Clearly, it became more and more difficult, as the world of the labor movement absorbed an increasing number of activities, to expect all segments of the expanded constituency to agree that their particular activity should symbolize Social Democratic principles and values to the detriment of other club functions.

The tension between performance and symbolizing ideology manifested itself with increasing clarity between 1890 and 1914. Regardless of how devoted to socialism they might be, most singers, for example, could not dispel the desire to perform well. The more they sang and improved, the more they enjoyed it. If they wanted to perfect their singing, they needed directors of talent and training. Few organized workers were musically educated or possessed the minimum skills required to direct a choral group. To solve the problem, the societies often went beyond their own labor movement circles to find competent conductors.

Directors were attracted in a number of ways, but it is not clear how many were active because of a prior commitment to the socialist labor movement. Commenting on the role of conductors, Franz Bothe, a leader in the Federation of Workers' Singing Societies, emphasized that "the gentlemen [directors] often come to us from another world, where the worker is not at home, and the world of the worker is alien to them [directors]. They do not have a feeling for the workers."[55] Statistical evidence supports the contention that directors constituted a rather substantial nonworker element. Of 2,060 directors in 1910, no less than 1,250, or 60 percent, listed themselves as "professional musicians." The other 40 percent were classified as amateur musicians, coming from 149 different occupations; many were from the free professions, but there was also a sprinkling of innkeepers, artisans, and workers. Some were schoolteachers, but in Prussia they were often prohibited by local regulations from all connections with the labor movement. Directors found their roles more appealing if they received a regular honorarium, and some musicians took directorships in workers' singing societies primarily to supplement their incomes. Of the active directors in 1910, 70 percent received a monthly honorarium ranging from less than five to twenty marks monthly. Although the sums were modest, they indicate that the societies, all with limited funds, valued directors who contributed substantially to the choir's musical achievements.[56]

The presence of professional musicians as directors in workers' singing societies reinforced the strength of the performance function. Directors, as well as talented members, often believed that the most important goal for a singing society was to achieve high quality in presenting choral music. Satisfaction in singing required, in turn, that the choral music chosen should also be aesthetically pleasing.[57]

Since the mass political songs of the labor movement seldom fulfilled the aesthetic expectations of those devoted to high artistic quality in performance, there was always pressure to use more of the established repertory of the German male choir tradition. When that happened, ideological symbolism suffered. The dominant trend in workers' choral societies throughout the Wilhelmian era was to give increasing importance to performance. Festival committees wanted to know how their choirs compared to other German singers, so professional musicians were engaged to submit critical evaluations. At a festival of the Württemberg Federation of Workers' Singing Societies in 1908 three critics were invited to submit their evaluations. Festival leaders proudly reported that the "critiques recognized the diligence, determination, ability, and the comrades' devotion to art."[58] The pursuit of excellence became more and more pronounced.

Giving preference to performance over ideology overlapped with what appeared to be an increasing influence of reformism in the singing societies in the years after the turn of the century. That overlap was not accidental. Social Democratic reformists were more likely than radical Marxists to accept the principle that the chief function of clubs was entertainment and recreation and not ideological expression. However, reformists did not need to create the desire in labor movement clubs to excel in performance. That desire came naturally with performing. But the reformist posture, unlike that of orthodox and radical Marxists, accepted the subordination of ideological representation without serious regrets.[59]

Emphasis on performance also created tension with sociability. One can see that same tension in nonsocialist clubs. As the choral societies in Weinheim an der Bergstrasse improved artistically, they made a greater separation between times set aside for performance and for sociability. In the beginning singing had served sociability; as time passed it was valued in and of itself.[60] The same tendency was apparent in the workers' singing societies. The tension became amply evident after the turn of the century, when a concerted effort began to get small choirs to merge with others. There were numerous reasons behind the drive for amalgamation, which was not, incidentally, restricted to the choral societies. Small choirs usually had limited musical and financial resources, but an abundance of sociability. Members were sometimes friends, knew each other well, and enjoyed practice sessions as times of togetherness. On the other hand, directors needed a large number of able singers if their choirs were going to perform choral music of high quality. Large singing societies offered a chance to bring together experienced voices and, therefore, greater musical range and flexibility. For that reason various leaders of the singing societies encouraged small choirs to merge and form larger ones.[61]

Around the turn of the century the encouragement turned into a high-pressure campaign sponsored by the executive committee of the national Federation of Workers' Singing Societies. But the small society was the haven of sociability. A club with substantially more than about twenty to twenty-five members began to lose its *Gemütlichkeit*. It is not surprising therefore that many rank-and-file members expressed considerable reluctance about mergers, and there were even clubs that preferred to withdraw from the national federation rather than amalgamate and lose their identity.[62] Advocates of amalgamation denounced the holdouts for their backwardness and *Vereinsmeierei*. In some cities, for example, Frankfurt am Main and Leipzig, a number of mergers took place after the turn of the century. But in Hamburg the societies were more defiant. They were scolded directly by Julius Meyer, president of the Federation of Workers' Singing Societies, in a speech in Hamburg in May 1912. "It is regrettable," he chided, "that small societies hold so firmly to [their] banners and names; they should see once and for all that only large societies are capable of achieving anything." He extolled the fact that a number of workers' singing societies had invited musical critics from outside to evaluate their concerts and urged his listeners to take that as an incentive to improve. To add weight to his argument he appealed to a prestigious name among the singers, stressing that "even the composer [Josef] Scheu thought that a society had to have at least 150 singers."[63]

Resistance to amalgamation was strengthened by the fact that several kinds of workers' clubs, especially the singing societies, had substantial numbers of "passive" members. By enrolling in a club as a passive member, a labor movement adherent could simultaneously support organizations of Social Democracy and satisfy a personal need for sociability among like-minded people. Clubs were pleased to enroll passive members as a way to collect more dues and to give an image of continuous growth and importance. The ratio of active to passive members varied dramatically, but in some instances it was exaggerated in favor of passive members. Out of 537 members in four singing societies in Schleswig-Holstein, no less than 415 were passive members! In the Ostland federation in 1907 there were 53 societies with a total of 1,924 active and

2,333 passive members.[64] These extremely high ratios of passive members seem to be exceptional. Depending on what they wanted from the societies, passive members could oppose or support mergers. Those who were there chiefly to support socialist organizations and express an ideological commitment were likely to look favorably on amalgamation because leaders throughout Social Democracy promoted it as a measure that would strengthen the labor movement. But passive members who looked on a club as a social organization had good reason to oppose mergers. They were especially vulnerable to the charge of *Vereinsmeierei.*[65]

The battle against *Vereinsmeierei* and for amalgamation went on throughout the associational life of the labor movement after the turn of the century. The Workers' Cycling Federation "Solidarity" decided at its conference in Erfurt in 1904 that instead of promoting new clubs, henceforth each locality (*Ort*) would have only one workers' cycling club. The resolution won approval among most members, but in Berlin and environs many clubs refused to abide by the decision. To preserve their independence, they abandoned the Workers' Cycling Federation "Solidarity" and founded their own workers' cycling league, which they called Freiheit. The new league, though comparatively small, stood for the preservation of the kind of club life, intimacy, and localism that made the organizations so appealing to many members. The swimming clubs adopted the same principle of one locality, one club, but without suffering any division as a consequence.[66]

After 1906 the fight for amalgamation among workers' educational clubs was carried on by the Social Democratic party's Central Education Commission. On the basis of its first survey, commission members concluded that the educational work of the labor movement suffered because of *Vereinsmeierei* and an excess of sociability in the clubs of singers and gymnasts.[67] The commission therefore assumed that educational societies would be more effective if they pooled their resources through amalgamation. The assumption was not entirely warranted; amalgamation, it turns out, could also be counterproductive. A report on the educational societies from 1912 indicated that after the merger of three societies into the Continuing Education Society for Hamburg-Altona (Fortbildungsverein für Hamburg-Altona), the new organization had only one clear advantage over the older clubs: It could use the Trade Union Building. Beyond that, however, the results of the merger were not encouraging. Members felt less and less responsibility for the new and much larger organization and they let direction fall into the hands of a few functionaries. General membership meetings, once very important in the life of the societies, were held less frequently and were very poorly attended. In short, the report concluded ruefully that the "inner cohesion among the members" had been lost. Enrollees in the educational programs could no longer feel that they belonged to a community, but simply attended courses as individuals. A vital ingredient of associational life had been lost.[68]

A vibrant life in the voluntary associations of the labor movement depended on a balance of club functions. Sociability, and all the frivolities that implied, could not be cast aside without undermining the whole structure. Personal attachments, familiarity, and fellowship among acquaintances created emotional bonds that were just as important for the vitality of the cultural world of the labor movement as party loyalty and ideological commitment.[69] Ideological symbolism and sociability could reinforce each other, but only on the assumption that once brought together by some common belief in the cause of the labor movement club members did not also insist on strict adherence to closely defined doctrines. The ideological symbols of labor movement clubs, as with all symbols, were appropriately broad and even ambiguous. They had to be. If any one function had won complete dominance, the associations would have lost their relevance for the personal needs of organized workers. All three central functions, though always in subdued competition, had to reach a balance if the associations were to serve their constituencies effectively and to attract other workers to the labor movement.[70]

4

Festivals

It would be easy to conclude that the leisure time activities sponsored within the labor movement were marginal both to the daily lives of organized workers and to the functions of the Social Democratic party and the free trade unions. There is something to be said for this conclusion, though it rests on assumptions that need to be examined if we are to avoid hasty judgments that may divert us from seeking a full and accurate understanding of the significance of the recreational, entertainment, and educational endeavors in the labor movement. The indisputable fact that work constituted the main activity of workers (and most other social groups as well), that work and activities directly related to it took up many more hours than could be given to organized leisure time activities, does not of itself explain the psychological or ideational significance of either kind of endeavor. To measure significance chiefly in terms of the proportion of time taken up by work in relation to leisure time activities would be excessively mechanistic and could lead to gross misjudgments. The stress on the centrality of work in the lives of workers, however salutary it has been as a corrective to an overemphasis on ideology and formal organizations, does not answer all questions about the behavior, beliefs, and values of organized workers.[1] It tells us where workers were physically and what they were doing, but not necessarily what they were feeling and thinking. Emphasis on the work process tells us what they routinely did, but does not yet demonstrate the commensurability of routine and meaningfulness. It is also possible to argue for their incommensurability, for rare and unusual events that may have occupied only a miniscule portion of a worker's time could nonetheless be of special significance precisely because, among other things, they were unique and stood out in bold relief against the background of the workaday routine. This is hypothetical, but it is appropriate to suggest that as work processes became more routine, and as work time and leisure time were increasingly separated, it became more likely that workers, even in skilled trades, looked with greater anticipation to their nonwork hours for meaningful experiences.[2]

Festivals were among those events that called special attention to the cultural world of the labor movement and attracted large numbers of participants and spectators. Although festivals and other kinds of celebrations were frequent occurences in the labor movement, they were not part of a daily routine. They were, nonetheless, an integral part of the labor movement milieu and, more important, they were invariably high points in the life of the sponsoring organizations. They gave a public presentation of the alternative culture in symbolic and recreational form.

Festivals present us with an opportunity to observe the public behavior of the movement's voluntary associations and to see how socializing, symbolizing beliefs, and striving for satisfaction in various kinds of performance were intermingled on these occasions. Many clubs participated in nearly all festivals sponsored by organizations within the labor movement and, in addition, almost every type of club held its own festivals at least once or twice annually. Festivals might be sponsored by a single club, by an ad hoc group of clubs, or quite commonly by the urban or regional leagues of the clubs. In addition, local organizations of the Social Democratic party (*Wahlvereine*) and of the free trade unions held numerous festivals.

Festivals were rich in symbols, ceremonies, and even ritual behavior, the evidence of which has led some commentators to interpret these occasions as religious phenomena.[3] This interpretation is based on a definition that assumes that rituals necessarily involve a relationship to sacred objects or beliefs in a supranatural world. These assumptions need not be shared. It is equally valid to distinguish between religious and secular rituals, what may also be called civic or political rituals.[4] The ceremonies at the festivals of the labor movement were instances of such secular rituals. They took place according to patterns that were repeated regularly at festivals throughout Germany and they embodied signs and symbols that signified the values and ideals of the labor movement. Although participants honored these ideals, they did not generally ascribe sacredness to the objects, signs, and symbols that represented the high principles of their movement. They showed respect before those symbols, but they did not worship them. They committed themselves to their cause, but their ceremonies were not imbued with a sense of holiness.[5]

The fact that festival rituals in the labor movement were essentially secular does not mean that they were less significant than religious ritual. In purely functional terms these secular ceremonies were comparable to religious rituals: They served to legitimate the substance of festivals and to provide the symbolic language that bound together the activities and programs as cohesive units. This was possible because ritual, secular or religious, is presentational. It presents something for acceptance and approval, not for discussion, debate, and resolution. Ceremonies at labor movement festivals employed music, rhetoric, and visual symbols to set forth values and ideas as if these were beyond all possible dispute. The nature of festivals needs therefore to be contrasted to the procedures followed at the congresses of the Social Democratic party and the free trade unions, where, despite the presence of certain limited ritualistic behavior, the assumption prevailed that delegates were gathered to present differing views, to engage in argumentation, and to reach resolutions through a rational process. That created the common image of the socialist labor movement as highly theoretical, devoted to Marxist ideology, rational and deliberative, and instrumentalist in method. The festival environment suggests strongly that we should modify that image by incorporating as well those dimensions that were ceremonial, emotional, and evocative.

By the end of the nineteenth century nearly every locality with an active labor movement could count on several festivals annually, with a number of them taking place during the summer months. The formal political festivals sponsored by the Social Democratic party organizations constituted a kind of socialist oppositional counterpart to the German calendar of patriotic festivals. Prior to the 1890s the most important party celebration had been the March Festival (*Märzfeier*), originally held to honor the outbreak of the revolution in 1848 but merged in the 1870s and 1880s with a memorial for the Paris Commune. This dual meaning did not last, however. By the end of the nineteenth century the link to the Paris Commune had weakened and 1848 became once again the sole center of attention at March festivals. After 1890 March festivals gave way to May Day demonstrations (*Maifeier*) as the most important explicitly political festival of the movement. In many localities the socialist labor movement also sponsored a Summer Festival, often in July, and, in late August, a Lassalle Festival served in certain areas as a socialist answer to the patriotic Sedan Day celebrations. Thus the time chosen for the festival was not Lassalle's birthday, which fell in April, but August 31, the date on which he died after suffering wounds in his famous duel in 1864. Lassalle Festivals were especially popular in the Rhineland and Westphalia.[6]

Many clubs in the labor movement were as energetic in sponsoring festivals as was the party itself. Indeed, looking back on the era after 1890 it would appear that a festival fever had overtaken the clubs of the movement. Regardless of what constituted its main activity, every type of organization found reasons to hold festivals. If no other reason presented itself, then annually there would be at least a Founders' Day Festival (*Stiftungsfest*). For most of the associations, but especially for singing societies and sports clubs, festivals were occasions that served the most diverse functions; they offered sociable fellowship, entertainment, drinking, opportunities for performance, as well as a way to express loyalty to the movement simply by being in attendance.[7]

Festivals created a feeling of belonging that could not be brought to life to the same degree by the more frequent business meetings of the party, trade unions, and auxiliary organizations. This sense of community could reach well beyond the local membership because festivals often attracted sympathetic visitors and delegations from neighboring towns, creating opportunities for people to become acquainted who otherwise would not meet. At a festival of the free trade unions in Aachen in July 1911 socialist visitors came from Maastricht, across the Dutch border, adding a touch of internationalism. They brought revolutionary posters and joined in the festival procession, led, according to a report in the local labor newspaper, by "a woman of the barricades, carrying the huge red party flag—and Aachen did not collapse!"[8]

Festivals were also family affairs. Women and children attended and participated, though they played only minor roles in the normal life of the party and trade unions. Even in the clubs of the labor movement women were seldom prominent, except in their own socialist feminist associations. The family character of festivals came to be true of May Day celebrations as well after the turn of the century. Since festivals frequently took place on Sunday, the one day of the week when most workers would be free from shop or factory, they were the only occasions when the extended constituency of the labor movement in a given locality had an opportunity to be together. They offered a retreat from the routine world of work nd household into a world of relaxed community of like-minded people.

As events for the whole family, festivals, including many May Day celebrations, offered something for everyone. Children and young people who had little or no comprehension of the social and political issues that animated the labor movement were offered a lively mixture of games and diversions. Paul Göhre attended several festivals during the summer of 1891 and at one in particular, in Siegmar, a small town near Chemnitz, he found a "genuine youth festival" with games, trinkets for children, target shooting, balloons, and many other diversions. A boisterous carnival atmosphere prevailed.[9] At other festivals serious matters might alternate with amusements, or they took place simultaneously in different parts of the festival grounds. Even labor movement journalists noted, with scarcely hidden irony, the unlikely conjunction of earnest ideological pronouncements and frivolous pastimes. There was entertainment for nearly everyone. For the local May Woods Festival (*Maiwaldfest*) of the Social Democratic party in Frankfurt am Main in 1908, the festival committee promised that

> the Offenbach Music Society, the Workers' Singing Society, and the Workers' Gymnastic Club will offer their very best so that no one will be bored. The Workers' Cycling Club will once again set up a booth; for those with a passion for shooting there will be a shooting gallery. For the little kids, children's games are planned and of course a carousel will not be lacking; there will also be no lack of sweets and toys. Everything that the festival committee can do is being done. Hopefully, the heavens will see to it that there will be good weather.[10]

Similarly, even a simple trade union festival in Aachen provided a round of diversions. In the words of an anonymous reporter, "there was bowling, shooting, throwing, exercising, swimming, cycling, riding, dancing, sitting and drinking, according to one's inclination, skill and means."[11] The games and amusements might vary from festival to festival, but the general pattern prevailed throughout the labor movement.

Most festivals combined opportunities for symbolic expression, performance, and socializing, although a few were given over almost exclusively to nonpolitical entertainment, amusements, and socializing. In 1898 the Free Wheels (Freie Radler), a cyclist club from Horn (a district of Hamburg), advertised a "Great Cyclist Festival" to take place in Horner Park that would include "pleasure rides [*Korsofahrt*], garden concert, a ball, hall and fancy riding, prize bowling for men, as well as entertainment games for women and children."[12] The swimming clubs in Hamburg went in for costume festivals at Fasching (Carnival), though they did not specifically call them Fasching celebrations. Declaring that there would be "fun in every corner," the Hamburg workers' swimming societies announced their "Great Costume Celebration" as a "beach festival in the realm of Prince Carnival" and went on to spell out the following attractions: master wrestlers and an acrobat would perform with perfection; a "world-famous *Bänkelsänger*" would appear with "enticing" presentations; and spectators could visit a museum with lore of the sea. In other places there would be raffles for sea monsters, with valuable prizes of carp, eel, and other goodies. An announcement for a similar festival in 1911 also played on images of the sea and the Fasching theme. Mermaids and Neptune were scheduled for big roles at the festival. To encourage the Fasching spirit of flirtation and changing partners, the announcement promised that "Neptune's court attendant will provide magnificent wedding cakes and sweets to be acquired through raffles. No limits will be placed on the fun; a polonaise will bring surprises of every kind and the 'aquatic justice of the peace' will get enough to do to keep his hands full. Naturally, without commitments for later times!!" Even with so much emphasis on amusements at certain festivals, political symbolism always played its part. The cyclists would carry emblems in red; club banners with labor movement slogans would be on display; and the above events in 1910 and 1911 were held in the Trade Union Building.[13]

Festivals took place as units. What they brought together came to belong together. What they left out did not belong. This should not be taken to imply that festivals reflected theoretical or practical consistency. It is not even concerned with that issue. It affirms only that people responsible for labor movement festivals had a sense of what was and what was not relevant and appropriate. This sense of relevance was acquired by living in the milieu and did not have to be derived from some well-articulated conception that prescribed the nature of labor movement festivals. Festivals were therefore important expressions of how leaders in various activities viewed themselves and their movement and how they wanted it to be understood. In fashioning a festival they marked out, almost spontaneously, the boundaries of the social-cultural world of the labor movement. The fact that most festival programs—May Day being the striking exception—were not officially recognized as statements of party or trade union policies in no way diminishes their meaningfulness as manifestations of the social-cultural milieu of the socialist labor movement. On the contrary, they were in one sense more meaningful because they reflected popularly held notions of local leaders as to what did and what did not belong. Festivals mirrored the fact that the culture of the labor movement was not drawn exclusively from socialist or working-class sources. It was eclectic; but its eclectic mixture came to constitute a meaningful whole. In that process festivals functioned as integrating events through which the mixture manifested itself as a meaningful social-cultural entity.

All labor movement festivals embodied political significance. They were public dramas, expressing in deed and symbol the values of the milieu to which they belonged. They were political even when their organizers denied all political intent. The labor movement was on public display, often in seemingly innocent clothing, but never lacking sufficient symbols to make a clear public declaration of political ideas and social values. In that functional sense they resembled the festivals of many other German associations; by traditions extending back decades German male choruses and gymnasts had used festivals to publicize their patriotic political goals.[14] This functional parallel was far outweighed, however, by the substantive contrasts between socialist festivals and those of other German organizations because labor movement festivals, even the least political of them, were established not only for entertainment but as a way to answer the claims of German nationalism.

The political implications of even the most innocent festivals did not escape the notice of the police, who looked suspiciously on any gathering of members of the labor movement. Festivals were watched closely. Well in advance of a festival organizational leaders had to obtain permission from the authorities to hold the event. They were normally expected to present a full statement of all planned activities. If part or all of the festival was to take place in a beer hall or restaurant, which was most often the case, then under normal conditions the owner also had to register the planned event with the police. Approval of labor movement festivals was seldom, if ever, automatic, and there were many instances when the gendarmerie prohibited some part of the planned program. In middle and northern Germany police were particularly strict during the 1890s, though application of the laws varied and in many parts of Germany severe restrictions remained in full force well after the turn of the century. Reports for 1902 on the festivals of the singing societies for all of Germany, for example, show that police had rejected about one-half of the requests for permission to hold a procession. Imperial Germany was, as one author has noted, a "state in which considerable importance was attached to what was said" as well as to what was done, and it followed that police felt it was especially important to censor everything that was to be presented at socialist festivals.[15]

Speeches, declamations, and plays in particular drew the attention of police. In 1904 police in Leipzig prohibited the performance of Friedrich Bosse's agitational play *The People Awake* (*Das Volk erwacht*) at the Twenty-fifth Founders' Day Festival of the Workers' Educational Society.[16] At a singing society festival for the district of the electorate of Hesse-Waldeck-South Hanover in July 1901, police rejected a parade request on the ground that public safety would be endangered. When the singers in the districts of Brandenburg and Lausitz planned a festival for July 1911 to take place in Forst, police allowed the festival, but banners with Social Democratic inscriptions were prohibited. Showing a highly refined but curious sense for differentiating the forcefulness of labels, the police disallowed the inscription "Free Singers" ("Freie Sänger"), but passed favorably on "Worker Singers" ("Arbeitersänger"). Finally, in a flurry of pendantry the police prescribed that the color red could not be used in the first letter of words on banners! On the same occasion the festival committee had secretly engaged a *bürgerlich* music authority to give a confidential evaluation of the singers' performance, but he was so intimidated by rumors and vague threats that he failed to appear.[17]

Even in the face of such obstacles Social Democrats preserved a sense of humor. They often found police anxiety amusing and openly mocked the fears of nonsocialists. The Social Democratic humor magazine *Der wahre Jacob,* hearing of police concern about an upcoming festival of the Westphalian workers' singing societies, sent a reporter to observe the dangerous situation. In his published account the reporter noted sarcastically that "the festival area itself was decorated with flags colored red with bourgeois blood." Even singing societies played tricks on policemen to make them look ridiculous. In 1894, when police in Mittweida refused to give permission for a festival, members of the workers' singing societies

nonetheless gathered in several large restaurants, sang some of
their songs, and then moved rapidly from place to place when the
arrival of the police seemed imminent.[18]

May Day festivals drew the heaviest fire from the authorities.
Processions might or might not be allowed. When they were permitted police often prohibited music and singing during the march.
May Day processions thus came to be thought of in Germany as
silent marches, and some historians, assuming that the silence was
always self-imposed, have interpreted this as evidence that these
processions took on sacred qualities. In fact, socialists played instruments and sang while marching whenever possible. In Leipzig,
for example, police for the first time authorized music in the procession in 1909 and four bands (*Musikkapelle*) marched and
played. In the following year, too, the procession in Leipzig moved
to the "tones of workers' songs," probably the "Marseillaise" and
the "Socialist March," the latter by Max Kegel.[19] During the 1890s
police had been especially opposed to speaking and singing in the
meeting halls themselves. No procession was permitted at a May
Day Festival in Frankfurt am Main in 1893 and, in addition, police
had proscribed singing and dancing as well as speaking. That left
only instrumental music. When the crowd became disorderly, a
local socialist leader who wanted to restore calm first had to request official permission before he could speak.[20]

The visible power of the state as represented in uniformed police
often aroused both fear and hostility among the participants. The
trade union leader Otto Buchwitz (1879–1964) first attended a
May Day Festival in 1895 in Morgenau (near Breslau) when he was
sixteen. That year the first of May fell on Sunday, which meant
that the authorities anticipated large numbers and correspondingly
dispatched a full force of policemen. The possibility of an angry
confrontation created a tense and oppressive atmosphere. Buchwitz was deeply impressed by the event as he wrote later in his
memoir.

> At the time it required much personal courage to participate in a
> festival of that nature because employers expelled without hesitation
> workers who celebrated May Day. . . . Attendance was not over-
> whelming, but there were nonetheless some hundred workers. At
> least one hundred policemen, mounted and on foot, were sent to
> Morgenau, so great at that time was the fear of the labor movement
> among the capitalist defenders of order. A comrade from Breslau,
> whose name I no longer remember, was supposed to give the festival
> speech. Still it is unforgettable to me how immediately upon the

opening of the meeting a civilian accompanied by several policemen
stepped to the head table to prohibit all speeches. An enormous
storm of protest began immediately with whistling and shouting
against the lackeys of reaction. The chairman and sergeant-at-arms
made an effort to restore order. They finally succeeded and the
festival went on, the assembled remaining in sociable companionship
[*gemütliches Zusammensein*] and cheerful song. Policemen and informers roamed among the tables to see whether anybody or at
anyplace a politically dangerous [*staatsfeindlich*] speech was being
made.[21]

Such occurrences were not unusual, although police in Silesia may
have been particularly severe. Long after the turn of the century
singing societies in Breslau still reported that their festivals were
sharply restrained by the police. Harassment was less pronounced
in the states of southern Germany, but in most areas of Prussia one
could always anticipate official hostility.[22]

The pressure of police surveillance was never fully removed, a
fact that always influenced the behavior of May Day celebrants.
Festival participants had learned from years of experience how to
adapt to the oppressive environment created by the omnipresent
Pickelhaube (spiked helmet). They had little choice. Adapting
meant avoiding confrontations; it implied moderate and acceptable
behavior. Social Democrats preferred to avoid violence, an atti-
tude that was understandable in the context of Imperial Germany.
But it also tamed them, compelling them to moderate the style, if
not also the substance, of their efforts to nurture a festival culture
as a counter to Germany's patriotic celebrations.[23]

Ironically, cooperation between local governments and festival
organizers was also possible. In a few instances singing societies
even enjoyed moderate success in obtaining financial subventions
from local governments. In December 1907 the Kaiserslautern city
government gave the Palatinate League of Workers' Singing Societies a subsidy of one hundred marks and, in addition, provided a
municipal hall at no charge. In Nuremberg in 1910 the city government granted the festival committee a subvention of fourteen hundred marks, threw in another eight hundred marks for decorating
the Bahnhofplatz, and saw to it that municipal buildings were
decked with flags. A year later in Esslingen, the Oberbürger-
meister, Dr. Mülberg, spoke at the opening ceremonies of a
workers' singing society festival and for his cooperation the festival
committee thanked him profusely. In the spring of 1914 the Munich municipal government authorized three thousand marks to

support an upcoming festival of workers' singing societies. Conservative Bavarians voiced strong criticism, but the state refused to intervene against the city's favorable action. But in 1907 the Görlitz city council had turned down a request by a festival committee for a subsidy of five hundred marks; the committee nonetheless had lauded the city police for behaving with distinction throughout the festivities.[24] Despite the above instances, financial support for labor movement festivals was rare. More often, local governments were cool or openly hostile.

Although labor movement festivals varied in certain substantive matters, in structure and style they tended to be similar. One can discern a common pattern, modified by special features to fit the needs and desires of particular kinds of organizations. The formats of printed festival programs give clues to the nature and dynamics of these occasions. Published programs ranged from a one-page listing to elaborate festival books of more than one hundred pages. The simple format was common before the turn of the century; the more elaborate books began to appear in the latter 1890s, though simple formats also continued to be used. Programs that consisted of only a few pages usually listed the essential information on the procession and the concert and might include the texts of a few songs for mass singing.

The larger books exploded with information and advertising. The festival book of the Rhenish League of Workers' Singing Societies in 1899 had sixty-two pages devoted to the program (it printed all song texts) and other information (including a railroad schedule) and another sixty-four pages of advertisements. Advertisers came from a wide spectrum, but beer halls, restaurants, and retail businesses in particular viewed it as a profitable investment to place announcements in festival books. This handsome *Festbuch* could be purchased for the comparatively modest price of twenty pfennigs, presumably because of the revenue acquired through advertising.[25] Very modest programs without advertising cost that much or more. Festival books also included informative articles. Short histories and descriptions of the host city or region reflected a certain local pride of the sponsoring clubs. The festival books of gymnastic organizations were likely to include articles of several pages on gymnastic techniques, club activities, and on "Turnvater" Jahn and the history of German gymnastics.[26]

For May Day festivals, central party headquarters printed pamphlets, usually entitled *Maifeier* (with a year), which could be distributed nationally and used to supplement the printed programs produced by local committees.[27] *Maifeier* for 1893 featured on the front cover a picture of a girl holding the May Day banner, accompanied by a poem by Leopold Jacoby. Inside an article explained the meaning of May Day (signed by W. L., presumably Wilhelm Liebknecht); a poem by Ernst Klaar glorified proletarians; a centerfold featured the "Goddess of freedom, equality, and brotherhood," surrounded and hailed by workers, women, and children, all waving flags inscribed with the words "Truth" and "Justice"; and, finally, there were several pages of inspiring quotations from international labor leaders. Such festival programs were not only guides to a particular event, but also revealed some of the contours of the movement's social-cultural milieu. They could also be souvenirs, reminding participants of times when they had expressed their convictions by marching, singing, eating, drinking, dancing, and gossiping with others who belonged to the same world.

Normally festivals lasted one day—Sunday or some national holiday—though the larger regional festivals might be planned for parts of two days and, in a few instances, they even spilled over to a third day. Large German restaurants were reserved or, if that was impossible, a large hall or even a park was used. In the years immediately before the First World War the amalgamated trade unions in a number of cities had managed to build their own central trade union buildings. These could then be used by affiliated clubs for special events and festivals. However, the overwhelming number of labor movement festivals were held in public parks or in the large halls or gardens of restaurants and beer halls. Thousands upon thousands attended, if we are to believe the estimates of both police and festival planners. In the last years before the war singers' festivals, even in moderate-size towns, drew large numbers. In 1911, at a regional festival in Erfurt, three thousand sang and eleven thousand actively participated. In Esslingen an estimated twenty thousand attended. In the following year twenty thousand attended a festival in Berlin, and at a regional festival in Ludwigshafen a reported forty-five hundred were active singers.[28]

On the eve of the festival day, or possibly on the subsequent evening, local groups hosted a *Kommers,* a gathering for conviviality, eating, drinking, and entertainment. Holding a *Kommers* was a tradition with all German associations, including student corporations, and the Social Democratic party itself normally held a *Kommers* on the evening of the opening of party congresses. At the *Kommers* of the congresses at Erfurt (1891) and Berlin (1892) Boleslav Strzelewicz entertained the assembled delegates with his

The centerfold from *Mai-Fest 1899,* a May Day pamphlet published and distributed by the Social Democratic party. Labor and the arts join hands in the interest
of freedom, as symbolized in a painting by Arnold Böcklin. Staatsarchiv
Düsseldorf.

Organized workers in the graphic trades and members of the Free Gymnasts (Freie Turnerschaft) in the procession at a May Day Festival in Hanau in 1910. Archiv der sozialen Demokratie, Bonn.

Members from District 19 of the Workers' Cycling Federation "Solidarity" lead the procession at a festival of workers' singing societies in Nuremberg in 1910. Wolfgang Ruppert (ed.), *Lebensgeschichten: Zur deutschen Sozialgeschichte 1850–1950* (Opladen: Leske Verlag und Budrich, 1980).

The procession returning to its starting point point at the May Day Festival in Hanau in 1910. Archiv der sozialen Demokratie, Bonn.

A festival of workers' singing societies held in Nuremberg in 1910. A horse-drawn float combines the celebration of beauty and freedom with Karl Marx's militant call for proletarian solidarity. Wolfgang Ruppert (ed.), *Lebensgeschichten: Zur deutschen Sozialgeschichte 1850–1950* (Opladen: Leske Verlag und Budrich, 1980).

A postcard showing proud members of the workers' gymnastic clubs honoring "Turnvater" Jahn. Archiv der sozialen Demokratie, Bonn.

The Social Democratic choral society "Harmony" (Liedertafel Eintracht) of Neumünster in 1881. It combined singing with illegal party activities. Archiv der sozialen Demokratie, Bonn.

The founding conference of the Workers' Cycling Federation "Solidarity" in Offenbach am Main at Pentecost, 1896. The lower row is comprised of members from the local club in Offenbach, while the upper row consists of delegates to the conference. Archiv der sozialen Demokratie, Bonn.

Flag of the Workers' Cycling Club of Hillentrup. Archiv der sozialen Demokratie, Bonn.

Members of a local club at the first South German Festival of Workers' Gymnastic Clubs held in Nuremberg at Pentecost, 1912. Archiv der sozialen Demokratie, Bonn.

The Social Democratic Party School in Berlin during the 1909–10 session. The following individuals are identified by number: (1) Emanuel Wurm; (2) Artur Stadthagen; (3) Franz Mehring; (4) Kurt Rosenfeld; (5) Heinrich Cunow; (6) Gustav Eckstein; (7) Rosa Luxemburg; (8) Heinrich Schulz; and (9) Friedrich Ebert. Internationaal Instituut voor Sociale Geschiedenis, Amsterdam.

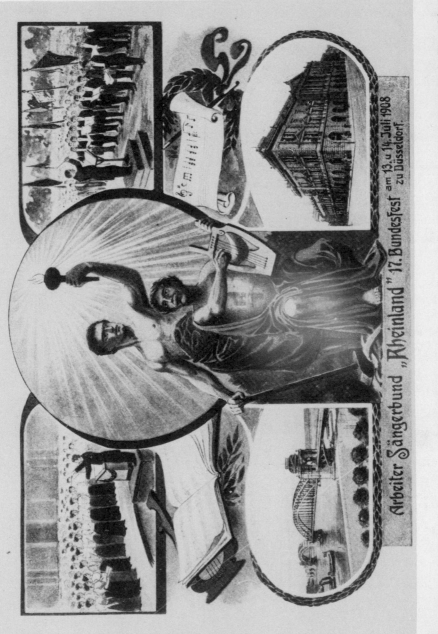

A postcard commemorating the seventeenth festival of the Rhenish League of Workers' Singing Societies in Düsseldorf in 1908. The symbolic unity of labor, enlightenment, and the arts is embodied in the two central figures, whose placement suggests that female and male choirs were of equal importance. Archiv der sozialen Demokratie, Bonn.

songs, couplets, and monologues. Strzelewicz, a man of quick mind and lively wit, mixed general humor with Social Democratic ideology and soon became one of the most popular entertainers in the labor movement world. His traveling troupe, the society "Forward" ("Vorwärts"), founded in 1893–94, was always in demand at *Kommers* and other events, and also sponsored its own independent programs.[29]

Reports on festivals seldom give particulars about their *Kommers,* though a special feature is mentioned occasionally. On the occasion of a regional gymnastic festival in Hanau the *Kommers* began at 7 P.M. with instrumental music performed by the Vorwärts Music Society (Musik-Verein-Vorwärts) and with choruses sung by the singing societies Vorwärts, Tone Blossoms (Tonblüte), Cheerfulness (Fröhlichkeit), Germania, Melomania, Concordia, and Humor, and the male choir of Langendiebach. The program consisted of fourteen items, alternating between instrumental music, choruses (including "O Schutzgeist alles Schönen" by Mozart), the consecration of the association flag (*Fahnenweihe*), and gymnastic displays (see Appendix B, section IV). A *Kommers* at the gymnastic festival in Lübeck (1913), similar in many respects, featured participatory singing of "Freedom Highly Honored" ("Die Freiheit hoch in Ehren"), a favorite of the workers' gymnastic clubs, a festival speech by *Turngenosse* Stelling, and a "handkerchief" gymnastic display by a club from Barmbeck.[30] In contrast to these occasions, May Day festivals did not feature *Kommers* because nearly every locality held its own May Day activities and thus people did not travel long distances or stay overnight to attend. The welcoming purpose of a *Kommers* did not apply.

Festival activities began in the morning. Singers' festivals are an example. During the morning singers from all participating choirs gathered to rehearse the songs to be presented at an afternoon concert. The mass choir would also rehearse, usually conducted by a musician who enjoyed a reputation as the most able of the directors. The number of singers involved could easily reach a thousand. Other participants might listen to the rehearsal. At the festival of the Rhenish League of Workers' Singing Societies in Ohligs in July 1899, the policeman assigned to control the event reported that "from 11:30 until almost 1 P.M. a rehearsal took place in the [Gasthaus] Schutzenburg which, with onlookers, included from 1,200 to 1,500 persons."[31] Sunday dinner followed the rehearsal. In the summer a distinct carnival atmosphere prevailed as people ate outside. Festivals that took place in parks or other open spaces had concessions with beer and food for sale. These concession stands were generally run by innkeepers whose regular business catered to followers of the labor movement.

Mornings at gymnastic festivals, as well as those of other sports clubs, were devoted to exhibitions of athletic skill. The sequence of events was determined well in advance by the sponsoring committee and printed as part of the festival program. Activities began early at sports festivals, usually by 7 or 7:30 A.M. (in 1910 at Langendiebach individual performances started at 6 A.M.!).[32] By midday gymnasts were also enjoying a large lunch.

By mid- or late afternoon a grand procession—if permitted by the police—would wend its way through the streets of the festival town and be joined by nearly all of the celebrants as well as occasional onlookers. Parades were a high point, and the larger the festival, the greater the attention to the details of the procession. The elements of ritualistic behavior were also most evident in the processions. The display of flags, banners, slogans, occupational insignia, and countless other symbols offered a visual representation of the contours of the social-cultural milieu of the labor movement. Processions presented the world of the labor movement as an ordered universe. The ceremonial process legitimated the inclusion of elements that Marxist-oriented theorists might otherwise have viewed with displeasure. As ritual, processions gave cohesion and order to festivals, bonding together what otherwise would have been loose-ended.

A predictable pattern for the procession developed by the middle of the 1890s. At the head were almost always the members of the workers' cycling clubs from the local town or district. They would be followed by the singers, grouped according to their choirs, and they in turn by marching bands, drum-and-bugle corps, sports clubs, and the local leaders of the Social Democratic party and free trade unions. When the Rhenish League of Workers' Singing Societies held its annual festival in Remscheid in 1903, the atmosphere in that industrial town was friendly and the singers put on a good show. "The high point of the festival," observed one sympathetic observer, "was the procession which moved through the town to the restaurant Schutzenfelde. Six marching bands accompanied the procession and many flags were carried. In front there were about 300 cyclists, bicycles decorated with flowers; with that there was a sense of vitality. The singers, about 4,000 strong, were greeted enthusiastically by residents all over the town."[33] Three years later, in 1906, the officer in charge of police surveillance at a festival of the same league made equally interesting observations.

> The procession was led by about 800 to 1,000 workers' cyclists carrying standards and emblems indicating their localities and the names of their clubs. The standard-bearers and the executive committee members [of the cyclists' clubs] wore red scarfs with gold fringes. The procession (including singers, cyclists, and gymnasts) consisted of 94 sections and there may have been in all 6,000 persons taking part in the procession. . . . Small marching bands had taken positions between the other clubs. In front of each club a schoolchild carried a banner with the club's emblem and its locality. The two large establishments where the festivities took place, the Stadthalle and the Driesenhof, were decorated with red flags with gold insets, red lanterns and garlands.[34]

Beauty and youth enhanced the legitimating force of the processions. Garlands of flowers were seldom lacking, and young children frequently led various processional segments. Similar forms were evident at almost all festivals of the party and labor movement clubs. The size and details varied, but cyclists, gymnasts, singers, and small marching bands participated. Exceptions were almost always a result of police prohibitions.[35]

Processions reveal a rich symbolism and certain ritualistic elements. Unless prohibited by police, red and gold colors provided both ideological identity and a bright visual stimulus. Members of the socialist labor movement believed sincerely that they had taken possession of the fight for liberty in Germany and so they routinely paid homage to "freedom." It could be expressed in different forms, but some representation of the "Goddess of Freedom" (*Freiheitsgöttin*) seems to have prevailed over all other possible modes. The goddess might be depicted on a canvas or, when horse-drawn display wagons were used, a young woman would be dressed in Grecian-style robes bearing other appropriate symbols. At a huge festival of singing societies in Nuremberg (1910) a float richly decorated with plants arranged on a series of terrasses had been prepared to honor freedom: "On top stands the Goddess of Freedom, in a white gown, a Jacobin cap on her head, the 'Freedom Banner' in her right hand, and supporting herself with her left hand resting on a lion as the symbol of power. A balustrade gives support behind, [and standing] to her right and left are busts of Marx and Lassalle."[36] Freedom, beauty, purity, and the French Revolution had all been clustered together to receive homage. We should not overlook the symbol of power in the above description. Even without such an explicit reference, the processions were, in themselves, expressions of strength and steadfastness, reinforcing the desired image of order and certainty.

Crafts, trades, occupations, the arts, forms of learning, and historical events can all be found represented in one form or another in festival processions. Viewers of the procession at a trade union festival in Aachen were treated to a veritable "trade union museum" as a display celebrating needlework led the way, followed by the banners and placards of brewers, painters, miners, metalworkers (the largest group), textile workers, and construction workers.[37] Processions became more elaborate as time passed, requiring considerable investments of time, energy, and money. Banners carried by marchers gave way to more elaborate floats on horse-drawn wagons. The eclectic cultural milieu of the labor movement manifested itself as a visual exhibition.

Processions gave a sense of visual unity to the eclectic collection, bringing together items that were not strictly socialist. This is well illustrated in the following long description of a procession at a festival in Gera (Thuringia) of the Osterland League of Workers' Singing Societies. Extra trains had been dispatched to bring in the participants; three huge halls had been rented; members from every segment of the labor movement joined in; and the small town of Gera jumped to the rhythm of the socialist movement.

Already at 1 P.M. the various choral societies were forming on the exhibition grounds. In the streets of the east-side suburbs there was much excitement as shortly after 2 P.M. the mighty procession began to move. Great throngs of people had taken positions on both sides of the route. While the houses were beautifully decorated in the workers' district of the town's east side and in the Debschwitz quarter, one did not notice much of that in the inner town; only here and there flags had been put out. The procession was divided into seven sections with more than 100 organizations marching. It was led by the executive committee of the Osterland League and the members of other committees; in this section there were ten wagons. In the second section the members of the Social Democratic party organization marched (unless they were in some other group), among whom one was pleased to see comrade Emanuel Wurm, Reichstag delegate for Reuss j[üngere] L[inie]. Many trade unions participated; a considerable number of these groups appeared in their occupational dress. The transport workers entered a display wagon entitled "Occupation" ["Der Beruf"] while the metalworkers' and the car-

penters' display was on "Industry." The textile workers entered a
festival display wagon along with a De-Smit Gruppe [*sic*]. The Consumer Cooperative wagon displayed commerce of the past and present, while the cyclists of Gera and vicinity illustrated the development of their organization with a display made up of bicycles. The
woodworkers [*Holzarbeiter*] illustrated the development of the German Woodworkers' Union with large boards on which were written
the membership figures for every five years. They also carried a
banner made from wood shavings which had just been consecrated
before the procession began. In addition, the league [of the singers'
societies] and the Singing Society of Gera-South, the Workers' Singing Society of Gera and the Free Singers of Zwötzen entered festival
wagons that illustrated "The Arts of Beauty," "The Consecration of
Song," the "Loreley," and the "Goddess of Freedom." These wagons offered very beautiful scenes because they were also surrounded
by appropriate groups of people, and especially attractive was a
group of children dressed in white with red sashes, carrying a lyre
decorated with flowers. It would take too much space to highlight
every group in this report; nonetheless, one remembers the workers'
youth groups who participated in extremely large numbers. The Es-
perantists aroused a bit of attention with their star banner; a number
of onlookers were certainly amazed by the relatively large number of
people devoted to the idea of a universal language. The local gymnastic league made a beautiful impression. Several hundred gymnasts, in matching uniforms, marched briskly and carried a whole
series of flags. The male gymnasts were then surrounded by female
gymnasts who in turn were carrying hoops decorated with flowers.
All of this gave the procession a wonderful touch of color and variety. It took a good three-quarters of an hour for the procession to
pass. Including the seven bands there were around 7,000 persons
involved; a splendid demonstration for the cause of workers' choral
music.[38]

This procession, as others, sought to present an aesthetically
pleasing and comprehensive image of the labor movement milieu.
Beauty, youth, the arts, recreation, work, occupations, trade
unions, the party, and ideology were symbolically integrated
through secular ritual. Such festivals, though sponsored by singers,
were produced as a kind of public theater by the movement as a
whole. The presence of Emanuel Wurm, well-known Social Democratic Reichstag deputy for the district including Gera, expressed
the collaboration between the party and the singers' festival.

Symbols of local identity were also prevalent. At Gera this was
evident in the occupations of special local significance. The same
was true at a Vogtland regional festival of singers in Zwickau in

July 1908, where display wagons illustrated mining and brewing. "The group of potterers made a splendid impression," according to one report, as "they appeared in the procession in blue working clothes, carrying a kiln." Themes of local history and custom were still more evident at a festival of Württemberg singers in Esslingen in 1911. Pairs of marchers wore traditional costumes from all of Württemberg's seventeen electoral districts, and one display wagon, featuring the "maid of Esslingen," illustrated the history of the town.[39] The cultural world of the labor movement had never disapproved of local loyalty. The absorption of regional patriotism, sharply differentiated from nationalism committed to the Imperial German state, was a feature that preserved a measure of attitudinal diversity in a Social Democratic movement that otherwise strove for centralization and uniformity.

Shortly after the procession ended, a festival program of music, declamations, plays, tableaux vivants, and other features began (see sample programs in Appendix B). Musical concerts were promoted especially by singing societies, but all labor movement festivals, including May Day, normally included a planned musical program. These ranged from the presentation of a few songs by a local singing society to extremely elaborate programs that included solos, duets, and quartets as well as choral performances. Mass singing of socialist songs would also be interspersed. Orchestral music would be performed by a marching band, or the festival committee may even have hired a small professional orchestra. The spoken word, unless prohibited, also had a place, at a minimum in a prologue, welcoming poem, or festival speech. Plays or humorous skits might be performed by a workers' theatrical club, while poems, humorous sayings, and couplets would be recited (see chapter 6). Programs were often diversified, but music and song always enjoyed a central and dominant place.

The development of concert programs from the early 1890s to 1914 illustrates the tension between the functions of taking pleasure in performance and symbolizing socialist ideology. During those years performance gained ground on symbolizing ideology and to a lesser degree also on socializing. These shifts took place gradually and unevenly, but they can be detected in changing preferences for different kinds of musical programming. The program material consisted of four types of music (not necessarily included at all festivals): (1) music from the standard repertory of the German male choirs; (2) choral music written by socialist composers and poets; (3) mass political songs of the labor movement (see chapter 5); and (4) instrumental music. Mass political songs were ideologically the most appropriate, but they were less suited to satisfy the desire of singers to excel in performance. This explains the fact (also noted by Werner Kaden) that as years passed fewer "freedom songs" appeared on festival programs.[40] By contrast, pieces from the standard German repertory of secular choral music enjoyed an increasingly important place on concert programs.

In interpreting festival programs it is important to stress that certain principles of exclusion were practiced uniformly throughout the socialist labor movement. Most notably, well-known nationalist songs did not appear, although their melodies were sometimes used to accompany socialist lyrics. While they avoided lyrics that would unmistakably have identified them with the nationalism of the Second Reich, they freely included music from regional or local cultural traditions.[41] With few exceptions, religious music also had no place in festival programs. On occasion directors would include religious choral music when they believed the aesthetic merit outweighed the religious content. Members of the labor movement who planned festival programs were self-consciously selective, and what they included had to meet broad standards of compatibility with their conception of what belonged in the movement. Festival programs were a mixture, but not an accidental mixture.

In the selection of choral music, two principles had to be considered: First, a piece ought to be of high musical quality, but still within the capacities of workers' singing societies; and, second, the lyrics could not be incompatible with the basic beliefs of the socialist labor movement. Choral conductors naturally enjoyed special distinction when their choirs performed and many of them were inclined to emphasize musical quality over ideological suitability. Because festival concerts offered the best opportunity for choirs to show how good they were, performers as well as conductors were irritated when audiences took to socializing. One musical reporter complained bitterly that at the huge singers' festival in Nuremberg (May 1910) the hall had poor acoustics and, furthermore, that "the audience, which for the most part did not listen, was noisy throughout, even those close to the podium."[42]

A carnival atmosphere distressed those who took seriously the performance of singers or athletes. Their distress arose from the boisterous cheerfulness of other celebrants. In 1905 the festival committee of the workers' singing societies in Hamburg invited a professional music critic to give an evaluation of the choral presentations. (The program is reprinted in Appendix B, Section III.) According to his uncharitable report, he encountered enormous obstacles just in finding a place to sit. After locating a vacant chair, he still did not find peace. He manifestly could not appreciate the jovial mood of the labor movement crowd, for he had come to carry out serious aesthetic business. He reported his misery in detail.

> The clanging of glasses and the jumbled noise of voices rolled out from the beer concession tents; playing children, for whom the art of singing is a triviality, pushed their way through the lines of listeners; here a young girl talks loudly and loosely about her sweetheart who, up front in all his singer's glory, adorns the podium; there a wife chatters with another about household matters—and above all of that waves of musical sound flow indistinctly. . . . During the instrumental concert a number of merry-go-rounds in the immediate area "work" along with the musicians; the robust organs of the merry-go-rounds were, according to my individual calculations, so much more powerful than the three dozen instruments of the . . . band that it would be an absurdity to try to offer a critique of the band's qualitative achievement. During other numbers by the band, singing groups which had settled comfortably in beer concession tents joined in lustily, and when a roving beer concessionaire brought out "another hundred mugs of beer" an enthusiastic "Long may he live!" [*"Hoch soll er leben!"*] roared forth, drowning out completely the tones of viola, bass, and violins. Not once during the presentation of the mass choir, which gave a good rendering of Uthmann's lovely "Spring's Arrival"—here I give at least one compliment—did all of those merry-go-rounds and pleasure pubs [*Lustschankeln*] put a stop to their noise.[43]

This poor soul never did file a musical critique of the concert, but, ironically, his newspaper story, inspired by frustration, demonstrated inadvertently how enormously successful the festival had been for other, equally important functions.

Emphasis on quality in performance meant that workers' singing societies would try to enlarge and diversify their repertories, and thus festival programs were sprinkled freely with the works of a large number of composers of traditional German choral music. Some composers appeared on the programs frequently, notably Franz Abt (1809–85), Friedrich Hegar (1841–1927), Konradin Kreutzer (1780–1849), Ferdinand Möhring (1816–87), Friedrich Silcher (1789–1860), and Max Weinzierl (1841–98). The choirs in the Federation of Workers' Singing Societies thus incorporated much of the same repertory used by the German Choral League (Deutscher Sänger-Bund), with the difference that the latter also emphasized songs of German nationalism as well as religious music. As an amalgamation of individual organizations, the German Choral League had been founded in 1862, as much to promote German unification as to advance singing. Intense patriotism continued to dominate the German Choral League, and except for the fact that they shared a certain repertory, the two choral associations had nothing more in common. The gap between them was further accentuated by the fact that the workers' singing societies performed music that was ideologically anathema to the German Choral League.[44]

At labor movement festivals choral music by socialist composers appeared prominently alongside the selections from Hegar, Abt, and Silcher. The juxtaposition is striking because of the musical similarities as well as the ideological differences. Musicians associated with the labor movement had learned to compose in the style of the traditional male chorus, and they continued to write in that form. It is important to note therefore that, with few exceptions, on the basis of musical style alone, audiences at labor festivals could not have distinguished pieces by socialists from those by others.[45] Socialist use of the melody of the "Marseillaise" was unique in Germany (see chapter 5), and that gave a somewhat distinctive musical character to festivals and other meetings. Combative political songs were always sung at celebrations sponsored directly by the party (May Day, March festivals, and Lassalle festivals, for example), but less often at festivals of singers and gymnasts.

The lyrics of choral music by socialist composers tended to be somewhat less militant than the mass political songs. These moderate choral pieces were still thought of as "tendentious choruses" (*Tendenzchöre*), and rightly so, for words and phrases distinctly symbolized a commitment to the socialist labor movement. *Freedom* was the key term, followed by words that spoke of enlightenment, optimism, and the dawning of a new age. If the lyrics of these choral numbers seem bland and uninspired in retrospect, they were, in the context of Imperial Germany, sufficiently sharp to proclaim the identity of the singers with the Social Democratic labor movement. Writing music that effectively served both agitational and aesthetic objectives was not easy; and while some critics complained about the mediocre quality of much of the socialist choral repertory, others expressed misgivings about lyrics that failed to carry a distinct socialist message.[46]

Workers' singing societies encouraged socialist musicians to compose new choral music to be sung at festivals and concerts. Shortly after its founding the Liedergemeinschaft called on musicians to send their choral compositions to an evaluation commission that would select the most worthy. Those chosen for distinction would be published in the federation's series, *Der freie Sänger*. Although socialist critics were frequently disappointed in the musical qualities of the compositions received by the commission, the enterprise helped to create a substantial body of Social Democratic choral music.[47] By the first decade of the twentieth century the cultural world of the labor movement included a considerable number of composers. Perhaps not all were deeply committed socialists, but they were sufficiently sympathetic to contribute their creative effort to the cause.

The most successful labor movement composer was Gustav Adolf Uthmann (1867–1920), a socialist of moderate views and, though a musical autodidact, a very prolific composer. Others included Carl Gramm, H. Buhr, Heinrich Pfeil, H. Riva, Otto Suchsdorf, Gutan, Jael, Cursch-Bühren, and Paul Büttner. Most of them made no mark in the general German musical world. That situation began to change slightly immediately prior to the First World War.[48] Franz Bothe, reporting to the general conference of the Federation of Workers' Singing Societies in June 1914, proudly told the delegates that several of their socialist composers were gaining recognition in the larger musical world. He noted also that at least two well-known *bürgerlich* composers, Ottomar Neubner and Grete Dietze, had been writing music for the workers' societies under pseudonyms. In the pursuit of the highest possible artistic quality for labor movement music, Bothe had even endeavored, though unsuccessfully, to persuade Richard Strauss to compose choral music for the Federation of Workers' Singing Societies.[49] Such aesthetic ambitions were not realized. The general musical world in Germany knew little or nothing about the socialist musicians who composed the choral works that appeared on the programs at workers' festivals.

Hardly a festival passed without one or more selections from the body of about four hundred *Tendenzchöre* composed by Uthmann in his lifetime, most of them before 1914. A likely choice would be "Upward to the Light" ("Empor zum Licht"), a text that shared the hortatory approach and optimistic mood that so typified the movement's mass political songs. Other favorites by Uthmann included "Storm" ("Sturm"), "Hymn to Freedom" ("Hymne an die Freiheit"), "Return of the Banished" ("Heimkehr des Verbannten"), "Song of Freedom" ("Freiheitsgesang"), "Toward Spring" ("Dem Lenz entgegen"), "Mankind Awake" ("Die Menschheit Erwachen"), and "Morning Glow" ("Morgenrot"). The lyrics for Uthmann's choral music were written by various socialist poets and, accordingly, reflected those optimistic notions that forecast the victory of light over darkness, labor over capital, truth over falsehood, and peace and harmony over war and conflict. The choral works by other socialist composers reflected essentially the same sentiments, seen, for example, in the popular "We Believe in Freedom's Victory" ("Wir glauben an der Freiheit Siege") by Otto Suchsdorf, in "Morning Call" ("Morgenzuruf") by the Austrian Josef Scheu, and in "Proletarian Lullaby" ("Proletarier-Wiegenlied") by Riva.[50] Uthmann's choral music had its first appeal in the 1890s among workers' choral societies in the Rhineland and then spread from there throughout the labor movement. Some localities had their own favorites. In Hamburg, a musical idyll, "The Smithies in the Woods" ("Die Schmiede im Walde"), appeared on festival programs repeatedly between 1896 and 1905 (see Appendix B, Section III). A freedom-loving blacksmith at work in the woods with his helpers is interrupted by a crashing noise made by the sword-bearing "god of war." In disgust and fearlessness the smithy breaks asunder the sword and the "god of war vanishes."[51] However romantic and idealistic, this piece and many like it reveal the popular forms in which socialist ideas were expressed. In hundreds of "freedom choruses" and "freedom songs" festival programs sought to transmit a mood of hope and confidence.

Concerts also included instrumental and orchestral music, often performed at the largest festivals by professional musicians hired for the occasion. Although instrumental music did not carry a message in words, musical choices and the popularity of various composers also reflected the cultural values of program planners. The most ambitious and serious symphonic music seldom appeared; preference went to waltzes, dances, marches, overtures, and orchestral arrangements of operatic arias. One can find music by Friedrich von Flotow, Franz Lehár, Felix Mendelssohn, Giacomo Meyerbeer, Johann Strauss, Giuseppe Verdi, and Carl Maria von Weber, to mention those played most frequently.[52]

Popular preference, however, went to the music of Richard Wagner. Overtures, arias, and orchestral arrangements from *Lo-*

hengrin and *Tannhäuser* were particularly favored. Between 1892 and 1905 festival programs of the workers' singing societies in Hamburg usually included at least one selection from a Wagnerian opera. At the singers' festival in Hamburg in 1904 the program highlighted this fascination in a special "Wagner Section" with four selections (from *Rienzi, The Flying Dutchman,* and *Tannhäuser*), and with five numbers in 1905 (from the same operas and also *Lohengrin*). At a regional festival of workers' singing societies in Limbach (Saxony), the orchestra began with the "Entrance of the Guests to the Wartburg" from *Tannhäuser* and later a concert singer named Bauer sang Wolfram's first song from the same opera. Wagner was no stranger to the milieu of the labor movement;[53] on the contrary, his music was absorbed rather deeply. He even had the honor of opening the congress of the Social Democratic party in Nuremberg (1908) when nine hundred singers sang the "Entrance of the Guests to the Wartburg" to the enthusiastic applause of the assembled socialist delegates.[54] The party's Central Educational Commission also reported, apparently with approval, that each year between 1908 and 1913 various labor movement associations had sponsored concerts especially devoted to the music of Richard Wagner. In September 1903 the later founder of Anthroposophy, Dr. Rudolf Steiner, lectured on "Richard Wagner's Goals" to the general assembly of the Freie Volksbühne, and in February 1908 the same organization held a special Wagner Festival.[55]

To point out that Richard Wagner's music played a role in labor movement culture is not to imply that all of his social and political values were also embraced. Even when lyrics from Wagner's operas were sung, that still did not mean that audiences were particularly aware of the composer's ideas. Nonetheless, the prominence given Wagner meant that his works could be assumed to belong to the social-cultural milieu of the labor movement almost as integrally as many of the choral works produced by socialist composers. Moreover, the incorporation of Wagner's music paralleled explicit sympathy for some of his social and cultural theories. The arguments in his essay of 1849, "Art and Revolution," offered ammunition for those involved in a critique of the cultural implications of capitalism. In this respect it is noteworthy that Wagner appealed as much to theorists on the radical wing of Social Democracy as to moderates and reformists. Hermann Duncker had already matured into an articulate radical when he drew directly on Wagner to support arguments about the cultural destructiveness of capitalism. Clara Zetkin, too, in developing the argument that a free and genuine artistic life could emerge only after the "capitalist yoke" had been broken and class conflicts transcended, cited Wagner's essay approvingly and at length. Although Duncker and Zetkin did not address themselves directly to the question of how Wagner's musical corpus might fit into the cultural programs of the socialist labor movement, they had ample opportunity to object to its inclusion if they had felt any reservations. However, no instance has been found of a German Social Democrat who went as far as George Bernard Shaw in *The Perfect Wagnerite*—trying to give the *Ring* cycle a more or less consistent socialist interpretation—but they freely incorporated much of his music and some of his ideas into their environment. This point is reinforced by a critical commentary on Wagner's *Parsifal* by Friedrich Caro in the journal of the Federation of Workers' Singing Societies. In referring to *Parsifal* as a "work of the crassest reaction," Caro revealed his generally pro-Wagnerian inclination by comparing it negatively to the greatness of *Götterdammerung*. The social-cultural milieu of the socialist labor movement was indeed an eclectic amalgam, the ingredients of which were amply manifest in festival programs.[56]

Festivals did not close when the program of music and speeches ended. There was more to come, a children's torch parade perhaps, probably a ball, and almost always fireworks. Dancing and fireworks were highly favored, with the exception that May Day festivals seldom included a ball. Torchlight parading to a polonaise, again, especially for children, could also be scheduled as part of the closing ceremony.[57] Here, too, labor movement organizations, including the political party, had absorbed the tradition of torchlight parades that had been associated with the cause of liberty and patriotism in Germany since early in the nineteenth century.

Processions, speeches, singing, plays, tableaux vivants, fireworks, and dancing, all coming in one sequence or another on the same day, created a sense of dynamism and excitement. The drama of such an event could make a lasting impression on the young. One veteran of the labor movement, Karl Grünberg, remembered years later many features of the May Day festivals he had attended in Rostock around the turn of the century. As he remembered,

Women made coffee; worker athletes showed off their skills; and the workers' singing [clubs] sang 'One People, One Heart, One Father-

land' ['Ein Volk, ein Herz, ein Vaterland']. Along with that there
were usually some comical female performers in roles with obvious
double meanings. Sometimes there would be a humorous one-act
skit in which police and informers would be ridiculed. Toward evening, when most of the men would appear and it would be getting
cool outside, they would move into the hall. There they danced to
the music of workers' songs. For the children there was still a torch
parade with light red lanterns on poles. For the conclusion there
were also tableaux vivants [*lebende Bilder*] with allegorical represen-
tations from the labor movement which made a deep impression on
me.[58]

Perhaps Grünberg's memory had mixed together several occasions,
but the spirit of his recollection fits well with the other evidence on
festivals. To what song he refers is not clear, though it would not
appear to have been a socialist political text, unless perhaps a song
of mockery. But he remembered the ambience, how politics and
amusement, performance and socializing were fused in labor
movement festivals, including those on May Day.

Festival planners obviously recognized a need to set aside time
that could be devoted exclusively to socializing and amusement for
amusement's sake. Symbolizing ideology and realizing satisfaction
in performance took precedence during the procession and in a
large portion of the concert programs. In reality, socializing went
on constantly throughout the festival day and for the great mass of
those in attendance it may have constituted the most meaningful
function of festivals. The inclination of people to talk and gossip,
laugh and drink, even during concerts, was irrepressible.

May Day festivals also reflected more and more a strong impulse
for participants to treat these occasions primarily as a time for
socializing. Contemporary socialists were fully aware of this tendency and it aroused some vigorous criticism. As the festive side of
May Day expanded, the purely ideological, combative side declined, and the whole event took on the character of an "ordinary
folk festival" (*allgemeines Volksfest*). With the passage of years,
May Day festivals became less and less distinctive; they assimilated
the features of the other labor movement festivals. What began in
a few places as a demonstration of militant workers leaving their
workplaces at great risk of losing their jobs changed gradually into
a family occasion for entertainment and socializing.[59]

Despite the increasing importance of performance and sociability, labor movement festivals never lost their political implications.
But many of the initial differences between the festivals of the

clubs and May Day diminished. As weapons of political propaganda, innocent-looking festivals of singers or gymnasts could sometimes be as effective as the presumably more militant May Day demonstrations. The involvement of the labor movement in cultural and recreational activities and its sponsorship of festivals improved its image among various middle-class groups. Police officers assigned to festivals noted that the good behavior of the processions could win the approval of the general public. Festival image building could have positive benefits for the labor movement. "Such festivals," observed Police Commissioner Koch, "serve Social Democracy as an appropriate means of getting around the gap that still separates the Social Democratic labor force and the burgher class [*Bürgerstand*]. Festivals have great selling power [*Werbekraft*] for the party. Yesterday I saw workers' singers, hats decorated with their festival tickets, in friendly contact with soldiers [*Husars*], lower officials of the postal service and the railroads, all in uniform. This indicates how the class of officials [*Beamtenklasse*] is getting closer and closer to Social Democracy. . . ."[60] To the authoritarian mind of Commissioner Koch it followed that festival processions should be prohibited. Social Democratic sponsors of singing societies and other clubs would have been pleased with his analysis because they always maintained that most party leaders failed to recognize the extent to which the activities of auxiliary organizations contributed to the political work of the movement. Their radical critics would have replied that this kind of appeal to middle-class groups only reinforced the contention that recreational clubs were diverting energies from the salient political task of mobilizing workers, not bourgeois, into the movement. But both sides could agree that festivals made an impact.

More than any other single event associated with the labor movement, festivals fused together diverse strands into living units that could be experienced by participants as coherent wholes. In a day's activities festivals brought together in one concentrated event many, if not all, of the ingredients of the social-cultural world of the socialist labor movement. They contributed to the substance and especially to the image of the Social Democratic labor movement as a solid phalanx of enthusiastic followers with a well-integrated set of political principles and cultural values.

5

Songs

Historically music and song have at one time or another played important roles in almost every aspect of life. Music has accompanied people at work, at play, at war; it can lend dignity to the ceremonies of the most humble as well as to those of the rich and powerful; it can add levity to the raucous behavior of drunken sailors or solemnity to religious services. Probably every social and political movement in European history has employed music in some manner. What can be learned from the music associated with movements and institutions varies from case to case. Here the musical dimension offers still another approach for identifying beliefs and sentiments to which followers of the labor movement were repeatedly exposed and to which they themselves gave indirect expression when they joined in singing the songs of Social Democracy. The mass political songs embody symbolisms, both literary and musical, that often reveal more about the emotional and intellectual texture of the movement than public speeches, newspaper articles, or party programs.

The study of political songs may be undertaken from a number of perspectives. Researchers primarily interested in ideologies, policies, and party programs will naturally focus on the ideas and sentiments expressed in lyrics. This has been the most prevalent approach of those who have written on the songs of the socialist labor movement in Germany.[1] Specialists in folk songs, ethnomusicologists, and musicologists examine the musical aspects in order to discover evidence of transmission, influence, and creativity. Modern political songs have been of little or no interest to musicologists and have held only a slight appeal for folklorists.[2] From still a third point of view, sociological or anthropological, the investigator's chief task is to analyze the various uses and functions of songs in a given society, community, or group. These questions are also uppermost in the minds of those writing the social history of music.[3] This approach is not concerned with the assumed aesthetic merits of either music or lyrics. A song in which no one finds aesthetic value may nonetheless serve social or political functions of considerable importance.

The approach in this chapter incorporates something from all three of the perspectives described above. Least attention is paid to the quality of the music itself, and the reasons for this will be abundantly clear. Nonetheless, the symbolic significance of various melodies as they related to the labor movement or groups in German society is of importance. More attention is given to an examination of texts that provide evidence as to what ideas were heard repeatedly and thus were likely to be embedded in the consciousness of Germany's organized workers. The focus is on two kinds of songs: socialist political songs for mass singing (*Massenlieder*), which were also widely known as "workers' songs" (*Arbeiterlieder*) and which everyone in the movement could participate in singing; and, second, strike songs, many of which grew directly out of labor disputes.

There was seldom, if ever, an occasion when the political songs served a primary aesthetic function. No doubt some members, perhaps many, found them beautiful and thus gained aesthetic satisfaction from singing or hearing the songs. But their primary function was not aesthetic. They were created to serve the labor movement and its affiliated organizations; the organizations did not exist to serve the songs. In their most important function mass political songs were symbols of identity and unity. As they helped to provide a sense of identity for people within the labor movement, so they also symbolized the differentiation of labor movement members from others in German society. But to be effective as a symbol of identity the melody as well as the text of a song had to become tightly linked to the labor movement in the minds of the general German public as well as in the sentiments of Social Democrats. One of the distinct drawbacks of writing new socialist words to well-known melodies was that the same popular melodies were used also by many nonsocialists for their club songs. When diverse groups in German society used the same melody, it could not become symbolic for the identity of any one group. For this reason only a few of the mass political songs—as melodies as well as words—became effective symbols of the Social Democratic labor movement.

Song texts served as instruments of communication and propaganda designed to arouse the consciousness of workers. This communicative function was taken seriously not only by the writers of socialist lyrics, but especially by the enemies of Social Democracy. For that reason the songbooks of the labor movement (*Arbeiterliederbücher*) fell under the ban during the era of the antisocialist legislation just as other socialist publications did.[4] In later years police would sometimes permit instrumental music at festivals while forbidding the singing of labor movement songs.[5] In many regions of Germany throughout the 1890s and well into the twentieth century labor movement organizations were required to provide local police with a detailed list of all items scheduled for festival programs. Even in Hamburg, where the authorities were comparatively tolerant, when the city council (*Bürgerschaft*) in 1903 passed a ruling that the local workers' gymnastic clubs were to be classified as political organizations, much of the argument rested on the fact that the song pamphlets (*Liederhefte*) of the clubs included such songs as Johann Most's "Who Hammers Brass and Stone?" ("Wer schafft das Gold zu Tage?").[6]

To what extent socialist political songs served socializing and entertainment functions among followers of the labor movement is difficult to determine. Such songs were not primarily designed to accompany casual socializing—for that they were too serious—but on occasion they served these purposes indirectly. Political songs were mixed together with entertainment features at every festival of the labor movement, and thus the propagandizing and socializing functions of song often overlapped. Otto Buchwitz remembered singing political songs together with fellow Social Democrats after leaving a May Day Festival in Breslau in 1895 (when he was sixteen!).[7] In a quite different context, Ernst Schuchardt, a rather hapless vagabond Social Democrat, tells of living in Magdeburg in cheap quarters above a tavern with a lower-class clientele mixed with organized workers as well as others. His report suggests that socialist political songs were sung as an accompaniment to drinking and socializing: "As in all such miserable quarters, alcohol was used heavily and there were also loud, excited discussions. In between there would be singing. Several times in an evening I heard notorious socialist songs like the '[Workers'] Marseillaise,' 'I Want to Be and to Remain a Son of the People' ['Ein Sohn des Volkes will ich sein und bleiben'], 'Who Hammers Brass and Stone?' ['Wer schafft das Gold zu Tage?'], or 'The Workers' Reveille' ['Die Arbeiterreveille'], etc."[8] Unfortunately, most sources that mention singing and socializing among organized workers are not as specific as Schuchardt, making it difficult to determine how often they may have sung Social Democratic political songs while spontaneously socializing. Schuchardt's testimony is especially striking because the titles he mentions were among the leading political songs of the movement.

A number of the political songs began with ceremonial functions, and others acquired such roles over time. Festivals and other special meetings of the labor movement frequently began with a kind of invocation—not a prayer, to be sure, but a song. The invocation was frequently a song of welcome, or one encouraging loyalty and adherence to the *Bund, Verband,* or *Verein.* There are numerous songs in the songbooks of the labor movement which carry the general title "League Hymn" ("Bundeslied"), or some variant, and most of these were sung at the beginning of festivals or meetings.

The large number of songbooks published by the various clubs and associations affiliated with Social Democracy attest to the significance of singing for the labor movement. These books are also the most important single source for the study of singing in the labor movement. Anthologies of songs with a labor orientation appeared in Germany as early as the late 1840s, but it was only in the 1860s and 1870s that song collections of the socialist labor movement appeared. A few more were published outside Germany in the era of the antisocialist legislation, and a veritable flood of "workers' songbooks" appeared between 1891 and 1914, when, with the outbreak of the First World War, there was once again an interruption in publishing until 1918. One expert has calculated that between 1870 and 1914 no less than 250 songbooks, some in many editions, were published either directly or indirectly by the Social Democratic labor movement and its affiliated voluntary associations.[9]

The collections of the labor movement fall into two broad categories: (1) the general Social Democratic songbooks, which included only strictly labor movement songs, and (2) the specialized collections of the voluntary associations (*Vereinsliederbücher*). The latter included both the standard political songs of the Socialist party and, in addition, songs of special interest to the particular activity in which the club members were engaged.[10]

With few exceptions the party collections included only songs that were unmistakably of the socialist labor movement. Editors of *Liederbücher,* such as Johann Most and Max Kegel, wanted to make sure that their collections served chiefly political and propagandistic functions. Except that an aesthetically appealing song might serve propagandistic purposes better than a song of mediocre quality, they were not primarily interested in the artistic quality of either the words or the music. In design and format the books were simple to the utmost degree. All were small enough to fit in a pocket, and easily carried and kept out of sight if necessary. They were normally published without special prefaces or introductory comments, in order, one suspects, to call as little attention as possible to the fact that they were closely linked with a party whose members had and might at any time encounter considerable police harassment. Thus, these publications were not party songbooks in a strict legal definition.[11] Nonetheless, no one could fail to discern the close identity between the *Liederbücher* and the Social Democratic party.

The songbooks of the ancillary organizations reflected an eclectic approach to the question of what should be included. The songbooks of the workers' gymnastic clubs, the socialist youth movement, and the workers' singing societies were all built on much broader principles than those that guided Most and Kegel in compiling anthologies for the party.[12] Although more inclusive, the eclectic approach also employed certain discernible principles of selection. The most obvious principle of exclusion prohibited songs with patriotic or religious content. Although melodies of patriotic songs were used with new texts, the patriotic texts themselves were almost universally excluded. The same exclusion held true for religious songs. For inclusion, the most common principle seems to have been to take traditional songs with popular appeal (*volkstümliche Lieder*) that were often and somewhat erroneously thought of as genuine *Volkslieder* in the nineteenth century.

In addition to such *volkstümliche Lieder,* each labor movement group had certain special club songs to include in the songbooks. Thus, *Der freie Turner* included a sizable number of songs that had long been part of the repertory of the German gymnastic tradition. The most nationalistic gymnastic texts were dropped, but those honoring the spirit of "Turnvater" Jahn or promoting "freedom" were retained. Of the seventy-nine items in the section entitled "Gymnastic Songs" ("Turner-Lieder") in *Der freie Turner,* no less than seventeen are also in the *Liederbuch für Deutsche Turner* (87th edition, ca. 1890), one of the major collections of the German gymnastic clubs.[13] In effect, the editors of *Der freie Turner* sought to retain those songs from the patriotic gymnastic tradition that were progressive (or harmless) and could be merged with a broad and loose interpretation of the labor movement's ideals.

Two examples will illustrate how socialist editors changed the wording slightly in order to salvage a song that they might otherwise have felt compelled to omit. In a song entitled "Gymnast's Delight" ("Turnerlust"), the traditional first verse and refrain are printed below under *A,* and the socialist modification of the refrain under *B.*[14] The alteration is slight but presumably thought to be sufficient to bring the text in line with the beliefs of the labor movement.

A

Was zieht dort unten das Thal entlang?
Eine Schaar in weissem Gewand!
Wie muthig brauset der volle Gesang!
Die Töne sind mir bekannt.
Sie singen von Freiheit und Vaterland,
Ich kenne die Schaar im weissen Gewand:

:: Hurrah! hurrah! hurrah!
Die Turner ziehen aus. ::

B

[Verse is identical with version A. The refrain is:]

:: Frei Heil! Frei Heil! Frei Heil!

Die Turner ziehen aus. ::

A

What moves down there along the valley?
A troop in white uniform!
How courageous sounds their vigorous song!
Those tones are known to me.
They sing of Freedom and the Fatherland.
I know this troop in their white uniform:

:: Hurrah! hurrah! hurrah!
The gymnasts are moving out. ::

B

[Verse is identical with version A. The refrain is:]

:: Freedom Hail! Freedom Hail! Freedom Hail!
The gymnasts are moving out. ::

A comparable change was introduced in a second song, "Tramping Song" ("Wanderlied"), in which one line in the original refrain— "Gymnast spirit, German spirit, faithful to the fatherland" ("Turnersinn, deutscher Sinn, treu dem Vaterlande")—was replaced with "Gymnast spirit, freedom's spirit, faithful to a free people" ("Turnersinn, freier Sinn, treu dem freien Volke.")[15] These changes were so minor that it is entirely conceivable that members of the workers' gymnastic clubs may well have alternated between the two versions on different occasions.

The songbooks constitute an enormously valuable source for probing the values and attitudes propagated among organized workers. The labor movement was a singing movement, and an organized worker who may never have read a page of Lassalle, Marx, Engels, Bernstein, Kautsky, or even Bebel probably participated on numerous occasions in singing songs that were common to the movement's clubs. In song, and especially in group singing, one simultaneously enjoyed the companionship of other people, expressed some ideological tendencies (often vague, to be sure), and could also find gratification by participating in simple artistic performances. Songs encourage an infinite repetition of ideas, and for that reason consciousness can be more deeply affected by song texts than by speeches that are heard once.

Six of the most important socialist songbooks have been analyzed systematically to identify both lyrics and melodies of songs that were widely used in the labor movement.[16] The results of the survey of these books is presented in two lists. The first gives the texts that appeared in at least three of the collections. The distinctive feature of the texts in Part I of the following list is that they all originated during the first decade of the active political labor movement, that is, within ten years following 1863. Part II includes songs that also appeared frequently in the songbooks of the labor movement, but which, for the most part, originated after 1890. The second list cites melodies to which three or more new texts were written by persons associated with the labor movement. This list of melodies is also compiled strictly from the same six *Liederbücher*. The lists of texts and melodies overlap to some extent, but not uniformly.

TEXTS OF LEADING MASS POLITICAL SONGS, 1864–1914*

Part I: Songs Originating in the First Decade, 1863–73

I. "Arbeiter, all erwacht" [4] "Workers, All Awake!" ("Auf-ruf an die Arbeiter" or "Arbeiter-Reveille"). Late 1860s or early 1870s. By "A Brunswick Worker" or Joh. Most. Melody: "Heil dir im Siegerkranz."

II. "Auf, und lasst die Fahne fliegen" [3] "Arise, and Let the Flags Fly" ("Fahnenlied"). Late 1860s. By August Geib. Melody: "Auf, ihr Brüder lasst uns wallen."

III. "Bet' und Arbeit" [5] "Work and Pray" ("Bundeslied" or "Arbeiterlied"). 1864. By Georg Herwegh. Melody: Several: one by Hans v. Bülow, most often sung to "Schles-wig-Holstein, meerumschlungen."

IV. "Brüder, reicht die Hand zum Bunde." [6: 2 variations] "Brothers, Embrace the League" (the same). Early 1820s. Anon. Melody: "Brüder, reicht die Hand zum Bunde."

V. "Freiheit, die ich meine" [3: two slight variations] "Free-dom That I Love" (the same, or "Freiheit"). 1813. By Max von Schenkendorf. Melody: "Freiheit, die ich meine."

VI. "Im schönen Mai, im jungen Mai." [4] "In Beautiful May, in Youthful May" ("Mailied"). Late 1860s. By August Geib. Melody: "Die Wacht am Rhein."

VII. "Ob Armuth euer Los auch sei" [3] "Is There for Honest Poverty" ("Trotz Alledem"). 1843. By Ferdinand Freilig-rath, from Robert Burns. Melody: "Als Noah aus dem Kasten war."

VIII. "Stimmt an das Lied der hohen Braut" [3] "Intone the Song of the Noble Bride" ("Das Lied der Arbeit"). 1868. By J. J. Zapf. Melody: Composed by Joseph Scheu (1868).

IX. "Was fluthet und strömt durch die Strassen dahin" [3] "What Flows and Streams Through the Streets Over There" ("Männer der Arbeit"). 1860s or very early 1870s. Anon. Melody: "Lützows wilde Jagd."

*In each part the list is alphabetical according to the first line of the texts. The number in brackets indicates in how many of the six *Liederbücher* the text appears. Common titles are given in parentheses. The date refers to the writing of the text. The melodies are also given, for the most part, according to the first lines of the texts to which they originally belonged. One exception has been made. No. XVI has been included although it appears in only two of these *Liederbücher* because other scholars insist that it was widely used. Cf. Nespital, *Das deutsche Proletariat in seinem Lied*, p. 48.

   X. "Wer nur den lieben Gott lässt walten" [3] "Whoever
       Lets God Almighty Master Things" ("Ermahnung"). Ca.
       early 1870s. By Max Kegel. Melody: "Schleswig-Holstein
       meerumschlungen."
   XI. "Wer schafft das Gold zu Tage?" [4] "Who Hammers
       Brass and Stone?" ("Das Lied der Arbeitsmänner").
       Early 1870s. By Johann Most. Melody: "Zu Mantua in
       Banden" ["Andreas Hofer Lied"].
  XII. "Wohlan, wer Recht und Wahrheit achtet" [5] "Boldly
       Now, Who Honors Truth and Justice" ("Arbeiter-Mar-
       seillaise"). 1864. By Jakob Audorf. Melody: "Marseil-
       laise."

Part II: Songs Originating in the Later Era
  XIII. "Auf, Sozialisten, schliesst die Reihen" [3] "Arise, Social-
       ists, Close Your Ranks" ("Sozialistenmarsch"). 1891. By
       Max Kegel. Melody: Composed by Carl Gramm.
  XIV. "Es stand meine Wiege im niedrigen Haus" [3] "My
       Cradle Stood in a Humble Abode" ("Ein Sohn des
       Volkes"). Ca. 1903–04. By Heinrich Pfeil. Melody: Com-
       posed by Peter Heinz.
   XV. "Ihr Männer all'," [3] "You Men, All of You" ("Acht-
       stunden-Marseillaise"). 1890. By Ernst Klaar. Melody:
       "Marseillaise."
  XVI. "Wir sind die Petroleure" [2] "We Are the Fire Bombers"
       ("Das Lied der Petroleure"). Originated 1878, not in
       Liederbücher until 1891. By Jakob Audorf. Melody: First
       melody from opera *La Fille de Madame Angot* by Charles
       Lecocq.

Two of the above texts appeared several decades before the
emergence of the organized socialist labor movement: "Brothers,
Embrace the League" ("Brüder, reicht die Hand zum Bunde")
and "Freedom, that I Love" ("Freiheit, die ich meine"). The
former came from Mozart's *Kleine Freimaurer Kantate* (1791), although the common text during the nineteenth century was a revision that appeared in the 1820s.[17] German voluntary associations
of many different kinds sang it on festive occasions as a musical
invocation. The same text, with only two or three words changed,
was taken over by the young socialist labor movement.

                Brüder, reicht die Hand zum Bunde,
                Diese schöne Feierstunde

Führ' uns hin zu lichten Höh'n.
Lasst, was irdisch ist, entfliehen,
Uns'rer Freundschaft Harmonieen
Dauern ewig fest und schön.[18]

Brothers, embrace the league,
May this beautiful festive hour,
Lead us to enlightened heights.
Let us flee the mundane world,
To harmonize our friendship,
May it last eternally firm and beautiful.

The ease with which the socialist movement incorporated these lyrics from Freemasonry is striking. At the same time two rather thorough revisions of the same song were written, and one in particular, by Jacob Stern, changed substantially the character of the text. Stern's version is permeated with the symbolic language of the labor movement. The last stanza is the high point.

Proletarier aller Lande
Schüttelt ab die Sklavenbande
Einigt euch zum Bruderbund!
Dass der Freiheit Banner wehen,
In den Tiefen, auf den Höhen,
Auf dem ganzen Erdenrund![19]

Proletarians of all lands
Shake off the chains of slavery
Unite yourselves in the brotherhood!
So that the banner of freedom waves,
In the valleys, on the peaks,
Over all the earthly planet.

With essentially no alterations, the labor movement had absorbed the text of "Freiheit, die ich meine," written by the patriotic and liberal Max von Schenkendorf (1783–1817) in 1813 in the midst of the Wars of Liberation. A few words were altered, but Social Democrats preserved the integrity of Schenkendorf's original text. The lofty mood of the first stanza is especially idealistic.

Freiheit, die ich meine,
Die mein Herz erfüllt,
Komm' mit deinem Scheine,
Süsses Engelsbild!
Magst du nie dich zeigen

Der bedrängten Welt?
Führest deinen Reigen
Nur am Sternenzelt?[20]

Freedom, that I love
That fills my heart to flowing,
Come now with all your brilliance,
Sweet angelic image!
Do you wish never to reveal yourself
In this world oppressed?
Are your rounds limited
To the starry heavens?

The absorption of Schenkendorf's ideals was complete, constitut-
ing a direct and explicit link between the labor movement and one
of the poetic and musical symbols of German patriotic liberalism as
it had been inspired by the fight against Napoleon's Imperial
France.

The other ten leading lyrics in Part I of the previous list in many
ways reflect the fact that they were written during the formative
years of the socialist labor movement. The cleavage between the
socialist labor movement and the liberal and democratic political
movements was completed organizationally only toward the end of
the 1860s. Many socialists continued to be intellectually and emo-
tionally attached to the liberal and democratic movements from
which they had only recently separated. Concomitantly, both
branches of the labor movement, Lassalleans and the Workingmen's Educational Societies, embraced the patriotic cause for a
united Germany. There were differences among socialists, but the
dominant opinion favored a Germany unified on the basis of
democratic principles. In the 1860s, before the Bismarckian solution to German unification had been realized, patriotic sentiments
were not alien to the youthful socialist movement. Alienation from
German nationalism became a marked characteristic only in 1870–
71 when socialists could not reconcile their democratic principles
with the Prussian-dominated German Empire. In the realm of socialist thought, ideas drawn from Ferdinand Lassalle were most
familiar and a personality cult held his name in sacred honor.

The Lassallean aura is amply evident in the text of Jakob Audorf's "Workers' Marseillaise" ("Arbeiter-Marseillaise," no. XII),
the quasi-official song of the Social Democratic labor movement in
Imperial Germany. The song made Lassalle the personal symbol of
the movement.

Wohlan, wer Recht und Wahrheit achtet,
Zu uns'rer Fahne steht zu Hauf:
Wenn auch die Lüg' uns noch umnachtet,
:: Bald steigt der Morgen Hell herauf! ::
Ein schwerer Kampf ist's, den wir wagen,
Zahllos ist uns'rer Feinde Schaar,
Doch ob wie Flammen die Gefahr
Mög' über uns zusammenschlagen,
    Nicht zählen wir den Feind,
    Nicht die Gefahren all',
    :: Der Bahn, der Kühnen, folgen wir,
    Die uns geführt Lassall'. :: [21]

Boldly now, who honors truth and justice,
To our banner come the throngs:
Even if lies still surround us with darkness,
:: Soon the morning brightness will shine through ::
It is a heavy fight that we are waging,
Countless are the troops of the enemy,
Even if flames and danger
May break loose over us,
    We do not count the number of enemies,
    Do not worry about danger,
    :: We follow the path of courage
    On which Lassalle leads us ::

Marx never enjoyed that kind of personal glorification in popular song. To be sure, Johann Most and others hostile to Lassalle tried to replace Audorf's refrain with one taken from a text by Freiligrath.[22] The effort failed; the Lassalle refrain appears in five of the six workers' songbooks surveyed in this study. Moreover, other Lassallean ideas permeated the lyrics of the "Workers' Marseillaise."

Das freie Wahlrecht ist das Zeichen,
In dem wir siegen, nun wohlan!
Nicht predigen wir Hass den Reichen,
:: Nur gleiches Recht für Jedermann :: [23]

The right to free elections is the sign,
Under which we are victorious, and now boldly!
Not hatred against the rich do we preach,
:: But equal rights for everyone ::

The final stanza alludes to Lassalle as the "sower" ("Säemann") and concludes with words of spiritual sanctification.

Ist auch der Säemann gefallen,
In guten Boden fiel die Saat,
Uns aber bleibt die Kühne That,
Heiliges Vermächtnis sei sie Allen![24]

Even if the sower has fallen,
The seed fell on good soil,
For us, however, remains the courageous act,
May it be a holy heritage for all of you.

The fact that Audorf's "Arbeiter-Marseillaise" held first place among all songs of the labor movement throughout the era of the Second Empire and well into Weimar cannot be stressed too much. Between 1875 and 1914 it was sung by the assembled delegates at the close of almost every Social Democratic party congress. Great ceremonial meaning is attached to any song that regularly closes meetings of significance. The repeated use of the "Arbeiter-Marseillaise" is all the more striking because German Social Democrats had not created elaborate liturgies and rituals to infuse their gatherings with symbolic meanings. But singing the "Arbeiter-Marseillaise" gained ritualistic meaning not only at the close of party congresses, but on numerous other occasions. More than any other single song, it embodied the spirit of the socialist labor movement.[25]

The words, symbols, and ideas in the mass political songs reflect many but not all of the impulses that inspired the German labor movement. Words and phrases that seem trivial when judged by the standards of high theory may nonetheless take on considerable meaning when understood as part of an informal matrix of sentiments and aspirations. The lyrics do not explain theories; they evoke emotions, arouse hopes, and allude to ideas. What emerges from the lyrics of socialist political songs is a mixed blend of evocative symbols and general labor movement notions.

With few exceptions the mode of expression was to address and exhort the workers directly. This hortative mode is characteristic of many political songs throughout the world, and may also be noted in the "Internationale." The obvious intent was to alter the consciousness of people who would sing and listen. The exhortations vary, although the most common is the call for an awakened political awareness, for solidarity, and class consciousness. By their very nature exhortations are simple and straightforward. As a result many of the texts have a one-dimensional character. Note the fol-

lowing, taken almost at random from verses in the sixteen songs
listed above: "Workers, all awake!" ("Arbeiter, all' erwacht!"),
"Arise, and let the flags fly" ("Auf, und lass die Fahne fliegen"),
"Brothers, embrace the league" ("Brüder, reicht die Hand zum
Bunde"), "Now stand together, man to man" ("Drum haltet fest
zusammen"), "Arise, Socialists, close your ranks" ("Auf, Sozialisten, schliesst die Reihen"), "Gather together your power"
("Rafft eure Kraft zusammen"), "Close the phalanx" ("Schliesst
die Phalanx"), "Man of labor, awaken and recognize your power!"
("Man der Arbeit, aufgewacht und erkenne deine Macht!"). The
one-dimensional character of the exhortations should not, however, be taken to imply that the songs were therefore not effective.
Hortatory modes may not inspire lyrics of great aesthetic merit,
but their intended function is to carry a message.

Whatever the particular message in the political songs of the
movement, workers were the recipients, not the agents. Socialist
workers do not even speak for themselves in most of the texts.
There are two exceptions, the first by H. Pfeil, "My Cradle Stood
in a Humble Abode" ("Es stand meine Wiege im niedrigen
Haus"), and the other by Audorf, "We Are the Fire Bombers"
("Wir sind die Petroleure"). But narrative and ballad forms were
not sufficiently direct to serve effectively as instruments of communication. Socialist authors in Imperial Germany preferred to use a
more direct form in carrying out the urgent task of arousing
workers to political and social consciousness.

Workers learned from many lyrics that they could be proud of
being workers. Translating Robert Burns, the spirited Scottish
poet of the common man, Ferdinand Freiligrath's verses in "Is
There for Honest Poverty" ("Ob Armuth euer Los auch sei")
encouraged self-esteem, inner confidence, and even defiance. Poverty is no cause for shame, but for pride.

> Ob Armuth euer Los auch sei,
> Hebt doch die Stirn, trotz alledem!
> Geht Kühn dem feigen Knecht vorbei,
> Wagt's arm zu sein, trotz alledem,
> Trotz alledem und alledem,
> Trotz niederm Plack und alledem,
> Der Rang ist das Gepräge nur,
> Der Mann das Gold, trotz alledem!
>
> Is there for honest poverty
> That hings his head, an' a' that?

The coward slave, we pass him by—
We care be poor for a' that!
For a' that, an' a' that,
Our toils obscure, an' a' that,
The rank is but the guinea's stamp,
The man's the gowd [gold] for a' that.[26]

Johann Most also gave workers cause for pride: Workers produce the wealth of the world and, even if it is taken from them, they are nonetheless the *sine qua non* for the increased welfare of society.

Wer schafft das Gold zu Tage?
Wer hämmert Erz und Stein?
Wer webet Tuch und Seide?
Wer bauet Korn und Wein?
Wer gibt den Reichen all ihr Brot
und lebt dabei in bitt'rer Noth?
 :: Das sind die Arbeitsmänner,
 das Proletariat::

Who hammers brass and stone?
Who raiseth from the mine?
Who weaveth cloth and silk?
Who tilleth wheat and vine?
Yet lives himself in sorest need?
 It is the men who toil,
 The Proletariat.[27]

Few texts in the whole corpus of mass political songs equaled the rhythmic power in Most's choice of language and his staccato style. In a different poetic style, but on a similar theme, the Austrian Joseph Zapf recounted the accomplishments of simple labor, from the struggles of primitive man, through the achievements of the Egyptians and Romans, to the nineteenth century when labor would break the bonds of the "capitalist yoke." Each stanza ends with a cheer, "Hail to Labor" ("Die Arbeit Hoch").[28]

The world of work is seldom depicted in socialist songs. When it is, the imagery alludes to traditional trades and occupations. Certainly, the language of traditional crafts had a familiar ring in popular poetic expression. When it flowed naturally from the pen of a man with poetic talent, the verses could be aesthetically pleasing. The second and third verses from Herwegh's "Work and Pray" ("Bet' und Arbeit") allude to such traditional crafts, the

world of preindustrial production, in language of simplistic beauty.
Herwegh tells the workers:

> Und du ackerst und du sä'st,
> Und du nietest und du näh'st,
> :: Und du hämmerst und du spinnst—
> Sag', o Volk, was du gewinnst? ::

> Wirkst am Webstuhl Tag und Nacht,
> Schlürfst im Erz- und Kohlenschacht,
> :: Füllst des Ueberflusses Horn,
> Füllst es hoch mit Wein und Korn. :: [29]

> And you till and you sow,
> And you rivet and you sew,
> :: And you hammer and you spin—
> But say, O folk, what do you win?

> You work at the loom day and night,
> In mine shafts you haul coal and ore,
> :: You fill the horn of plenty to overflowing,
> Fill it full with wine and grain. ::

In Most's "Wer schafft das Gold zu Tage" there are direct references or allusions to blacksmiths, weavers, farmers, miners, and
producers of luxury goods, all preindustrial forms of labor. And
Joseph Zapf too, in "Die Arbeit Hoch," recounted the history of
work to modern time with only one allusion to modern industrial
production.

One should not conclude, however, that songwriters addressed
themselves only to the world of traditional craftsmen or modern
skilled workers. Language referring to all workers permeates the
lyrics. August Geib, in "Auf und lasst die Fahne fliegen" calls on
"Proletarier," and in "In Beautiful May, in Youthful May" ("Im
schönen Mai, im grünen Mai") he appeals to "the people of toil,"
to the "proletarian," and to the "army of poverty" ("Armuth Hee-
resbahn"); the anonymous poet of "What Flows and Streams
Through the Streets Over There" ("Was fluthet und strömt durch
die Strassen dahin") glorifies "those figures in simple dress," the
"men of labor"; and in "You Men, All of You" ("Ihr Männer
all' ") Ernst Klaar specifically associates the "people of labor" and
the "Proletariat" with factories.[30] Except for occasional references
to the *Volk,* the terms *worker* and *proletarian* occupy a central
place as concepts of social class. It is also important to note that
although there are allusions to crafts, the term *artisan* (*Hand-*

werker) itself has no place in the lyrics of these songs of the labor movement.

Nature's world still provided many of the symbols for good and bad. August Geib rhapsodized about spring, associating it with the founding of the labor movement. The last two stanzas are particularly rich in nature imagery.

> Auf, aus der Werkstatt, aus dem Schacht!
> Es strahlt die Welt in Frühlingspracht!
> Bleibt nicht in dumpfer Nacht zurück!
> Nehmt Antheil an der Erde Glück.
>   :: Hurrah, im schönen jungen Mai::
>   :: Nimmt stark und kühn das Volk, das Volk Partei!::
>
> Im schönen Mai, im jungen Mai,
> Erhebt der Arbeit Volk sich frei!
> Die Saat, im Frühling ausgestreut,
> Der Sommer reif zur Ernte beut!
>   :: Hurrah, im schönen jungen Mai usw.:: [31]
>
> Arise, out of the workshop, out of the mine!
> The world radiates in the splendor of spring!
> Linger not in night's stifling darkness!
> Join in the happiness of earth.
>   :: Hurray, in beautiful youthful May::
>   :: With strength and courage the people take up their cause::
>
> In beautiful May, in youthful May,
> Working people arise to free themselves!
> The seed, sown broadly in spring,
> Ripens in summer for a bountiful harvest!
>   Refrain repeats

In Max Kegel's "Socialist March" ("Sozialistenmarsch") the whole world of nature joins in the joy of the new emancipatory movement.

> Auf, Sozialisten, schliess die Reihen!
> Die Trommel ruft, die Banner wehn.
> Es gilt die Arbeit zu befreien,
> Es gilt der Freiheit Auferstehn!
> Der Erde Glück, der Sonne Pracht,
> Des Geistes Licht, des Wissens Macht,
> Dem ganzen Volk sei's gegeben!
> Das ist das Ziel, das wir erstreben. [32]

Arise, Socialists, close your ranks!
The drums call, the banners wave.
The cause is to make labor free
The cause is the resurrection of Liberty!
Happiness on earth, the brilliance of the sun,
The light of the mind, the power of knowledge,
To all the people, should these belong!
That is the goal for which we strive.

Freedom itself is identified with nature in Max von Schenkendorf's "Freiheit die ich meine."

Auch bei grünen Bäumen
In dem lust'gen Wald,
Unter Blüthenträumen
Ist dein Aufenthalt.[33]

Also near the lush green of the trees
In the delightful woods,
Amidst floral dreamings,
There's your place of abode.

Such imagery gave the impression that the goals of the labor movement were sanctified by and in full harmony with the natural world.

The milieu created by the lyrics is a polarized world. To some degree, the language of conflict is infused in nearly every song. The degree varies immensely, but the fundamental structure is "we" against the enemy—exploiters, the rich, the oppressors, and others. A spirit of enmity, hostility, struggle, anger, contempt, and outrage is summoned through a varied vocabulary: "Contempt for the enemy" ("Dem Feind zum Hohn"), "Battle Red" ("Schlachtenroth"), "Fight" ("Kampf"), "Servility" ("Knechtschaft"), "Yoke of Slavery" ("Sklavenjoch"), "Capitalist Yoke" ("Kapitales Joch"), "Slavery's Misery" ("Not der Sklaverei"), "Tyrant's Blood" ("Tyrannenblut"), "Holy War" ("Heiliger Krieg"). The same Jakob Audorf who wrote the seemingly moderate words of the "Arbeiter-Marseillaise" could also, with considerable cleverness, write "Wir sind die Petroleure," verses overflowing with irony, insolence, sarcasm, contempt, and defiance. But the defiance is symbolic. The workers are not admonished and exhorted, but socialists (and by implication workers) declare an outrageous eagerness to incinerate the world around them. The tone is mocking and ironic. By identifying with the legendary "Petroleuses" of the last days of the Paris Commune in 1871, Audorf created a sense of literalness drawn from historical example. But to set fire to cities and villages is to create light, to spread enlightenment. This symbolic meaning did not make the lyrics seem any less dangerous, especially since Audorf wrote the text in 1878 as the antisocialist law was being enacted. It was as if Audorf openly and mockingly told authorities and proper German burghers that Social Democrats were every bit as dangerous as the new law declared them to be.

> Schon brennt es in den Städten
> So licht und frank und frei,
> Man spürt, dass es von Nöthen
> Auch auf den Dörfern sei.
> Es leuchtet in dem Heere schon,
> Man ist vor Staunen stumm,
> Trotz Sub- und Ordination
> Brennt hell Petroleum.
> ∷ Hier Petroleum, da Petroleum,
> Petroleum um und um,
> Lasst die Humpen frisch voll pumpen,
> Dreimal hoch Petroleum. ∷ [34]

> Already it is burning in the cities
> So bright and frank and free,
> One also feels that of necessity
> It's in the villages, too.
> Light penetrates even the army,
> One is dumb with amazement,
> Despite subordination and ordination,
> Petroleum is burning brightly.
> ∷ Here petroleum, there petroleum,
> Petroleum everywhere,
> Let's pump the tankards full again,
> Three hails to petroleum. ∷

Few mass political songs matched "Wir sind die Petroleure" for cleverness and colorful, combative imagery.

The goals of the labor movement were often expressed in general, abstract, and lofty language. Pastoral images enhanced the beauty and high idealism of the struggle for freedom, justice, truth, and equality. On a more concrete level the goal was to raise the oppressed out of "pain and misery," and for Joseph Zapf it was to break the "capitalist yoke." The most specific goals mentioned were universal suffrage, in texts from the 1860s, and the eight-hour day. The latter is the major point of Ernst Klaar's "You Men, All of You" ("Ihr Männer all' "), written in 1890 at the time when the international socialist movement had just recently made the eight-hour day a central demand. Klaar's text is also interesting because it is one of the few to reflect the changing issues and conditions affecting the socialist movement. It is the only one of these texts that uses the term *Fabrik,* and its allusions to socialist internationalism are explicit. But, as the last verse indicates, Klaar also expected the state to solve the social problem and pleads, presumably to those in power, to *give* the eight-hour day to the workers.

Schon rafft sich rings in allen Ländern
Empor das Proletariat—
Das Loos der Armen soll sich ändern,
Und ändern soll sich's durch den Staat.
O, wenn wir fest zusammenstehen,
Wer will uns weigern unser Recht?
Empor, empor, du neu Geschlecht,
Lass trotzig deine Banner wehen!
    Gebt den Achtstundentag!
    Verkürzt der Arbeit Plag!
    Zum Siegeszug
    Die Trommel schlug.
    Acht Stunden sind genug![35]

Already on all sides and throughout the world
The proletariat rises up together—
The fate of the poor is to be changed,
And to be changed through the state.
O, if we stand together firmly,
Who will be able to refuse us our right?
Upward, upward, you new generation,
Defiant let your banner wave!
    Put in the eight-hour day!
    Reduce the misery of toil!
    To our victorious march
    The drum now beats.
    Eight hours are enough!

The lyrics of mass political songs reveal that, with few exceptions, they were written by political leaders and ideologues interested in broad goals. Workers are called on, but particular trades and crafts are forgotten. Names of places and persons are extremely rare. Events are seldom mentioned; time itself is not a necessary backdrop. The story in mass political songs is in the future, the optimistic future, not in the past, and only to a limited extent in the present. At the root of all these characteristics was a basic fact: The purpose and function of songs was to arouse political awareness, create a sense of solidarity, and drill general principles into the minds of German workingmen.

The total impact of socialist songs also depended, as with all songs, on their musical qualities. Only three of the previous sixteen songs—numbers VIII, XIII, and XIV—were sung to melodies specifically composed by labor movement musicians. All three of the composers—Josef Scheu, Carl Gramm, and Peter Heinz—wrote a considerable amount of music for the Austrian and German Social Democratic movements. They did not, however, create a unique musical style. In musical terms they belonged to the tradition of composers who for decades had written for male choirs, composing hymnlike anthems, marches, and sentimental melodies. Only after the First World War did socialist composers experiment with new musical styles.[36]

The natural way to meet the need for melodies was to parody older songs, a practice common throughout Germany and other countries. For what reasons an individual socialist author chose a particular tune is seldom discernible from documentary sources. If, however, the repertory of parodied melodies is counted and classified systematically, certain patterns become evident that suggest explanations for some of the choices. The following list of the thirteen most parodied melodies provides a basis for searching for the rationale underlying melody selections.

LEADING MELODIES*

    I. "Marseillaise" [14] C. J. Rouget de Lisle, 1792.

    II. "Zu Mantua in Banden" [12] "In Mantua in Chains" ("Andreas-Hofer-Lied"). L. Erk, from a popular tune. 1849.

    III. "Strömt herbei, ihr Völkerscharen" [11] "Stream For-

---

*Included are melodies that appear in the six songbooks with three or more different texts written to them. The melodies are rank-ordered according to the number of texts. The greatest number of texts (fourteen), were written to the melody of the "Marseillaise." The number of texts is in brackets, followed by frequently used titles, the composer's name, and approximate date of composition.

ward, Populous Throngs" ("Rheinlied"). Johann Peters, 1840s.

IV. "Der Papst lebt herrlich in der Welt." [10] "The Pope Lives Sumptuously in This World."

V. "Sind wir vereint zur guten Stunde" [7] "We Stand United in Good Time" ("Bundeslied"). Georg F. Hanitsch. 1815.

VI. "Brüder, reicht die Hand zum Bunde" [6] "Brothers, Embrace the League" ("Bundeslied"). Mozart. November 15, 1791.

VII. "Auf, ihr Brüder lasst uns wallen" [6] "Arise, Brothers, Let's Move On" ("Fahnenlied" or "Vaterlands Sänger"). Joseph Hartmann Stuntz. Ca. 1830.

VIII "Frisch auf, Kameraden, aufs Pferd" [6] "Arise, Comrades, to Your Mounts." Dr. Christian Jakob Zahn. 1797.

IX. "Es braust ein Ruf wie Donnerhall" [6] "A Roar Goes Forth Like a Thunderbolt" ("Die Wacht am Rhein"). Karl Wilhelm. 1854.

X. "Deutschland, Deutschland über alles" [5] "Germany, Germany Above All" ("Das Lied der Deutschen"). Haydn, composed for a text by L. A. Haschka. "Gott erhalte Franz den Kaiser" as Austrian National Hymn. 1797.

XI. "Freiheit, die ich meine" [4] "Freedom, That I Love" Karl Groos. 1818.

XII. Crambambuli, das ist der Titel" [4] "Crambambuli, That is the Title."

XIII. "Ein feste Burg ist unser Gott" [3] "A Mighty Fortress Is Our God." Martin Luther. 1520s.

The above two lists contain a total of twenty-one different melodies. Three of them were original compositions by socialist musicians, leaving eighteen that were parodied. It is a striking fact that at least ten out of the twenty-one came directly from patriotic traditions that were so powerful in Germany during the middle decades of the nineteenth century. Many of these patriotic songs had appeared first during the Wars of Liberation; another group originated in the 1840s and 1850s. No other cluster of melodies came from another identifiable ideological tradition. Only one melody, "A Mighty Fortress" ("Ein feste Burg"), came from a religious tradition. (Moreover, that seems to have been the only religious hymn to serve as a tune for a labor movement text.)[37] One melody came from Freemasonry, two were traditional comic songs (*Scherzlieder*), one was an old drinking song, one came from an operetta, and one was taken directly from Schiller's play, *Wallensteins Lager*.

An explanation is needed for the fact that so many labor movement texts were sung to melodies with patriotic connotations. Four possible explanations deserve special consideration. The first is that socialist authors wanted to use melodies that were well-known and possessed certain stirring qualities. Melodies of the patriotic tradition tended to have the qualities either of hymns (anthems) or marches, the former inspiring moods of exhaltation and solemnity, the latter arousing a sense of masses of people in movement. To be sure, socialists wanted to employ symbols that would express the dignity and worthiness of their undertakings, and to that end hymnlike melodies were appropriate. They also wanted to infuse a mood of action and dynamism; stirring march melodies served that purpose. However, if these musical qualities had been the uppermost reason for choosing certain melodies, then socialists had a large repertory of popular melodies from which to choose and the predominance of patriotic tunes would not be so obvious.

Patriotic melodies could also be used in order to disguise the true content of the song. Normally, there was little substantive advantage to be gained by such camouflaging, although outwitting the police gave socialists special pleasure during the years under the antisocialist law. Surveillance police might think socialists were singing "Watch on the Rhine" ("Die Wacht am Rhein") when in fact they had in mind August Geib's "Im schönen Mai, im jungen Mai." However, as a general explanation for the use of patriotic melodies, this camouflage theory has numerous weaknesses. The first use of patriotic melodies preceded a time when the labor movement had any serious need to disguise its songs.[38] Moreover, had socialists been particularly concerned, even during the antisocialist law, to disguise their songs, they would not have used the well-known and easily recognized "Marseillaise" so widely and intensively. Finally, Social Democrats could have disguised the content of their songs just as convincingly by using nonpatriotic melodies. Indeed, few policemen would have been seriously misled for long by this kind of deception.

It would be easy to assume that socialists used patriotic melodies as a means of ridiculing German national sentiment. There is one text, "Active Duty with the Lyre" ("Der Dienst an der Leyer"), clearly written to satirize German patriotism by contrasting the glorification of war to the misery and suffering of a wounded soldier. The first verse very effectively expresses biting sarcasm and mockery of "Die Wacht am Rhein."

> Es tönet nicht wie Donnerhall,
> Wie Schwertgeklirr und Wogenprall;
> Es ächzt wie schriller Todesklang
> Die Leyer und der heis're Sang:
> :: Dort draussen über'm deutschen Rhein,
> Da blieb mein Glück, da ruht mein Bein. :: [39]

> It does not sound like thunderbolts,
> Or like swords clashing and waves crashing;
> It groans like the shrill noise of death
> The harp and the coarse singing:
> :: There, on the other side of the German Rhine,
> There remains my joy, there lies my severed leg. ::

So far as can be determined, this text appeared only in Johann Most's *Proletarier-Liederbuch,* in which there is also a different kind of satire on "Die Wacht am Rhein." In the latter case, however, the substance of "Die Wacht am Rhein" is satirized not only in the words, but by singing the satirical text to a drinking song, "Crambambuli." The burlesque effect is doubled. The first verse shows that the early socialists were not wanting in wit.

> Die Wacht am Rhein, das ist der Titel
> Des Liedes, das im Schwange geht.
> Es ist ein ganz probates Mittel
> Für Einen, der sonst Nichts versteht.
> Darum bei Mond- und Sonnenschein
> Sing' ich nur stets die Wacht am Rhein,
> Die wi—Wa—Wacht am Rhein, die Wacht am Rhein. [40]

> The Watch on the Rhine, that is the title
> Of the song that is now in fashion.
> It is perfectly suited
> To anyone who otherwise understands nothing.
> That is why, by moonlight and sunlight
> I always sing only the Watch on the Rhine,
> The wi—Wa—Watch on the Rhine,
> The Watch on the Rhine.

Close examination of the other texts written to patriotic melodies shows that they were not consciously written to ridicule German patriotism. To be sure, it might have seemed ironic at first to hear organized workers singing Social Democratic propaganda to patriotic melodies, but as years and then decades passed the ironic effect could not be sustained.

A fourth explanation pertaining to the use of patriotic melodies must be strongly emphasized. German patriotism in itself was by no means incompatible with the social reform goals of the young labor movement. In the 1860s "Deutschland, Deutschland über alles," "Schleswig-Holstein by Seas Surrounded" ("Schleswig-Holstein meerumschlungen"), and "Die Wacht am Rhein" were not yet musical symbols for the kind of German Empire that came into being in 1870–71. Before Germany became a unified and powerful state, most patriotic songs were thought of simultaneously as "freedom songs."[41] This applied especially to songs that came out of the Wars of Liberation. That earlier union of liberationist and patriotic ideals dissolved as the political context in which the songs were sung changed. The first major change came in 1870–71, followed much later by the events of 1914–18 and of 1933. But in the 1860s members of the young German labor movement lived in an environment in which most Germans assumed that liberationist principles and patriotic sentiments worked in harmony. There was thus a subtle ideological symbolism at work when early socialists wrote new texts to tunes of patriotism. Through musical symbolism they were linked to an older German liberationist tradition that embodied love of country as well as love of freedom.[42]

If it is noteworthy that melodies associated with German patriotism were so frequently sung with labor movement lyrics, it is an even more striking feature that the melody that accompanied the greatest number of socialist texts came from French republican patriotism—the "Marseillaise." Fourteen new texts to one melody found in six *Liederbücher* is certainly striking evidence. But there were more. For example, already in 1849 Ferdinand Freiligrath had written "Be Quick to the Tune of the Marseillaise" ("Frisch auf zur Weise von Marseille"), a song that does not appear in any of the six collections concentrated on here, but which workers' singing societies sometimes sang and which became more prominent only after the First World War.[43] And the labor movement's most popular song, Audorf's "Boldly now, Who Honors Truth and Justice" ("Wohlan, wer Recht und Wahrheit achtet"), was written to the "Marseillaise" and was known popularly as the "Workers' Marseillaise" ("Arbeiter-Marseillaise"). This widespread and intensive use of the "Marseillaise" is all the more impressive because no other group in German society did likewise, and certainly not after 1870–71. Within the context of Imperial Germany the music of the "Marseillaise" became an integral possession of the socialist labor movement community.[44]

The melody of the "Marseillaise" was a powerful and meaningful symbol for German Social Democracy. Throughout most of the nineteenth century, in France as well as in much of Europe, its tones were understood as a call to radicalism, republicanism, and emancipation through revolution. When Social Democrats took over the melody of the "Marseillaise," they took possession— within Germany, that is—of Europe's most powerful musical symbol of revolution. The "Marseillaise" became the national anthem of France only in 1879, that is, of republican France. That did not undermine the song's liberationist implications for other Europeans.[45] The symbolic implications of the "Marseillaise" were, to that degree, not substantially different from those of early German patriotic songs—both carried, in different ways, emancipatory connotations. The difference was that in Imperial Germany other groups did not use the melody of the "Marseillaise" and for that reason it could contribute to the labor movement's sense of cohesion and identity.

The opposite is also notable. That is, melodies that clearly belonged to nonsocialist groups and ideologies within German society could not become identified with the labor movement. As long as "Die Wacht am Rhein" and "Deutschland, Deutschland über alles" remained vigorous songs of German nationalism for the population as a whole, their melodies could not become the unique property of the labor movement. The words that Social Democrats had written to "Deutschland, Deutschland über alles" might speak socialism, but the musical tones sent out contrary signals. Using current melodies of vibrant German nationalism created symbolic ambiguity, not clarity.

It is significant that in the history of the German Social Democratic labor movement, and later of the Communist movement, only four melodies have served as clear and decisive symbols of identity. Literally hundreds of songs have been repeatedly sung in the labor movement, but most have lacked some essential ingredient needed to serve as a symbol of identity. The first was the "Marseillaise." It enjoyed a long career as a musical symbol for Social Democracy. The second was Carl Gramm's music to Max Kegel's "Sozialistenmarsch." It enjoyed a shorter career and before the First World War never succeeded in displacing the "Arbeiter-Marseillaise." Nonetheless, the "Sozialistenmarsch" had widespread appeal; it had been composed by a socialist sympathizer and it was easily remembered, though a bit difficult to sing. The third song was, of course, the "Internationale." Though it was known in Germany as early as the mid-1890s, it only became widespread there in the last years before the First World War.[46] It had to wait until the revolutionary era at the end of the First World War to come into its own as the musical hallmark of socialist internationalism in Germany. The "Internationale" has enjoyed the longest career. The fourth song was "Brothers, On to the Sun, On to Freedom" ("Brüder, zur Sonne zur Freiheit"), but it appeared only after the First World War, rapidly became popular, and has retained much of its symbolic appeal.

The songs discussed thus far were formal pieces, written largely by socialist authors intent on presenting a positive statement in the cause of the labor movement. The strike songs in the following list differed in many ways from the mass political songs. Strikers' songs reflected a wide emotional range. Whereas songs of the party tended toward optimism, the lyrics in strikers' songs expressed sorrow as well as optimism, resignation as well as hope, weariness as well as a will to fight. In these texts workers are seldom exhorted as in the political songs, but they presumably speak for themselves or about themselves. When they are exhorted, as in "Listen You Good People of Crimmitschau" ("Hört, ihr braven Crimmitschauer," no. IV), it is clear that the speaker is one of them, a *Streikgenosse*. The level of abstraction changes. Strikers' songs project a sense of immediacy, of time and place, of pain and strength.

STRIKE SONGS[47]

   I. "Es braust ein Ruf so schnell wie Pest" "A Roar Goes Forth as Swift as the Plague." Anon. 1889. Melody: "Die Wacht am Rhein."

  II. "Glück auf, Kameraden, durch Nacht zum Licht" "Good Luck, Comrades, from Darkness to Light" ("Internationales Knappenlied"). Heinrich Kämpchen. Melody: "Frisch auf, Kameraden, aufs Pferd."

 III. "Heilige Nacht—Heiss tobt die Schlacht" "Holy Night— the Heated Battle Goes on" ("Weihnachtslied der Ausgesperrten"). "H. J." [H. Jäckel]. Ca. 1900. Melody: "Stille Nacht, Heilige Nacht."

  IV. "Hört, ihr braven Crimmitschauer" "Listen, You Good People of Crimmitschau" ("Hört, ihr lieben Streikgenos-

sen"). Anon. 1903. Melody: "Als die Römer frech gewor-
den."

V. "In Sachsen liegt ein Städtchen" "In Saxony There Is a
Small Town" ("Um den Zehnstundentag muss werden erst
gestritten"). Anon. 1903. Melody: "Im Böhmen liegt ein
Städtchen."

VI. "In Löbtau sitzt bei ihrem Kinde" "In Löbtau She Sits with
Her Child" ("Löbtau-Lied"). Anon. Late 1890s. Melody:
"Bei ihrem schwer erkrankten Kinde."

VII. "Still ruht der Saal" "The Hall Rests Silently" Anon. Ca.
1903. Melody: "Still ruht der See."

At the time of the miners' strike in 1889, several songs appeared
in the Saarland and the Ruhr expressing the sentiments of striking
workers. "A Roar Goes Forth as Swift as the Plague" ("Es braust
ein Ruf so schnell wie Pest," no. I) parodied "Die Wacht am
Rhein" and illustrates perfectly the features of many strike songs.
Authorship of the text is unknown, though it is likely that one
person, perhaps in collaboration with a few others, was chiefly
responsible. There is specificity and immediacy in the text; a story
unfolds. The first verse immediately identifies an event, the location, the workers' leader, their organization, their emotions, and
their determination.

> Es braust ein Ruf so schnell wie Pest,
> Der Warken sitzet im Arrest.
> Vom Bildstock bis zu Von der Heydt
> Sind wir gerührt in tiefem Leid
> /: Kam'raden, wir müssen einig sein,:/
> /: Fest stehn wir treu zum Rechtschutzverein:/[48]
>
> A roar goes forth as swift as the plague,
> That Warken is under arrest.
> From Bildstock to Von der Heydt
> We are moved to deepest sympathy
> /: Comrades, we must be united,:/
> /: We stand, loyal and firm, by the Protection Union:/

Subsequent stanzas tell us that "twenty-four thousand men" joined
the cause, that their trusted representatives (*Vertrauensmänner*)
were involved, and the miners were at one with Warken, "a man
of honor," as he served his sentence. The verses reflect a spontaneous, unpolished style and uneven use of language. The text is

not intended to be poetry; it is an announcement, a news story, a trade union ballad, with a strong declaration of purpose.

During the same year a song of a different character gained popularity among striking miners (no. II). The author was Heinrich Kämpchen (1847–1912), himself a miner who lived near Bochum. Influenced by the labor movement, Kämpchen played an active leadership role in the Ruhr during the strike of 1889, and for that the employers blacklisted him. In Kämpchen's verses there is an amalgam of phrases and imagery common to miners on the one side and to the Social Democratic movement on the other. He fused those two strands. However, both in style and content his text is closer to the lyrics of socialist party songs than to a strikers' song like "Es Braust ein Ruf so schnell wie Pest." The first line begins with the customary miners' greeting, "Good Luck" ("Glück auf"), and ends with a favorite slogan of socialist optimism, "from darkness to light." Terms from the world of mining are less dominant than themes that stress toughness, solidarity, brotherhood, persistence, human rights, a fearless confrontation of the enemy, and confidence in an ultimate victory that will bring freedom.[49]

In the textile strike in Crimmitschau (1903) songs emerged, spontaneously it appears, and were transmitted orally as well as in print. Striking workers in Crimmitschau parodied "Silent Night, Holy Night" ("Stille Nacht, Heilige Nacht") in a text that exudes bitter sarcasm (no. III).

> Heilige Nacht—Heiss tobt die Schlacht,
> Und es blitzt und es kracht.
> "Friede auf Erden!" die Christenheit singt,
> Während der Arme das Schwert mutig schwingt,
> /: Kämpfend für Freiheit und Glück. :/[50]
>
> Holy Night—the heated battle goes on,
> And it flashes and it roars.
> "Peace on Earth" the Christians sing,
> While the poor bravely wield the sword,
> /: Fighting for freedom and joy.:/

In this instance use of a Christian musical symbol, especially cherished during the Christmas season, sharpened the cutting edge of the song. Christian hypocrisy was the central object of the strikers' scorn and hostility.

Musical parody in *Streiklieder* turned not only on bitterness; it could also be used to express a secure confidence that striking workers can stop the production system. There is a subtle ironic twist in the use of the melody of "The Lake Rests Silent" ("Still ruht der See") for another Crimmitschau strike song (no. VII).

> Still ruht der Saal, die Stühle schweigen,
> Der Schützen liegt in guter Ruh.
> Ihr wolltet eure Macht uns zeigen,
> Nun schliesset eure Buden zu!

> Still ruht der Saal und die Maschinen
> Sowie die ganze Transmission.
> Man darf nicht reden von Verdienen,
> Denn's ist ja nur ein Sündenlohn.[51]

> The hall rests silently, the looms are quiet,
> The shuttle lies in sweet repose.
> You wanted to show us your power,
> Now you can close the stalls of labor.

> The hall rests silently and also the machines
> As well as all the transmission belts.
> One should not speak about earnings,
> For they are no more than a starvation wage.

Subsequent verses tell how quiet it is in the firm's accounting office, but also how a decision to fight lies ahead for the workers. A sense of humor about the struggle is also evident in the manner in which the Crimmitschau workers parodied the well-known "Song of the Eel" ("Das Lied vom Aal"), in which Saxon carding girls (*Krempelmädchen*) were chided for having eaten eel, considered too pretentious for their station in life. Herring was thought more fitting.

> In Sachsen liegt ein Städtchen,
> Das kennt fast jedermann,
> Da gibt es Krempelmädchen
> Ein ganzes Bataillon.

> Kartoffeln esst und Hering
> Zu jedem Mahl des Tags;
> Das ist die beste Nahrung
> Für Mädchen euren Schlags!

> In Saxony there is a small town,
> That almost everybody knows,
> There you find the carding girls,
> A complete batallion.

[A carding girl] eats potatoes and herring
At every meal of the day;
That is the best nutrition
For girls of your particular type.

The first and the third stanzas of the strikers' song (no. V) show
how closely it was patterned on "Das Lied vom Aal."[52]

In Sachsen liegt ein Städtchen,
Das kennt fast jedermann,
/: Da gibt's ein Arbeitsvölkchen
Von siebentausend Mann.:/

Umsonst war alles Bitten
Um den Zehnstundentag,
Muss werden erst gestritten,
Eh man's erkennen mag.

In Saxony there is a small town,
That almost everybody knows.
/: There you find a working people
Of seven thousand men.:/

In vain was all our pleading
For the ten-hour day,
But first there must be a struggle,
Before they'll give it recognition.

Imitation is the key to this as well as to other *Streiklieder*. They
followed more closely the pattern of the parodied song; and they
dealt with what was familiar, local, and personal.

Strikers' songs could also be sad and mournful. Such is the
"Löbtau-Lied" (no. VI) that seems to have emerged around 1898
in Dresden during a masons' strike. It is a sentimental ballad that
tells the story of "the wife of a workingman" and how unmercifully
her life is saddened by an undeserved and brutal fate. Her
daughter, "Klein-Gretchen," awakens, having dreamt of seeing
her father in prison and asks what he had done to be so maltreat-
ed. Did he murder? Violate the moral code? What crime did he
commit? No, he committed no crime, but only let his full wrath get
hold of him when he "once was drunk." Then he became a victim
of the law. In the German Reich, the mother tells her child, the
severest methods are immediately used against working people. By
contrast, continues the ballad, the "smooth scoundrels" get by
with everything. Upper-class criminals live in comfort and splen-

dor. It is a song of resentment, despair, sadness, frustration, anger, pain, and even self-pity.[53]

The glowing optimism so prevalent in mass political songs is either muted or totally lacking in the songs of strikers. When optimism is expressed, it concerns specific and limited goals, such as confidence that the ten-hour day will be won (in "Hört, ihr braven Crimmitschauer" and "Still ruht der Saal"). Strikers' songs were undeniably closer to the life experiences of workers than were party lyrics. A marked psychological distance separated the two types of song. That distance highlights the fact that the emotional world of organized workers had many dimensions. The two types of songs were not, however, in contradiction. On the contrary, it should also be noted that some qualities of the political songs were also embodied in the strike lyrics, notably the call for unity, solidarity, and determination; that is, some influences of the socialist labor movement are certainly evident in strike songs. They contrast most sharply with the party songs in mode of expression, style, specificity, and variability in moods.

In their various functions the songs discussed above contributed to defining the contours of the social-cultural milieu of the labor movement in Imperial Germany. It is particularly important to stress that the songs highlight the complexity of the relationship between the Social Democratic labor movement and the rest of German society. The labor movement existed within German society and could not help but draw on that culture. Music and song reflected the complexity of those relationships with just as much accuracy and subtlety as theoretical articles and parliamentary debates. The style and form of the culture of the labor movement are just as integral to its nature as its official doctrines. In musical style the cultural milieu of the labor movement was hardly distinguishable from other elements of German society.

But there was an important exception: By using the melody of the "Marseillaise" the labor movement simultaneously symbolized its devotion to a long European revolutionary tradition and declared its uniqueness within German society. During the Second Reich no native melody embedded in German culture could have served that dual function. And even when Carl Gramm and Max Kegel produced the "Sozialistenmarsch," with its own melody as well as text, it could not equal the "Marseillaise" as a symbol of unique identity because it lacked a distinctive musical style.

Two functions deserve special comment in conclusion. With respect to the ideas communicated in the political songs, it is striking

how little substantive change in themes and ideas can be detected
between 1864 and 1914. Part of the explanation lies in the fact that
many of the most successful songs were written during the first
decade of the organized labor movement in Germany and their
repeated use implied stability and ideological continuity. But even
the texts written in the later decades seldom departed markedly
from the general spirit already evident in the early texts. To be
sure, later texts did not glorify Ferdinand Lassalle as did the "Arbeiter-Marseillaise." Several new texts reflected a heightened
sense of the international brotherhood of all workers. Others occasionally referred to new issues, such as the eight-hour day, another
reflection of the German labor movement's participation in the
Second International. On the whole, however, one cannot detect
in the mass political songs a direct reflection of tendencies toward
radicalism or reformism. The texts from the early period are, in
every important respect, just as radical in some instances and just
as moderate in others as the songs that were written in the later
era. Even the increasing penetration of Marxism on a theoretical
level had little, if any, reverberation in the most popular song
lyrics.

What is the implication for the communicative function of mass
political songs? A gradual and subtle shift in the nature of the
communicative function took place over several decades. In the
early years the texts communicated the general notions of a new
social and political movement. The songs contained ideas that were
then comparatively novel and they reflected, broadly speaking,
current levels of thinking in the young labor movement. As the
same songs continued to be sung, the communicative function inevitably changed. In later decades it shifted to reaffirming and
stabilizing notions that came from an earlier epoch; they did not
necessarily reflect current levels of thinking in the movement by
the beginning of the twentieth century. This highlights one of the
difficulties inherent in the use of songs by dynamic social-political
movements. Such movements undergo changes, sometimes rapidly, in goals and outlook. By contrast, the song that is truly appealing—words and music as a unit—will remain in the repertory
along with lyrics that may have become antiquated. Constant renew-
al and updating is required if the communicative function is to
retain its vitality. The communicative function of a song text may
never cease entirely, but its importance declines dramatically once
the message in the text is a commonplace among those who sing
and listen. Insofar as it continues to play a role, the communicative

function does nothing more than to conserve established notions. From this examination of the party's political songs, it seems clear that the conserving dimension far outweighed the innovative aspect by the end of the nineteenth century. The fact that the communicative function declined in importance did not mean, however, that the songs themselves became less important.

These conclusions need to be modified in connection with strikers' songs. Unlike party songs, strike songs were not created with the intention that the whole labor movement should sing them. The texts generally emerged out of the milieu of a particular economic action or set of events. The communicative function was thus related directly to a specific time and place. To be used in new situations, it was necessary to alter the text slightly to fit different circumstances. Communication was thus preserved as a primary function. The many variants to strikers' song texts that have been discovered show that, in fact, it was common to adapt them to new circumstances. By contrast, the political song lyrics were not susceptible to such adaptations. They were written to have universal appeal throughout the labor movement. Through strike songs workers also expressed their sense of solidarity, but solidarity with a group that was familiar, immediate, and limited in size.

The symbolic and ceremonial functions of the party's political songs gained more meaning with the passage of time. The texts of numerous songs, at least the first stanzas, became a familiar part of festivals, meetings, and party congresses. The symbolic meaning of a labor movement song was not dependent on a literal comprehension of its lyrics, but on familiarity and a sense that it belonged and fitted into the movement. The early success of a substantial number of socialist songs written during the first decade of the labor movement meant that they grew in meaning as the labor movement itself grew in size and political significance. By the last decade of the nineteenth century, Audorf's "Arbeiter-Marseillaise," first sung in 1864, symbolized the movement's stability and strength through its own parallel longevity. It gave a certain historical justification to the whole movement. The fact that the melody of the "Marseillaise" was used with many other songs made the symbolic impact even more pervasive. By singing the "Arbeiter-Marseillaise" and other *Massenlieder* participants declared not so much *what* they believed, but *that* they believed and that they *belonged.*

6

The Uses of Poetry and Drama

Declamations, poetry recitations, and amateur theatrical performances enjoyed a prominent place on the programs at many kinds of labor movement gatherings. They were featured at nearly all festivals, though on many occasions, especially May Day celebrations during the 1890s and even later, police were quick to prohibit the spoken word in almost any form. Nonetheless, from its beginning in the 1860s, the labor movement—Lassallean and Eisenacher wings alike—recognized the usefulness of these artistic forms for both the dissemination of ideas and entertainment.[1] In a number of those early political organizations amateur theatrical divisions were founded as a means to ensure that presentations would be available and as a way for individuals to nurture their personal acting ambitions. Unlike the singers and gymnasts, actors in the labor movement had to struggle to enlarge their numbers and to gain comparable recognition from the party and trade unions. Acting demanded more personal commitment, time, and energy of the individual participants than did choral singing or gymnastics and for that reason alone it is understandable that workers' theatrical clubs did not flourish to the same degree. Moreover, there were other obstacles to overcome, notably a Social Democratic preference for the higher artistic quality of the professional theater, a point that will be treated below at greater length. It is even difficult to determine precisely the extent to which workers' theatrical clubs were established and maintained themselves, but the numbers were comparatively small. In 1899 the Federation of Workers' Associations (Bund der Arbeitervereine), a local Leipzig organization, reported that out of twenty-seven workers' associations, only seven had special dramatic divisions. As late as 1908 the newly founded Federation of Workers' Theatrical Clubs had only fifteen member clubs; by 1913 the number of affiliated clubs rose to sixty-six, with a total membership of 985. That is the best count available. The federation viewed itself as an integral part of the labor movement, and reaffirmed this by requiring that all individual members belong to either the Social Democratic party or one of the free trade unions.[2]

Numerical limitations did not dampen the enthusiasm of participants in the workers' theatrical clubs. In some cities, especially Leipzig, they were more active than in others. These amateur actors believed that despite their small numbers they played a significant role within the social-cultural milieu of the labor movement. Heinrich Lange, an active member of a workers' theatrical group in Leipzig, has left a brief account of the enthusiasm of young socialist workers who wanted to act.

> It was always noteworthy what our dramatic department achieved. The director, the master shoemaker August Scheibs, did not have it easy, rehearsing the roles, getting the costumes, putting on makeup and, as a rule, also taking part in the acting. Practices could only be held after work in the evening. But the members were full of enthusiasm for their task. For example, there were two young market assistants, Zschocher and Massias; I saw them one day coming along the Petersteinweg, the one pushing, the other pulling his wheelbarrow, so that they could walk next to each other. Completely immersed, they did not notice me, and then I could hear that they were practicing a scene from a piece in which they were to perform—and they were doing that in the midst of the hustle and bustle of a large city.[3]

These two were certainly exceptional—therefore Lange noticed and remembered the incident—and yet their experience reflected the sense of engagement that young people could feel as they became involved in the milieu of the socialist labor movement.

In the 1860s and 1870s there were as yet only a few plays written specifically for the labor movement, and the amount of socialist prose and poetry was also very limited. For the most part the earliest presentations were comedies or farces, but occasionally, as in Barmen in 1872, the actors would perform classical drama; in this instance they performed *Kabale und Liebe* by Schiller, an author immensely influential in Social Democratic circles.[4] Eventually, after the turn of the century, socialist writers had produced a rather large body of literature in all three genres. Each had its own place, but plays and skits in particular were prominent at festivals and other gatherings to serve both as entertainment and as instruction in socialist principles and values. Large and small audiences watched and listened as amateur actors presented their counterpart to the performances of singers, gymnasts, and cyclists.

The development of a body of socialist dramatic, poetic, and prose literature took time and had to overcome several serious obstacles. Despite the difficulties, the Social Democratic labor movement gradually began to accumulate a literature of its own, highly tendentious to be sure, but nonetheless integral to its social-cultural milieu. The literature produced within and for the movement never won, with some rare exceptions, any recognition among the general German public. Indeed, Social Democratic cultural commentators looked on their own socialist literature as artistically inferior, and accepted it primarily and often exclusively because of the message it carried.

Most authors of socialist literature were themselves modest about the artistic merits of their work. This was fitting no doubt because for them belletristic writing was a sideline, a hobby to be cultivated primarily for political reasons while they earned their livings in other occupations. A remarkable number of well-known Social Democratic leaders wrote plays, poems, short stories, and even novels. There were early precedents for this aspiration to combine socialist politics with belles lettres, beginning with Friedrich Engels, Ferdinand Lassalle, and Jean Baptiste von Schweitzer. (Engels' early dramatic writing remained unpublished and unknown to the Social Democratic movement.[5]) Lassalle chose the adventurous and controversial figure of the Reformation era, Franz von Sickingen, as the subject of his literary effort and structured it as an historical tragedy in verse form. One dramatic work hardly sufficed to win Lassalle a reputation as a writer of belles lettres and, although the play was known in socialist circles, its first performance came only in 1876, and after that its significance lay simply in the fact that it was part of Lassalle's intellectual biography.[6] Schweitzer, a bit more modest than Lassalle, did not aspire to create a tragedy, but limited himself to writing agitational plays and humorous skits, all with a didactic purpose. One of his first pieces, a novel entitled *Lucinde or Capital* (*Lucinde oder das Kapital*), from 1863, contained excerpts from Lassalle's social and political writings. Two humorous skits from a few years later marked a practical starting point for the Social Democratic tradition of incorporating socialist ideas in short plays that could be presented at gatherings by amateur performers. Schweitzer composed *A Rascal* (*Ein Schlingel,* 1867) and *A Goose*

(*Eine Gans,* 1869) to present the essentials of Marx's *Capital* in language that could be grasped quickly.[7] In the first a worker, too obviously named "Red" ("Roth"), easily outwits and outdebates his employer and the latter's assistant in all matters of economic theory by drawing heavily on Marx's recently published *Capital.* Since Schweitzer had written *A Rascal* to be recited rather than performed, the original had to be adapted for the stage. Both of these plays, simultaneously humorous and didactic, were performed in the late sixties and appeared on programs in subsequent decades. As for Schweitzer, he continued to write farces and comedies after he resigned as president of the Lassallean General Association of German Workingmen in 1871.[8]

Other members of the early Lassallean movement combined political and organizational commitments with literary aspirations. Friedrich Wilhelm Fritzsche (1824–1905), one of the organization's founding members and later a Social Democratic Reichstag deputy, published a volume of poetry in 1876 under the pseudonym F. W. Dornbusch. Except for an occasional reprint of a few poems, his work quickly passed from view. Another early Lassallean, the Reichstag deputy Wilhelm Hasenclever (1837–89), who after 1878 moved steadily toward anarchism, brought out a collection of poems, *Love, Life, Struggle* (*Liebe, Leben, Kampf. Gedichte*) in 1876, some of which were subsequently anthologized. The poetry of August Geib (1842–79), published as early as 1864, enjoyed considerable popularity and some of his lyrics were put to music.[9] One of the most prolific writers among the early Lassalleans, Karl Frohme (1850–1933), also enjoyed a long tenure as a Social Democratic Reichstag deputy (from 1881 to 1924!). He began his poetic publications in 1872 with a collection called *An Everlasting Wreath* (*Ein Immortellenkranz*), continued a few years later with *Festive Hours* (*Feierstunden*) and the *Magic Bullet* (*Freikugeln*), both published in 1876, contributed to a Social Democratic anthology of poetry (1893), and added one more in 1910, *Arise!* (*Empor!*).[10] In artistic terms August Otto-Walster (1834–98) surpassed the above and his output included a large number of prose works, the most popular of which was the novel *At the Loom of Time* (*Am Webstuhl der Zeit,* 1870), as well as poetry. Although an effective speaker, Otto-Walster did not hold a parliamentary seat but made his personal contribution to the labor movement through journalism. He also broke with the General Association in 1869, along with several other Lassalleans, to join the Social Democratic Labor party (Eisenachers), the newly transformed organization of the

Union of Workers' Educational Societies in which August Bebel
and Wilhelm Liebknecht were, and continued to be, the most effective leaders.[11] Still another Lassallean political leader, August
Kapell, composed a short agitational play, *Dr. Max Venison-Cow
or the Hypocrite's Office* (*Dr. Max Hirschkuh oder Das Amt des
Heuchlers*)—a satirical polemic against the views of the liberal
reformer Dr. Max Hirsch—for the Founders' Day Festival of the
General Association in 1872.[12] With that, Kapell's belletristic career reached its apex, though he played an active role in the move
to unify Lassalleans and Eisenachers in 1875 and for one session
(1877–78) held a Reichstag seat for the unified Social Democratic
party.

In contrast to the Lassalleans, the early Eisenachers included
only a few who were both political leaders and literary aspirants.
Their most prolific writer, Robert Schweichel (1821–1907), attended party congresses and coedited the *Demokratisches Wochen-
blatt* with Wilhelm Liebknecht, but never emerged as a political
leader. Only Wilhelm Blos (1849–1927) achieved a leading political reputation in the Social Democratic movement and also wrote
and published extensively. But Blos specialized in historical works,
especially on revolutions, and only once turned to belles lettres to
write a novel about the socialist movement at the time of the
antisocialist law. His histories enjoyed a certain popularity among
the users of workers' libraries, though his novel could not compete
with the works of popular fiction writers.[13]

Later, during the Wilhelmian era, there were some notable examples of Social Democratic political figures who wrote extensively. Among these the most talented was clearly Emil Rosenow
(1871–1904), a socialist Reichstag deputy from 1898 to 1904—at
age twenty-seven the youngest in the house—and also an energetic
campaigner who had spoken no less than fifty-three times during
the election of 1893. Rosenow wrote novels, poems, and drama,
and was the one Social Democratic playwright who succeeded with
the professional theaters, especially with his four-act comedy *Kater
Lampe.* His untimely death only two years after its successful pre-
miere in Breslau cut short a promising and unique career in both
politics and belles lettres.[14] Finally, it is also notable that a number
of young men who later came into prominence wrote agitational
plays prior to the First World War: Erich Mühsam (1878–1934)
published several pieces, including a four-act comedy; Wilhelm
(Willi) Münzenberg (1889–1940), later important in Communist
publishing, wrote a radical play, *Children from the Depths* (*Kinder*

der Tiefe) in 1913 that reportedly was performed on several occasions; and Ernst Däumig (1866–1922), a leading revolutionary shop steward in 1918–19, composed a radical piece for May Day celebrations (*Maifeier*).[15]

Political leaders with literary ambitions, though noteworthy as examples of the labor movement's early involvement with literature, constituted only a portion of the total number of socialist authors. The majority of these writers tried to earn a living within the labor movement, especially after 1890, when the number of socialist and trade union newspapers and periodicals expanded rapidly. This growth created positions for editors, feuilletonists, and part-time reporters. Some socialist authors even tried to survive as free-lance writers, but at considerable risk because the honoraria were comparatively modest in the world of the labor movement. Nonetheless, Social Democratic journalism, in addition to serving a basic political communicative function, also provided employment and publishing opportunities to numerous socialist authors.[16]

Among the possible positions with the labor movement press, perhaps the most desirable was to be on the staff of one of the specialty journals, such as *Die neue Welt,* the party's cultural and entertainment weekly (founded in 1876); *Die neue Zeit,* the party's main theoretical organ; the *Sozialistische Monatshefte,* the voice of reformism; or *Der Zeitgeist* (founded in 1908), the ambitious and substantial educational monthly of the Metalworkers' Union. Nearly all of the best-known socialist authors contributed to or at one time worked on *Die neue Welt,* a preferred position because it facilitated the publication of their own belles lettres. These included Robert Schweichel, Hermann Thurow, Ernst Preczang, Manfred Wittich, Emil Rosenow, Franz Diederich, Ludwig Lessen (editor, 1900–1919), and many others.[17] *Die neue Zeit* and the *Sozialistische Monatshefte* required reviews and critical essays and seldom published the belletristic writings of socialist authors. Humor magazines, of which there were a number in the labor movement, also offered regular positions for a few socialist writers. In the early 1870s Max Kegel edited the first of these magazines, *Der Nussknacker* (*The Nutcracker*). Then for a few years he edited another journal of the same genre, *Hiddigeigei* (Dresden, 1879–81), and between 1882 and 1888 took over the *Süddeutscher Postillon,* a humor magazine owned at that time by Louis Viereck. From 1888 until his death in 1902 Kegel coedited *Der wahre Jacob,* a kind of official satirical journal of the party.[18]

However, most socialist authors who held positions with the

movement's press worked for one of the party's many local newspapers. These were steady positions, though not the most attractive for writers who valued artistic as well as political topics. Nonetheless, socialist writers often had limited choices, and so one finds that Max Kegel edited the Chemnitz *Freie Presse* (1873–78), Manfred Wittich the Leipzig paper, *Der Wähler* (1890–94), and Franz Diederich the Dortmund *Arbeiterzeitung* (1891–96). When socialist authors joined the staff of a party newspaper, they frequently found it more congenial to take special responsibility for literature and the arts as feuilleton editors. Such positions were held, for example, by Franz Diederich on the *Sächsische Arbeiterzeitung* and Ludwig Lessen for a short time on *Vorwärts* (1904–5). Even Emil Rosenow, the most successful socialist dramatist, earned his living as a journalist, first as an editor of the Social Democratic *Chemnitzer Beobachter* (1892–99) and then for about a half year as chief editor of the *Rheinisch-Westfälische Arbeiterzeitung* in Dortmund.[19]

Only a few socialist writers pursued occupations independent of the labor movement. One of the most prolific writers of agitational drama, Friedrich Bosse (1848–1919), was a master painter in Leipzig, although he may also have made much of his living through his journalistic and functionary roles in local labor movement organizations. Another socialist writer, Richard Cramer (1844–1915), known chiefly by his pseudonym, Rudolf Lavant, apparently never joined the Social Democratic party, although he published his poetry in its journals and participated for many years in the Leipzig Workers' Educational Society. But Lavant preferred personal anonymity, in great part because he worked in a business as a bookkeeper and subsequently in managerial and marketing capacities. Social Democratic political leaders knew Lavant well and showed their trust in him by selecting him to edit their movement's first official anthology of poetry.[20]

Some socialist authors were no doubt writers of considerable talent, but on the whole it is generally agreed by literary historians of all persuasions that most of the work had limited aesthetic merit. Among contemporary Social Democrats this negative evaluation rested on the general presupposition that literature with an obvious political or social message could not also be of high artistic quality. Most socialist critics shared this view, even when they also valued the work of socialist authors for its propagandistic value. They commonly assumed that politics and art—good art, that is— were two different realms.

Social Democratic intellectuals and social commentators, with few exceptions, had absorbed their aesthetic principles directly from the German culture of which they were otherwise so deeply critical, and yet they showed little or no uneasiness about this ironic situation. In failing to develop a special set of socialist or Marxist aesthetic principles, they passed up an opportunity to clarify their relationship to all of the arts. Lack of an innovative socialist approach in artistic matters also had consequences for the political endeavors of the whole movement. Socialist labor leaders wanted an art that would serve their movement, but they had absorbed aesthetic ideas that effectively precluded the possibility that the two realms could be joined satisfactorily. On the basis of traditional artistic principles, no theoretical foundation could be found on which to create a labor movement literature that could serve aesthetic as well as political needs.

Numerous Social Democratic commentators had drawn the conclusion that art and politics were two completely independent realms. Paul Ernst already held this view during the early 1890s when his rhetoric appeared to place him on the left wing of Social Democracy.[21] This view was shared by several who wrote literary criticism in *Die neue Zeit* in the 1890s and following—Eduard Bernstein, Heinrich Ströbel, Friedrich Stampfer, and Franz Diederich.[22] There were also cultural spokesmen within Social Democracy who were politically radical, but who believed that aesthetic considerations and artistic works were fundamentally unrelated to material realities such as social class. Rudolf Franz could declare that artistic matters had nothing whatsoever to do with class, that a "proletarian aesthetic is a piece of nonsense."[23] This forthright denial of any connection between social conditions and artistic production and judgments, in addition to being blatantly anti-Marxist, rested on the idealist assumption that artistic values are absolute.

Franz Mehring and some of his collaborators on *Die neue Zeit* took the opposite position. In critical reviews of modern literature, especially after 1908, they omitted substantially all aesthetic criteria and evaluated literature according to standards of political and social relevance.[24] This was part of Mehring's effort to develop a socialist literary criticism based on historical materialism. Although Mehring's approach may have prevailed in *Die neue Zeit,* it seldom appeared in the criticism in the other journals of the socialist labor movement. Even if Mehring had succeeded in persuading his fellow Social Democrats that his critical mode was correct, this tactical victory would not have overcome the common assumption about the dichotomy between politics and art. This notion was also embedded in Mehring's thinking, and the reasons for his position need to be explored briefly.

Despite his immense learning and his intense desire to construct a literary criticism on a Marxist foundation, Mehring could not break away from the assumption that there was something incompatible about modern proletarian politics and literature of merit. To be sure, Mehring's Marxism led him to the general principle that literature is socially determined, essentially by the conflict of classes. In making this direct connection between the social-economic base and literature, he took one decisive step toward developing a theory of Marxist aesthetics, but stopped short of its fuller development. He limited his thinking in a decisive way: He assumed the near-universality of the aesthetic principles inherent in German classicism. This narrowed his aesthetic vision drastically. As one consequence he focused his criticism almost exclusively on matters of content, leaving form out of the discussion as an element that was either unchangeable or peripheral. He assumed that literature, as a reflection of the social-economic base, would of necessity express conflict and manifest strong partisan features. An analysis of the content, therefore, meant much more to him than attention to style. Mehring was still left with a dilemma: Since he accepted the classical German definition of what was artistic, he could not find a way to give an aesthetic endorsement to most contemporary literature by socialist authors. He approved of the content, but artistically socialist literature could not measure up to classic prescriptions. What he could embrace substantively disappointed him artistically. He could have solved this problem had he used his historical materialism to aid in redefining the meaning of *artistic* and *aesthetic*. He wanted contemporary literature to reflect the historical role of the proletariat, but in a traditional aesthetic mold.[25]

Mehring's artistic preference for classical writers did not mean that he failed to point out serious flaws in nonsocialist authors. Indeed, he interpreted what he called Schiller's "aesthetic idealism" as an expression of "political resignation" and related it to the political capitulation of the German bourgeoisie after the middle of the nineteenth century. At the same time Mehring viewed most of Enlightenment literature as an expression of the bourgeois struggle for emancipation, in essence a class struggle, which resembled the contemporary struggle of the German proletariat. In contrast to that earlier *bürgerlich* literature with its sense of struggle and optimism, contemporary literary movements, especially naturalism, were nothing more than modern belletristic manifestations of the spirit of resignation.[26]

In view of Mehring's general principles it is not surprising that he concluded that the arts, literature especially, could not play a role in proletarian emancipation comparable to what they had performed for the bourgeoisie.[27] We can see the dilemma he faced but could not solve. Since he demanded that the content of literature should be appropriate to the development of social classes, it followed that proletarian mores and socialist ideology had to be embodied in modern literature. But his traditional aesthetics compelled him to disapprove of such a direct literary manifestation of ideology. He had no choice but to live with an unsatisfactory polarity: on the one side his commitment to the working class and socialist politics, but on the other his intellectual preoccupation with modern nonsocialist literature, whose style he could endorse while simultaneously rejecting its implied or explicit social and political values.[28]

Only a few Social Democrats rejected the dominant assumption of the incompatibility of artistic merit and socialist political content. Otto Krille, the talented young writer from a working-class background, argued that "tendentious art" (*Tendenzkunst*) had far more aesthetic value than most Social Democrats recognized.[29] Emanuel Wurm, Social Democratic Reichstag deputy, and Hermann Duncker, later to become a leading Communist party intellectual, both applied the same principle to songs, contending that socialist "tendentious songs," scorned by many conductors of workers' singing societies, were as valuable aesthetically as other forms.[30] But the most spirited and informed arguments in defense of "tendentious art" were presented between 1910 and 1912 by the Dutch poet Herman Heijermans (1864–1924), under the pen name Heinz Sperber. He argued that many of the great writers of the past, including Sophocles, Shakespeare, and Goethe, had produced "tendentious art," but that this fact was now overlooked because the ideologies they had espoused were no longer relevant and therefore had lost their power to arouse passions. Sperber's interpretation provoked some sharp rebuttals and a spirited debate that, in itself, highlighted the uniqueness of his views and the extent to which most Social Democrats were wedded to traditional aesthetic assumptions.[31]

The special difficulties involved in attempting to create a unique socialist literature can be illustrated briefly by reference to anthologies of poetry sponsored by the Social Democrats. The first major collection appeared in 1884, published under the auspicies of the party's political leaders. To edit the volume, entitled *Vorwärts,* they chose Rudolf Lavant. In the preface to *Vorwärts* Lavant described it as a "collection of the best worker poetry" available, consisting of "poems of battle" which were part of the "great world-historical struggle of the disinherited against the propertied, of the oppressed against the oppressor, of the outlawed against the powerful, of those who long for knowledge against those who monopolize learning. . . ."[32] Except for the fact that hardly any of the "worker poetry" he included had been written by workers, and only a portion of it by socialists, his claim still had some merit. He had brought together in the anthology much of the poetry of German radicalism, drawn from the diverse currents of left liberalism, free thought, antimilitarism, the spirit of 1848, and the early socialist movement. It included selections from well-known poets of political democracy and of unorthodox cultural views—Ferdinand Freiligrath, Georg Herwegh, Heinrich Heine, Georg Weerth, and Hoffmann von Fallersleben, for example. There were many others as well whose names are seldom remembered today—Ludwig Pfau, a Forty-Eighter and a volunteer in the patriotic German uprising against the Danes in Schleswig-Holstein; Friedrich von Sallet, an insubordinate professional officer whose fame as an atheist came from the enormous popularity of his book *Laienevangelium* (1842); and Adolf Glassbrenner, also a Forty-Eighter and one of the most humorous and biting satirists of his time. The anthology thus merged the socialist labor movement with German radicalism generally. It gave precedence to political propagandistic purposes over aesthetic considerations, and it defined a broad spectrum of enemies, while bringing together all friends of the labor movement under the rubric "worker poetry." One is impressed, reading in *Vorwärts,* with how intensely the maturing Social Democratic labor movement drew on almost everyone who had been at one time or another in conflict with the established order.

Several years later, in 1893, the Social Democratic movement supported still another publication of what they called "worker poetry," a five-volume set published by the Dietz house in Stuttgart. Seven well-known socialist authors were included: Wilhelm Hasenclever; Karl Frohme; Rudolf Lavant; Max Kegel; Adolf Lepp (1847–1906), a former Lassallean who continued to write partisan poetry after ceasing active political work; Jakob Audorf,

Lassallean author of the lyrics of the "Workers' Marseillaise"; and Andreas Scheu, the Austrian socialist whose verses were also popular in the German labor movement.[33] Regardless of how important these seven authors were in the Social Democratic movement, none qualified in artistic terms for much attention from those socialists who fashioned the educational and cultural programs of the labor movement. Instead, when educational organizations sponsored special literary evenings, it was not the works of the Hasenclevers, Frohmes, and Audorfs that were presented, but the literature of Goethe, Schiller, Kleist, Ludwig Anzengruber, Gottfried Keller, Detlev von Liliencron, Arthur Schnitzler, Alfred Tennyson, and Fritz Reuter, to name some of the most prominent. Similarly, in the libraries of the labor movement librarians generally urged their clientele to read prose and poetry by the latter, and rarely works by socialist belletristic writers.[34]

To put the matter as succinctly as possible, in the social-cultural milieu of the socialist labor movement, poets like Hasenclever were to be used but not studied; poets like Goethe were to be studied but seldom could be used. Only a few, such as Freiligrath and Herwegh, qualified to be both used and studied. They came from an earlier era, one that preceded, for the most part, the actual founding of the socialist labor movement. With few exceptions, the socialist movement before the First World War did not produce writers whose poems simultaneously satisfied both the political and the aesthetic expectations of Social Democratic cultural commentators. This created a constant problem: If the editor of an anthology of poetry gave precedence to literary considerations, the political effectiveness suffered, and the reverse would also be true.

This dilemma manifested itself with special force early in the 1890s when the Executive Committee of the Social Democratic party authorized Karl Henckell, already a well-known German literary figure and at that time close to the socialist movement, to revise *Vorwärts,* the collection compiled initially by Lavant. Henckell's collection, entitled *Buch der Freiheit* (*Book of Freedom*), differed so radically from Lavant's *Vorwärts* that it must be considered an entirely new publication. Henckell believed, as he stated in the preface, that artistic standards should not be compromised and he therefore reduced substantially the number of poems that were explicitly political.[35] He stressed classical authors at the expense of radical writers like Weerth and Pfau. Moreover, as a friend of the German naturalists he included a very generous sampling of their poetry. Parts of the table of contents read like a catalog of German naturalist writers, including Otto Erich Hartleben, Arno Holz, Wilhelm Arent, Heinrich Hart, Julius Hart, Detlev von Liliencron, and Otto Julius Bierbaum. With an obvious lack of modesty, Henckell also included thirty-five of his own poems, by far the largest number by any single author. He even included Michael Georg Conrad, who just two years previously had published a scathing attack on the cultural views of Social Democracy.[36]

Whatever high artistic principles *Buch der Freiheit* may have embodied—even that might be questioned—it could not serve the uses the Executive Committee had in mind when they chose Henckell as editor. In effect, he had included in an official anthology poets who could be studied but not used. He had believed erroneously that his own artistic taste would serve as an adequate guide for the selection of poems in an anthology for the socialist labor movement. Despite its assumed superior aesthetic standards, *Buch der Freiheit* could not be as valuable to the political functions of the movement as were the two earlier collections.[37]

The difficulties apparent in trying to create a body of socialist poetry were paralleled in the theatrical realm. Party intellectuals gave much more encouragement to the Freie Volksbühne (People's Free Theater) movement, which sponsored performances by classical as well as some modern dramatists for labor movement members, than to the dramatic efforts of socialist dramatists and amateur workers' theatrical clubs. The Freie Volksbühne movement must be viewed as an archetypical example of those socialist-dominated organizations that were designed to transmit to workers what Social Democratic leaders considered to be the best of established European and German culture. The most successful Freie Volksbühne was in Berlin, but similar organizations were founded in other cities. Some foundered from the beginning, as in Leipzig, Frankfurt, and Cologne, while others were reasonably successful for a few years, as in Bielefeld, Breslau, Hanover-Linden, Kiel, and Hamburg.[38] The organizations operated in several ways, but normally they contracted for performances with professional theaters and sold tickets to labor movement associations at sharply reduced prices. In Berlin, despite severe internal conflicts that led to a major split and the founding of the Neue Freie Volksbühne (The New People's Free Theater) late in 1892, the original organization had considerable success and could even afford to build its own theater in the years immediately prior to the First World War.[39]

The Freie Volksbühne in Berlin rarely performed plays by socialist authors because their writing did not appear to meet the high artistic standards of the professional theater. Friedrich Stampfer, who sat on the committee that selected the plays for performance, claimed in later years that at the beginning he diligently read every script submitted, hoping to make a great discovery, but soon became discouraged and then decided easily for classical authors and for a few well-known modernists, such as Ibsen, Strindberg, and Hauptmann.[40] The two socialist exceptions to this rule were Emil Rosenow and Ernst Preczang (1870–1949). Rosenow's *Kater Lampe,* which was not, however, a play with special socialist content, was produced in 1906. The Freie Volksbühne presented two pieces by Preczang, *Sein Jubiläum* in 1897, and *The House in the Back* (*Im Hinterhause*), the latter in 1903 in the Metropole Theater in Berlin.[41]

In addition to writing agitational drama while working simultaneously as a labor movement journalist, Preczang also aspired to write for the professional stage in Germany. He never realized that ambition. Although he worked off and on as a free-lance writer, he still had to rely almost exclusively on the labor movement press for his livelihood. His output included lyric verses and short stories, as well as a substantial number of plays.[42] Despite his close association with the socialist labor movement, he did not automatically portray workers as courageous heroes of the class struggle. A spirit of pessimism and resignation, reminiscent of the naturalists, pervades *The House in the Back.*[43] One of the leading characters, Wilhelm Gensicke, a disabled factory worker in his fifties and depressed by his physical incapacities, contemplates and then actually commits suicide. The young labor functionary Hermann Petzold, though presumably a man with ideals and socialist convictions, leaves the scene of the economic and political struggles in a spirit of personal adventure. He tells Klara, the young woman in love with him—she is Gensicke's daughter—that he is happy to leave because, for a while, that will give him personal freedom. He is enthralled by the prospect of little or no responsibility and is eager to experience a life that is unpredictable. He speaks in great rhetorical flourishes about his wandering future: "Where will I be tomorrow? Where the day after tomorrow? Where in a month? It is wonderful not to know that. To think: something could pop up out of nowhere—suddenly, very suddenly. Something completely new."[44] The play has a certain psychological power and persuasiveness, perhaps because it offers no easy solutions to complex human problems, although it does depict the personal defeats of the workers and their families as a consequence of the alienating conditions under which they must work and live. In contrast to the overwhelming majority of political plays by socialist authors, *The House in the Back* met the dramatic standards that directors of the Freie Volksbühne had established for their productions.

The Freie Volksbühne societies were certainly a part of the labor movement milieu, and their policies and expectations highlight some of the dilemmas inherent in Social Democratic cultural programs. They went further than the other organizations in the world of the labor movement in divorcing art from politics. It is not that they played down their affiliation to the socialist labor movement, but that the substance of their main activity—sponsoring drama productions—seldom had any direct symbolic link to the movement. Franz Mehring, for many years a leading light of the Freie Volksbühne in Berlin, prepared socialist commentaries on forthcoming plays which were distributed to subscribers.[45] Except for these and for the fact that audiences were entirely from the labor movement—the performances were scheduled almost exclusively for Sunday afternoons, when workers normally would be free to attend—such events were indistinguishable from the regular productions of the professional stage. They were a bridge between German culture and the social-cultural milieu of the labor movement, but a bridge on which the traffic moved only in one direction. For the story of the drama that was written for and performed by amateurs within the milieu of the labor movement one needs to look elsewhere to plays that appeared on the programs of special events and which dealt with modern social and political themes from a Social Democratic point of view.

Regardless of the negative aesthetic criticism of the writings of most socialist authors, this body of literature, especially drama, served an important function within the social-cultural milieu of the labor movement.[46] To be sure, the effectiveness of plays and skits in disseminating the values of the movement cannot be measured, but it can be described by looking more closely at several of the dramatic pieces that we know were performed, usually at one or more of the festivals.

The exact size of the repertory of Social Democratic drama is difficult to establish with certainty because some plays were performed but never published, while others may have been lost entirely. One estimate is that during the decade of the 1890s alone there were some thirty Social Democratic plays in circulation. Many more appeared after 1900. Three Social Democratic publishing houses issued special series of socialist theatrical pieces: In Berlin the party's Vorwärts press published seventeen titles between 1894 and 1917; Adolf Hoffmann's house, also in Berlin, issued twenty-one between 1893 and 1914; and in Leipzig the Richard Lipinski Press brought out fifty-one between 1901 and 1914.[47] These numbers are inflated to some degree because certain titles were reissued, but at the same time other presses affiliated with the labor movement also published theatrical pieces not counted here. The bibliography of a recent study lists some eighty-four titles for the period 1890 to 1914, which does not count those that appeared earlier, though it does include a few that may have had only tenuous links to the socialist movement.[48] It is reasonable to estimate that the total repertory between the 1860s and 1914 reached one hundred titles, and certainly no less than eighty. In either case it represented a substantial body of social-political drama and, within the bounds of that genre, offered considerable choice to festival planners and amateur performers.

This repertory of Social Democratic theatrical pieces reflected the full spectrum of the political and social ideas current in the labor movement as a whole, from the moderate right to the radical left, and constituted a major expression of the spirit of the alternative culture. In a detailed analysis of some fifty socialist plays that appeared after 1890, and with reference to many more, Dietmar Trempenau divides the corpus into "radical-combative" drama on the one side and "reconciliatory-integrationist" on the other. He refines this scheme further by introducing additional differentiations under the two major headings.[49] The result is an instructive thematic classification based, to be sure, on Trempenau's own interpretation of where each play fits ideologically. What is especially significant is that Trempenau's work documents the degree to which Social Democratic theater embodied nearly every nuance of ideology and outlook in the labor movement. He also suggests that this kind of early Social Democratic didactic political theater, which continued well into the 1920s, may be related to the more artistically sophisticated *Lehrstück-Versuche* of Bertolt Brecht. Although Trempenau does not pursue this possibility, a few years earlier Peter von Rüden hinted strongly that a link existed between Boleslav Strzelewicz's theatrical troupe and the dramatic ideas of Erwin Piscator and Brecht.[50] If future research ever demonstrates this suggested link, it will greatly enhance the historical significance of a genre of drama that hitherto has received essentially no critical attention from literary specialists. This is not the place to attempt such a demonstration, but rather to explore several of the plays for their content and place in the social-cultural milieu of the socialist labor movement.

The political prestige and ideological significance of Ferdinand Lassalle lived on in several short socialist plays. One of these, performed at a Lassalle Festival in Ohligs in 1896, is especially striking because it combined Lassallean ideas, Greek symbols, and popular visual techniques. This allegorical love story, *Demos and Libertas or The Unmasked Deceiver* (*Demos und Libertas oder: Der entlarvte Betrüger*), published in 1876 by an anonymous author, gave a summary and paraphrase of the ideas found in Lassalle's popular pamphlet *Science and the Workers* (*Die Wissenschaft und die Arbeiter*). The four characters—Demos, Libertas, Scientia, and Parisitus—do not portray individual personalities but types, in this case clothed in the garb of Greek antiquity. Demos, the embodiment of a democratically minded worker, wins the love of Libertas (wearing the symbolic Phrygian cap of the French Revolution), the daughter of Scientia, against the pretensions of Parasitus, a scoundrel representing bourgeois capitalism. At first floundering and confused about the cause of his misery, Demos, coming under the influence of Scientia, gradually achieves clarity and wins Libertas because Scientia herself favors the union of freedom with workers, not with the bourgeoisie. The obvious message of the allegory (as in Lassalle's pamphlet) is that if a union of the working class and freedom is to become a reality, if workers are to be emancipated, this can only be accomplished in close collaboration with science.[51]

To enhance their visual impact, festival plays were frequently produced with accompanying tableaux vivants. For Scientia's closing monologue in *Demos und Libertas,* the anonymous author called for a tableau vivant consisting of five groups of performers to represent salient aspects of a future communist society. In the first group, workers—both male and female—would be busy at machines to symbolize "communist labor." In the second, men and women would listen intently to a speaker while two people would hold ballot boxes to signify the legislative and legal importance of popular assemblies. A third group was to consist of children receiving instruction from a person holding a crucifix in one hand and in the other an open book in which the audience could read the words "Science—not faith." This group signified the principle according to which youth would be instructed in the future society. A fourth group (depicting marriage and the family in the future) was to show a young mother, held lovingly by her husband, rocking a child on her lap, while nearby a young man would seek to win the affection of a bashful girl. The final group consisted of performers representing Frenchmen, Englishmen, Germans, Italians, Slavs, and others, all standing over the shattered arms of war, reaching out to each other to symbolize the "brotherhood of nations in the communist society." Before the curtain was to fall, the final four groups would gradually encircle the first group of workers, creating the image of a complete and "harmonious unity." A huge red flag would wave gently over the stage as the five scenes of the tableau vivant would pass before the audience.[52]

Socialist authors and performers frequently employed such elaborate tableaux vivants to enliven their presentations. When the local Social Democratic organization for the first Berlin electoral district sponsored a Memorial Service (*Gedächtnisfeier*) on October 1, 1892, to commemorate the second anniversary of the expiration of the antisocialist law, the estimated three thousand celebrants in the Feen-Palast watched and listened as Gajus Mucius Scävola declaimed his twelve-part "epic-dramatic poem," *Twelve Years of Banishment or the Exile's Return Home* (*12 Jahre der Verbannung oder Des Ausgewiesenen Heimkehr*) while members of the Society for the Popular Arts (Verein für volkstümliche Kunst), under the direction of their club chairman Fritz Hansen, presented tableaux vivants to illustrate each scene. The epic tells the story of an expelled Social Democrat, how he endured persecution and deprivations, and culminates with his triumphant and jubilant return. Little is known about the author's identity—the pseudonym Scävola was taken presumably to symbolize fearless political opposition—except that he was born in 1859 into a middle-class family in Berlin, where he attended a gymnasium, studied architecture, but soon turned to writing. Social Democratic leaders showed their confidence in him by issuing many of his subsequent pieces through the party's official publishing house, Vorwärts.[53] *Twelve Years of Banishment* had several more performances, one at a May Day Festival in Rostock in 1896 and another at a Lassalle Festival in Solingen in 1897. It may have been presented even more often because it so pointedly reinforced popular labor movement images of the "heroic era" and could be staged with either simple or intricate tableaux vivants, depending on local talent and resourcefulness.

The Goddess of Freedom was a common subject of tableaux vivants.[54] At a May Day festival in Pöhlau (1898), a prologue was accompanied by a tableau entitled "Homage to Freedom." It showed laborers paying allegiance to the goddess, who was sitting on a throne with Marx and Lassalle on either side of her. To help celebrate their second anniversary, the members of the Freie Volksbühne in Berlin planned a celebration at the Muggelsee and set up a tableau vivant on a small galley close to the lake shore. The tableau gave an historical presentation of forms of slavery, while the Goddess of Freedom took a dominant place in the middle of the boat. Tyranny, in the costume of Mephistopheles, lay at her feet, held down by the first of a modern industrial wage earner. Alongside the galley swam a "gigantic dolphin" on which Greek men and women stood with harps and goblets. In their midst was Arion, the first dithyrambic poet, singing the praises of the "new freedom." All tableaux vivants were structured to highlight antinomies, for example, freedom versus tyranny and capital versus labor. This dualistic structure and the usual depiction of freedom as a Greek goddess, as well as still other allegorical forms, had been absorbed from older German and European traditions. Here, as with many other aspects of the alternative culture of the labor movement, socialists filled old forms with new content and different meanings.[55]

Amateur theatrical groups in the labor movement varied considerably, but wherever they existed they were called on to take responsibility for presenting political plays and declamations. In Leipzig the drama section of the Workers' Educational Society served the movement with special vigor, in part because of the exceptional abilities of Friedrich Bosse, the author of some fourteen socialist agitational dramas and a leading figure in local Social Democratic educational and entertainment activities. Little is known of Bosse's personal life except that he was born in Hessen (a village in Brunswick), the son of a peasant and wheelwright, and was already a master house painter when he settled permanently in Leipzig in 1874. Under the antisocialist law Leipzig Social Democrats were forced to abandon their former party organization and created the Association for Workers' Continuing Education (Fortbildungsverein für Arbeiter) as a front for a reduced level of political activity. With the expulsion of many leading Social Democrats from Leipzig, Bosse took over as chairman of the organization between 1881 and 1890 and during the latter part of that decade began to write socialist agitational plays, at first under the pseudonym Heinrich Friedrich. His productivity as socialist playwright reached its apex during the 1890s, while he also edited the *Sturm-*

glocken (1894–96) and *Der freie Bund* (1899–1902), both devoted
to popular education among workers.[56] Bosse wrote many of his
pieces as special festival plays (*Festspiele*), a fact that ties them to a
particular time and makes them potentially more interesting as
historical documents than as dramatic writing. Since they frequently treat prominent issues in the labor movement, they illustrate the way Social Democratic politics intersected with and influenced the artistic aspirations of socialist educational leaders.[57]

Bosse employed a number of techniques and embodied contrasting ideological tendencies in his theatrical pieces. To some extent
his plays may be viewed as a reflection of the diverse sentiments
and opinions in the socialist labor movement itself. In his first
festival play, *The Old and the New* (*Die Alten und die Neuen*), a
short piece in verse form, Bosse fashioned a dialogue between
Hans Sachs and Ulrich von Hutten on one side and, on the other,
the chairman of the Association for Workers' Continuing Education in Leipzig, that is, the organization which Bosse himself
chaired. Toward the close of the piece, as Sachs and Hutten are
about to return to heaven, Bosse has Sachs speak confidently
about the future of the association, but the central message is a
humanitarian exhortation: to strive always to make progress; to be
helpful to one another in life; to nurture what is good and beautiful; and always to be prepared to stand up for enlightenment
(*Aufklärung*). In the same spirit Ulrich von Hutten's closing
homily admonishes the members to avoid error—what kind he
does not say—serve the public welfare, and promote scientific
knowledge. "Seek to raise the thinking of humans so that they will
strive for truth and justice, and that they will fight with heightened
earnestness to curb selfishness and hypocrisy."[58] The dominance of
bland Enlightenment humanitarianism in this play may be explained in part by the fact that Bosse wrote it to be performed in
1888, at a time when Leipzig police still imposed heavy censorship
on organizations assumed to be affiliated with Social Democracy.
The same explanation may apply also to *May Day* (*Der erste Mai*),
a play Bosse wrote in 1890 for the first May Day celebrations in
Leipzig in support of the eight-hour day. This would have been
after the Reichstag had declined in February of that year to renew
the antisocialist legislation, but several months before the law was
to expire officially on September 31, 1890. While the play pro-
motes the cause of the eight-hour day, its underlying message
strongly favors social harmony. Reconciliation and peaceful collaboration between workers and owners is achieved in the play

through the mediation of a progressive-minded, socially concerned lawyer and the good will of an enlightened second-generation entrepreneur. The conclusion stresses the partnership between capital and labor, avoids combative sentiments, and has nothing to say about the necessity of class struggle to achieve working-class emancipation.[59]

In sharp contrast to the conciliatory mood in the above pieces, Bosse took a much tougher line only two years later (1892) in the play *In the Struggle* (*Im Kampf*). The play offers a kind of cross section of attitudes and modes of behavior among workers in Germany in the early 1890s. To make his points amply clear, Bosse employed the rather simple technique of giving the characters names that would symbolize good and bad qualities. The good workers are called "Rock" ("Fels") and "Fight" ("Kämpf"), while those with undesirable features bear equally revealing names, such as "Impetuous" ("Rasch") for an unsteady type and "Clever" ("Kluge") for the opportunist. The factory owner is called "Coldhead" ("Kalthaupt"), his director is "Intriguer" ("Schleicher"), but the liberal-minded lawyer is "Good Hans" ("Guthans"). A certain tension builds up in the course of the play, in great part because Bosse does not simply pit good workers against bad owners, but shows conflicting attitudes and hostilities among workers as well as among people on the side of capital. Certainly, *In the Struggle* captures a number of sentiments and conflicts that were evident within the socialist labor movement at the time. Bosse's achievement, it should be stressed, is most apparent in his ability to condense leading issues of the day and to encourage viewers to favor the official positions of the Social Democratic party.[60]

Bosse's plays, whether they leaned to the moderate or radical sides, could be counted on to arouse some kind of response. They also aroused the suspicions of the police. On the occasion of the Twenty-fifth Founders Day Festival of the Leipzig Workers' Educational Society in 1904 the theater division intended to perform Bosse's *The People Awake!* (*Das Volk erwacht!*), a play that employed music and visual aids to portray the rising consciousness of the lower classes. The police in Leipzig moved in, however, and prohibited the theatrical part of the program, implying that in their eyes such agitational drama could be dangerously effective.[61] On other occasions police seem to have raised no objections against the performance of plays that were equally radical. Indeed, Bosse's *In the Struggle,* in itself a more combative play, had been performed in Leipzig in 1892, apparently without police interference. On the other hand, some plays may never have been presented because of their revolutionary spirit. Trempenau believes, for example, that the one-act drama *Miners* (*Bergarbeiter*) by Lu Märten had only one performance because it embodied such a radical revolutionary point of view.[62]

The forthright nature of these agitational plays suggests that at a minimum they reinforced ideas and sentiments already held by participants in the socialist labor movement. Most of the pieces could be presented in less than an hour, so that they did not overtax the attention span of the audiences. To be at all successful, plays for purposes of social and political education had to have exciting plots in addition to partisan themes and a well-paced dialogue. Authors naturally hoped that their pieces would be suitable for repeated performances. There were limits, however, as to how often an agitational play could be presented without running the danger of boring festival audiences. In contrast to the political songs, which because of their melodies could be and were expected to be sung again and again, plays with blatant propagandistic purposes, if repeated several times to the same constituency, were unlikely to sustain the interest of even the most devoted members. Some of the plays must have fallen flat because they consisted almost entirely of expository dialogues, even monologues, with little or no action.

The plays that appear to have been performed most often were humorous skits or farces. These too could, and often did, carry a strong partisan theme, but one can see that in farces humor served as the counterpart of melodies in songs. Humor embellished the propagandistic text. Farces and comedies were also short and frequently ridiculed political authorities, the police, and other enemies of Social Democracy. One of the more successful farces, *The Newspaper Trial or The Daughter of the State Attorney* (*Press-Prozesse oder die Tochter des Staatsanwaltes*) had been written by Max Kegel in 1876. It was performed three times in the same year and continued to enjoy popularity among amateur theater groups; one could see it, for example, at the May Day Festival in Solingen in 1893 (see Appendix B, section I). In it Kegel depicted, with apt humor and satire, the persecutions, arrest, and imprisonment of a dissident newspaper editor.[63] Unfortunately, the sources do not tell us enough about the nature of most of the humor. Printed programs often indicate that a "humorous presentation" would be given, but exact titles are seldom listed so that we cannot describe the humor itself. It is clear, nonetheless, that humor in many forms constituted an important part of most programs and contributed to the spirit of belonging within the social-cultural milieu.

The striking fact is that socialists and trade unionists made intensive use of various forms of literature, poetry, and drama especially, to broadcast their criticism of contemporary German society and to promote their views of an alternative. Although Social Democratic intellectuals showed little or no interest in the artistic potential in political poetry and drama, the corpus of this literature expanded substantially in the Wilhelmian era and served the labor movement in diverse ways at nearly every meeting and public event. But the artistic potential itself remains a matter of conjecture. Even if Social Democratic views on matters of aesthetics had not been so traditional, it would still be impossible to assert that the authors of agitational drama would have been stimulated or able to improve the artistic quality of their work. There were other obstacles. For example, restrictions on public performances in Imperial Germany meant that for the most part declamatory and theatrical presentations reached people who were already within the labor movement. Amateur socialist theatrical troupes were not free to perform openly in the streets, as were agitprop groups during the Weimar years. The latter showed considerable inventiveness at times, especially in combining simple musical accompaniment with their short skits and plays. The amateurs before the First World War lived in a world of tight restraints that did more to discourage than to stimulate such inventiveness. They also lived within a social-cultural milieu that in reality dissuaded them from thinking of themselves as artists and accepted them chiefly as useful adjuncts to serve the primary political and economic goals of Social Democracy.

7

Teaching and Learning

It has been evident in the preceding chapters that party members and trade unionists recognized that considerable care had to be taken in stating the principles that would guide the activities of various clubs and in selecting material for festivals and other public occasions. The emancipatory work of the labor movement could be helped or hindered, depending on how well each affiliated group or activity fit into the larger ideological and organizational framework. In no endeavor, however, was the need for ideological clarity and carefully defined goals and procedures greater than in the programs established to promote *Bildung,* that is, education and cultivation among organized workers. Use of the term *Bildung* itself, rather than the more prosaic *Erziehung,* implied at least an indirect link to the hallowed Humboldtian tradition that viewed learning and cultivation as means for the development of the complete individual. In contrast to most recreational and service associations, in which substantive issues of political principle were often peripheral to the main functions of the organizations, educational programs were established on the assumption that their central goal was to disseminate the principles of the Social Democratic party and the free trade unions. Through the educational programs socialists and unionists could define the central core of a special labor movement social-cultural milieu. The educational programs may in fact be one of the most reliable indicators we have of what leaders believed the intellectual foundation of their movement should be. Chance and accident were not to play a role in the selection of instructional subject matter. This was serious study, not entertainment.

What has been argued earlier in this book, that the social-cultural milieu of the labor movement offered an alternative model of society, applies with special force to the educational and cultural programs. Within this area, commonly referred to as *Arbeiterbildung* (workers' education and cultivation), one can detect both countercultural and integrative tendencies. That is, there were different conceptions of what should constitute *Arbeiterbildung*, to whom it should be directed, and what it should seek to achieve. In the years between 1890 and 1914 the labor movement established an increasingly large and flourishing system of educational programs and libraries. This upsurge belonged to a tradition that had imbued Social Democracy with a special pedagogical character. The German socialist labor movement began within the framework of workers' educational societies that had been founded by liberals as early as the 1840s and were especially significant during the 1860s. The story of how these workers' educational societies were detached from their liberal origins and became the foundation for the socialist labor movement has been part of every history of organized labor in Germany.

In the 1860s liberal leaders viewed these societies as ways to compensate for inadequate primary education and to help raise workers to respected positions in life. The societies were to contribute to the general progress of modern humanity.[1] Two pedagogical forms were used: systematic courses of instruction, in which pupils enrolled much as in any school, and public lectures. In the systematic courses the common subjects were reading, arithmetic, penmanship, physical education, singing, drawing, and German grammar; a substantial number of societies also offered more advanced courses in drafting, geometry, algebra, English, French, bookkeeping, stenography, and history. Public lectures, on the other hand, often went beyond the elementary and practical subjects and could be used to introduce audiences to recent developments in various fields of learning. Liberal ideological principles could be infused easily into public lectures on social and political topics. The lecture system enjoyed considerable popularity. Within one year alone, 1864, over 1,000 lectures were sponsored by thirty-three workers' educational societies in Prussia (436 in natural science; 120 in applied science; 118 on the arts and literature; 329 on politics, economics, and social science; and 80 on other themes).[2]

With the reorientation of many of the workers' educational societies and with the hostility of the young socialist movement to the German Empire as fashioned in 1870–71, the pedagogical tasks of the organizations became far less important than their political functions. While a number of the original liberal societies continued to exist in their old form, they were overshadowed by the public prominence of the two socialist political parties. Those original societies that continued to exist outside of the socialist labor movement became more and more identified with lower-middle-class elements and less with workers.[3] They escaped dissolution at the time of the antisocialist legislation in 1878 when nearly all organizations, educational as well as others associated with Social Democracy, were abolished.

In the overall history of the labor movement's educational role, the seventies and eighties thus mark a low point between the original intensity of the sixties and the rapid and extensive growth of socialist-oriented educational societies at the turn of the century. During the 1890s educational programs were reestablished or expanded in many cities, but not in all. The entertainment and recreational clubs, discussed in earlier chapters, emerged earlier and with much greater strength. The nineties were founding years for those clubs, while the decade preceding the First World War witnessed the most rapid expansion of the educational programs.

Until the end of the nineteenth century Wilhelm Liebknecht played the most important role in defining Social Democratic attitudes on education and cultivation. Although he enjoyed a reputation for being a Marxist, he had failed, even more than Franz Mehring, to work out a consistent theory of education on those premises. In reality Liebknecht put together a mixture of ideas from liberalism, Humboldtian neohumanism, and quasi-Marxism into his special brand of Social Democratic educational ideology.[4] This does not mean that he took over existing systems without modification or that he did not adapt them with reasonable effectiveness to the needs of the socialist labor movement. His version of educational and cultural theory could not have been accepted by any other movement in Germany, and, if it did not fulfill what subsequent historians have seen as Marxist prescriptions concerning educational principles, he nonetheless provided a workable definition of what socialist educational and cultural policy ought to be. In 1872 he had expounded his views in a popular speech and pamphlet, *Wissen ist Macht—Macht ist Wissen* (*Knowledge Is Power—Power Is Knowledge*), and, although his thought shifted somewhat, the basic lines had been developed there. In that speech he launched a severe attack on the existing system, stressing that the state exploited *Bildung* to support the power of the ruling class, that superficiality characterized current German *Kultur,* and that the German school system, despite its comparatively high international standing, was nonetheless one of three major institutions designed to make people stupid (the other two were the army and the popular press).[5] All of this implied a need for total change: "As long as the present state and society continue to exist, there is no *Kultur,* no *Bildung,* no popular education." Since all other groups in society had failed, he drew the conclusion that *"Social Democracy is in the most eminent meaning of the word the party of Bildung."* And then, seemingly reversing the Humboldtian prescription, he declared that the correct way was not "Through *Bildung* to Freedom," but *"Through Freedom to Bildung,"* that is, only in a free state could genuine *Bildung* be achieved.[6]

Nineteen years later, in 1891, on the occasion of the founding of the Berlin Workers' Educational School, Liebknecht applied his general notions to the specific issue of the new institution. Now the emphasis on *Bildung* for political purposes came out more clearly. Addressing some four thousand people in the Brauerei Friedrichshain, Liebknecht set forth the radical goals of the school with his usual flair for revolutionary rhetoric. The overriding goal of the school, he declared, was to prepare workers to carry on the struggle for emancipation, not to make them learned specialists filled with superfluous information. For a model he drew heavily on the earlier Workers' Educational Society in Leipzig, in which he had been an active member and which he described as having been a "kind of agitational school." The new Workers' Educational School in Berlin would make up for what workers had missed in the public elementary school and, in addition, would sponsor scholarly lectures and theatrical performances. In the course of emancipating themselves, Liebknecht contended, workers would also emancipate the arts. Although Liebknecht did not try to spell out an ideal curriculum, he emphasized the need for practical subjects such as stenography (so that workers could keep accurate records of their meetings) and German language (to improve their speaking and writing). No matter what the subject matter might be, Liebknecht stressed, the courses had to be fashioned so that a Social Democratic victory in the economic realm would be accompanied by vast gains for workers in the intellectual sphere. Workers, he insisted, made the best agitators for the socialist cause because they possessed something that even the most intelligent and committed middle-class socialists lacked—proletarian education. Closing with a flourish, Liebknecht declared that "we only want to open the Temple of Knowledge to workers so that they will be capable of fighting for their emancipation." The school would not play down or try to ameliorate class differences, and if that should ever happen, Liebknecht announced that he would disavow the whole endeavor.[7]

Liebknecht's speech reflected much of the tone that initially surrounded the Workers' Educational School in Berlin, and in reality it is true that the school, and others like it founded in the early 1890s, did offer an alternative program of instruction for members of the labor movement. The school went from crisis to crisis for several years until toward the end of the century a reorganization laid the basis for steady growth.[8] Viewed from the perspective of later historians with radical inclinations, the Berlin school may appear to have been a failure because it did not offer a systematic and consistent Marxist program of study. Seen, however, within the context of a Social Democratic movement that had just emerged from the restrictions of the antisocialist legislation and that continued to face renewed threats of state oppression, the Berlin school embodied features that could contribute significantly to the work of emancipation. This interpretation assumes, to be sure, that emancipation is a process, and that, as such, activities that at one time were fitting and even effective may appear in a later period to be functionally inadequate or ideologically misguided.

Many of the ambiguities common to the social-cultural milieu of the labor movement were also evident in the curriculum of the Berlin school. While it emphasized social science, economics, history, speaking practice, and natural science—literature received much less attention—these were taught from varying ideological perspectives. The teaching staff came generally from the large body of party journalists, writers, and intellectuals who lived in Berlin, whether radicals, centrists, or reformists. During 1898–99, the staff included Conrad Schmidt, Richard Calwer, Bruno Borchart, Paul Kampffmeyer, Max Schippel, as well as Emil Roth, a sympathetic Berlin attorney, and Rudolf Steiner, who later became renowned not as a socialist, but as the founder of Anthroposophy.[9] For a while Steiner taught a substantial percentage of the school's courses and at that time may have influenced considerably the direction of the school. His deep interest in religion and literature shows up clearly in the curriculum for 1901–02 (see Table 2). After Steiner left the teaching staff, the courses on religion were dropped. The teaching staff between 1907 and 1910 once again included several of the well-known party members from both the reformist and radical wings: Max Maurenbrecher, the articulate revisionist, taught history, also with a certain emphasis on religious

Table 2
Berlin Workers' Educational School
Courses of Instruction for 1901–2*

Discipline	Course Content	Teacher	Evening
Second Quarter 1901			
History (103)	Origin and history of various religions	Dr. Rud. Steiner writer	Monday
Law (36)	German imperial and Prussian state constitutions	Victor Fränkl attorney	Tuesday
National Economy (25)	Cooperatives	Miss F. Imle	Thursday
Speaking Practice (52)	Reports and discussion on themes of society, trade unions, and intellectual life	Dr. Rudolf Steiner writer	Friday
Fourth Quarter 1901			
History (51)	Literature among primitives and in antiquity	Dr. R. Steiner writer	Monday
Natural Science (23)	Energy theory	Dr. R. Hasse	Tuesday
National Economy (62)	Policy matters on tariffs, commerce, and exchange	Georg Bernhard, writer	Thursday
Speaking Practice (84)	Practice in speaking and in writing papers	Dr. Rudolf Steiner, writer	Friday
First Quarter 1902			
History (76)	History of literature in Christian Middle Ages	Dr. Rud. Steiner writer	Thursday
National Economy (78)	Selected chapters from banking and the stock exchange	Georg Bernard, writer	Thursday
Speaking Practice (55)	Practice in speaking and in writing papers	Dr. Rud. Steiner writer	Friday

*The numbers in parentheses under "Discipline" indicate the average attendence at lectures.

*Source:*Arbeiter–Bildungsschule Berlin, *Jahres-Bericht über die Thätigkeit vom 1. April 1901 bis 31. März 1902* (Berlin, 1902), pp. 2–3.

themes; Ernst Kreowski, literary critic for socialist periodicals, lectured on the history of literature; Julian Borchardt and Max Grunwald concentrated on economics; S. Rosenfeld and Simon Katzenstein both gave courses on various aspects of law; Heinrich Schulz, the prominent Bremen radical, and Alexander Conrady specialized in history; and Mrs. Regina Ruben treated the history of literature.[10]

The school's constituency came largely from the ranks of organized labor. Moreover, it should be emphasized that as time passed an increasing number of enrollees belonged to both the party and a trade union, and a very small percentage belonged only to the party. The trade unions clearly provided the most significant organizational base for the student body of the Berlin school. The more striking feature is, however, that by 1909–10 nearly nine out of every ten students held membership in a trade union or the party and nearly two out of three belonged to both (see Appendix C, Table 2). As the table on age distribution indicates, the overwhelming majority—consistently over two-thirds— were in their twenties (see Appendix C, Table 1). A final striking feature is the curious fact that despite the increasing number of women in the courses, their portion of the total enrollment reached its peak at 12 percent in 1901–2 and then dropped drastically in subsequent years (see Appendix C, Table 3). The explanation lies in part in the growth of socialist women's organizations, but also in the fact that the school failed to provide courses designed to appeal to the particular needs of women.

A few years after the turn of the century Social Democrats showed a new and intensified commitment to creating programs for education and cultivation. In particular, a number of those on the radical wing of the party, notably Otto Rühle, Heinrich Schulz, and Clara Zetkin, wanted to upgrade and intensify educational endeavors among socialists and workers. This concern generated more discussion about *Arbeiterbildung,* on what premises it rested, how it should be shaped, and what it ought to achieve. Although highly refined positions were elaborated on these issues, two main orientations stood out. The most important position paralleled the strident propositions that had been presented by Liebknecht, but often went much farther than he did in stressing the fundamental political and ideological nature of workers' education. *Arbeiterbildung* was to serve workers' emancipation, to be sure, and that could only be achieved, according to this view, by instilling workers with the principles and theories of the socialist movement—often explicitly identified as Marxism—so that all the opinions of organized workers would fit consistently into a socialist framework. In sharp contrast, the other position held that general education and a more pluralist approach to curriculum design would better serve the emancipatory goal because it would encourage the worker-students to think critically for themselves. These contrasting orientations appeared repeatedly in the discussions that took place as new programs were planned and instituted.

In the context of this new interest, several decisive steps were taken in 1906 which greatly influenced the nature of educational programs in the labor movement. In preparation for the party congress at Mannheim in 1906, Clara Zetkin had been charged with drafting a full report on the whole educational issue. Although discussion on this matter was cut short at Mannheim and Zetkin could not present a full report, the delegates nonetheless created the party's Central Educational Commission, charged with developing general educational guidelines and with generating new programs for the movement as a whole. The membership of the commission reflected the ideological currents in the party itself, as it included two prominent revisionists, Eduard David and Georg von Vollmar, but a larger number from the radical wing—Karl Korn, Franz Mehring, Heinrich Schulz, Clara Zetkin—with Hugo Heimann as chairman (August Bebel represented the party's Executive Committee at the commission's meetings).[11] In the same year the Social Democratic party established its own Party School in Berlin, and it too gained a position of considerable significance. Its first instructional session began on November 15, 1906, and ran for approximately six months. Finally, the General Commission of the Free Trade Unions founded the Trade Union School in Berlin and its first classes were held from August 20 to September 15, 1906.

The salient controversial issues concerning principles, methods, and goals of *Arbeiterbildung* all came to the fore in the initial stages of the above three institutions. Although the most obvious lines of demarcation corresponded broadly to the larger debate between reformists and orthodox Marxists, especially on specific matters of economic and social theory, it is important to point out that these ideological lines were not carried over into discussions on the arts. At the first meeting of the Central Educational Commission, Heimann emphasized that he and his comrades could not avoid the issue of "whether our activity should be directed toward instruction in the ideology of the party or toward general enlightenment."[12] On that point, Bebel and Zetkin knew precisely where they stood. Both insisted that the school should focus on "enlightenment in the sense of partisan knowledge" (*parteiwissenschaftliche Aufklärung*), although Zetkin also strongly recommended the inclusion of instruction in the natural sciences. Advocates of the partisan political principles dominated the discussions and only Vollmar argued at that time that socialists should not condemn all "bourgeois educational endeavors," but should appreciate some of their efforts.[13]

Commission members agreed that they needed to debate the fundamental principles more thoroughly. The discussion at the second meeting (June 24, 1907) revealed once again a basic cleavage, but with individual formulations. Korn argued vigorously that curricular emphasis should be on economics, history, and socialism, with only secondary importance given to the natural sciences. Nothing more would be needed, and he expressed deep misgivings about including other subjects. According to his harsh and narrow opinion, the arts, literature, and related humanistic studies were either irrelevant or harmful.[14] In no way second to Korn in radical ideology, Zetkin nonetheless reflected a broader vision and contended that everything should be included that could in any way help to raise the proletariat. Political and trade union struggles deserved top priority, she agreed, but other topics also had their uses. For example, she made a particularly ingenious argument for the arts as a functional substitute for religion: "More and more religion loses its position with the proletariat; therefore, as a substitute, we must offer artistic works that embody our conception, otherwise the workers would be driven into the arms of religious mysticism, such as prevails among the bourgeoisie. And so we must give consideration to a rational art that reflects our world view."[15] No one pursued the implications of Zetkin's substitution hypothesis, in great part, one suspects, because it is doubtful that any member of the commission believed that Social Democrats could create works that combined artistic merit with genuine socialist content.

The discussion shifted again to the need to emphasize courses that would directly encourage the readiness and ability of workers to carry on the class struggle. When the revisionist Eduard David tried to persuade his fellow members that all fields of learning and art related to socialism, Zetkin shot back by repeating the underlying radical theme that *Arbeiterbildung* should give priority to subjects that would promote the "combative capacities of the proletariat." Bebel agreed fully. Although he hesitated categorically to exclude all humanistic subjects, Bebel harbored serious suspicions about humanists, explaining that "people who are especially pleased to speak on art and similar things come for the most part from the bourgeois world." Even Franz Mehring, who might be expected to give serious consideration to the relationship between the arts and socialist politics, observed that "the theater and art must remain in the background [because they] lead easily to foolishness [*Versimpelung*] and indifference toward serious endeavors." Despite the presence of the reformist voices of David and Vollmar, Heinrich Schulz, one of the most energetic members of the commission, spoke for the majority when he said that he wanted "out-and-out education for the class struggle [*ausgesprochene Klassenkampfbildung*]" and anything that did not fit that formula he dismissed as totally irrelevant.[16] That continued to be Schulz's theme, as a few years later he wrote that "precisely that knowledge is of the greatest significance which can make a worker completely clear about his position in the present and about himself as a fighter for his class for a better future."[17] In principle, therefore, most of the members of the Central Educational Commission fully intended to promote a politically inspired, propagandistic educational program within the labor movement. That constituted the core of what they understood by *Arbeiterbildung*.

To implement their principles, members of the commission worked out an overall plan that involved the establishment of a system of extension courses (*Wanderkurse*) and the publication of guides on how local educational committees could best sponsor cultural programs.[18] They also needed to find out what programs already existed and, to that end, they sent out 1,123 questionnaires in February 1907: 447 to executive committees of Social Democratic political organizations; 530 to branches of the free trade unions; and 146 to representatives of the socialist feminist associations. Only 404 questionnaires, slightly more than one-third, were completed and returned: 144 from Social Democratic political organizations; 191 from trade union cartels; 33 from individual trade unions; 27 from feminist groups; and 9 from general labor movement educational organizations.[19]

The results of the survey are obviously incomplete, possibly inflated as well, and do not reveal why so many questionnaires went unanswered. To be sure, in some towns leadership in the above organizations overlapped so extensively that one completed questionnaire would suffice for a whole locality. The most thorough data came from the larger towns, that is, the major centers of existing educational endeavors.[20] One can only speculate, but labor movement organizations in small towns may not have responded because they had little or nothing to report concerning educational and cultural programs. In any case, the results were discouraging, and the Central Educational Commission could not avoid the conclusion that it had much to do if its principles were to be realized. Table 4 in Appendix C summarizes the answers to the question of whether organizations were doing anything to promote education.

The survey results, despite their assumed incompleteness, give some interesting clues about the nature of the movement's educational endeavors as of 1907. Clearly, the trade unions constituted the single most important organizational base on which to build such programs, considerably more significant in this respect than the party itself. The implications of that fact for the ideological orientation of *Arbeiterbildung* contradicted almost directly the principles laid down so stridently by the members of the Central Educational Commission. The reformist reality of the trade union base confronted head-on the radical rhetoric of most commission members. The survey also showed that the single lecture was the format used most frequently. Lecture topics reflected chiefly the political and social interests of the labor movement. Socialism stood at the top of the list, trade unions next, followed by natural science, history, economics, technology, cooperatives, social welfare legislation, and German literature. These might be the right topic headings, but members of the Central Educational Commission had to wonder whether the content fit their idea of the kind of knowledge that needed to be disseminated to further the class struggle. Most organizations reported that they lacked the resources to sponsor artistic presentations, although 110 indicated that they had held recitation evenings and several had put on concerts and other musical events.[21]

Just as orthodox Marxists and radicals seemed to dominate the deliberations of the Central Educational Commission, so they came also to shape the nature of the Party School, which opened on November 15, 1906. However, at the outset their control was in no way a foregone conclusion. For example, Rosa Luxemburg, who later became one of the Party School's most renowned and influential teachers, initially expressed deep suspicions because she feared that reformist cultural advocates would quickly gain an upper hand.[22] She had reason to be fearful. Prior to the school's opening a debate had already erupted as to what principles would determine its practice. One of the key phrases in the debate was "bourgeois knowledge" (*bürgerliche Wissenschaft*), understood to include nearly everything that did not belong within that quasi-official corpus of writings and authors endorsed broadly by the Social Democratic movement. Max Maurenbrecher, originally selected to be on the teaching staff of the Party School, launched the exchange in the summer of 1906 with arguments that favored a kind of general education based on pluralist assumptions. Although Maurenbrecher assured his readers that he recognized that the Party School had to contribute to the long-range interests of the labor movement, he disapproved of a curriculum that served primarily, if not exclusively, propagandistic and agitational goals. Franz Mehring counterattacked with the sweeping proposition that the Party School had no reason to bother with the "rotten rubbish of *'bürgerliche Wissenschaft,'* " and Heinrich Knauf repeated the standard argument that "above all the Party School should provide learned armament [*wissenschaftliche Ausrüstung*] for agitators."[23] Although they were fighting a losing battle, reformists like Maurenbrecher, Franz Laufkötter, and Eduard Bernstein continued in the following months and years to express serious misgivings about a Party School devoted wholly to a one-sided approach to the study of society, economics, and history.[24] When the issue came before the party congress in 1908, Rosa Luxemburg, Max Grunwald, Clara Zetkin, Paul Lensch (at that time still a radical), and Wilhelm Pieck (recently a student at the Party School) answered the charges that Maurenbrecher and Kurt Eisner had raised against the one-sided nature of the curriculum. The outcome of the discussion offered the revisionist critics of the school little or no consolation. What commenced as a debate on the issues soon deteriorated into essentially a series of personal attacks on Maurenbrecher.[25] The mood of the delegates had not favored Maurenbrecher and Eisner and the Party School remained under the tight control of orthodox Marxists.

A victory for radicals and orthodox Marxists in the conflict over the Party School did not give them educational control throughout the labor movement. On the contrary, for in the free trade unions advocates of an intensified educational program held sharply different pedagogical views. For many years the trade unions had been sending their members to the Berlin Workers' Educational School, but with considerable misgivings. Trade unionists felt estranged from the Berlin school's strong theoretical and historical orientation, which did not meet the practical needs of their members. They expressed their distrust of the Berlin school in various ways, often by referring to it derisively as a "War Academy" for party comrades. Despite their unhappiness and their special instructional needs, trade unionists were slow to develop an educational program of their own. As late as 1902, at the congress of the Free Trade Unions in Stuttgart, Christian Tischendörfer sought in vain to interest his fellow delegates in a school for trade union functionaries. At that time both Carl Legien and Theodor Leipart showed no interest in a plan for special courses for trade unionists, but Tischendörfer continued his campaign in the following years.[26]

The educational system envisaged by Tischendörfer was both pragmatic and pluralist. He specifically warned against the tendency, which he found also in trade union libraries, to make available only literature that reflected one point of view. One-sided learning harmed students, he argued, because it would "hinder a worker from developing his own judgment in economic matters and inadvertantly justifies the opinion of independent observers that workers in the free trade unions are held to a rigidly defined outlook. That approach fails to engender a learning that has strength, but leaves a confusion of concepts which can be tossed about as chaff by every strong gust of wind."[27] Tischendörfer then appealed for intellectual pluralism and for trade unionists to be more tolerant of educated persons who would be needed to teach courses in the new program. Chiding his fellow trade unionists for a certain antiintellectualism, he noted that "today it is an undeniable fact that even in the free labor movement, which strives for enlightenment and freedom, wisdom and clarity, there is often no greater crime than to get ahead of others intellectually."[28] Tischendörfer's sentiments were shared by many other trade unionists who expressed little or no hostility to *bürgerliche Wissenschaft*. They articulated an overriding concern to ensure that their educational programs would serve the practical needs of trade unions and improve the effectiveness of the membership.[29] In this way trade union educational principles contrasted with and even contradicted the intellectual world that the Central Educational Commission and the Party School hoped to create.

The practices of the Party School and the Trade Union School also invite comparison. It is clear that both were designed to train elites for various roles in the labor movement. Of the two, the Party School chose its students more selectively and implemented a more intense course of study. It sponsored one semester annually, lasting six months during the fall and winter. By contrast, the Trade Union School held terms ranging from four to six weeks at three different times during the year. Its courses were, on the whole, less thorough and less demanding than those in the Party School. Both institutions recruited students only from within the labor movement, but the Party School used a more elaborate screening system and limited the number of admissions to about thirty for each semester, while the Trade Union School admitted as many as seventy to each of the three terms held annually. Candidates for admission to both schools were first recommended from the local level. Recommendations for the Party

School were made primarily by local Social Democratic committees; for the Trade Union School most frequently by the central
committees of local trade union cartels. Local organizations scru-
tinized their nominees with great care, trying to make sure that in
return for sponsoring and subsidizing a person at one of the
schools the labor movement would get a "graduate" of special
training, commitment, and usefulness. Persons known to be slow
learners were not recommended. Others of wavering loyalty were
unlikely to be good investments. The schools were not set up to
convert new disciples, but to train those already devoted fully to
the labor movement. In the years between 1906 and 1914 the
Party School taught about 240 students, while 1,287 trade unionists went through the twenty-two instructional terms at the Trade
Union School. In addition, political organizations and the Labor
Secretariats for Female Workers also sent an unrecorded number
of students to the Trade Union School.[30]

The faculty of the Party School wanted to emphasize studies on a
comparatively advanced level of theory (see Table 3). By contrast,
courses in the Trade Union School were intentionally designed to
relate directly to the day-to-day activities of the unions (see Table
4). The contrast in the pedagogy of the two schools is evident in
the course titles themselves. Choice of instructor also played a
crucial role in determining the theoretical level of a course, a fac-
tor noted carefully by directors of the Party School. Both faculties
remained quite stable in the years between 1907 and 1914. In the
Party School the core faculty included Luxemburg, Mehring, Hein-

Table 3
Social Democratic Party School
Courses of Instruction for 1909–10

Course Title	Total Semester Hours	Instructor
National Economy	230	Rosa Luxemburg
History of Social Development	144	Heinrich Cunow
Oral and Written Expression	120	Heinrich Schulz
Labor Law and Social Legislation	76	Artur Stadthagen
German History	72	Franz Mehring
Natural Science	46	Emanuel Wurm
Penal and Civil Law	48	Hugo Heinemann and Kurt Rosenfeld
Newspaper Technology	16	Heinrich Schulz
Municipal Politics	12	Emanuel Wurm

*Source: Protokoll über die Verhandlungen des Parteitages der Sozialdemokratischen Partei Deutschlands.
Abgehalten in Magdeburg vom 18. bis 24. September 1910 (Berlin, 1910), p. 58.*

Table 4
Trade Union School
Courses of Instruction for First Term, August 20–September 15, 1906

Course Title	Hours of Instruction and Discussion	Instructor
History and Theory of the German Trade Union Movement	12 + 8	Karl Legien
The Opposing Trade Unions in Germany	8 + 4	Paul Umbreit
The Trade Union Movement Abroad	8 + 4	Eduard Bernstein
Insurance Legislation	8 + 4	Robert Schmidt
Labor Protection	12 + 4	Paul Umbreit
Industrial Labor Contracts	8 + 4	Simon Katzenstein
National Economics	16 + 8	Max Schippel
Cartels and Entrepreneurial Combinations	8 + 4	Richard Calwer
Introduction to Statistics	8 + 4	Max Schippel
Trade Union Literature	4 + 2	Johannes Sassenbach
Bookkeeping and Commercial Trade	4 + 2	Buchwald

Source: Fritz Gumpert, *Die Bildungsbestrebungen der freien Gewerkschaften* (Jena, 1923), p. 19.

rich Cunow, Heinrich Schulz, Artur Stadthagen, Emanuel Wurm, Hugo Heinemann, and Kurt Rosenfeld, and for short periods they were joined by Rudolf Hilferding, Anton Pannekoek, and Hermann Duncker. If they were not all radicals, they leaned in that direction. This contrasts strikingly with the faculty of the Trade Union School, where reformists were predominant—Eduard Bernstein, Paul Umbreit, Karl Legien, Robert Schmidt, Simon Katzenstein, Max Schippel, Richard Calwer, and Johannes Sassenbach.

Were the schools effective? In terms of training committed Social Democrats for positions in the labor movement, especially for the party itself, the Party School could claim considerable success. Of 141 students who attended between 1906–7 and 1910–11, 101 held positions in the socialist labor movement. Of that number there were 32 newspaper editors, 23 union functionaries, 13 Social Democratic party secretaries, and 11 functionaries in the labor secretariats. Of the 40 who held no official positions in the labor movement, 22 returned to their former trades, 6 were women with no specified occupation, 4 were independent entrepreneurs, and 3 lived outside of Germany.[31] Unfortunately, comparable data on graduates of the Trade Union School are unavailable. There is no way to speculate intelligently on the subsequent occupations of the students, although they were a larger group and, for that reason alone, may collectively have played an important role.

The intellectual impact of the schools is even more difficult to evaluate. The dominance of orthodox Marxists and radicals as teachers in the Party School did not ensure that the pupils would share their ideological predilections. In 1911, when Franz Mehring and Rosa Luxemburg organized a special series of debates among the students, they were dismayed to learn that a substantial number of the participants propounded revisionist views. Luxemburg expressed deep disappointment, and Mehring is reported to have complained, "Nah, then the whole Party School actually has had no purpose."[32] Mehring may have been too pessimistic, for there were numerous radicals among the students, including Wilhelm Pieck, later to become a leading member of the German Communist party and ultimately the first president of the German Democratic Republic. Still other former students of the Party School had radical careers as Spartacists and Communists, notably Karl Schulz, Gustav Naumann, Georg Schumann, Rosi Fröhlich (née Wolfstein), Jakob Walcher, and Georg Röder. In addition, the political convictions of Hermann Remmele and Wilhelm Koenen drew them into the Independent Social Democratic party.[33] On the other side ideologically, August Winnig and Fritz Tarnow had been students in the Party School, and clearly neither had imbibed the radical spirit. At the time of the debate in 1911, Josef Lübbring, Heinrich Sierakowsky, and Franz Mitzkat, none of whom gained prominence in the socialist movement, all had taken reformist stands.[34] On balance, Luxemburg and Mehring had cause to be concerned. Even under the best of conditions, that is, within an institution controlled by the left wing of Social Democracy, orthodox Marxists were unable to exercise the sweeping kind of ideological influence that they believed should permeate the whole social-cultural milieu of the labor movement.

The Trade Union School never faced that kind of contradiction. The faculty endorsed most of the pragmatic goals and reformist principles of the trade unions. To be sure, some members of the union movement believed that the Trade Union School should be purged of reformist teachers. One delegate to the conference of the Free Trade Unions in 1906, Kloth, argued strenuously that Richard Calwer and Max Schippel should not be appointed as instructors because of their favorable views on tariffs and cartels. But his was a lonely voice. No action was taken against Calwer and Schippel and both continued to teach at the school for many years.[35] That pattern remained the norm. Several years later some Social Democrats complained that insufficient efforts were made to ensure that teachers at the Trade Union School were also members of the Social Democratic party. When that issue came before the eighth national congress of the free trade unions in Dresden, Karl Legien himself led the move to delete all political prerequisites for teachers in the school. To make his case, Legien drew a doubtful parallel between instruction in the natural and social sciences, arguing that since the quality of teaching in hygiene did not depend on membership in the Social Democratic party, neither would it make any difference for those giving courses in economics and welfare legislation.[36] Legien's comments accurately reflected the sentiments of that very large segment of the labor movement that refused to believe that it had an ideological obligation to reject everything associated with *bürgerliche Wissenschaft* and to cut itself off totally from other segments and dimensions of German society.

While the two elite schools enrolled about sixteen hundred pupils in the years between 1906 and 1914, many thousands of organized workers attended lectures and courses sponsored by local labor movement associations and by the party's Central Educational Commission. But throughout Germany these programs faced numerous difficulties, the nature and severity of which varied from place to place. The few competent lecturers in any locality were quickly overworked, and many localities felt they had no one who could present knowledgeable lectures. Speakers had to make special efforts to arouse and hold workers' attention. Long working hours, poor wages, and unemployment all contributed to low attendance and indifference. Trade union respondents to the questionnaire of the Central Educational Commission almost universally blamed the "miserable working conditions" as the main obstacle hampering their educational undertakings. Others complained that even organized workers were distracted from serious educational participation by excessive "club idiocy" (*Vereinsmeierei*), especially among the workers' singing and gymnastic societies, and by clubs for trivial entertainments (*Klimbimvereine*). Socialist feminists charged that their educational efforts were insufficiently supported by "party comrades," no doubt an accurate estimation since it is generally agreed that many socialist men were often indifferent about female participation. Finding suitable rooms for lectures and classes also posed a constant problem. Almost without exception lectures took place in the large halls of restaurants and beer halls.[37] The atmosphere was relaxed, frequently too relaxed since owners made it a precondition that food and drink could be served during meetings, including lectures. Throughout Germany labor movement audiences at most lectures and cultural events refreshed themselves with food and drink as they listened to presentations on socialism, natural science, and hygiene. The air was heavy with the smell of tobacco, beer, and schnapps. With bodies already weary from long hours of toil, concentration must have been difficult if, in addition, one had to overcome both the interruptions of waiters and a gentle alcoholic drowsiness.[38]

Regardless of the obstacles, programs for education and cultivation increased steadily (see Appendix C, Table 5). In a common pattern throughout Germany, trade union cartels and party organizations cooperated by forming local educational commissions which then directed many, if not all, of the projects. By 1911 there were 244 of these local educational commissions, spending some 681,290 German marks on educational and cultural programs.[39] The party's Central Educational Commission attempted to guide and encourage the local efforts. Beginning in 1907 it published an annual guide, entitled *Ratschläge und Winke,* outlining what it thought to be appropriate material for educational courses, festival programs, special evenings featuring drama and music, as well as hints for the movement's libraries.

To expand on local efforts and to ensure that its ideological preferences would be presented in lectures, the Central Educational Commission instituted a system of extension courses (*Wanderkurse*) in 1907 (see Appendix C, Tables 6 and 7). These too expanded steadily, except for the slowdown during 1911–12 because of the Reichstag election, although the absolute number of persons who attended the lectures is rather modest. Female participation was particularly disappointing, in part because no courses were specifically designed to meet the special needs and interests of women.[40]

The initial curriculum of the extension program stressed two closely related subjects: "Developmental Stages of Economic Life" and "Basic Concepts of Political Economy." In both, Marxist principles formed the foundation. Two young Marxist intellectuals, Otto Rühle and Hermann Duncker, were among the initial instructors and continued to constitute the core of the teaching staff between 1907 and 1914. Julian Borchardt, just as young and no less devoted to Marxism, also gave courses in basic economics for several years. During the first year the teachers also included Max Schutte (on general political party history), Hermann Wendel (on Social Democratic history), and Hermann Muller (on the history of trade unions). In the following years the commission diversified the offerings and increased the number of instructors.[41]

Table 5
Extension Courses for 1912–13

Course Title	Instructor
Economic Foundations of Socialism (Erfurt Program)	Hermann Duncker; Otto Rühle; Julian Borchardt; Reimes
Stages of Economic Development	Rühle; Reimes
Basic Concepts of Political Economy	Duncker; Rühle
Historical Materialism	Borchardt
History of Socialism to the Beginning of the Nineteenth Century	Duncker
History of German Social Democracy	Rühle
History of the German Trade Union Movement	Anon.
German History from the End of the Middle Ages to the French Revolution	Rausch
German Classical Literature	Poensgen-Alberty
History, Theory, and Programs of the Bourgeois Parties in Germany	Borchardt; Reimes
Constitutional Questions	Reimes
National Insurance System	Anon.
Basic Problems of Education	Rühle
Lecturing Techniques	Poensgen-Alberty
Objectives of the Plastic Arts (with slides)	Poensgen-Alberty
Science (with slides)	Engelbert Graf
History of Evolution in Science	Graf
Introduction to Biology	Duncker
From Primitive Animals to Man	Graf
On Knowing Mankind	Duncker
Germany's Fate in the Various Eras of the Earth's History	Graf
Illness and the Proletariat	Duncker
Development of Industrial Dominance	Woldt
The Modern Industrial Plant	Woldt
A Technical Excursion through Germany's Large Industry	Woldt

Source: Protokoll über die Verhandlungen des Parteitages der Sozialdemokratischen Partei Deutschlands (Berlin, 1913), pp. 39–42.

In addition to the extension courses, which it ran directly, the Central Educational Commission sent out detailed advice to local organizations on how to sponsor special cultural events, recitation evenings, drama and opera performances, and other musical presentations.[42] For the most part the commission simply expanded what was already a long tradition of musical and literary programs in the labor movement. Nonetheless, the recommendations of the Central Educational Commission provide striking evidence to support the view that the intellectual world that radicals and orthodox

Marxists created within the German labor movement did not constitute a coherent unity, but was in fact a multifaceted amalgamation.
On the one hand they fought strenuously to establish the hegemony
of Marxist thought against the pretensions of *bürgerliche Wissenschaft,* but on the other they embraced the world of art, literature,
and music which the same "*bürgerliche* tradition" had created. The
commission certainly did not recommend everything German society viewed as its culture, but it included so much that it seems clear
that even the radical members were blind to the fact that by this
approach they were inadvertently weakening the ideological world
they wanted to create with courses in socialism, social science, and
history. Table 6 gives an indication of the extent to which certain
authors and composers were preferred within the labor movement.

   Names carry symbolic meanings and associations and provide
vital clues as to what belongs and is appropriate to a given context.
The names of writers and composers who had a place on labor
movement artistic programs were also signals about how to understand the nature of German socialism. Since these programs obviously enjoyed the approval of those labor leaders most concerned
with promoting workers' education, participants and observers
were justified in believing that the works performed had an approved place in the social-cultural milieu of the labor movement. It
can certainly be understood that Heine, Herwegh, and Freiligrath
should have a place in the intellectual world of the labor movement. But why Kleist, Anzengruber, and Liliencron? One could
make a firm link to Beethoven, but had the cultural leaders not yet
discovered that Richard Wagner's commitment to revolution had
been superficial at best and that Bayreuth had become the shrine
for a new mystical German nationalism? The intellectual world
that orthodox Marxists and radicals wanted to create centered on
socialist theory, the social sciences, the history of labor, and
closely related subjects. One word, "Marxism," symbolized what
they consciously desired. In reality, however, they helped to create
a diffuse and variegated alternative culture that was more latitudi-
narian than ideologically coherent. Once again it is appropriate to
point out that even radicals within Social Democracy tended to
assume a sharp separation between political issues, to which they
ascribed high priority, and the artistic realm, to which they assigned a peripheral role.

   Making books, pamphlets, and periodicals available to their
members became an important part of the educational projects of
many organizations within the labor movement. Trade unions of

Table 6

Artistic Programming, 1910–13

Year	Poetry Evenings	Musical Programs	Recitation and Artistic Evenings
1909–10	Goethe, Schiller (40), Heine (10), Freiligrath (20), Herwegh, Hauff, Anzengruber, Keller, Busch, Liliencron, Schnitzler, Negri, Gorki, *Arbeiterdichter;* in all, 97 evenings.	Evenings for Beethoven, Mozart, Schubert, Schumann, Mendelssohn, Richard Wagner; concerts of vocal, instrumental, symphonic chamber music; evenings for the violin and *Volkslieder;* in all, 135 performances.	Without set programs (recitations, cabaret, *Münchener Scharfrichter,* Variety Evening, political-satirical); in all, 180 evenings.
1910–11	Busch, Freiligrath, Goethe, Hans Sachs, Henckell, Heine, Liliencron, Reuter (14), Seume, Tolstoy, modern writers, Russian poets; in all, 54 evenings.	Beethoven, Schumann, Wagner, Wolf (Hugo); vocal, instrumental, violin concerts; *Volkslieder* evening; in all, 151 performances.	Without set programs (recitations, *Lieder zur Laute,* ballads, varied evenings, *Münchener Scharfrichter,* humorous and political-satirical evenings); in all, 211.
1911–12	Busch, Ebner-Eschenbach, Goethe, Heine, Ibsen, Kleist, Reuter, Hans Sachs, Tennyson, modern poets, March poets, Russian poets; in all, 22 with 11,572 in attendance.	Beethoven, Händel, Liszt, Mendelssohn, Mozart, Wagner; concerts of vocal and instumental music, *Lieder* evenings; in all, 97 performances with 58,115 in attendance.	Without set programs (recitations, *Lieder zur Laute,* ballads, varied program, humor evenings); in all 212 with 94,825 in attendance.
1912–13	Busch, Hebbel, Heine, Keller, Krille, Liliencron, Reuter, Rosenow, Schiller, Thoma; in all, 28 with 8,556 in attendance.	Beethoven, Mozart, Wagner; concerts of vocal and instrumental music; *Lieder* evenings; in all, 159 performances with 84,513 in attendance.	Without set programs (recitations, *Lieder zur Laute,* ballads, varied evenings, humor evenings, family evenings); in all, 297 evenings with 104,271 in attendance.

Source: Protokoll . . . Magdegurg (1910), p. 52; *Protokoll . . . Jena* (1911), pp. 50–51; *Protokoll . . . Chemnitz* (1912), p. 49; *Protokoll . . . Jena* (1913), pp. 38–39.

highly skilled workers, such as printers and bookbinders, started collections as early as the 1850s and 1860s. The workers' educational societies of the 1860s also developed small book collections to complement their instructional courses. The early socialist political organizations—Lassallean and Eisenacher, and after 1875 the unified Socialist Workers' party—were not yet involved in setting up libraries in the sixties and seventies. In the labor movement as a whole there were only a handful of organizational libraries when the antisocialist law went into effect in 1878 and the ensuing oppression cut off the possibility that new ones would be founded.[43] The growth came in the nineties, and especially after the turn of the century, when individual trade unions, trade union cartels, party organizations, and local educational commissions showed an increasing awareness of both the need to provide their members with reading material and the presumed ideological advantages in doing so.

Regardless of the different sponsoring organizations, the collections were all referred to as "workers' libraries" (*Arbeiterbibliotheken*) and viewed as an integral part of the labor movement milieu. Numerically, the free trade unions and not the Social Democratic party created the overwhelming majority of these libraries, many of which originated as small collections of specialized literature particularly suitable for training union functionaries and agitators. A number of local party organizations also began to build their own collections, some of which became quite substantial, but most lacked resources to develop large and diversified holdings. By the turn of the century two major organizational models were evident: the single-organization library, and the centralized library, established as an amalgamation of several preexisting collections. The latter came into being when socialists and trade unionists realized that small libraries belonging to one organization confronted many obstacles that limited their efficiency and effectiveness.[44] The trend toward library centralization began at the turn of the century, but only made rapid progress after 1906 when the Central Educational Commission and local educational commissions pushed vigorously for mergers. The expansion of workers' libraries is reflected in the data on the growing number of centralized collections. By 1914, 748 localities reported no less than 1,147 workers' libraries, of which 591 were centralized and the other 556 belonged to individual organizations. Collectively they held 833,857 volumes, of which 532,904 were in the centralized collections and 300,953 in the individual libraries.[45]

The maintenance of most workers' libraries in the nineties required little more than a few hours of attention weekly. Small collections were usually kept in a cabinet or bookshelf, stored in the inn that served as the organizational locale, in a member's home, or in the trade union building. As collections expanded, those responsible had to find more suitable space and, in exceptional cases, special rooms were rented to house the larger libraries. The library of the Social Democratic party organization in Lindenau (a Leipzig suburb) started in 1898 as a small collection housed in the restaurant Stadt Altenburg, the locale where the socialists held their meetings. In 1900 the party organization moved to the inn Zwei Linden and the bookcase went along. The library then grew rapidly, in part, one assumes, because Gustav Hennig, the librarian, devoted himself to the task with pride and energy. By 1905 bookcases in the restaurant no longer sufficed, and independent rooms were leased. Growth continued, a youth section was added, and by 1908 still better quarters were leased.[46] Most workers' libraries grew during the same period, though only a few matched the Lindenau success story.

The existence of a collection did not in itself assure that the books would be easily accessible to workers. Workers' libraries were open for lending only a few hours each week, usually in the evenings and Sunday mornings. Geographic location also played a decisive role in affecting how many organized workers could make use of a collection. Recognizing accessibility as a serious problem, the Central Educational Commission of the party established extension libraries (*Wanderbibliotheken*) as a way to take books to the workers.[47] Only a few libraries had reading rooms, but these too had very limited hours. In Elberfeld, for example, the reading room opened for only a few hours on Wednesday evenings. Nonetheless, a reading room greatly enhanced a library's appeal. In Frankfurt am Main use of the Central Workers' Library doubled shortly after it acquired a reading room. But these were the exceptions. Out of 547 central workers' libraries as of 1911, only 87 reported that they had reading rooms.[48]

Although the majority of workers' libraries were still comparatively small operations in the early twentieth century, they were rapidly becoming a specialized business with an accompanying sense of professionalism. Initially, the small collections were tended by interested members who volunteered their time to the cause. By 1914 at least 365 libraries were able to provide salaries—at varying levels, to be sure—to staff members.[49] In 1909 the association of workers' libraries founded its own professional journal, *Der Bibliothekar,* which reported regularly on the status of labor movement libraries throughout Germany and carried a wide variety of bibliographical, technical, and ideological articles. The larger centralized libraries discovered that they needed staff members who were well trained both in library techniques and in the history and theory of the socialist labor movement. To fill this need special training courses for librarians were planned, and the first was held in Berlin between May 11 and June 29, 1914. This course consisted chiefly of a series of bibliographical lectures on the literature in various fields.[50] The training course was clearly to be designed as a means of ensuring that those in charge of workers' libraries would be fully informed about what reading material would be appropriate in labor movement libraries. The special brand of professional training for workers' librarians revealed once again the extent to which the social-cultural milieu of the labor movement could be both an imitation of the rest of modern society and at the same time a world unto itself.

In principle workers' libraries were to be instruments in the emancipatory struggle of the working class, to support the goals of the party and the trade unions, and to aid serious socialist learning, not primarily to offer reading for escape and diversion. The radical formulation of the principle, as expressed by Heinrich Schulz, stressed that the libraries were created to supply workers with "weapons" to be used in the "fight for freedom" by providing books that would "awaken their [the workers'] sympathy for socialism and simultaneously inflame their desire to fight for socialist ideals," and not to advance some "indiscriminate general education."[51] A more moderate formulation, given by Ernst Mehlich, one of the most prominent and effective promoters of workers' libraries, emphasized that "our libraries have first the general purpose of satisfying the reading needs of the working class [*Arbeiterschaft*]. But in particular they should serve serious learning, that is, the political and trade union instruction of the workers. Without underestimating the significance of light reading [*Unterhaltungsliteratur*], our major objective still must be to interest workers in serious literature [*belehrende Literatur*]."[52]

To implement these principles the libraries had to acquire the right kind of books, and workers had to be encouraged to select and read them. From the beginning, promoters of the collections assumed that the holdings would consist overwhelmingly of works in the social sciences and on the Social Democratic labor movement. Trade unionists argued strongly that their libraries should specialize in economics, technology, social policy, and statistics. The libraries were to acquire all essential literature directly related to trade unions—statutes, union journals, conference proceedings, and other published reports—on the assumption that these would be the most important reading for union members.[53] Libraries founded by socialist party organizations paid less attention to trade union literature and more to socialist theory and party histories, but both they and trade unionists acted on the assumption that the libraries existed to serve the movement ideologically and that the holdings would be suited to that purpose.

To make available books on socialist theory, labor history, and trade union practices did not in itself guarantee that workers would read them. When Social Democrats began in the 1890s to pay attention to what materials were borrowed from the libraries, they made some unhappy discoveries and concluded that workers needed additional guidance in choice of reading matter. Examination of the circulation records of several libraries revealed that their users turned to fiction and light reading far more frequently than to books on socialism or the social sciences.[54] For those who had assumed that sharp-witted workers would automatically concentrate on socialism and social theory, these findings were very disappointing. Workers apparently needed more encouragement and guidance so that they would reach enthusiastically for materials that would give them intellectual ammunition for the class struggle.

Guidance was forthcoming from many quarters. The labor movement press advertised and reviewed publications from the major socialist publishing houses. Social Democratic speakers frequently stressed the importance of reading the works of major socialist authors.[55] The librarians themselves were always prepared to give advice. "The librarian," wrote Gustav Henning, director of the successful Lindenau library, "must be a guide who leads the reader along the path from what is good to what is the very best."[56] His first principle stressed the need to exclude undesirable literature, a view shared by the sponsors of workers' libraries throughout Germany. They wanted to wean workers away from everything they thought to be "trash" (*Schundliteratur*). That included, in their judgment, the works of some of Germany's most popular writers, E. Marlitt (pen name for Eugenie John), W. Heimburg (pen name for Berte Behrens), Nataly von Eschtruth, and even Karl May.[57] Hennig indeed purged the library in Lindenau of all books by May, and other socialist librarians shared his practice; Karl May does not appear on the list of authors borrowed from workers' libraries.

For a while the purifiers believed that they would be able to reform the reading habits of their clients. The labor secretariat in Mannheim proclaimed proudly that "the struggle of the trade unions against trash of all kinds, higher and lower, is being carried on successfully by our library." Despite their optimism and diligence in censoring books and magazines, librarians had little reason in fact to conclude that they were reforming the reading habits of workers.[58] To the extent that a worker depended entirely on the local labor library for reading material, the fight against "trash" had some chance of temporary success. But "trash" could be picked up on the open market in many inexpensive publications. It is estimated that around 1900 there were in Germany and Austria forty-five thousand book peddlers who were the chief suppliers of reading material to some twenty million people. Thousands of organized workers appear to have purchased "trash" from these peddlers, a fact that highlights the magnitude of the task of reform undertaken by the sponsors of workers' libraries.[59]

Library administrators applied the exclusionary principle to far more than "trash." They seldom included works on social science by authors who were known to be indifferent or unsympathetic to socialism and the labor movement. On religion, the shelves held chiefly the publications of freethinkers, socialists, and other critics of the traditional Christian confessions. Historical studies by political dissidents were clearly favored over those by liberals, and books by out-and-out conservatives were never to be found. On all political, social, and economic topics, most labor movement educationalists had no qualms about restricting the holdings to books they believed to be correct. Clients had to be protected from wrong ideas as well as from smut. The principle of exclusion did indeed offer guidance by limiting, and to that extent also predetermining, choices. Labor movement libraries were needed, Ernst Mehlich argued, as a means for keeping workers away from the public *Volksbibliotheken* (people's libraries) which were run frequently by patriotic or religious librarians. Failure to provide alternatives to the *Volksbibliotheken* would be tantamount to handing workers over to the enemy.[60]

The other side of the exclusionary principle were the positive recommendations on what to read and acquire for workers' libraries. Rank-ordered lists were prepared to give systematic guidance for developing collections. Heinrich Schulz, under the auspices of the Central Educational Commission, compiled the most ambitious and flexible of these guides. He designed it on the stair-step principle, moving from a minimum collection upward to much more sophisticated and inclusive holdings. Built on a graduated cost scale, it began with a list of ten items considered absolutely essential and could be purchased for a total of ten marks.[61] Moving to higher levels, the lists were built on the cumulative principle, until they culminated in a collection that would cost five hundred marks. Gustav Hennig published a similar model catalog for workers' libraries, but on a more modest scale and with less ideological rigor. He made concessions to the general interests of users, so that his least expensive list—for five marks—included, in addition to works by Engels and Kautsky, an anthology of short stories, a travel account, and Wilhelm Bölsche's popularization of evolutionary theory.[62] Librarians appear to have become increasingly confident in making recommendations on what to read, and others also wrote and lectured on the subject. Giving unsolicited advice had become so common that Ernst Mehlich felt compelled to warn subscribers to the professional publication of the workers' libraries that "every form of tutelage is of course to be avoided. Nothing is more repugnant to adults than school masterism [*Schulmeisterei*]."[63] Repugnant or not, library staff members had been busy censoring workers' reading for many years and would continue to do so.

The actual pattern of borrowing from workers' libraries disappointed socialist leaders and even left the impression that organized workers seldom heeded the advice they had been given. Moreover, with few exceptions, the number of users never rose to become a substantial percentage of an organization's membership. Table 7 in Appendix C reveals that only printers and bookbinders used their trade union libraries in substantial percentages. Although the table cannot claim to represent a cross section of all workers' libraries, the pattern it discloses fits with other evidence on borrowing practices. The obvious but not surprising conclusion is that unskilled workers used the libraries much less than the skilled.[64]

More distressing to Social Democratic observers than the low percentage of organized workers using most libraries were the data on reading choices. Precisely that kind of material most urgently recommended by socialists—serious social-scientific studies—stood extremely low on lists of users' preferences. The earliest investiga-

tions revealed this apparent indifference toward socialist and social-scientific publications, and the pattern never changed, as all
subsequent enquiries confirmed. Although most libraries were well
supplied in socialism and the social sciences, organized workers
preferred fiction and, often, history and natural science. On the
basis of numerous reports from workers' libraries for the years
1908 to 1914, Langewiesche and Schönhoven have compiled an
extensive table that classifies the topic distribution of over a million borrowed books. In summary form, their conclusions are as
follows: 63.1 percent of borrowed books were belletristic; 9.8 percent were books for youth (most of which were also belletristic);
6.8 percent were in history; 6.6 percent in the natural sciences; 5.0
percent were collected works (including many collections of fiction); and only 4.3 percent were in the social sciences. The remaining 4.4 percent included books in philosophy, religion, law, and
miscellaneous subjects.[65]

A closer look at exactly what books in the social sciences were
borrowed shows that they seldom included the major socialist classics. Workers interested in informing themselves about socialism
and social science understandably turned to popularizations and
other easily comprehended works. They found in Bebel's *Die Frau
und der Sozialismus* (*Women and Socialism*) a book that superbly
fulfilled their needs. It almost invariably headed the list of the
most frequently borrowed works on socialism and social science.
Without Bebel's book, one researcher has observed, most libraries
would have shown almost no circulation of materials in the social
sciences.[66] Moreover, it must be emphasized that workers' librarians interpreted the category of serious literature in socialism and
the social sciences very broadly. Thus, they included in this category Leo Deutsch's two autobiographical accounts of his adventures in Russian detention, *Viermal entflohen* (*Four Times Escaped*) and *16 Jahre in Sibirien* (*16 Years in Siberia*). Though nonfiction, these were, as one commentator on workers' reading
noted, highly sensational and inadequate as introductions to socialism. (Lassalle's pamphlets and Karl Kautsky's *Karl Marx's ökono-
mische Lehren* were borrowed at a much lower rate than the
above.)[67]

Within the category of historical studies, librarians included two
popular works by Otto von Corvin, *Pfaffenspiegel* (*Preacher's Mir-
ror*) and *Gekrönte Häupter* (*Crowned Heads*), filled with gossipy
stories about the scandalous lives of priests and princes. Corvin's
books were vehemently polemical, designed to arouse passions

against the churches and clergymen in particular. In the judgment of Pfannkuche, Corvin's *Pfaffenspiegel,* which ran second to Bebel in popularity, should not have been classified as a serious work of nonfiction because it was read, he believed, as "pornographic literature." Less sensational than Corvin, but no less partisan, were the other books of history that enjoyed some popularity. They belonged to a standard corpus of Social Democratic historiography, including two works by Wilhelm Blos, *Die französische Revolution* (*The French Revolution*) and *Die deutsche Revolution, 1848–49* (*The German Revolution, 1848–49*), Wilhelm Zimmermann's *Geschichte des grossen Bauernkriegs* (*History of the Great Peasant War*), and Lissagary's *Geschichte der Kommune von 1871* (*History of the Commune of 1871*).[68] These were clearly some of the most serious books borrowed, but even they, though prosocialist, were not particularly well suited to introduce readers to the larger realm of socialist thought.

Social Democratic recommendations on belles lettres also exercised little demonstrable influence on workers' reading preferences. Guides on what should be read gave highest priority to German classical authors, secondly to nineteenth-century radical writers, especially Heine and Freiligrath, and thirdly to modern schools of literature. However, nearly every survey of borrowed books showed the opposite: The modernists stood first and the classics last. This evidence contradicted directly Franz Mehring's contention of the early 1890s that German workers would prefer the classics to modern schools like naturalism because the pessimism of the latter was incompatible with the spirit of a rising class of revolutionary proletarians. Like so many Social Democratic intellectuals, he convinced himself that his personal preferences overlapped with the inclinations of the working-class constituency of the labor movement. In fact, Emile Zola, the naturalist par excellence, appealed to the tastes of organized German workers and held first or second place on most lists of borrowed fiction.[69]

Paralleling the popularity of Zola throughout the era from the early 1890s to 1914 were the works of Friedrich Gerstäcker (1816–72), a prolific writer of travel and adventure stories. Himself a world traveler, Gerstäcker had spent time in North and South America, had accompanied Duke Ernst von Coburg-Gotha on a trip through Egypt and Abyssinia in 1862, and took his readers into a world of excitement in exotic places. In this respect his work belongs to the same genre as Leo Deutsch's accounts of adventures in Siberia and other nonfictional travel literature that so much appealed to German readers generally and to the users of workers' libraries in particular. The works of Jules Verne were also exceedingly popular. Circulation figures that suggest that users of workers' libraries looked to literature for adventure, excitement, and escape are supported by the direct autobiographical testimony of numerous workers and socialists.[70]

Librarians in the labor movement could not disregard users' tastes without endangering the appeal of their collections. This created a dilemma for Social Democrats who hoped that workers' libraries would be used by the rank and file to arm themselves intellectually for the emancipatory struggle. But if their libraries failed to provide the kind of material most borrowers wanted, reading workers would turn to nonsocialist libraries (especially the *Volksbibliotheken*) where they would be exposed to influences hostile to the labor movement. On the other hand, by increasing the size and range of belletristic writings they ran the risk of acquiring more and more literature about which they were skeptical, but would seem to sanction by making it available. Nonetheless, holdings in fiction, travel, and exploration had to be increased if the libraries were to satisfy some of the strongest wishes of their regular users. Recognizing these realities, sponsors of the libraries rationalized that diversified collections would appeal to an even wider audience and that once drawn to the libraries by a desire for fiction, the new patrons would at times also pick up books on economics and socialism.[71] As a consequence of this trend most labor movement libraries gradually began to look like general collections as their holdings in social science constituted a constantly decreasing percentage of the total.[72]

The fact that the users of labor movement libraries did not fulfill the expectations of Social Democratic intellectuals does not mean that the workers were either dull-witted or ideologically hostile to socialism. There is nothing inherently incompatible between holding advanced or radical political views and also preferring to read fiction and other belletristic writings for instruction and relaxation. Some historians have tried to draw specific conclusions about the mentality of organized workers from the data on borrowing patterns in workers' libraries, but this can be very misleading. Organized workers were exposed to ideological indoctrination from many sides, and it may have been a mark of their balanced intellectual interests that they chose to read fiction on their own. Moreover, newspapers of the party and trade unions made up a large part of the reading material of workers, perhaps the largest, and these publications were a constant source of information on socialism and related subjects.[73]

Comparisons are also instructive. Workers compared favorably to other Germans in their choice of reading matter, although proportionately fewer workers were heavy library users than were people of the *Bildungsbürgertum* (middle class of education and cultivation). In most other respects, however, there were great similarities. Workers' preference for belletristic writings (72.9 percent of all borrowings) corresponded to the "international library standard," which ranged from 60 to 80 percent. In Germany the lower middle class seems to have borrowed fiction at a slightly higher rate than workers did. Workers neglected the classics no more than did a sampling of *bürgerlich* readers, and they read Heine and Freiligrath more frequently.[74] Their interests were as diverse as those of the middle classes generally, and there appears to have been no single type of reader among organized workers.

The fact that the borrowing choices of organized workers resembled general patterns does not explain why they seemed to pay so little attention to the advice of labor movement educationalists. The answer probably lies in the realities of working-class life, in such things as limited educational preparation, long working hours, fluctuating employment, geographic mobility, cramped living quarters, and a natural psychological need for recuperation through various forms of entertainment and recreation. Educational deficiencies could be a major problem. A worker such as the locksmith M. Przybelski read Bebel and Kautsky, but he preferred to relax with lighter fare—Zola, Tolstoy, Gorki, and Otto von Corvin. But when he attempted to read Immanuel Kant, he had to admit "that already by the fourth page my head was in a whirl and I had to give it up. . . ."[75] The same would have happened to many middle-class readers. With high expectations Otto Buchwitz borrowed Marx's *Capital* from a workers' library in Dresden. "But back home I found out," Buchwitz tells us, "that in order to understand 'anything,' I first had to buy a dictionary of foreign terms. Only many years later was I able once again to begin to study this standard work with greater success."[76] Many obstacles stood in the way of workers who wished to follow the advice of their socialist mentors. It is not necessary to argue that they lacked commitment or were reformists at heart in order to explain the fact that they borrowed Gerstäcker's works more frequently than Kautsky's. Employed workers had very little leisure time, and what they had they often wished to spend relaxing with family, friends, or on

Sunday walks. To toil six days of the week and then spend the better part of the seventh day reading Kautsky called for more devotion to socialism than most people, including the party intellectuals, would have had.

Advice from labor movement intellectuals constituted but one of numerous pressures that could influence reading choices. Nonsocialist influences were very strong, especially on young workers. Selections were sometimes made for reasons that appear to be irrelevant. Pfannkuche even concluded that three factors influenced workers' reading: public lectures, beautiful book bindings, and the lending hours of the libraries. Accidents of availability always played a role. Otto Dikreiter enjoyed reading on Sunday afternoons, but his only source for books was the local Catholic priest, who loaned him the *Hausschatz,* a Catholic family periodical that serialized, among other things, the adventure stories of Karl May. Dikreiter was impressed, as he reported: "I uncritically accepted everything as genuine that Karl May related as his own experiences. . . ." Adelheid Popp remembered that as a child she indiscriminately read everything that came her way. Chance even determined the reading material of the young Heinrich Holek, although he grew up in a socialist household.[77]

Reading aloud, whether from a newspaper or book, was an especially effective way for workers to learn about history and the social sciences and to become familiar with belles lettres. To what extent reading aloud was practiced is difficult to determine, but it was common among some groups. German cigar workers, for example, often had someone read aloud as they worked, and Engelsing has established that a substantial portion of their reading included socialist literature. Various socialist leaders—Julius Bruhns, Hermann Molkenbuhr, Paul Löbe, and Walter Ulbricht, for example—have told about how as young boys they read aloud to cigar workers or sometimes at home to their fathers.[78] Otto Buchwitz reported the same practice among weavers in Zittau.

Often in autumn and winter, fifteen, also sometimes twenty, handweavers would come together in the evening in the house of a colleague. We took along the bobbins and spun yarn for the next day's work. One of us would be chosen to read from a book; someone else would take over his work. In a certain sense those were our schooling evenings. We were all socialists and trade unionists. On these evenings contemporary problems and the goals and the struggles of the Social Democratic party were heatedly discussed.[79]

Testimony of this kind confirms once again that socialist ideas spread among workers far more effectively by word of mouth and in groups than through individual reading.[80]

Whether devised by radicals, orthodox Marxists, or reformists, the programs for the political education and cultivation of workers fit comfortably into the configuration of the social-cultural milieu of the labor movement that has been explored in the earlier chapters. According to that pattern, diversity held its own against total uniformity, the indigenous habits and preferences of workers often frustrated the lofty goals of Social Democratic reformers, ideological vagueness tended to win out over theoretical precision, and traditions from various segments of German *bürgerlich* society and culture were carried over into the labor movement. At the same time the whole milieu, and the programs for political education in particular, spelled out the main principles of that alternative view of society and culture that so threatened many middle-class Germans. Viewed as a whole the total program, from reformist to radical, may not have offered a self-consistent social blueprint, but therein lay part of its genius. Like the social-cultural milieu of which they were a part, the educational and cultural programs were broad enough to appeal to increasingly large numbers of German workers. If these workers did not automatically imbibe everything that was presented under the rubric of *Arbeiterbildung,* they nonetheless declared their preference for that alternative vision of society, however they understood it, by joining unions and the party, or simply by attending labor movement lectures, courses, and festivals.

8

Conclusion:
The Labor Movement Milieu
and Its Meaning

The meaning of the social-cultural world of the labor movement can be interpreted from a number of perspectives. Viewed from within, the dominant perspective of the preceding chapters, the milieu reveals a striking diversity, numerous contradictions, and a certain lack of self-confidence. But it also possessed a central core of shared beliefs and values, although these were often expressed in terms that today may sound like vague clichés. Within the milieu everyone could agree that they were Germany's most sincere and devoted advocates of freedom, equality, and brotherhood, and that one had to apply the latter with special force to fellow workers and socialists. These were not hollow phrases within the milieu, but their prominence itself illustrates the fact that both in substance and style the world of the labor movement drew heavily on the same *bürgerlich* society and culture that Social Democrats also criticized so consistently and bitterly. Viewed from within, one can see that the social-cultural milieu lacked the tight cohesiveness that is sometimes implied in the phrase "Social Democratic subculture." On the other hand, when placed within the context of the larger society, the internal diversity and even the contradictions appear to be less significant than the differences that separated the socialist labor movement from most segments of Imperial Germany. Both of these perspectives need to be explored in order to elucidate further the meaning and implications of the preceding chapters on the social-cultural milieu.

Certain trends within the milieu reveal much about its inner character. The popularity and steady growth of many of the ancillary associations, especially of singers and gymnasts, meant that by the eve of the First World War the network of clubs and programs enrolled many thousands of organized workers. Although most of these associations were not recognized legally as official affiliates of the party or the trade unions, in reality they fit so tightly into the whole labor movement that they were easily taken to represent the accepted views of Social Democracy. As new types of ancillary associations for varying activities were added and as the whole network increased numerically, it exercised a correspondingly greater influence on the mood and tone of the whole labor movement milieu. The trend toward increased emphasis on excellence in performance in workers' singing societies, for example, would not have been so pronounced had the choirs failed to grow and to centralize. A greater emphasis on achieving high-quality performances implied less attention to symbolizing ideology, and programs of the singing societies often gave only token recognition to the politically strident freedom songs of the movement. If this development—in no way limited to the singing societies—seemed to parallel the ideological thrust of revisionism, it had its own inner dynamic. Nonetheless, the impression that reformism had a special hold within many of the ancillary associations was not entirely mistaken. Reformism almost always gained in the Social Democratic labor movement when socialist ideology took a secondary position. Thus, the paradox in the inner development of the auxiliary clubs was that as they grew and followed the trend toward centralization—pressed on them by numerous Marxists as well as reformists—they could simultaneously be more effective as organizations for recruitment and less reliable as disseminators of the party's official ideology.

The trend toward amalgamation of the voluntary associations and toward the centralization of all educational and cultural programs, especially marked after the founding of the Central Educational Commission in 1906, brought with it greater official emphasis on uniformity in the social-cultural milieu and less appreciation of local traditions and indigenous working-class mores. Although there is no evidence to show that local customs were immediately and negatively affected by the policy from above that favored uniformity, it may be that standardization actually increased the psychological distance between the social-cultural milieu and the daily lives of workers. That remains an open question. The evidence does demonstrate that amalgamation and centralization of educational and artistic programs were means by which socialists sought to create a standardized labor movement culture on the national level. Despite the weaknesses and contradictions that those policies may have had (and which recent scholars have analyzed), the educational and artistic programs constituted an essential part of the overall Social Democratic alternative to existing German society.

The alternative culture offered by the labor movement, as embodied in its own social-cultural milieu, was itself permeated by eclecticism. The integrative coherence that many Social Democrats believed they had achieved by the early 1890s in those aspects of socialist thought that concerned economics, politics, and social policy had no parallel for their approach to literature, music, and the visual arts. If the extent to which Marxism influenced and shaped the political and economic thinking of Social Democrats is debatable, the evidence seems overwhelming that it did not determine their cultural views. Historians have understandably focused much of their attention on the role and significance of Marxism in the life of the Social Democratic movement. This emphasis is fully justified in studies of the party's development, its programs, and the theoretical debates that took place within it. There is no question but that Marxism was a central concern of political and theoretical leaders, that many sought to propagate it and to bring party practice into line with its precepts.

As one leaves the core of Social Democratic political leaders who held positions on the party's executive committee, as Reichstag deputies, or as writers for important party periodicals, and turns to the free trade unions and the auxiliary associations of the movement, the concern with Marxism recedes into the background. However significant Marxism may have been for Social Democracy's official programmatic statements on theory, it failed to provide an ideological thread that could tie together the diverse elements of the labor movement milieu into a cohesive whole. Even the passage of time and the ever-increasing familiarity with Marxism after 1890 did not make a noticeable difference in the significance of Marxism for the whole of the social-cultural milieu. In the 1860s Lassalle's pamphlets and speeches had already enjoyed widespread popularity, and because of their agitational value they continued to be used in great quantities. Many workers could read them and grasp the essential points. Among Social Democratic thinkers, Marxism, as a more powerful system of analysis, displaced Lassallean thought at the center of ideological deliberations. But the penetration of Marxism was limited largely to the higher levels and did not permeate uniformly the whole fabric of the labor movement. Despite the adoption in 1891 of the Erfurt Program, which embodied Marxism as the official party doctrine, and despite the debate that raged between revisionists and orthodox Marxists, life on the associational level continued with little attention to what was taking place on the olympian heights of socialist theory. The symbolism of associational life seldom alluded to Marx, Engels, or Marxism. At party congresses, and occasionally at other large meetings, busts of Marx and Lassalle shared honored positions on either side of the podium, but at the festivals of singers and gymnasts Lassalle's name was more often hailed than Marx's. Throughout the nineties numerous localities still held Lassalle Festivals, but no one seems ever to have thought of holding a Marx Festival. Clubs were named for Lassalle, "Turnvater" Jahn, and even Fichte, but not for Marx. In workers' libraries book borrowers seldom turned to works on Marxism or, for that matter, on socialist theory generally.

All of the above is understandable in view of the difficulties involved in comprehending Marxism, and the fact that rank-and-file members failed to absorb it does not diminish the ideological significance of the theory. What is highly significant, however, is that the most advanced Social Democratic thinkers neglected to develop a fully rounded cultural theory on a Marxist foundation. There were several reasons for this deficiency, the least important of which was the fact that numerous reformists were active in promoting educational and artistic programs. Reformists and revisionists could be expected to encourage organized workers to take possession of the best and most progressive aspects of the arts as they existed in Europe at the time. That was entirely consistent with their general principles. The burden of creating a new socialist cultural conception lay with those who proclaimed their full devotion to Marxism. Clearly, it was people like Franz Mehring who should have transformed their inherited assumptions about the arts and aesthetics in accordance with Marxist theory. But Mehring never freed himself from the classical aesthetic principles that he had learned as an educated German and which he never subjected to basic questioning. Despite his intense personal interest in literature, Mehring, like other Social Democratic thinkers, assumed that the arts and politics belonged to different realms and assigned the former to a comparatively low rank on his hierarchy of priorities. In Mehring's view there were two important educational tasks for socialists to accomplish. First, organized workers should be exposed to the best—in artistic terms—that German and European culture had to offer and, second, they should be made to understand that what is aesthetically superior is often politically reprehensible. In this way workers would acquire a knowledge of the arts, especially the various genres of literature, and their lives would be enriched, while at the same time they would learn to distrust the political ideas and practices associated with *bürgerlich* culture.

Most Social Democratic thinkers, whether reformists or orthodox Marxists, relegated artistic and cultural issues to the periphery because economic and political matters were uppermost in their minds. The Central Educational Commission of the party had an explicit mandate to develop a broad educational and cultural theory for the movement, but it never undertook to do so. Had it tried seriously to formulate a cultural theory, it might well have failed since its members spoke with anything but one voice. The guidance offered by the commission for the movement's educational and artistic programs reflected the fact that commission members believed that, except for the need for courses in social science, history, and socialism, the artistic program of the labor movement should be essentially a system of selecting and transmitting material from well-established German culture.

The possibility that workers, in conjunction with Social Democracy, might develop a unique culture of the labor movement, one that would draw its inspiration directly from the lives of workers themselves, had no place in the assumptions of the Central Educational Commission. Nor did anyone else among the leading intellectuals of Social Democracy articulate a view that would have encouraged the participants in the associational life of the movement to believe in their own potential. Many of the intellectuals were from middle-class backgrounds and were still influenced by the principles of their educational experiences and by the general assumption that uneducated people were unlikely to produce anything of value. The upshot was that Social Democratic theorists on culture were more likely to be discouraging than encouraging with respect to the efforts of amateur musicians, artists, actors, and writers within the labor movement. In this respect it is especially noteworthy that Adolf Levenstein, an educated German with a genuine interest in what workers tried to create, was not a Social Democrat. In the course of carrying out a large survey of opinions held by organized workers, Levenstein developed an extensive correspondence with many of the respondents and discovered among them amateur writers and painters. He then made much of their work public, chiefly by editing anthologies, but also by sponsoring an exhibition of paintings.[1] The social-cultural milieu of the labor movement would have been greatly enhanced if Social Democrats had been equally sympathetic to the amateur endeavors of their organized followers.

There were theoretical reasons for the indifference of Marxists. They assumed that conditions under capitalism militated against genuine artistic creativity, that a free and authentic human culture could emerge only when socialism had overcome the existing system. Within capitalism artistic work would be treated like any other product of the marketplace. Clara Zetkin explained in 1911, that the foundation of capitalist production "is the enslavement of human labor, both manual and intellectual. As long as labor remained enslaved by capitalism, science and art could have no freedom."[2] In one way or another this basic principle found its way into essays and speeches that touched on the arts and education. In this view the culture of everyday life, the values that workers expressed in behavior and casual attitudes, could have no significance for socialist culture.

The theory of stages also played a role in thinking about workers and culture. Not only was a socialist revolution a precondition for the emergence of a free and human culture, but the organized working class had to get full possession of the existing *bürgerlich* culture before a further stage could develop. Zetkin explained how the theory of stages applied to the arts with the succinct comment that "every rising class finds its artistic models in the apex of the earlier development. The Renaissance drew on the art of Greece and Rome, German classical art drew on antiquity and the Renaissance. . . . Socialism is the logical extension and transformation of cosmopolitan liberalism, which was the intellectual property [of the bourgeoisie]. The art of socialism—so to speak—will be an extension of the grand, classical, bourgeois art. . . ."[3] Socialists and workers had to know bourgeois culture, had to understand it, and build on it as a model for their own culture of the future. They could not go around bourgeois culture. They could not create a truly new and unique culture based on the life experience of the proletariat.

Socialist commentators before the First World War never discarded the above assumptions. As a consequence they were content to promote cultural consumption as a way for workers to take possession of bourgeois culture and to make their lives more interesting and meaningful. Workers had much to learn and absorb. Although learning required effort on the part of organized workers, it cast them into an essentially passive role. Workers received; they did not create. They were to receive the best that high culture could offer, not to be content with amateurish mediocrity. Even a radical like Heinrich Schulz encouraged workers to seek high culture and to turn their backs on inferior amateur performances.[4] Radicals and orthodox Marxists, as well as reformists, found theoretical reasons for disseminating much of inherited German culture among organized workers.

The above theories did not in fact dictate and shape all of the realities of the social-cultural milieu of the labor movement. On the contrary, for the promotion of programs that emphasized the *bürgeilich* cultural inheritance only increased the diverse character of that milieu. Had the world of the labor movement included only the political and economic activities of the party and the trade unions it would have manifested an underlying dualism, but with all of the other ingredients that were present and that have been described in the main chapters of this book, the milieu became exceedingly complex. Despite the fact that it had no single unifying intellectual focus and that it brought together seemingly contradictory elements, the social-cultural milieu of the labor movement was not simply a random collection of elements assembled indiscriminately by accidents of time, place, and personality. Participants in the clubs developed a sense that some things seemed to belong and others did not. One could draw from the heritage of the Wars of Liberation, but not everything from that legacy could be accepted. One could herald radical democrats of the mid-nineteenth century, but the strong German patriotism of some of them had to be shunned. One could select pieces from most of the operas of Richard Wagner—he did have a "revolutionary" past—but not from *Parsifal*. One could draw on the repertory of Germany's male choral societies, but socialist singers had to cull out those lyrics that were unacceptable in a broad ideological sense.

In a similar way labor movement organizations could cooperate with some nonsocialist groups, but not with others. In Jena the trade union cartel encouraged its members to attend the entertainment evenings of the Comenius Society, an organization for the promotion of popular education, and the two organizations discussed what should be on the programs. In Bremen the cartel and the local educational commission of the party cooperated for several years with the Society for Popular Performances (Verein für Volkskunstabende) and the Goethe League (Goethebund), a society for the promotion of the arts. (Franz Diederich, editor of the Social Democratic *Bürgerzeitung,* had been one of the founding members in 1900 and sat on the board.) Formal collaboration ended in 1905, however, after radicals, led by Heinrich Schulz, launched a successful campaign against further cooperation on the ground that it undermined working-class integrity to affiliate with a *bürgerlich* organization. The decision to withdraw officially from the Goethebund has been taken as evidence of radicalization in Bremen, but in fact the subsequent artistic programming of the local Social Democratic educational commission did not differ markedly from that of the Goethe League. Moreover, the reformists in Bremen, still an important segment of the social-cultural milieu, continued to believe in the suitability of such cooperation.[5] If anything, the Bremen experience only underlined the apparent heterogeneity of the world of organized labor.

The binding together of the disparate elements of the alternative culture was accomplished more by symbolic expression than by formal theory and official programs. Festivals and other gatherings played a pervasive and decisive role in presenting a symbolic configuration that made the movement appear as a cohesive and internally consistent entity. Festival processions encompassed the milieu's heterogeneity, but within a ritual form that arranged the symbols as a visual demonstration of oneness, not multiplicity. As participants in those secular rituals, members of the party, trade unions, singing societies, and gymnastic clubs, to name only the most obvious, generated *togetherness* on a massive scale. They were bonded together by being together, by presenting themselves to each other and to a larger public as a unified body with a homogeneous set of values and principles. For this reason the movement's eclecticism and derivativeness were less harmful than the critical tone in several of the above chapters implies. Symbolic unity carried far more social power than did logical consistency. The melody and lyrics of the "Workers' Marseillaise," heard and sung in the movement for half a century, symbolized both the cohesion and durability of the socialist labor movement and its distinctness from the rest of German society.

The language of social class also exercised its symbolic power to give cohesion to the milieu. In particular, *worker* (*Arbeiter*) became the central code word that could be used with different connotations. Participants used it to refer to the social-economic class of dependent wage earners, to be sure, and in that objective sense workers constituted the overwhelming majority of the labor movement's followers. No one can seriously question the fact that Social Democracy—as party, trade unions, and ancillary associations— was based chiefly on the support of a substantial portion of the German working class. Likewise, a sense of worker solidarity, even of class conflict, contributed in some important measure to the feeling of unity in the labor movement. However, *worker* was used in more than that restricted sense. It came loaded with ideological connotations that also carried paradoxical implications. In its most common usage *worker* symbolized anyone and anything that belonged within the milieu of the Social Democratic labor movement. This broad ideological usage, in conjunction with the ubiquitous *comrade* (*Genosse*), sanctioned the presence of a substantial number of middle-class people, found especially among the movement's intellectuals, in a party that proclaimed both its confidence in the necessity and ability of workers to emancipate themselves and its unrelenting hostility to everything bourgeois and capitalist. In that way *worker*—as an ideological symbol rather than as a sociological category—instead of implying exclusion, dissolved the significance of class distinctions for everyone within the movement's milieu. When used with reference to German society as a whole, the term *worker* implied intense social conflict; but within the milieu of the labor movement it meant the opposite— harmony and unity. It is unlikely that middle-class socialists deluded themselves into believing that they had literally altered their place in the hierarchy of social classes, but they often wrote and spoke as if they believed an objective change had taken place. They wrote "workers' poetry," belonged to "workers' clubs," and affirmed their solidarity with the ultimate victory of workers. This symbolic usage of *worker* became so commonplace that participants accepted it as a self-evident truth. In that way both the image and the reality of cohesiveness in the milieu of the labor movement manifested themselves in the pervasive usage of a symbolic vocabulary.

Of no less importance for binding together the eclectic social-cultural milieu of the labor movement was the open and sometimes fierce hostility of German governments—federal, state, and municipal—and of large segments of the German population. Indeed, the external wall of oppression, emanating from the various levels of government, did as much as any other element to hold together the cultural milieu of the labor movement. Persecution of Social

Democrats did not cease when the special antisocialist legislation lapsed in 1890; it simply took on different forms. Although oppressive governmental practices failed to halt the growth of labor movement associations, the constant threat of persecution or minor harassment intensified the sense of solidarity, of the need to moderate internal conflicts in order to confront the common enemy with the greatest possible strength.

In the face of this hostility, the social-cultural milieu of the socialist labor movement offered the vision and, in considerable part, the actuality of an alternative culture in the midst of the social realities of Imperial Germany. The genius of this alternative culture lay in its capacity to synthesize the particular interests and needs of proletarians with principles of universal humanitarianism. Although its constituency came almost entirely from the ranks of the Social Democratic party and the free trade unions, and although socialist theorists, especially Marx and Lassalle, directly influenced the party's official ideology, the social-cultural milieu as a whole drew its intellectual and artistic substance from what its sponsors viewed as the best and most progressive elements of European culture. Workers and their families brought with them many of their own values and ways of doing things, but they did not mold the larger milieu of the labor movement into a purely working-class culture. On the contrary, the ongoing process of selection, absorption, and adaptation meant that during the Imperial era the alternative culture of the socialist labor movement sustained its ties, even if tenuously, to numerous segments of German society and to particular traditions of German culture. Even the most outspoken Marxists in the movement did not fundamentally fault this process, but accepted it as appropriate and did what they could to guide it, while reformists and moderates encouraged a broad pluralism. Whatever its weaknesses, and they were numerous, the social-cultural milieu of the labor movement offered a genuine alternative, an alternative that appealed not only to workers, but to many others who took seriously its broad humanitarianism.

APPENDIX A
List of Complete Festival Programs

A. *SÄNGERFESTE* (SINGERS' FESTIVALS)

Anhalt (1908). 7. Bundesfest. Program in *Arbeiter-Sängerzeitung*, no. 22, August 15, 1908, p. 7.

Chemnitz (1910). "Festkonzert des Sängerfestes 1910 in Chemnitz in der Festhalle." In: Kaden, *Arbeitersängerbewegung im Gau Chemnitz*, pp. 308–9.

Dortmund (1911). *Fest-Schrift zum Gau-Fest am 6. August 1911 in den Anlagen des 'Fredenbaum' zu Dortmund* (Dortmund: Buchdruckerei A. Gerisch, 1911).

Giebichenstein bei Halle (1896). "Arbeiter-Sängerbund der Provinz Sachsen und Anhalt, Samstag den 28. August 1896, Saalschlossbrauerei zu Giebichenstein bei Halle. V. Grosses Sängerfest." In: Arbeiterliedarchiv, Deutsche Akademie der Künste zu Berlin (DDR).

Görlitz (1907). "Schlesischer Arbeiter-Sängerbund," *Arbeiter-Sängerzeitung*, no. 18, September, 1907, p. 4.

Gotha (1914). *Festbuch zum X. Gausängerfest am 30., 31. Mai, 1. Juni Pfingsten 1914 in Gotha* (pub. by Deutscher Arbeiter-Sängerbund Gau Thüringen 1914).

Hamburg (1891). "Sänger-Fest (2. Bundesfest) am 23. und 24. August 1891." (This and subsequent Hamburg programs are from the Staatsarchiv Hamburg, Politische Polizei, S2338, Bd. 1.)

Hamburg (1892). "Drittes Bundesfest zur Feier des einjährigen Bestehens des Bundes, Sonnabend, den 2. April 1892."

Hamburg (1894). "Viertes Stiftungs-Fest (Siebentes Bundes-Fest), Montag, den 19. November 1894."

Hamburg (1895). "Achtes grosses Bundes-Sängerfest auf der 'Viktoria-Festwiese,' Stückenstrasse und Langenrehm, Barmbeck. Sonntag, den 14. Juli 1895."

Hamburg (1896). "Fest-Programm zum 9. Bundes-Sänger-Fest des Arbeiter-Sängerbundes von Hamburg, Altona, Wandsbek und Umgegend. 2. Tag: Montag, den 10. August 1896."

Hamburg (1897). "Fest-Programm zum 10. Bundes-Sänger-Fest des Arbeiter-Sänger-Bundes von Hamburg, Altona, Wandsbek u. Umgegend. 1. Tag: Sonntag, den 8. August 1897."

Hamburg (1898). "Programm zum Elften grossen Bundes-Sängerfest. Sonntag, den 7. und Montag, den 8. August 1898."

Hamburg (1899). "Programm zum 12. Gr. Bundes-Sänger- u. Volks-Fest II. Tag: Montag, den 14. August 1899."

Hamburg (1900). "Programm zum XIII. grossen Bundes-Sänger- und Volksfest am Sonntag, den 19., und Montag, den 20. August 1900."

Hamburg (1902). "Programm zum 15. Gr. Bundes-Sänger u. Volks-Fest am Sonntag, den 3., und Montag, den 4. August 1902."

Hamburg (1903). "Sechzehntes Bundes-Sänger- und Volks-Fest im Etablissement 'Horner Park,' Besitzer: G. Schaardt, am Sonntag, den 9. August 1903."

Hamburg (1904). "Fest-Schrift zum XVII. Bundesfest. Sonntag, den 7., und Montag, den 8. August 1904."

Hamburg (1905). "Programm zum XVIII. Bundes-Sängerfest, Sonntag, den 6. August und Montag, den 7. August 1905."

Leipzig (1909). *Festbuch zum Bundes-Konzert. Sonntag den 8. August, nachmittags 3 Uhr, in der Festhalle zur 500-Jahresfeier der Universität Leipzig* (Messplatz) (pub. by Gauvorstand, 1909).

Limbach. (1907). "Bezirks-Konzerte des Westsächsischen Arbeiter-Sängerbundes," *Arbeiter-Sängerzeitung,* no. 19, December 1907, p. 5.

Mittweida (1894). "Programm für das Conzert zum Sängerfest in Mittweida den 22. Juli 1894." In: Kaden, *Arbeitersängerbewegung im Gau Chemnitz,* p. 285.

Ohligs (1899). *Fest-Buch zu dem am Sonntag, 16. Juli 1899 zu Ohligs stattfindenden 8. Bundes-Stiftungsfeste in sämmtlichen Räumen der "Schützenburg" nebst Ausstellungshalle* (Krefeld, 1899). In: Staatsarchiv Düsseldorf, Landesamt Solingen, no. 525.

Rostock (1895). Mecklenburgischer Arbeiter-Sängerbund. "Programm zum II. Bundesfest am Sonntag, den 11. August 1895 in den Räumen des 'Thalia-Theaters' zu Rostock." In: Arbeiterliedarchiv.

B. *TURNFESTE* (GYMNASTIC FESTIVALS)

Fechenheim (1911). *Festbuch zur Bannerweihe verbunden mit Bezirks-Spieltag am 24., 25. und 26. Juni 1911* (Fechenheim, 1911). In: Archiv der sozialen Demokratie.

Hamburg (1903). "Programm zur Feier des Zehnjährigen Bestehens des Arbeiter-Turnerbundes. Mittwoch, den 20. Mai 1903."

Hamburg (1904). "Fest-Programm zum 6. Kreis-Turnfest des 3. Kreises des Arbeiter-Turnerbundes. Abgehalten am Sonntag, den 31. Juli und Montag, den 1. August 1904." (The 1903 and 1904 Hamburg programs are from the Staatsarchiv Hamburg, Politische Polizei, S3784.)

Hanau (1907). *Festbuch zum III. Kreisturnfest des IX. Kreises des Arbeiter-Turner-Bundes am 6., 7. und 8. Juli 1907 in Hanau am Main* (Frankfurt a.M., 1907). In: Archiv der sozialen Demokratie.

Langendiebach (1910). *Fest-Buch zum 9. Bezirksturnfest am 9. 10. 11. Juli 1910 in Langendiebach* (1910). In: Archiv der sozialen Demokratie.

Lübeck (1913). *Fest-Schrift zum X. Kreisturnfest in Lübeck. Abgehalten am 26., 27. und 28. Juli 1913* (n.p., 1913) In: Archiv der sozialen Demokratie.

Stuttgart (1907). *Festprogramm zum Kommers und III. Stiftungsfest zu Ehren der Delegierten vom 8. Bundesturntag 1907 in Stuttgart. Samstag 18. Mai (Pfingstsamstag) im Festsaal der Liederhalle* (n.p., 1907). In: Archiv der sozialen Demokratie.

Würzburg (1905). *Festschrift zum sechsten Kreisturntag nebst zweitem Kreisfest. Würzburg 10.–13. Juni 1905.* Arbeiter-Turnerbund, 7. Kreis Bayern. (n.p., 1905). In: Archiv der sozialen Demokratie.

C. *MAIFEIER* (MAY DAY FESTIVALS)

Aachen (1895). "Programm der Mai-Feier von 1895: Arbeiter-Bildungsvereine für Aachen und Umgegend." In: Klöcker, *Die

Sozialdemokratie im Regierungsbezirk Aachen vor dem 1. Weltkrieg, pp. 308–12. (The following Aachen programs are all from Klöcker.)

Aachen (1903). "Programm der Mai-Feier von 1903: Sozialdemokratischer Verein."

Aachen (1904). "Programm der Mai-Feier von 1904: Mai-Feier 1904. Programm."

Aachen (1908). "Maifeier 1908 beginnend am 1. Mai abends 7 Uhr auf dem Frankenberger Bierkeller."

Burscheid (1894). "Programm zur Maifeier Burscheid 1894." In: Staatsarchiv Düsseldorf, Landesamt Solingen, no. 519.

Ohligs (1897). "Programm für die Maifeier in Ohligs." In: Staatsarchiv Düsseldorf, Landesamt Solingen, no. 525.

Pöhlau (1898). "Programm zur Maifeier 1898 in Feldschlösschen Pöhlau." In: Kaden, *Arbeitersängerbewegung im Gau Chemnitz,* pp. 288–89.

Solingen (1893). "Maifeier 1893. Solingen am Sonntag, den 7. Mai, Nachmittags 4 Uhr." In: Staatsarchiv Düsseldorf, Landesamt Solingen, no. 519.

Solingen (1894). "Maifeier 1894 in der St. Seb.-Schützenhalle zu Solingen, am Sonntag, den 6. Mai, Nachm. punkt 5 Uhr." In: Staatsarchiv Düsseldorf, Landesamt Solingen, no. 519.

Wald (1897). "Programm für die Maifeier in Wald." In: Staatsarchiv Düsseldorf, Landesamt Solingen, no. 525.

D. *LASSALLE-FEIER* AND *SOMMERFESTE* (LASSALLE AND SUMMER FESTIVALS)

Lassalle-Feier Ohligs. (1895). "Programm zur Lassalle-Feier Ohligs 1895." In: Staatsarchiv Düsseldorf, Landesamt Solingen, no. 519.

Lassalle-Feier Solingen. (1896). "Programm zur Lassalle-Feier 1896." In: Staatsarchiv Düsseldorf, Landesamt Solingen, no. 519.

Lassalle-Feier Solingen. (1897). "Lassalle-Feier 1897." In: Staatsarchiv Düsseldorf, Landesamt Solingen, no. 525.

Sommerfest Einsiedel. (1890). Reprinted in Göhre, *Drei Monate Fabrikarbeiter,* pp. 98–100.

Sommerfest Solingen. (1895). "Sommerfest der Sozialdemokratischen Partei des Kreises Solingen. Programm." In: Staatsarchiv Düsseldorf, Landesamt Solingen, no. 519.

Sommerfest Solingen. (1900). "Programm zum Sommerfest 1900 der sozialdemokratischen Partei des Kreises Solingen. Abgehalten Sonntag, den 5. August 1900 in sämmtlichen Lokalitäten und Gartenanlagen des Itterthaler Volksgarten zu Ober-Itter bei Wald." In: Staatsarchiv Düsseldorf, Landesamt Solingen, no. 525.

E. MISCELLANEOUS FESTIVALS

Herbstfeier. Berlin (ca. 1912). "Herbstfeier einer Gewerkschaft in Berlin." Zentralbildungsausschuss der Sozialdemokratischen Partei Deutschlands, *Winke und Ratschläge, Winterprogramm 1912/13* (Berlin: Vorwärts, [1912]); two programs, pp. 32–33, 34.

Märzfeier. Chemnitz (1874). In: Kaden, *Arbeitersängerbewegung im Gau Chemnitz*, p. 279.

Märzfeier. Dresden (1876). "Programm zur Gedächtnisfeier zur Erinnerung an die Volksbewegung von 1848 und 1871." Reprinted in Knilli and Münchow, *Frühes deutsches Arbeitertheater*, pp. 166–67.

Schwimmfest. Berlin (July 1901–July 1911). Programs for seventeen festivals of workers' swimmers from Berlin and the immediate vicinity. (All copies are housed in the Archiv der sozialen Demokratie.)

Schwimm-Fest. Hamburg. (1911). Arbeiter-Schwimm-Verein für Hamburg-Altona u. Umgegend, "Programm zum Lokalen Volkstümlichen Vereins-Schau-Schwimmen am Sonntag, den 20. August 1911." In: Staatsarchiv Hamburg, Politische Polizei, S16940.

Sportfest. Brunswick (1914). Arbeiter-Sportfest. Sonntag, den 5. Juli, Sonnabend, den 11. Juli, Sonntag, den 12. Juli, Sonntag, den 19. Juli [1914] (Brunswick, [1914]). In: Archiv der sozialen Demokratie.

Stiftungsfest. Berlin (1872). "Stiftungsfest. Sonnabend, den 10. August 1872." Allgemeiner deutscher Arbeiter-Verein. Reprinted in Knilli and Münchow, *Frühes deutsches Arbeitertheater*, pp. 156–57.

Stiftungs-Fest. Leipzig (1904). Arbeiterverein Leipzig. "XXV. Stiftungs-Fest im Etablissement Sanssouci, Sonnabend, den 20. Februar 1904." In: Arbeiterliedarchiv.

Stiftungsfest. Berlin (ca. 1912). "Künstlerischer Unterhaltungsabend und Stiftungsfest eines sozialdemokratischen Vereins in einem Vororte Berlins." In: Zentralbildungsausschuss der Sozialdemokratischen Partei Deutschlands, *Winke und Ratschläge. Winterprogramm 1912/13* (Berlin, [1912]), pp. 33–34.

APPENDIX B
Sample Festival Programs[a]

I. PROGRAM FOR MAY DAY FESTIVAL, SOLINGEN, 1893[b]

MAIFEIER 1893
SOLINGEN
Am Sonntag, den 7. Mai, Nachmittags 4 Uhr
[On Sunday, May 7, afternoon, at 4 P.M.]
in den prachtvollen Anlagen und Sälen des Herrn F. W. Bungards,
Grünwald
[in the lovely gardens and halls of Mr. F. W. Bungards,
Grünwald.]

I. Theil
[Part I]

1. "Jubelfestmarsch" v. Latann (Sol. Feuerwehr-Kapelle Abth.
   I.)[c]
   ["Jubilation Festival March" by Latann (Solingen Fire Bri-
   gade Band, Section I)]

---

[a]The information on composers in the notes is drawn from the biographical en-
tries in the following: Ewens, *Lexikon des Chorwesens;* Friedrich Herzfeld, *Ull-
stein Lexikon der Musik* (Frankfurt am Main, Berlin, Vienna 1965); and Oscar
Thompson (ed.), *The International Cyclopedia of Music and Musicians* (London,
New York, Toronto, 1975).
[b]In: Staatsarchiv Düsseldorf, Landesamt Solingen, no. 519.
[c]Karl Latann (1840–88). As a military bandmaster in Wilhelmshaven for many
years, he composed numerous marches and dances.

2. Ouvertüre zum "Volksfest" von Carl (Sol. Feuerwehr-
   Kapelle Abth. I)
   [Overture to "People's Festival" by Carl (Solingen Fire Bri-
   gade Band, Section I)]
3. "Seid gegrüsst" von Kohlmann (M.-G.-V. "Eintracht"-Merscheid.)
   ["Greetings" by Kohlmann (Male Singing Society "Concord" of Merscheid.)]
4. "Der Rheinenthusiast." (Tenorsolo)
   ["The Rhine Enthusiast." (Tenor solo)]
5. Aria aus *Lucia v. Lammermoor*. (Orchester)
   [Aria from *Lucia di Lammermoor*. (Orchestra)]
6. "Arbeitermarseillaise." (Vorwärts-Wald)
   ["Workers' Marseillaise." (Onward [Singing Society] of
   Wald)]
7. "Wenn hoch in den Wipfeln" von Fischer (Freiheit-Solingen)
   ["Up High in the Treetops" by Fischer (Freedom [Singing
   Society] of Solingen)]

****

8. PRESSPROZESSE
oder
DIE TOCHTER DES STAATSANWALTS
Schwank in 2 Aufzügen von Max Kegel[d]
Personen:

Felsenstein, Red. der soz.	Klara, seine Tochter
Arbeiter-Zeitung "Blitz"	Pietsch ⎱ Polizisten
Merkur, Expedient	Lehmann ⎰
Wolfskopf, Staatsanwalt	Setzerlehrling

Ort der Handlung: Eine bedeutende Provinzstadt.

---

8. THE NEWSPAPER TRIAL
or
THE DAUGHTER OF THE STATE ATTORNEY
Farce in 2 Acts by Max Kegel
Characters:

Felsenstein, editor of the	Klara, his daughter
socialist workers' paper	

[d]See pp. 141–42, 157–58.

  Lightning   Pietsch, policeman
 Merkur, dispatching clerk Lehmann, policeman
 Wolfskopf, state attorney Apprentice typesetter
   Location: an important provincial city

   ****

 9. "Zum Maienfest" (Chorlied) (Text umstehend)[c]
  ["On the May Festival" (Choir song) (Text on other side)]

II. Theil

 10. "Vorstädter-Walzer" v. Rixner[f] (Orchester)
  ["Suburban Waltzes" by Rixner (Orchestra)]
 11. "Festrede"
  ["Festival Speech"]
 12. "Sozialistenmarsch" von Gramm.[g] (Freiheit-Solingen u. Vorwärts-Wald)
  ["Socialist March" by Gramm (Freedom [Singing Society] of Solingen and Onward [Singing Society] of Wald)]
 13. "Achtstunden-Couplet"
  ["Eight-Hour Couplet"]
 14. "Wiener Schwalbenmarsch" von Schögel (Orchester)
  ["Viennese Swallows March" by Schögel (Orchestra)]
 15. "Fritzchens erste Liebe" von Kron[h] (Vorwärts-Wald)
  ["Little Fritz's First Love" by Kron (Onward [Singing Society] of Wald)]
 16. "Der alte und neue Kurs" (Couplet)
  ["The Old and the New Course" (Couplet)]
 17. "Der Geister Erwachen" von Heinr. Riever (Freiheit-Solingen)

  ["The Spirits Awaken" by Heinrich Riever (Freedom [Singing Society] of Solingen)]

[c]The title is printed incorrectly on the festival program, but on the reverse side it carries the proper name, "Zum Maifest." It is to be sung to the melody of "Deutschland, Deutschland über alles" and the text embodies the major demands of the Second International as first formulated at the conference in Paris in 1889. The author of the lyrics is not identified.
[f]Joseph Rixner (1825–1913), composer of songs and choral music.
[g]See pp. 118–19. Except for the fact that Carl Gramm composed several melodies for Social Democratic songs, little is known about his life.
[h]Louis Kron (1842–1907). His humorous pieces for male choirs were very popular at the end of the nineteenth century.
[i]The correct form of his name is apparently Bela Keler, which itself is a pseudonym for Adalbert von Keller (1820–82), a composer of popular light music. His pieces appear on numerous programs of workers' festivals.

18. "Lustspiel-Ouvertüre" von Keler-Béla[j] (Orchester)
    ["Comedy Overture" by Keler-Béla (Orchestra)]
19. "Es hapert wo!" (Couplet)
    ["It Goes Badly!" (Couplet)]

III. Theil

20. "Dem schönen Heil." Lied von Neidhardt[j] (Orchester)
    ["To the Life Beautiful." Song by Neidhardt (Orchestra)]
21. "Frei der Sang, frei das Wandern" v. Hunger[k] (Eintracht-Merscheid.)
    ["Free the Song, Free the Wandering" by Hunger (Concord [Singing Society] of Merscheid)]
22. "Am Rhein." (Tenor-Solo.)
    ["On the Rhine" (Tenor solo)]
23. "Vermischte Nachrichten." Potpourri von Kiesler. (Orchester)
    ["Miscellaneous Reports." Potpourri by Kiesler. (Orchestra)]
24. "Der letzte Generalmarsch" v. Müller (Vorwärts-Wald)
    ["The Last General March" by Müller (Onward [Singing Society] of Wald)]
25. "Zwei Herzen und ein Schlag." Polka für 2 Trommler (Orchester)
    ["Two Hearts and One Beat." Polka for 2 drummers (Orchestra)]
26. "Die 3-Gläser" v. Fischer (Freiheit-Solingen)
    ["The 3 Glasses" by Fischer (Freedom [Singing Society] of Solingen)]
27. "Die schöne Helena." Quadrille v. Strauss (Orchester)
    ["Beautiful Helen." Quadrille by Strauss (Orchestra)]
28. "Lebendes Bild"
    ["Tableau Vivant"]

[j]Probably Karl Neidhardt (b. 1872), a hornist in the orchestra in Sondershausen and composer of choral and orchestral music.
[k]Probably Karl Hunger (1863–1906), who wrote music for male choirs and himself directed choirs in different cities. See Ewens, *Lexikon des Chorwesens*, p. 120.

II. PROGRAM FOR MAY DAY FESTIVAL, AACHEN, 1903[a]
SOZIALDEMOKRATISCHER VEREIN
MAI-FEIER 1903
PROGRAMM

Abtheilung I
[*Part I*]
Vokal- und Instrumental-Concert
[Vocal and Instrumental Concert]

Abtheilung II
[*Part II*]

1. Eröffnungsmarsch
   [Opening march]
2. "Frühlingsruf"   (vorgetr.   vom   Arbeiter-Gesang-Verein
   "Lyra")[b]
   ["The Call of Spring" (presented by the Workers' Singing Soci-
   ety "Lyra")]
3. "Gruss an den ersten Mai" (Solo-Quartett "Lyra")
   ["Greetings to the First of May" (Solo Quartet "Lyra")]
4. "Das höchste Gut" (Solo-Vortrag)
   ["The Highest Good" (Solo presentation)]
5. Musik-Piece
   [Music piece]
6. "Gruss an den Mai" (vorgetr. vom Arbeiter-Gesang-Verein
   "Lyra")
   ["Greetings to May" (presented by the Workers' Singing So-
   ciety "Lyra")]
7. Allgemeines Lied[c]
   [General singing]
8. Theaterstück
   [Play]

[a]Reprinted from Klöcker, *Die Sozialdemokratie im Regierungsbezirk Aachen,* p.
313.
[b]This is probably the "Frühlingsruf" by Andreas Scheu that appears in *Der freie
Turner,* 9th ed. (Leipzig, 1907), pp. 86–87.
[c]On separate pages the program included the lyrics of two popular songs of the
labor movement: August Geib's "Im schönen Mai, im jungen Mai," sung to the
melody of "Die Wacht am Rhein" (see pp. 109, 118), and Ernst Klaar's "Ihr
Männer all'," sung to the melody of the "Marseillaise" and popularly known as
the "Achtstunden-Marseillaise" (see pp. 110, 121).

Mai-Feier
Soziales Drama in 3 Aufzügen von Ernst Däumig[d]
Personen:

1. Martha Neuberg. 2. Die Mutter Martha's. 3. Gustav Neuberg, Bäckermeister, Martha's Bruder. 4. Fritz Albers, Redakteur. 5. Dr. Richard Bär, Arzt, Freund von Fritz Albers. 6. Schulze. 7. Gebbardt, Arbeiter-Vorstandsmitgl. des Gewerkschaftskartell. 8. Arbeiter. Zeit: Gegenwart.
    1. und 2. Aufzug: Am Abend vor dem 1. Mai.—3. Aufzug: Am 1. Mai. *Während dem Theaterstück bleiben die Thüren Geschlossen.*

Pause

[*May Day Festival*
Social Drama in 3 Acts by Ernst Däumig
Characters:
1. Martha Neuberg. 2. Martha's mother. 2. Gustav Neuberg, Master Baker, Martha's brother. 4. Fritz Albers, editor. 5. Dr. Richard Bär, doctor, friend of Fritz Albers. 6. Village Mayor. 7. Gebbardt, worker, member of the Executive Committee of the Trade Union Cartel. 8. Workers. Time: The Present
Acts 1 and 2: On the eve of May 1.—Act 3: On May 1. *The doors remain closed during the presentation of the play.*
[Intermission]

Abtheilung III
[*Part III*]

1. Musik-Piece
   [Music piece]
2. "Leiter-Pyramide" des Arbeiter-Turn-Verein
   ["Ladder Pyramid" by the Workers' Gymnastic Club]
3. "Bete und arbeite"[e] (vorgetr. vom Arbeiter-Gesang-Verein "Lyra")
   ["Work and Pray" (presented by the Workers' Singing Society "Lyra")]

[d]See p. 141, and especially Trempenau, *Frühe sozialdemokratische und sozialistische Arbeiterdramatik*, pp. 115–17.
[e]By Georg Herwegh; see pp. 109, 116–17.

4. "S'ist alles nur Komödie" (Vortrag)
   ["It's All Only a Comedy" (recitation)]
5. "Die rauhe Faust" (Solo-Vortrag)
   ["The Clenched Fist" (Solo presentation)]
6. "Photograph und Bauer" (Komisches Duett)
   ["Photographer and Peasant" (Comical duet)]
7. Allgemeines Lied
   [General singing]
8. "Das biedere Herz" (Solo-Vortrag)
   ["The Upright Heart" (Solo presentation)]
9. *August Kommt* (Ensemble-Scene)
   [*August Comes* (Ensemble scene)]

III. PROGRAM FOR SINGERS' FESTIVAL, HAMBURG, 1905[a]

*ARBEITER-SÄNGERBUND VON HAMBURG-ALTONA UND
UMGEGEND
PROGRAMM ZUM XVIII. BUNDES-SÄNGERFEST*
—Sonntag, den 6. August 1905—
Chor- und Orchester-Dirigent: Herr H. Hansen-Tebel

1. "In Treue fest!" Grosser Festmarsch   Machts[b]
   ["Faithful and Firm!" Great festival march]
2. Fest-Ouvertüre   Lortzing[c]
   [Festival overture]
           Kanonenschlag
           [Canon blast]
3. "Freiheitschor" (Grosser Chor)   Mozart
   ["Freedom Chorus" (Large choir)]
4. "Mondnacht auf der Alster," Walzer   Fétras[d]
   ["Moonlit Night on the Alster," Waltzes]
5. "Frühlingswanderlied"   H. Bohl
   Erster kl. Chor. Dirigent Herr A. Dick. Mitwirkende:

[a]In: Staatsarchiv Hamburg, Politische Polizei, S2338. See pp. 93–94 for the report by the frustrated music critic in Hamburg who tried to listen to this program.
[b]Either Karl Machts (1846–1903), music director in Hanover and later Jena, or Ludwig Machts (1850–1904) of Jena, where he was a musical director and taught school.
[c]Albert Lortzing (1801–51), famous German composer, especially for his opera *Zar und Zimmermann*.
[d]See p. 248, n. 41.

Troubadour, Loreley, Frei von 1891, Lassallea-Ottensen, Former-Liedertafel, Viola-Ottensen, Gerber-Gesangverein von 1885, Egalité-Eimsbüttel, Eimsbütteler Männer-Gesangverein, Glasmacher-Ottensen, Maurerarbeitsleute-Altona, Hafenarbeiter-Altona, Quartett Widerhall, Freiheit-Langenfelde, Freiheitsklänge-Altona, Vorwärts-Langenlohe-Elmshorn, Vorwärts-Pinneberg, Humor-Rellingen, Frohsinn-Barmstedt, Arbeiter-Gesangverein Eintracht-Elmshorn.

["Tramping Song of Spring"
First-class choir[e]: Director Mr. A. Dick. Participating [choirs]: Troubador, Loreley, Free of 1891, Lassallea of Ottensen, Molders' Singing Circle, Viola of Ottensen, Tanners' Singing Society of 1885, Equality of Eimsbüttel, The Eimsbüttel Male Singing Society, Glass Makers of Ottensen, Workers in Stone of Altona, Dockworkers of Altona, The Echo Quartet, Freedom of Langenfelde, The Tones of Freedom of Altona, Onward of Langenlohe and Elmshorn, Onward of Pinneberg, Humor of Rellingen, Cheerfulness of Barmstedt, The Workers' Singing Society "Concord" of Elmshorn.]

6. "Grosse Fantasie" aus der Oper "Lohengrin"   R. Wagner
   ["Great Fantasy" from the opera *Lohengrin*]
                    Kanonenschlag
                    [Canon blast]
7. "Dem Lenz entgegen" (Grosser Chor)   G. A. Uthmann[f]
   ["Spring's Arrival" (Large choir)]
8. Ouvertüre zur Oper "Die Zigeunerin"   Balfe
   [Overture from the opera *The Gypsy Woman*]
9. "Vorwärts in die weite Welt"   Ed. Köllner[g]
   Zweiter kl. Chor. Dirigent Herr Johs. Kohfahl. Mitwirkende: Stradella, St. Pauli-Liederkranz von 1883, Norddeutsches Männerquartett von 1901, Morgenroth, Männer-Gesangverein Echo, Unter Uns v. 1884, Einigkeit v. 1890, Liedertafel der Kutscher von öffentl. Fuhrwesen, Liedertafel der Ewerführer.

[e]The five classes of choir do not necessarily represent a hierarchy of quality, but are based on some other principle for grouping various singing societies, perhaps their sizes.
[f]See pp. 96–97.
[g]Edmund Köllner (1839–91), singer, music teacher, and composer of choruses that were very popular at one time with German male choirs.

["Onward into the Wide World"
Second-class choir. Director M. Johs. Kohfahl. Participating [choirs]: Stradella, Saint Pauli Song Circle of 1883, North German Men's Quartet of 1901, Morning Glow, Male Singing Society Echo, Together of 1884, Unity of 1890, Song Circle of Coachmen in Public Transportation, Song Circle of Coastal Pilots.]

10. "Die beiden Grenadiere," Ballade (Baryton-Solo)
                                                    R. Schumann
["The Two Grenadiers," Ballad (Baritone solo)]

11. "Wie hab' ich sie geliebt"   F. Möhring[h]
Dritter kl. Chor. Dirigent Herr C. Schulz. Mitwirkende: Herwegh, Eiche von 1897, Liberté, Treue-Eilbeck, Freiheit von 1892, Sängerlust, Vorwärts (Hamburger Fortbildungsverein), Liedertafel der Kupferschmiede.
["Oh, How I Loved Her"
Third-class choir. Director Mr. C. Schulz. Participating (choirs): Herwegh, Oak of 1897, Liberty, Faithful of Eilbeck, Freedom of 1892, The Joy of Singing, Onward (Hamburg Continuing Educational Society), Singing Circle of the Coppersmiths]

12. "Stephanie-Gavotte"   Czibulka
["Stephanie Gavotte"]

13. "Lenzesmahnen"   C. H. Döring[i]
Fünfter Kl. Chor. Dirigent Herr A. Seybold. Mitwirkende: Eichenkranz-Alt-Rahlstedt, Männer-Gesangverein-Billwärder, Eintracht-Schiffbek, Hoffnung-Kirch-Steinbek, Unverdrossen-Bergedorf, Nieverzagt-Bergedorf, Eintracht-Sande, Bruderhand von 1899-Sande.
["Vernal Warnings"
Fifth-class choir. Director Mr. A. Seybold. Participating [choirs]: Oak Wreath of Alt-Rahlstedt, Male Singing Society of Billwärder, Concord of Schiffbek, Hope of Kirch-Steinbek, Unwearied of Bergedorf, Never Despondent of Bergedorf, Concord of Sande, Hand of Brotherhood of 1899 of Sande.]

14. "Sorgenlose Stunden," Potpourri   Stetefeld

[h]Ferdinand Möhring (1816–87), organist and music teacher in Neu-Ruppin who enjoyed great success as composer for male choirs in Germany. His music also appears on numerous programs of workers' festivals.
[i]Carl Heinrich Döring (1834–1916), teacher at the Dresden conservatory and composer of piano exercises and many popular pieces for German male choirs.

["Carefree Hours," Potpourri]
> Kanonenschlag
> [Canon blast]

15. a) "Aennchen von Tharau"
> Grosser Chor
   b) "Untreue"
   [a) "Annie of Tharau"
> Large choir
   b) "Unfaithful"]   Silcher[j]
16. "Die Schmiede im Walde," Tongemälde   Michaelis[k]
    ["The Smithies in the Woods," Tone poem]
17. "Auf der Eisenbahn," Galopp   André
    ["On the Train," Gallop]

****

—Montag, den 7. August 1905—

Chor- und Orchester-Dirigent: Herr H. Hansen-Tebel
[Choir and Orchestra Director: Mr. H. Hansen-Tebel]

1. "Krönungsmarsch" aus der Oper "Der Prophet."
> G. Meyerbeer
   ["Coronation March" from the opera *The Prophet*]
2. Ouvertüre zur Oper "Oberon"   C. M. v. Weber
   [Overture to the opera *Oberon*]
3. "Die Reveille," Charakterstück   Eilenberg[l]
   ["Reveille," Character piece]
4. "Fantasie" aus der Oper "Margarethe"   Gounod
   ["Fantasy" from the opera *Faust*]
5. "Ouvertüre zur Oper "Das Glöckchen des Eremiten"
> Maillart[m]
   ["Overture" to the opera *The Bells of the Hermits*]

[j]Friedrich Silcher (1789–1860), famous founder, in 1829, of the first singing circle (*Liedertafel*) in Germany and successful composer of vocal music.
[k]See p. 97.
[l]Richard Eilenberg (1848–1925), composer of entertainment music and for male choirs.
[m]Louis Maillart (1817–71), French opera composer whose greatest success was *Das Glöckchen des Eremiten* in 1856. The original title in French is *Les Dragons de Villars*.

6. "An der schönen blauen Donau," Walzer   J. Strauss
    ["On the beautiful blue Danube," Waltzes]
7. Vorspiel und Szenen a.d. 2. Akt der Oper "Der Evangeli-
    mann"   Kienzl[n]
    [Prelude and Scenes from the second act of the opera *The
    Apostle*]
8. Quadrille in militärischem Stil   Fétras
    [Quadrille in military style]
9. Ouvertüre zur Oper "Rienzi"   R. Wagner
    [Overture to the opera *Rienzi*]
10. Erinnerung an Wagners "Tannhäuser"   V. Hamm
    [Reminiscence of Wagner's *Tannhäuser*]
11. Grosse Fantasie aus der Oper "Der fliegende Holländer"
                                                    R. Wagner
    [Great Fantasy from the opera *The Flying Dutchman*]
12. "Einzug der Gäste auf der Wartburg," aus "Tannhäuser"
                                                    R. Wagner
    ["Entrance of the Guests into the Wartburg," from *Tann-
    häuser*]
                    Kanonenschlag
                    [Canon blast]
13. "Hymne an den Freiheitssang"   Ed. Köllner
    Grosser Chor mit Orchester
    ["Hymn to Freedom's Song"
    Large choir with orchestra]
14. Ouvertüre zu "Robespierre"   H. Litolff[o]
    [Overture to *Robespierre*]
15. "Frühlingszeit"   C. Wilhelm[p]
    Vierter kl. Chor. Dirigent Herr Th. Strobel. Mitwirkende:
    Oberon von 1891, Frisch auf von 1885, Uhlenhorster
    Männer-Gesangverein von 1892, Freundschaftsbund von
    1892, Quartett Freundschaft von 1896, Unverzagt-
    Gr.-Borstel, Beethoven, Helvetia, Hansa.
    "Spring Time"

[n]Wilhelm Kienzl (1857–1941), Austrian composer of some nine operas, of which
The Apostle (1894) was the most successful.
[o]Henry Charles Litolff (1818–1891), pianist and composer, born in London of an
Alsatian father and an English mother, wrote operas as well as music for piano
and orchestra. He founded a successful music publishing house.
[p]Probably Carl Wilhelm (1815–73), music director in Krefeld, who composed for
male choirs and is most renowned for "Die Wacht am Rhein," which he wrote in
1854.

[Fourth-class choir. Director Mr. Th. Strobel. Participating [choirs]: Oberon of 1891, Arise of 1885, The Uhlenhorst Male Singing Society of 1892, Friendship League of 1892, Friendship Quartet of 1896, Undismayed of Gr.-Borstel, Beethoven, Helvetia, Hanse.]

16. Grosse Fantasie aus der Oper "Carmen"   G. Bizet
    [Great Fantasy from the opera *Carmen*]
17. "Estudiantina," Walzer   Waldteufel[q]
    ["Estudiantina," Waltzes]
        Kanonenschlag
        [Canon blast]
18. "Sturmbeschwörung," Grosser Chor   Dürrner[r]
    ["Stormy Evocation," Large choir]
19. "Die Schmiede im Walde," Tongemälde   Michaelis
    ["The Smithies in the Woods," Tone poem]
20. "Bum-Bum," Galopp   Resch
    ["Bum-Bum," Gallop]

[q]Emil Waldteufel (1837–1915), pianist and composer, after 1865 Director of Court Balls under Napoleon III. "Estudiantina" was one of his popular dances for orchestra.
[r]Johannes Dürrner (1810–59), a student of Mendelssohn, who moved to Edinburgh in 1844 to become music director. He wrote much for male choirs; "Sturmbeschwörung" enjoyed great popularity among German male choirs.

IV. PROGRAM FOR GYMNASTIC FESTIVAL, HANAU, 1907[a]

KREISTURNFEST DES IX. KREISES DES
ARBEITER-TURNER-BUNDES
am 6., 7. und 8. Juli 1907 in Hanau am Main
PROGRAMM ZUM KOMMERS, 6. Juli 1907
7 Uhr Abends am Festplatz
KOMMERS
Musik: Offenbacher Musik-Verein "Vorwärts." Die Massen-Chöre werden von den Gesangvereinen Vorwärts, Tonblüte, Fröhlichkeit, Germania, Melomania-Hanau, Konkordia und Humor-Kesselstadt, sowie Männerchor-Langendiebach vorgetragen.
[Music: Offenbach Music Society "Onward." The mass choral music will be presented by the Singing Societies Onward, Tone

[a]In: Archiv der sozialen Demokratie, ATUS, Bonn-Bad Godesberg.

Blossoms, Happiness, Germania, Melomania of Hanau, Concordia and Humor of Kesselstadt, as well as the male choir of Langendiebach.]

1. Festmarsch mit Fanfaren und Kesselpauken   A. Müller
   [Festival march with fanfares and kettel drums]
2. Jubel-Ouvertüre   Bach
   [Jubilation overture]
3. "Die Fahne, die wir heut entfalten," Massenchor mit Orchester   Weinzierl[b]
   [The Flag That We Unfurl Today," mass choir with orchestra]
4. Übergabe der Fahne und Ansprachen
   [Presentation of the flag and speeches]
5. Stabübungen der Freien Turnerschaft Hanau a. M.
   [Exercises on the gymnastic bars by the Free Gymnasts of Hanau am Main]
6. "O Schutzgeist alles Schönen," Massenchor mit Orchesterbegleitung   Mozart
   ["Oh Spirit of Protection of All That Is Beautiful," mass choir with orchestral accompaniment]
7. Turnerische Aufführungen der Freien Turnerschaft Offenbach a. M.
   [Gymnastic display by the Free Gymnastic Club of Offenbach am Main]
8. "Maiglöckchen," Solo für Tubaphon   Seele
   ["Little May Bell," solo for tuba]
9. "Im Krug zum grünen Kranze"
   ["The Pitcher at the Green Wreath"]
10. "Heut ist heut," Massenchöre   Zöllner[c]
    ["Today Is Today," mass choirs]
11. Musikalisches Allerlei   H. Winter
    [Musical medley]
12. Massenpyramiden, gestellt von 200 Turnern und Turnerinnen
    [Mass pyramid formed by 200 male and female gymnasts]

[b]Max Weinzierl (1841–98), choir director and orchestra conductor in Mödling (near Vienna) and composer of music for male choirs. His music appears on many festival programs of the labor movement.
[c]I have been unable to determine which of the several prolific choral composers by the name Zöllner wrote this particular piece.

13. "Goldene Rosen," Walzer   Krug
    ["Golden Roses," Waltzes]
14. Reigenfahren des Arbeiter-Radfahrer-Vereins "Union" Ha-
    nau a. M.
    [Show riding by the Workers' Cyclist Club "Union" of Ha-
    nau am Main]
15. "Ein fideles Schützenfest." Grosses hum. Tongemälde mit
    25 Nummern von Finke.
    ["A Jolly Shooting Festival." Great humorous tone poem
    with 25 numbers by Finke.]

****

Sonntag, 7. Juli 1907, Vormittags 7 Uhr Vereins-Wertungsturnen
          von 11 ¼ Uhr an: FRÜHKONZERT
Nachmittags von ½ 3 Uhr an: Massenfreiübungen, Festrede, Schau-
  turnen der Kreisvereine, Damenturnen, Wettspiele, Konzert
  und Volksbelustigungen aller Art.
[Sunday, July 7, 1907, 7 A.M. Judging of gymnastic clubs.
          From 11:15 A.M.: EARLY CONCERT
Afternoon from 2:30 P.M.: Mass calisthenics, festival speech, exhibition displays by the gymnastic clubs of the district, female
  gymnastics, competitions, concert and popular pleasures of all
  kinds.]

****

Montag, 8. Juli 1907, Turnfahrt . . .
[Monday, July 8, 1907, gymnasts' excursion . . .]
Nachmittags 4 Uhr auf dem Festplatz
[Afternoon, 4 P.M., at the Festival Square]

GROSSES VOLKS-FEST

1. "Hie guet Brandenburg," Fanfaren Marsch   Henrion
   ["Hail, Good Brandenburg," Fanfare march]
2. Ouvertüre zur Operette "Frau Buna"   Linke
   [Overture to the operetta *Frau Buna*]
3. Reigenfahren des Arbeiter-Radfahrer-Vereins "Union."
   [Show riding by the Workers' Cycling Club "Union."]
4. Musikalische Rundschau, Potpourri
   [Musical panorama, Potpourri]
5. "Frei wie des Adlers mächtiges Gefieder"   Marschner[d]

["As Free as the Mighty Feathered Eagle"]
6. "Der flotte Trompeter," Polka-Solo   Rixner
   ["The Lively Trumpeter," Polka solo]
7. Turner, Aufführungen (Stabübungen)
   [Gymnastic displays on the bars]
8. "Romaneska"   Zikoff
   ["Romanesque"]
9. "O Wald, mit deinen duft'gen Zweigen"   Haeser
   ["O Forest, with your Fragrant Boughs"]
10. "Libella," Tongemälde   Kiesler
    ["Libella," Tone poem]
11. Pyramiden
    [Pyramids]
12. "Muss i'denn," Chor   Silcher
    ["Must I Then," choir]
13. Ein Prosit der Gemütlichkeit
    [Cheers to joyous fellowship]
    ABENDS 11 UHR GROSSES BRILLANT-FEUERWERK
    [EVENING, 11 p.m., A HUGE AND BRILLIANT FIRE-
    WORKS DISPLAY]

[d]This choral piece by Heinrich Marschner (1795–1861) remained a popular favorite among male choirs in Germany, although most of Marschner's instrumental music lost its appeal.

APPENDIX C
Educational Programs

1. AGE DISTRIBUTION OF MEMBERS: WORKERS' EDU-CATIONAL SCHOOL, BERLIN
2. TRADE UNION AND PARTY MEMBERSHIP: WORK-ERS' EDUCATIONAL SCHOOL, BERLIN
3. DISTRIBUTION BY GENDER IN COURSE ENROLL-MENTS: WORKERS' EDUCATIONAL SCHOOL, BERLIN
4. NUMBER OF ORGANIZATIONS WITH EDUCATIONAL PROGRAMS, 1907
5. OVERVIEW OF LOCAL EDUCATIONAL PROGRAMS IN THE LABOR MOVEMENT
6. LABOR MOVEMENT EXTENSION COURSES (*WANDER-KURSE*)
7. USER FREQUENCY IN SELECTED WORKERS' LIBRAR-IES

Table 1
Age Distribution of Members:
Workers' Educational School, Berlin[*]

Year	to 20 No.	to 20 %	20–30 No.	20–30 %	30–40 No.	30–40 %	40–50 No.	40–50 %	over 50 No.	over 50 %	Total
1898–99	34	8.9	264	68.9	75	19.6	8	2.1	2	0.5	383
1901–2	84	13.5	416	66.8	105	16.8	16	2.6	2	0.3	623
1907–8	143	8.5	1162	69.0	316	18.8	58	3.4	5	0.3	1684
1909–10	120	8.4	945	65.9	310	21.6	51	3.6	7	0.5	1433

[*]In each year there were a number of members who did not record their ages: in 1898–99, 76; in 1901–2, 71; in 1907–8, 336; and in 1909–10, 115.

Source: Arbeiter-Bildungsschule Berlin, *Jahres-Bericht,* for 1898–99, 1901–2, 1907–8, 1909–10.

Table 2
Trade Union and Party Membership:
Workers' Educational School, Berlin

	Total Membership	SPD Members	%	Trade Union Members	%	In SPD and in Trade Unions	%	Total Organized	%	Total Party	%	Total in Trade Unions	%	No Data Given	%
1898–99	459	19	4.1	171	37.3	116	25.3	306	66.7	135	29.4	287	62.5	153	33.3
1901–2	694	26	3.7	275	39.6	201	29.0	502	72.3	227	32.7	467	67.3	192	27.7
1907–8	2,020	40	2.0	534	26.4	1,072	53.1	1,646	81.5	1,112	55.1	1,606	79.5	374	18.5
1909–10	1,548	71	4.6	349	22.6	944	61.0	1,364	88.1	1,015	65.6	1,293	83.5	184	11.9

Source: Arbeiter-Bildungsschule Berlin, *Jahres-Bericht*, for 1898–99, 1901–2, 1907–8, 1909–10. The column "In SPD and in Trade Unions" includes only those who held dual membership and excludes the figures in the two columns to the left.

Table 3
Distribution by Gender in Course Enrollments°
Workers' Educational School, Berlin

Year	Women		Men		Total
	No.	%	No.	%	
1898–99	69	10.9	565	89.1	634
1901–2	124	12.1	904	87.9	1,028
1907–8	151	5.6	2,569	94.4	2,720
1909–10	200	7.6	2,447	92.4	2,647

°This table is based on enrollment in courses and not on membership data which are the basis for most of the other tables on the Berlin Workers' Educational School. The course enrollment totals are larger than the membership totals used in other tables.

Source: Arbeiter-Bildungsschule Berlin, *Jahres-Bericht,* for 1898–99, 1901–2, 1907–8, 1909–10.

Table 4
Number of Organizations with Educational
Programs, 1907°

Type of Organization	Yes	No	In Part
SPD Political Organizations	52	41	44
Trade Union Cartels	104	30	57
Feminist	17	4	5

°The table includes no information from 50 of the 404 reporting organizations. This omission is presumed to be the result of over-laps.

Source: "Das Ergebnis der Umfrage," 3. Vollmar Archive, IISH.

Table 5
Overview of Local Educational Programs in the Labor Movement

Year	Localities with Courses	Courses	Lectures	Enrollees
1909–10	151	288	—	32,816
1910–11	177	345	2,879	45,873
1911–12	127*	243	1,857	34,336
1912–13	215	420	2,510	44,146

*The drop for 1911–12 reflects the preoccupation with the election campaign of 1912.

Source: Protokolle of the congresses of the Sozialdemokratische Partei Deutschlands for 1910, 1911, 1912, 1913. Reports by the Zentralbildungsausschuss.

Table 6
Labor Movement Extension Courses (*Wanderkurse*)

	1907–8	1908–9	1909–10	1910–11	1911–12	1912–13
Number of Localities	29	57	115			
Number of Courses	44	57	128	122	128	206
Number of Lectures	323	419	682	733	654	941
Number of Participants	5,493	8,969	24,360	21,529	19,844	29,836
Female Participants	200	666	1,775	2,759	2,247	4,754
Distribution by Age:						
15–20	149		1,882	2,358	2,627	3,109
21–30	2,120		7,502	7,595	7,519	11,376
31–40	1,945		6,102	5,885	5,856	8,967
41–50	509		1,879	1,845	1,887	3,101
over 50	106		603	592	555	735
no data	864		6,392	3,254	1,380	2,868

Source: Protokolle of the congresses of the Sozialdemokratische Partei Deutschlands for 1908, 1909, 1910, 1911, 1912, 1913. Reports by the Zentralbildungsausschuss.

Table 7
User Frequency in Selected Workers' Libraries

	Year	Number in Organization	Number of Readers	Percentage
Bibliothek des Vereins der Buchdrucker				
(Leipzig)	1895			26
	1896			27
	1897			26.7
Buchdrucker-Gehilfen-Verein, Breslau	1895	395	180	45.6
	1897	430	205	47.7
Gutenberg-Verein, Stuttgart	1897–98	550	192	34.9
Vereinsbibliothek der Buchbinder,				
Hamburg	1898	297	125	42.1
Bibliothek der Metallarbeiter,				
Nürnberg	1898	2,000	170	8.5
Gewerkschaftsbibliotheken, Munich	1899	8,306	2,200	26.5
Zentralbibliothek, Hamburg	1902	30,043	691	2.3
	1903	29,939	988	3.3
Zentral-Arbeiterbibliothek, Bielefeld	1906	14,033	300	2.1
	1907	14,477	?	?
	1908	12,641	1,043	8.3
	1909	12,669	754	6.0
	1910	16,015	828	5.2
	1911	16,497	893	5.4
	1912	17,355	874	5.0
	1913	17,947	1,054	5.9
Vereinigte Bibliothek, Meissen:				
Buchdrucker	1910			25
Baugewerbe	1910			4
Handels- und Transportarbeiter	1910			< 4
Bibliothek des Holzarbeiterverbands,				
Berlin	1911	28,000	2,000	7.1
Zentralbibliothek, Bremerhaven	1911		835	10
Zentralbibliothek, Halle a. d. S.	1911		1,288	7–9
Zentralbibliothek, Bremen	1912–13	30,000	2,624	< 8.7

Source: Compiled from Pfannkuche, *Was liest der deutsche Arbeiter?*, pp. 19, 30, 31, 34, 42, 44–45; *Siebenter Bericht des Hamburger Gewerkschaftskartells und Vierter Bericht des Arbeitersekretariats Hamburg für das Geschäftsjahr 1903* (Hamburg, 1904), p. 27; *Der Bibliothekar* 3 (May 1911):271, (October 1911):343, and 4 (June 1912):449; 5 (October 1913):655; 6 (March 1914):715; and Wilhelm Nitschke, "Wie und nach welcher Richtung entwickelt sich das Lesebedürfnis der Arbeiterschaft?" *Sozialistische Monatshefte* 17, Part I (1913):366.

Notes

CHAPTER 1

1. Guenther Roth, *The Social Democrats in Imperial Germany. A Study in Working-Class Isolation and National Integration* (Totowa, N.J., 1963).
2. Serious doubts have been expressed about the appropriateness of the subculture concept for German Social Democracy by Gerhard A. Ritter, "Workers' Culture in Imperial Germany: Problems and Points of Departure for Research," *Journal of Contemporary History* 13 (1978):169, and, more recently and more extensively, by Richard J. Evans, "Introduction: The Sociological Interpretation of German Labour History," in Richard J. Evans (ed.), *The German Working Class, 1888–1933* (London and Totowa, N.J., 1982), pp. 18–30. My reservations were first developed in "Social Democratic Cultural Organizations in Imperial Germany," a paper presented at the American Historical Association Convention in December 1974.
3. I have drawn on M. Rainer Lepsius, "Parteiensystem und Sozialstruktur: zum Problem der Demokratisierung der deutschen Gesellschaft," in Wilhelm Abel et al. (eds.), *Wirtschaft, Geschichte und Wirtschaftsgeschichte. Festschrift zum 65. Geburtstag von Friedrich Lütge* (Stuttgart, 1966), pp. 371–93.
4. Roth, *The Social Democrats in Imperial Germany*, pp. 160–61.
5. Ibid., pp. 8, 49, 58, 167, 193–211, 249, 288, 290.
6. For example, Dieter Groh, *Negative Integration und revolutionärer Attentismus: Die deutsche Sozialdemokratie am Vorabend des Ersten Weltkrieges* (Frankfurt am Main, 1973).
7. Cf., for example, Mary Nolan, "The Socialist Movement in Düsseldorf, 1890–1914" (diss., Columbia University, 1975), chap. 6, pp. 25, 69. Nolan's dissertation, extensively revised, has appeared as *Social Democracy and Society. Working-class Radicalism in Düsseldorf, 1890–1920* (Cambridge, Eng., 1981). I have retained my references

to the dissertation because the revisions either rearranged or omitted some of the original text that happened to be especially relevant to my research. Also, Willi Breunig, *Soziale Verhältnisse der Arbeiterschaft und sozialistische Arbeiterbewegung in Ludwigshafen am Rhein, 1869–1919* (Ludwigshafen, 1976), p. 298.

8. Carl E. Schorske, *German Social Democracy, 1905–1917* (Cambridge, Mass., 1955), pp. 108–10.

9. I intentionally do not use *working-class culture* or *worker culture*, though some have applied these terms to the Social Democratic labor movement. These concepts have stimulated considerable debate and discussion from many points of view. Cf. Dieter Langewiesche, "Arbeiterkultur in Österreich: Aspekte, Tendenzen und Thesen," in Gerhard A. Ritter (ed.), *Arbeiterkultur* (Königstein/Ts., 1979), pp. 40–57; Wolf Lepenies, "Arbeiterkultur. Wissenschaftssoziologische Anmerkungen zur Konjunktur eines Begriffs," *Geschichte und Gesellschaft* 5 (1979):125–36; Sidney Pollard, "Englische Arbeiterkultur im Zeitalter der Industrialisierung," Ibid., pp. 150–66; Peter N. Stearns, "The Effort at Continuity in Working-Class Culture," *Journal of Modern History* 52 (December 1980):626–55; the essays by Chas Critcher and Richard Johnson in John Clarke et al. (eds.), *Working-Class Culture* (London, 1979), pp. 13–40, 41–71; and Klaus Tenfelde, "Anmerkungen zur Arbeiterkultur," in Wolfgang Ruppert (ed.), *Erinnerungsarbeit. Geschichte und demokratische Identität in Deutschland* (Opladen, 1982), pp. 107–34.

10. My exposition draws on Ralf Dahrendorf, *Class and Class Conflict in Industrial Society* (Stanford, Cal., 1959), pp. 157ff.; Donald N. Levine and Robert Cooley Angell, "Integration," in *International Encyclopedia of the Social Sciences* 7 (1968):372–86; and Werner S. Landecker, "Types of Integration and their Measurement," *American Journal of Sociology* 56 (January 1951):332–40.

11. Dieter Fricke, *Die deutsche Arbeiterbewegung 1869 bis 1914. Ein Handbuch über ihre Organisation und Tätigkeit im Klassenkampf* (Berlin, 1976), pp. 245, 526, 672.

12. Cf., for example, the collection of documentation to prove the threat by W. Ilgenstein, *Die Gedankenwelt der modernen Arbeiterjugend*, 4th ed. (Berlin, 1913).

13. See Ralf Dahrendorf's chapter on the "Faulted Nation" and his statement that "the society of imperial Germany was consistently determined by faults to such an extent that it must be described as volcanic," in *Society and Democracy in Germany* (New York, 1967), pp. 46–60, 51.

14. I am not disputing the reality of *Sammlungspolitik*, the attempt to join together all nonsocialist parties in a united front, but do contest the implication that attempts on the part of government and party

leaders reflected a basic social and cultural coherence throughout Imperial Germany.

15. These observations have been implicit (or explicit) in the work of a number of historians. The inadequacies of German political culture are at the heart of Fritz Stern's essay on "The Political Consequences of the Unpolitical German," reprinted in Stern, *The Failure of Illiberalism* (New York, 1972), pp. 3–25. Note also David Blackbourn's comment that "Wilhelmine Germany's economic dynamism contrasted strongly with its inability to develop a mature political and constitutional system," in "The Problem of Democratisation: German Catholics and the Role of the Centre Party," in Richard J. Evans (ed.), *Society and Politics in Wilhelmine Germany* (London, 1978), p. 160. Cf. also Geoff Eley's conclusions in *Reshaping the German Right* (New Haven, 1980), pp. 349–56.

16. This interpretation is suggested in part by Dahrendorf's effort to work out a "coercion theory of society," in *Class and Class Conflict*, pp. 162ff. My objective is not to arrive at a general theory of society—Dahrendorf's goal—but more modestly to find a formulation that allows one to generalize about Imperial Germany.

17. Christoph Klessmann, *Polnische Bergarbeiter im Ruhrgebiet, 1870–1945* (Göttingen, 1978), pp. 16–17, 59–60, 62–68, 187–89.

18. How the intensity of trade union conflict varied from time to time and place to place is succinctly summarized by Klaus Saul, "Zwischen Repression und Integration. Staat, Gewerkschaften und Arbeitskampf im kaiserlichen Deutschland 1884 bis 1914," in Klaus Tenfelde and Heinrich Volkmann (eds.), *Streik* (Munich, 1981), pp. 209–36.

19. Cf. Alex Hall, *Scandal, Sensation and Social Democracy* (Cambridge, Eng., 1977), pp. 24, 41–48; and "By Other Means: The Legal Struggle Against the SPD in Wilhelmine Germany, 1890–1900," *The Historical Journal* 17 (1974):365–86.

20. Klaus Saul, "Der Kampf um die Jugend zwischen Volksschule und Kaserne," *Militärgeschichtliche Mitteilungen* 1 (1971):99–100.

21. Ibid., pp. 106, 109, 113–15, 124–25.

22. Klaus Saul, *Staat, Industrie, Arbeiterbewegung im Kaiserreich* (Düsseldorf, 1974), esp. pp. 66–98, 188–394.

23. Stressed by Adelheid von Saldern, "Wilhelminische Gesellschaft und Arbeiterklasse: Emanzipations- und Integrationsprozesse im kulturellen und sozialen Bereich," *Internationale wissenschaftliche Korrespondenz* 13 (December 1977):469–505.

24. For example, Michael Grüttner, "Working-Class Crime and the Labour Movement: Pilfering in the Hamburg Docks, 1888–1923," in Evans (ed.), *The German Working Class, 1888–1933*, pp. 54–79, makes the fascinating, though not entirely persuasive, argument that petty thievery contributed not only to self-assertion but also to emancipation.

25. Jochen Loreck, *Wie man früher Sozialdemokrat wurde* (Bonn–Bad Godesberg, 1977), esp. pp. 247–54.
26. See chapter 7. In order to capture some of the atmosphere of Social Democratic discourse, I have retained the German term *bürgerlich,* especially when seeking to present a discussion from the perspective of participants within the world of the labor movement. The term is not part of my own analytical vocabulary because it is too broad and too rich in connotations, and for those reasons also it is nearly impossible to find an adequate English equivalent.

CHAPTER 2

1. James S. Roberts, "Wirtshaus und Politik in der deutschen Arbeiterbewegung," in Gerhard Huck (ed.), *Sozialgeschichte der Freizeit* (Wuppertal, 1980), pp. 123–39.
2. An overview of these organizations may be found in Hartmann Wunderer, *Arbeitervereine und Arbeiterparteien. Kultur- und Massenorganisationen in der Arbeiterbewegung (1890–1933)* (Frankfurt/New York, 1980), pp. 29–76; and in Adelheid von Saldern, "Wilhelminische Gesellschaft und Arbeiterklasse: Emanzipations- und Integrationsprozesse im kulturellen und sozialen Bereich," *Internationale wissenschaftliche Korrespondenz* 13 (December 1977):469–505.
3. Under the general heading "Die Entwicklung der Arbeiter-Sportvereine," the Social Democratic cultural supplement *Die neue Welt* ran the following series of articles in 1910: M. Labbé, "Die Arbeiter-Radfahrer-Vereine," no. 29, pp. 227–30; F. Locke, "Die Arbeiter-Rudersport-Vereine, no. 29, p. 230; Karl Liess, "Die Arbeiter-Segler," no. 30, p. 235; Fritz Wildung, "Die Arbeiter-Turner," no. 30, pp. 235–38; G. Zepmeisel, "Die Arbeiter-Schwimmer," no. 31, pp. 243–44; and Paul Strumpf, "Die Arbeiter-Athleten-Bund," no. 31, p. 244. These were followed in the same publication by Paul Kupfer, "Der Arbeitersängerbund und seine Bedeutung für die Arbeiterschaft," no. 22 (1911), pp. 171–72; and Erwin Hoselbarth, "Arbeiter-Wander-Vereine," no. 21 (1911), p. 164. Peter von Rüden, *Sozialdemokratisches Arbeitertheater (1848–1914)* (Frankfurt am Main,1973), pp. 82ff. and 176ff.; Siegfried Nestriepke, *Geschichte der Volksbühne in Berlin* (Berlin, 1930), pp. 152–54.
4. Herbert Schwartze, "Zur Geschichte der Arbeiter-Samariter-Bundes," in Kurt Kühn (ed.), *Ärzte an der Seite der Arbeiterklasse* (Berlin, DDR, 1973), pp. 38–59; Konrad Beisswanger, *50 Jahre Freidenkertum* (Nuremberg, [1930]); and Jochen-Christoph Kaiser, *Arbeiterbewegung und organisierte Religionskritik* (Stuttgart, 1981), pp. 81–125, for a more detailed discussion of the proletarian freethinkers' movement.
5. This typology is a modification of that presented by Charles K. War-

riner and Jane Emery Prather, "Four Types of Voluntary Associations," *Sociological Inquiry* 35 (Spring 1965):138–48. Other works on voluntary associations that have been especially helpful include: C. Wayne Gordon and Nicholas Babchuk, "A Typology of Voluntary Associations," *American Sociological Review* 24 (1959):22–29; Arthur P. Jacoby and Nicholas Babchuk, "Instrumental and Expressive Voluntary Associations," *Sociology and Social Research* 47 (July 1963):461–71; Arnold Rose, "Voluntary Associations in France," in his *Theory and Method in the Social Sciences* (Minneapolis, Minn., 1954), pp. 74–115; and Orvoell R. Gallagher, "Voluntary Associations in France," *Social Forces* 36 (December 1957):153–60.

6. Thomas Nipperdey, "Verein als soziale Struktur in Deutschland im späten 18. und frühen 19. Jahrhundert," in Hartmut Boockmann et al., *Geschichtswissenschaft und Vereinswesen im 19. Jahrhundert* (Göttingen, 1972), pp. 9–12, 17.

7. Wolfgang Meyer, *Das Vereinswesen der Stadt Nürnberg im 19. Jahrhundert* (Nuremberg, 1970), p. 266; Heinz Schmitt, *Das Vereinsleben der Stadt Weinheim an der Bergstrasse* (Weinheim a. d. B., 1963), p. 30.

8. Schmitt, *Weinheim*, pp. 223–24.

9. Nipperdey, "Verein," pp. 15, 18; Meyer, *Nürnberg*, pp. 69, 254; Hermann Freudenthal, *Vereine in Hamburg* (Hamburg, 1968), p. 26.

10. Schmitt, *Weinheim*, pp. 31, 107.

11. Victor Noack, *Der Deutsche Arbeiter-Sängerbund* (Berlin, 1911), pp. 75, 81. On the trend toward specialization, see Nipperdey, "Verein," pp. 23–26.

12. Rüden, *Arbeitertheater*, pp. 27–29.

13. Freudenthal, *Hamburg*, p. 197; Noack, *Arbeiter-Sängerbund* (1911), pp. 68, 74–75, 81; Wolfgang Schmierer, *Von der Arbeiterbildung zur Arbeiterpolitik. Die Anfänge der Arbeiterbewegung in Württemburg 1862/63—1878* (Hanover, 1970), p. 254; Werner Kaden, *Die Entwicklung der Arbeitersängerbewegung im Gau Chemnitz des Deutschen Arbeitersängerbundes von den Anfängen bis 1933* (Zwickau, 1966), pp. 51, 57.

14. In promoting socialist singing societies, Josef Scheu, the Austrian musician, argued for the artistic, ideological, and social advantages, in *Die Arbeiter-Gesangvereine und ihre Bedeutung für die sozialdemokratische Partei* (Dresden, n.d.). See also Walter Fillies, "Die Arbeitersängerbewegung. Ein Beitrag zur Klassengeschichte der Arbeiterschaft" (diss., University of Rostock, 1922), p. 47.

15. The earliest singing divisions in the 1860s drew heavily on musical material of the Deutsche Sängerbund (German Choral League). See Arno Kapp, *Vom Gesang der Handwerksgesellen zum ersten deutschen Arbeitergesangverein unter Bebel* (Halle [Saale], n.d.), pp. 26–30. On the repertory of German male choirs, see Otto Elben, *Der*

Volksthümliche deutsche Männergesang, 2nd. ed. (Tübingen, 1887), passim.

16. Cf. Schmierer, *Von der Arbeiterbildung zur Arbeiterpolitik,* p. 254; Rüden, *Arbeitertheater,* pp. 57–58; the imposition of the law retarded the emergence of the workers' gymnastic movement by a decade, according to Fritz Wildung, *Handbuch des Arbeiter-Turnerbundes* (Leipzig, 1911), p. 1; Noack, *Arbeiter-Sängerbund* (1911), pp. 44, 75, 81. See n. 27 for explanation concerning two editions of this work by Noack.

17. Kaden, *Arbeitersängerbewegung im Gau Chemnitz,* pp. 58–61; Arno Kapp, "Die politische Funktion der Arbeitersänger unter dem Sozialistengesetz (Ausnahmegesetz der Jahre 1878–1890)." (Typewritten manuscript, 42 pages, n.d.; copy in Arbeiterliedarchiv.)

18. The pattern is drawn from evidence in Noack, *Arbeiter-Sängerbund* (1911), pp. 68, 74, 75, 81, 83; Kaden, *Arbeitersängerbewegung im Gau Chemnitz,* pp. 60–61.

19. For example, the "Freundschaft-Sängerbund" in Weimar, as described by Kurt Thomas, *Arbeitergesang-Arbeitermusik* (Weimar, 1974), pp. 16–17.

20. Cf. Meyer, *Nürnberg,* pp. 27–32; Wildung, *Handbuch des Arbeiter-Turnerbundes,* pp. 128–30, 156, 164, 178, 197, 216, 236; "Vereinswesen," in *Allgemeine deutsche Real-Encyklopädie für die gebildeten Stände,* 15 vols. (Leipzig: Brockhaus, 1868), vol. 15, pp. 63–64.

21. Quoted in Kaden, *Arbeitersängerbewegung im Gau Chemnitz,* p. 98.

22. Ibid.

23. "Politics is excluded" was written into the *Statuten der Freien Turnerschaft an der Kieler Förde* (Kiel, 1904), p. 3, and the *Statut der "Freien Turnerschaft" in Fechenheim a. M.* (n.p., 1904), p. 3. On the heavy hand of the police during the 1890s, see Richard Kötzschke, *Geschichte des deutschen Männergesanges hauptsächlich des Vereinswesens* (Dresden, 1926), p. 212; and Alex Hall, "By other Means: The Legal Struggle against the SPD in Wilhelmine Germany 1890–1900," *The Historical Journal* 17 (1974):365–86. For the Cologne area there are police reports on the workers' gymnastic clubs in Günter Bers and Michael Klöcker, *Die sozialdemokratische Arbeiterbwegung im Kölner Raum 1890–1895* (Wentorf bei Hamburg, 1976), pp. 379–81, 415–19.

24. E. Loening and O. Loening, "Vereins- und Versammlungsfreiheit," *Handwörterbuch der Staatswissenschaften,* 8 vols. 4th ed. (Jena: Gustav Fischer, 1923–28), vol. 8, pp. 554–55.

25. Kurt Koszyk, "Die sozialdemokratische Arbeiterbewegung 1890–1914," in Jürgen Reulecke (ed.), *Arbeiterbewegung an Rhein und Ruhr* (Wuppertal, 1974), p. 167; Mary Nolan, "The Socialist Movement in Düsseldorf, 1890–1914," chap. 2, pp. 68–69.

26. Loening and Loening, "Vereins- und Versammlungsfreiheit," pp. 554–55.

27. Victor Noack, *Deutscher Arbeiter-Sängerbund. Entstehung, Kampf und Aufstieg* (Berlin, 1931), pp. 45–48, 53–54. This work, an extensive revision of the first edition of 1911, reached page proofs but was never published. I used one of the few extant copies of the 1931 version in the Arbeiterliedarchiv. Since my text includes material from both versions, I cite the year along with the title. Cf. also summary of various attempts against workers' athletic clubs, in Heinz Timmermann, "Geschichte und Struktur der Arbeitersportbewegung 1893–1933" (diss. in typescript, Marburg-Lahn, 1969), pp. 28–35.

28. Detailed account of the campaign in Klaus Saul, "Der Kampf um die Jugend zwischen Volksschule und Kaserne. Ein Beitrag zur 'Jugendpflege' im Wilhelminischen Reich 1890–1914," *Militärgeschichtliche Mitteilungen* 1 (1971):97–125. On the basis of extensive archival material, Saul has also analyzed the campaign of the state, parties, and employers against the free trade unions and the Social Democratic party in *Staat, Industrie, Arbeiterbewegung im Kaisserreich. Zur Innen- und Aussenpolitik des Wilhelminischen Deutschland 1903–1914* (Düsseldorf, 1974). A critical survey of the government's campaign appeared anonymously as "Der Jungdeutschlandbund," *Arbeiter-Schwimmerzeitung* 14 (November 1, 1913), pp. 81–83.

29. Cf. Gerhard A. Ritter and Klaus Tenfelde, "Der Durchbruch der Freien Gewerkschaften Deutschlands zur Massenbewegung im letzten Viertel des 19. Jahrhunderts," in Heinz Oskar Vetter (ed.), *Vom Sozialistengesetz zur Mitbestimmung* (Cologne, 1975), pp. 93–95; Schorske, *German Social Democracy,* pp. 118–22.

30. Noack, *Arbeiter-Sängerbewegung* (1911), pp. 14–18; Kaden, *Arbeitersängerbewegung im Gau Chemnitz,* pp. 78–83.

31. Horst Ueberhorst, *Frisch, frei, stark und treu. Die Arbeitersportbewegung in Deutschland 1893–1933* (Düsseldorf, 1973), pp. 18–23; Wildung, *Handbuch des Arbeiter-Turnerbundes,* pp. 11–17. Organizational matters were treated with deep seriousness, as illustrated by the debates at the regional conference of the Saxon gymnastic clubs in 1894: *Protokoll vom Kreisturntag des 4. Turnkreises (Sachsen) des Arbeiter-Turnerbundes Deutschlands, abgehalten am 14. und 15. Mai 1894* (Dresden, 1894), pp. 8–14.

32. Timmermann, "Geschichte und Struktur der Arbeitersportbewegung," p. 16; C.F., "Der Arbeiter-Radfahrerbund 'Solidarität,' " *Arbeiter-Sportfest* (Brunswick, 1914), pp. 13, 15; newspaper clippings from *Vorwärts*, March 22, 1908, and *Der Arbeiter-Radfahrer*, February 1, 1910 (Beilage), in Staatsarchiv Hamburg, Politische Polizei, S4316, Bd. 2.

33. G. Zepmeisel, "Die Arbeiter-Schwimmer," *Die neue Welt*, no. 31 (1910), pp. 243–44.

34. Ueberhorst, *Frisch, frei, stark und treu*, p. 111; Fritz Heine, "Die

Arbeitersportbewegung" (Typescript manuscript, in Archiv der sozialen Demokratie), pp. 3–6.

35. On the cyclists' enterprises, see M. Labbé, "Die Arbeiter-Radfahrer-Vereine," *Die neue Welt,* no. 29 (1910), pp. 227–30; and C.F., "Der Arbeiter-Radfahrerbund 'Solidarität,' " pp. 15–16. On the gymnastic and athletic federations, see Wildung, *Handbuch des Arbeiter-Turnerbundes,* pp. 369–93; clipping from *Vorwärts* (September 15, 1911), Staatsarchiv Hamburg, Politische Polizei, S138a.

36. Clippings (on cyclist federation) from *Hamburger Echo,* May 25, 1904, in Staatsarchiv Hamburg, Politische Polizei, S4316, Bd. 2; Wildung, *Handbuch des Arbeiter-Turnerbundes,* p. 25; clipping (on athletic association) from *Vorwärts,* September 15, 1911, in Staatsarchiv Hamburg, Politische Polizei, S13822. *Protokoll der 3. Generalversammlung des Deutschen Arbeiter-Sängerbundes* (Berlin, 1914), p. 10.

37. Freudenthal, *Hamburg,* pp. 423–24.

38. Ibid., pp. 424, 465.

39. Wolfgang Pahncke, "Traditionen der Rostocker Arbeiter-Turn- und Sportbewegung," *Wissenschaftliche Zeitschrift der Universität Rostock, Gesellschafts- und Sprachwissenschaftliche Reihe* 13 (1964):292. Karl Frey, prominent leader of the workers' gymnastic clubs, doubted in 1894 the wisdom of rapidly opening the clubs to women. *Protokoll vom Kreisturntag des 4. Turnkreises (Sachsen),* p. 22. Jean H. Quartaert points to a general reluctance on the part of male Social Democrats to accept full female participation, in *Reluctant Feminists in German Social Democracy, 1885–1917* (Princeton, N.J., 1979), pp. 153–60, 199–200.

40. Noack, *Arbeiter-Sängerbund* (1931), p. 85. On male hesitation concerning mixed choirs, Kaden, *Arbeitersängerbewegung im Gau Chemnitz,* p. 66.

41. The fact that workers' singing societies had established special women's choirs was stressed as a unique feature among German choral societies by Hans Staudinger, *Individuum und Gemeinschaft in der Kulturorganisation des Vereins* (Jena, 1913), p. 114.

42. Schmitt, *Weinheim,* pp. 31, 107; Heinrich Husmann, "Lebensform und ihr Wandel beim Arbeiter in Hamborn," *Rheinisch-Westfälische Zeitschrift für Volkskunde* 4 (1957):32.

43. Dieter Wuerth, "The Politics and Sociology of Organized Labor in a Middle-Sized German Town: Göppingen 1910–1919" (diss., Univ. of Wisconsin, 1974), pp. 85, 86–87.

44. Freudenthal, *Hamburg,* pp. 455–56, 460–63.

45. Arbeiter-Sängerbund vom Hamburg, Altona und Umgegend, "Statistisches Verzeichniss der Mitgliederschaft, Mai 1896." Staatsarchiv Hamburg, Politische Polizei, S2338, Bd. 2.

46. Noack, *Arbeiter-Sängerbund* (1911), p. 54; Kaden, *Arbeitersängerbewegung im Gau Chemnitz,* p. 290.

47. Clipping from *Hamburger Echo*, September 6, 1905, in Staatsarchiv Hamburg, Politische Polizei, S4316, Bd. 1; Noack, *Arbeiter-Sängerbund* (1911), pp. 35, 44; Kaden, *Arbeitersängerbewegung im Gau Chemnitz*, p. 108; Rüden, *Arbeitertheater*, p. 183.

48. Hans-Joachim Schäfers, *Zur sozialistischen Arbeiterbildung in Leipzig 1890 bis 1914* (Leipzig, 1961), p. 72; police report, dated May 22, 1894, in Staatsarchiv Hamburg, Politische Polizei, S4316, Bd. 1; Wuerth, "Göppingen," pp. 189–90.

49. Wuerth, "Göppingen," pp. 181–83; Marie Bernays, "Berufswahl und Berufsschicksal des modernen Industriearbeiters," *Archiv für Sozialwissenschaft und Sozialpolitik* 35 (1912):127.

50. Hans Schuster, *Arbeiterturner im Kampf um die Jugend. Zur Geschichte des revolutionären Arbeitersports 1893–1914* (Berlin, DDR, 1962), p. 31.

51. Cf. W. Troeltsch and P. Hirschfeld, *Die deutschen Sozialdemokratischen Gewerkschaften* (Berlin, 1905), pp. 11–12; Otto Hommer, *Die Entwicklung und Tätigkeit des Deutschen Metallarbeiterverbandes* (Berlin, 1912), pp. 55–56; Schmierer, *Von der Arbeiterbildung zur Arbeiterpolitik*, p. 60; Staudinger, *Individuum und Gemeinschaft*, p. 119.

52. Timmermann, "Geschichte und Struktur der Arbeitersportbewegung," pp. 31–32; Noack, *Arbeiter-Sängerbund* (1931), pp. 45–48, 53–54; Saul, "Der Kampf um die Jugend zwischen Volksschule und Kaserne," p. 105.

53. Evidence on founding clubs as satellites in Wildung, *Handbuch des Arbeiter-Turnerbundes*, pp. 14, 256–57, 282; Schuster, *Arbeiterturner im Kampf um die Jugend*, p. 19; Noack, *Arbeiter-Sängerbund* (1911), pp. 41, 44–45, 49, 68, 74–75; Kaden, *Arbeitersängerbewegung im Gau Chemnitz*, pp. 52–53, 57.

54. Noack, *Arbeiter-Sängerbund* (1911), pp. 37–38, 40, 63; Wildung, *Handbuch des Arbeiter-Turnerbundes*, pp. 152, 155–56, 167–68; Ueberhorst, *Frisch, frei, stark und treu*, p. 24; Meyer, *Nürnberg*, pp. 159–60.

55. Staudinger, *Individuum und Gemeinschaft*, pp. 113–14.

56. Noack, *Arbeiter-Sängerbund* (1911), p. 47; Wildung, *Handbuch des Arbeiter-Turnerbundes*, pp. 181–82, 196, 200, 253–54; report on a Stuttgart club, in *Arbeiter-Turn-Zeitung*, February 15, 1897, p. 84 (hereafter cited as *ATZ*); *25 Jahre Arbeiter-Samariter-Bund E.V. Kolonne Hamburg 1907–1932* (n.p., n.d.), p. 5; Schwartze, "Zur Geschichte des Arbeiter-Samariter-Bundes," pp. 38–39.

57. "Das Schwimmen" (n.s.), *Arbeiter-Sportfest*, p. 17.

58. See sampling of complaints and explanations in Noack, *Arbeiter-Sängerbund* (1911), p. 74 and passim; Ueberhorst, *Frisch, frei, stark und treu*, pp. 23, 25; "Partei und Deutsche Turnerschaft," *ATZ*, August 24, 1913; "Singende Proletarier," (by "t"), *Arbeiter-*

Sänger-Zeitung, December 1907, p. 3; Schuster, *Arbeiterturner im Kampf um die Jugend,* p. 15; clippings in Staatsarchiv Hamburg, Politische Polizei, S4316, Bd. 1 (*Hamburger Echo,* June 21, 1896, on workers' cycling clubs), and Bd. 2 (*Hamburger Echo,* December 29, 1905, for statement by Karl Frey).

59. Report by "K. K." in *ATZ,* October 15, 1908, p. 314.
60. Schäfers, *Zur sozialistischen Arbeiterbildung,* p. 26; Rüden, *Arbeiter-theater,* pp. 98–100; Noack, *Arbeiter-Sängerbund* (1911), p. 5.
61. For Düsseldorf, Nolan stresses the cooperative relationship between party and trade unions on the one side and the clubs on the other. Referring specifically to educational programs, singing societies, theater societies, athletic clubs, and consumer cooperatives, she says that "the Socialists viewed all of these institutions . . . as integral aspects of the movement." Nolan, "The Socialist Movement in Düsseldorf, 1890–1914," chap. 6, p. 25.
62. Scheu, *Die Arbeiter-Gesangvereine,* pp. 13–14; Noack, *Arbeiter-Sängerbund,* pp. 11, 78–79.
63. Vernon L. Lidtke, "Socialism and Naturalism in Germany," *American Historical Review* 79 (February 1974):14–37.
64. Cf. "Protokoll über die Verhandlungen des IV. Bundes-Turntages am 21. u. 22. Mai 1899 in Nürnberg," *ATZ,* July 1, 1899, p. 102; M. Blumtritt, "Arbeiter-Turnvereine und Gewerkschaften," *ATZ,* October 1, 1900 (Beilage), 133.
65. Wildung, *Handbuch des Arbeiter-Turnerbundes,* p. 60; "Die Arbeiter-Turnerbund, eine 'politische' Organisation," *ATZ,* October 15, 1908, pp. 312–13.
66. Ueberhorst, *Frisch, frei, stark und treu,* pp. 113, 296; clipping from *Vorwärts,* July 5, 1903, Staatsarchiv Hamburg, Politische Polizei, S4316, Bd. 2, emphasized the contribution of cyclists in the election.
67. Konrad Beisswanger, "Sozialdemokratie und Freidenkertum," *Der Atheist* 3 (October 20, 1907):333–34. The statutes of the proletarian freethinkers' organization specifically stated that anyone could join who "Stands on the ground of the modern labor movement . . ." *Statut des Zentral-Verbandes der proletarischen Freidenker Deutschlands* (Nuremberg, n.d.), p. 4. Cf. the following elaborations on the argument that the Proletarian Freethinkers should be recognized as official spokesmen of the labor movement: Beisswanger, *50 Jahre Freidenkertum,* pp. 17–19; Beisswanger, "Freidenkertum und Arbeiterbewegung," *Der Atheist* 4 (January 12, 1908):14; "50 Jahre Freidenkerverein," *Der Atheist* 7 (October 15, 1911):315; Karl Wilh. Schmidt, "Freidenkertum und Arbeiterbewegung," *Der Atheist* 2 (April 22, 1906):125–26.
68. A concerted effort was made to try to persuade the Social Democratic party to drop its principle that "religion is a private matter" and to take up the fight against Christianity, especially against church

membership. That is the theme of the following unsigned articles in *Der Atheist:* "Religion ist nicht Privatsache!" 1 (March 19, 1905):87–88; "Erklärung der Religion zur Privatsache," 6 (September 18, 1910):298–99, and (October 2, 1910):317–18; " 'Religion ist Privatsache'—ein Schwindel," 7 (December 3, 1911):370–71; and "Sozialdemokratie, Kirche und Religion," 8 (October 27, 1912):321–23.

69. Cf. Vernon L. Lidtke, "August Bebel and German Social Democracy's Relation to the Christian Churches," *Journal of the History of Ideas* 27 (April–June 1966):245–64.

CHAPTER 3

1. Arbeiter-Bildungsschule Berlin, annual report for 1898–99 (title page missing), p. 10, and *Jahres-Bericht über die Tätigkeit vom 1. Oktober 1909 bis 30. September 1910* (Berlin, 1910), p. 18.
2. Kaden, *Arbeitersängerbewegung im Gau Chemnitz*, p. 107.
3. Compiled from documents and newspaper clippings in Staatsarchiv Hamburg, Politische Polizei, S16940.
4. Wildung, *Handbuch des Arbeiter-Turnerbundes*, p. 162.
5. Reports on youth activities in Elberfeld-Barmen and Hanover in *Arbeiter-Jugend*, February 27, 1910, p. 67, and March 12, 1910, p. 83. Further reports for 1910 in *Arbeiter-Jugend:* from Bielefeld, February 26, 1910, p. 66; from Cologne, March 12, 1910, p. 83; from Kiel, March 25, 1910, pp. 99–100; from Sorau, April 23, 1910, p. 131; from Dresden, June 18, 1910, p. 194; from Lübeck, July 20, 1910, p. 243; and from Nuremberg, August 13, 1910, p. 250. In Hamburg, by 1910, there were twenty branches of the youth organization, each holding weekly meetings, discussion evenings, and supplied with a small collection of books. During the first quarter of 1910 these groups participated in the following activities (numbers in parenthesis are total attendance): 50 lectures (1,319); 21 visits to museums, etc. (446); 162 reading and discussion evenings (2,631); 94 events with indoor games (1,879); 112 events of outdoor games (3,631); 52 entertainment and parents' evenings (1,278); 62 meetings (1,855); 6 singing evenings (171); 53 outings (1,018). Reported in *Arbeiter-Jugend*, August 27, 1910, p. 275, by Rud. Lindau.
6. Freie Turnerschaft Hammerbrook-Rotenburgsort, *Mitgliedsbuch* (Hamburg, n.d.), pp. 14–15.
7. See, Arbeiter-Radfahrer-Verein "Vorwärts," *Mitgliedsbuch* (Hamburg [1890s]); and Arbeiter-Radfahrer-Verein, "Vorwärts," *Mitgliedsbuch* (Hamburg, n.d.).
8. Clipping from *Hamburger Echo*, March 24, 1910, Staatsarchiv Hamburg, Politische Polizei, S16940.
9. Wilhelm König, "Turnen und Kneipe," *ATZ*, May 15, 1902, pp. 109–10.

10. At least the official publication of the Workers' Chess Societies, the *Deutsche Arbeiter-Schachzeitung,* gives no indication in its reports for the years 1909–12 that frivolity and drinking were part of their milieu. The first article in the first issue stressed the value of chess as a counter to the "inconsequentiality and emptiness of beer-stool politics." Joseph Domberger, "Schach, ein Kulturfaktor," *Deutsche Arbeiter-Schachzeitung,* January 1, 1909, p. 5.

11. Due to police regulations, marching through a town was often impossible or highly regulated as in the case of an outing planned by the Freie Turnerschaft of Hammerbrook and Rotenburgsort (in Hamburg) when participants could march, but without "pipes and drums." Clipping from *Hamburger Echo,* September 2, 1902, Staatsarchiv Hamburg, Politische Polizei, S3784, Bd. 1.

12. Report signed by "D.V." in the *ATZ,* July 15, 1896, p. 4.

13. See n. 9.

14. Members of workers' associations were instructed by their Social Democratic leaders on how to engage in relaxation in ways that were beneficial to mind and body. Youth groups were given the following "rules" for Sunday hiking: go on foot, not by train; go all day, not just half a day; do not stop at taverns; do not go too far, thirty kilometers for a full day, fifteen for a half day; only beginners think that beer and spirits will increase energy; smoking is unsuited for hiking; singing is excellent, but not *Gassenhauer* (street songs). W. Wollmann, "Wander-Regeln," *Arbeiter-Jugend,* July 3, 1909, pp. 138–39.

15. Schmitt, *Weinheim,* p. 159.

16. Siegfried Reck, *Arbeiter nach der Arbeit* (Lahn-Giessen, 1977), p. 137, who cites the phrase from the collection by Adolf Levenstein.

17. Schmitt, *Weinheim,* p. 159; Wuerth, "Göppingen," p. 86.

18. These points are made in the fine article by James Roberts, "Wirtshaus und Politik in der deutschen Arbeiterbewegung," in Huck (ed.), *Sozialgeschichte der Freizeit,* pp. 123–39.

19. Paul Göhre, *Drei Monate Fabrikarbeiter und Handwerksbursche* (Leipzig, 1891), pp. 93–94.

20. Ernst Schuchardt, *Sechs Monate Arbeitshaus. Erlebnisse eines wandernden Arbeiters,* 2nd. ed. (Berlin, [1907]), p. 7.

21. Hermann Engst, "20 Jahre turnerischen Vereinslebens in Leipzig," *ATZ,* September 1, 1899, pp. 126–28; and Hermann Engst, "Rückblick auf die Entwicklung der freien Turnbewegung in Leipzig," *ATZ,* March 15, April 1, and April 15, 1911, pp. 97–98, 117–18, 135–36, resp.

22. A.B. "Ein Beitrag zur Geschichte aller Arbeiter-Turnvereine," *ATZ,* January 1, 1898 (Beilage), p. 10.

23. Arbeiter-Bildungsschule Berlin, report for 1898–99 (see n. 1), p. 1.

24. Zentralkommission für das Arbeiterbildungswesen von Hamburg-

Altona und Umgegend, *Geschäftsbericht für das Jahr 1911/12* (Hamburg, [1912]).

25. The organization Verband der freien Gast- und Schankwirte also published a newsletter, *Der freie Gastwirt*, printed in editions of 11,000 copies by 1913. Fricke, *Die deutsche Arbeiterbewegung 1869 bis 1914*, p. 461.

26. Wildung, *Handbuch des Arbeiter-Turnerbundes*, pp. 216–17, 291.

27. Ibid., p. 100; Pahncke, "Traditionen der Rostocker Arbeiter-Turn- und Sportbewegung," p. 291; Nolan, "The Socialist Movement in Düsseldorf," chap. 6, p. 57.

28. "Die Lokalfrage für die Arbeiterturnvereine," *ATZ*, August 1, 1908, pp. 227–28; Wildung, *Handbuch des Arbeiter-Turnerbundes*, pp. 410–13; Schlüter, "Der Bau eigener Turnstätten für Arbeiterturnvereine," *ATZ*, October 15, 1911, pp. 330–31.

29. Sources for club names: Noack, *Arbeiter-Sängerbewegung* (1911), passim; Deutscher Arbeiter-Sängerbund, Gau Leipzig, *Festbuch zum Bundes-Konzert, Sonntag den 8. August 1909* (Leipzig, 1909), pp. 36–38; Arbeiter-Sängerbund Hamburg, Altona und Umgegend, *Statistisches Verzeichniss*, for May 1896, and the first quarters of 1902 and 1910, Staatsarchiv Hamburg, Politische Polizei, S2338, Bd. 2; "Statistischer Bericht über den Turnbetrieb innerhalb des Arbeiter-Turnerbundes vom 1. Januar bis 31. Dezember 1898," *ATZ*, May 1, 1899, pp. 61–66; and *Statistischer Bericht über den Mitgliederbestand und den Turnbetrieb innerhalb des Arbeiter-Turnerbundes vom 1. Januar bis 31. Dezember 1910* (Leipzig, [1911]), pp. 2–58.

30. Since a complete statistical survey of names for all clubs is not possible, and since there is no system by which a valid representative sample can be made, the following list of names of workers' gymnastic clubs from 1910 provides one indicator of the distribution of names.

Name	*Number of Clubs Using Name*
Freie Turnerschaft	643
Arbeiter-Turnverein	235
Jahn (used in various forms)	112
Vorwärts	80
Frisch auf	53
Freiheit	28
Eiche	35
Including:	
Eichenkranz (13)	
Grüne Eiche (1)	
Deutsche Eiche (1)	
Germania	20
Fichte	12

The following were also found in small numbers: Einigkeit, Eintracht, Frei Heil, Brüderschaft, Frankonia, Froh und Frei, Frohsinn, Freundschaft, Gut Heil, Bahn Frei; the following represented by one club each: Mehr Licht, Weisse Rose, Phoenix, Erholung, Fortschritt, Saxonia, Harmonie, Hiltonia, Gleichheit, Morgenrot, Glück auf, and Frohe Zukunft. Compiled from: *Statistischer Bericht über den Mitgliederbestand und den Turnbetrieb innerhalb des Arbeiter-Turnerbundes vom 1. Januar bis 31. Dezember 1910* (Leipzig, [1911]), pp. 2–58.

31. Pahncke, "Traditionen der Rostocker Arbeiter-Turn- und Sportbewegung," p. 291.
32. "Protokoll über die Verhandlungen des IV. Bundes-Turntages am 21. u. 22. Mai 1899 in Nürnberg," *ATZ*, July 1, 1899, p. 103.
33. Elben, *Der volkstümliche deutsche Männergesang*, p. 188.
34. Cf. George L. Mosse, *The Nationalization of the Masses* (New York, 1975), pp. 42–43, 131–32; Erich Langer, "Das Vereinsleben," in Franz Josef Ewens (ed.), *Deutsches Lied und Deutscher Sang* (Karlsruhe and Dortmund, 1930), pp. 356–57; Kötzschke, *Geschichte des deutschen Männergesanges*, p. 298.
35. For example, at workers' gymnastic festivals in Würzburg (1905), Mainz (1906), and Hanau am Main (1907), and Fechenheim (1911): *Festschrift zum sechsten Kreisturntag nebst zweitem Kreisfest. Würzburg 10.–13. Juni 1905* (n.p., n.d.[1905]); *Festbuch zum siebenten Bezirks-Turntag nebst 10jährigem Stiftungs-Fest und Fahnen-Weihe der Freien Turngemeinde Mainz vom 21.–23. Juli 1906 zu Mainz* (Mainz, 1906); *III. Kreisturnfest des IX. Kreises des Arbeiter-Turner-Bundes am 6. 7. und 8. Juli 1907 in Hanau am Main* (Frankfurt am Main, 1907); *Festbuch zur Bannerweihe verbunden mit Bezirks-Spieltag am 24. 25. und 26. Juni 1911* (Fechenheim, 1911), p. 3.
36. Noack, *Arbeiter-Sängerbund* (1911), p. 85.
37. Ibid., p. 75.
38. Heinrich Holek, *Unterwegs. Eine Selbstbiographie* (Vienna, 1927), p. 130.
39. "Touristenverein 'Die Naturfreunde,' " *Arbeiter-Sportfest*, p. 22.
40. Hartmann Wunderer, "Der Touristenverein 'Die Naturfreunde'—eine sozialdemokratische Arbeiterkulturorganisation (1895–1933)," *Internationale wissenschaftliche Korrespondenz* 13 (December 1977):512, 515.
41. Deutscher Arbeiterstenographenbund, *Protokoll des 10. Bundestages vom 5. bis 8. April 1912 in Berlin (Gewerkschaftshaus)* (Freiburg i. B., n.d.), pp. 6, 8–9, 10.
42. Cf. Ueberhorst, *Frisch, frei, stark und treu*, pp. 192–94.
43. "Haben die Arbeiter-Turnvereine eine Berechtigung den Namen 'Jahn' zu führen?" *ATZ*, September 1, 1904, p. 206.
44. The following illustrate the concern with Jahn: "Was bezweckt die Turnkunst?" *ATZ*, February 15, 1897 (Beilage) p. 8; "Wie sind

Turnübungen zu betreiben?" *ATZ*, September 1, 1897, pp. 21–22; "Auch ein Beitrag zur Jahnfeier," *ATZ*, December 1, 1902, pp. 236–38; Karl Blind, "Zur Erinnerung an den Turnvater Jahn," *ATZ*, October 15, 1903, pp. 213–14; "Episoden aus Jahns Leben," *ATZ*, September 15, 1903; K. L., "Episoden aus Jahns Leben," *ATZ*, January 15, 1903; M. Blumtritt, "Deutschland zur Zeit Friedrich Ludwig Jahns," *ATZ*, June 1, June 15, July 1, July 15, August 1, and August 15, 1908; Josef Kliche, "Friedrich Ludwig Jahn und das deutsche Turnwesen," *ATZ*, April 15, 1901; Bruno Schubert, "Mit Jahn oder gegen Jahn?" *ATZ*, August 15, 1911; Fritz Wildung, "Jahnfeier," *ATZ*, July 1, 1911; and "Johann Gottlieb Fichte," *ATZ*, May 15, 1912.

45. "Turnvater Friedrich Ludwig Jahn, die 'Roten' von 1848 und die 'Roten' von heute," *ATZ*, December 15, 1894, pp. 41–42.

46. *Protokoll vom Kreisturntag des 4. Turnkreises (Sachsen) des Arbeiter-Turnerbundes Deutschlands abgehalten am 14. und 15. Mai 1894* (Dresden, 1894), pp. 3–4.

47. Ibid., p. 8.

48. A. Schauder, "Eine Pilgerfahrt zu Jahns Grabstätte in Freiburg a. U.," *ATZ*, November 1, 1905 (Beilage), p. 311.

49. Ueberhorst, *Frisch, frei, stark und treu*, p. 195.

50. Ibid., p. 49; cf. also Schuster, *Arbeiterturner im Kampf um die Jugend*, pp. 54–56, who does not believe that competitive gymnastics (*Wett-Turnen*) contradicted socialist principles.

51. The resolution is reprinted in Wildung, *Handbuch des Arbeiter-Turnerbundes*, p. 27; and Ueberhorst, *Frisch, frei, stark und treu*, p. 50.

52. Wildung, *Handbuch des Arbeiter-Turnerbundes*, pp. 42–43; Ueberhorst, *Frisch, frei, stark und treu*, pp. 50–51. For the conflict within the workers' swimming clubs on these issues, see "Fünfzehn Jahre Arbeiter-Schwimmer-Bund," *Arbeiter-Schwimmerzeitung* 13 (December 1, 1912), pp. 83–85.

53. Clipping from *Vorwärts*, April 5, 1907, quoting *Die Athletik. Organ des Arbeiter-Athleten-Bundes Deutschlands*, Staatsarchiv Hamburg, Politische Polizei, S13822; also, "Die Arbeiter-Athletenbund," *Arbeiter-Sportfest*, pp. 26–28.

54. Clippings from *Hamburger Echo*, April 15, 1910, and April 15, 1914, Staatsarchiv Hamburg, Politische Polizei, S16940. For the critic's statement, see "Das Schwimmen," *Arbeiter-Sportfest*, p. 17.

55. *Protokoll der 3. Generalversammlung des Deutschen Arbeiter-Sängerbundes. Abgehalten zu Leipzig am 14. und 15. Juni 1914* (Berlin, 1914), p. 48.

56. Noack, *Arbeiter-Sängerbund* (1931), pp. 63–64. On the question of schoolteachers as directors, see Kötzschke, *Geschichte des deutschen Männergesanges*, p. 212; Johannes Schult, *Die Hamburger Arbeiterbewegung als Kulturfaktor* (Hamburg [1954]), p. 109; and the *Proto-*

koll of the general conference of 1914 (n. 55), pp. 34–35. For the workers' singing societies in the Chemnitz district, Kaden gives the following occupational classification of directors: fifty-seven were "factory workers" (miners, woodworkers, weavers, [*Weber, Wirker*], cigar workers, etc.); fifty-two were musicians, music directors, choirmasters, musical entrepreneurs; twenty were artisans (turners, plumbers, tailors, painters, etc.); and thirteen were civil servants (*Beamte*). *Arbeitersängerbewegung im Gau Chemnitz,* p. 107.

57. Schult, *Die Hamburger Arbeiterbewegung als Kulturfaktor,* p. 110. A service organization, such as the Workers' Samaritan Federation, also faced the problem of how to attract and hold nonsocialist experts without undermining the organization's ideological principles and their appeal to the working class. To perform first-aid service adequately they needed doctors and therefore had to play down their political commitments. Alfons Labisch, "The Workingmen's Samaritan Federation (Arbeiter-Samariter-Bund) 1888–1933," *Journal of Contemporary History* 13 (1978):302–3.

58. Noack, *Arbeiter-Sängerbund* (1911), p. 93. Singing societies in Hamburg also hired music critics to evaluate performance (see chapter 4).

59. See the following statement by F.S. (probably Friedrich Stampfer) in "Kunst und Klassenkampf," *Freie Volksbühne* 15 (1910–11):18: "It is not the opinion [*Gesinnung*] that makes the artist, but ability [*das Können*]. If he can embody an opinion, a thought, a bit of life in a work of art, then he is an artist. Praise be to *Tendenzkunst* [opinionated art] when the *Tendenz* is ours and the art is great art. But *Tendenz* is still not art and can in no way replace art." It should be stressed that, contrary to the opinion of some historians, subordinating ideological expressions to the needs of performance did not mean that the singing societies were "depoliticized," only that they did not embrace radical politics. See also Dieter Dowe, "The Workingmen's Choral Movement in Germany before the First World War," *Journal of Contemporary History* 13 (1978):280–82.

60. Schmitt, *Weinheim,* p. 158.

61. Cf. Staudinger, *Individuum und Gemeinschaft,* p. 117; Paul Kupfer, "Der Arbeitersängerbund und seine Bedeutung für die Arbeiterschaft," *Die neue Welt,* no. 22 (1911), pp. 171–72.

62. Noack, *Arbeiter-Sängerbund* (1911), pp. 34–35.

63. Clipping from *Hamburger Echo,* March 21, 1912, Staatsarchiv Hamburg, Politische Polizei, S2388, Bd. 2.

64. Noack, *Arbeiter-Sängerbund* (1911), pp. 42, 59.

65. In Hamburg, the "passive members" were the most vigorous opponents of the merger of several choirs; clipping from *Hamburger Echo,* March 9, 1912, Staatsarchiv Hamburg, Politische Polizei, S2338, Bd. 2.

66. *Arbeiter-Sportfest,* pp. 15, 16.

67. "Das Ergebnis der Umfrage," p. 9. Typescript copy in Vollmar Archive, no. 240, International Institute for Social History, Amsterdam.

68. Zentralkommission für das Arbeiterbildungswesen von Hamburg-Altona und Umgegend. *Geschäftsbericht für das Jahr 1911/12* (Hamburg [1912]), p. 8. Among the singing societies around Chemnitz, Kaden, *Arbeitersängerbewegung im Gau Chemnitz,* pp. 123, 301–03, believes that there was increased attention to sociability after 1900, a concomitant to his view of the growing influence of revisionism in the Social Democratic movement. That is an impressionistic judgment, which he supports with references, but hardly sufficient to prove that there was a definitive trend. In Nuremberg it appears that there was a new form of specialized workers' club, completely devoted to pleasure and socializing. They are identified as "Workers' clubs," but it is not entirely clear that they were affiliated with the socialist labor movement. The "Alpenrausch" was founded in 1897, and in 1899 two more, "Atonia" and "Gemütlicher Achter," appeared. Meyer, *Nürnberg,* p. 69.

69. Cf. Breunig, *Soziale Verhältnisse der Arbeiterschaft und sozialistische Arbeiterbewegung in Ludwigshafen am Rhein 1869–1919,* p. 298, on the importance of sociability for bringing about and sustaining solidarity in the party in Ludwigshafen.

70. This analysis is not drawn from Adelheid von Saldern, but she stresses the role of the voluntary associations in politicizing workers who otherwise would have remained aloof from the labor movement, in "Wilhelminische Gesellschaft und Arbeiterklasse," pp. 483–84.

CHAPTER 4

1. The comparatively recent emphasis on the history of "daily life" (*Alltagsleben*) is a manifestation of the trend to counter the traditional focus on ideology and organizations. See Jürgen Reulecke and Wolfhard Weber (eds.), *Fabrik. Familie. Feierabend. Beiträge zur Sozialgeschichte des Alltags im Industriezeitalter* (Wuppertal, 1978); Jürgen Kuczynski, *Geschichte des Alltags des Deutschen Volkes 1600 bis 1945. Studien,* 5 vols. (Berlin, DDR, 1980–82); and two articles by Alf Lüdtke, "Alltagswirklichkeit, Lebensweise und Bedürfnisartikulation," in H.-G. Backhaus et al. (eds.), *Gesellschaft. Beiträge zur Marxschen Theorie,* no. 11 (Frankurt am Main, 1978), pp. 311–50, and "Rekonstruktion von Alltagswirklichkeit—Entpolitisierung der Sozialgeschichte?" in Robert Berdahl et al., *Klassen und Kultur* (Frankfurt am Main, 1982), pp. 321–53.

2. This view would appear to be implicit in much of the recent literature on workers and leisure. See the essays in Gerhard Huck (ed.), *Sozialgeschichte der Freizeit. Untersuchungen zum Wandel der Alltagskultur in Deutschland* (Wuppertal, 1980); see also William J. Baker, "The

Making of a Working-Class Football Culture in Victorian England," *Journal of Social History* 13 (1979):241–51.

3. For example, Friedrich Giovanoli, *Die Maifeierbewegung* (Karlsruhe, 1925), argues that May Day festivals were religious in character.

4. Sally Moore and Barbara Myerhoff make persuasive arguments for the concept of secular ritual, in "Introduction: Secular Ritual: Forms and Meanings," in Sally F. Moore and Barbara G. Myerhoff (eds.), *Secular Ritual* (Assen/Amsterdam, 1977), pp. 3–24; while Robert Bocock, *Ritual in Industrial Society. A Sociological Analysis of Ritualism in Modern England* (London, 1974), p. 60, insists on the religious nature of ritual.

5. Cf. Mosse, *The Nationalization of the Masses,* pp. 164, 181–82, who, despite an effort to find liturgical dimensions in Social Democratic festivals, concludes that the movement's rationalist assumptions predominated. See also my essay on "Social Class and Secularisation in Imperial Germany. The Working Classes," *Yearbook of the Leo Baeck Institute* 25 (1980):21–40, and the interesting reflections by Gottfried Korff, "Volkskultur und Arbeiterkultur. Überlegungen am Beispiel der sozialistischen Maifesttradition," *Geschichte und Gesellschaft* 5 (1979):83–102.

6. Kurt Koszyk, "Die sozialdemokratische Arbeiterbewegung 1890 bis 1914," in Jürgen Reulecke (ed.), *Arbeiterbewegung an Rhein und Ruhr* (Wuppertal, 1974), p. 153; Nolan, "The Socialist Movement in Düsseldorf," chap. 6, pp. 48–49.

7. Source material on labor movement festivals is scattered and uneven. Many documents contain references and brief descriptions of festivals, but copies of complete programs that list all events, including specific concert numbers, are much more difficult to find. Appendix A gives a full list of the complete and detailed programs that have been used in this study. To avoid lengthy and repetitious citations, abbreviated references are made to these programs as listed in the appendix. Sources that report on what happened at festivals but do not provide an itemized and complete list of events and presentations are not included in the appendix and are cited in the usual fashion.

8. Cited in Michael Klöcker, *Die Sozialdemokratie im Regierungsbezirk Aachen vor dem I. Weltkrieg* (Wentorf bei Hamburg, 1977), p. 364.

9. Göhre, *Drei Monate Fabrikarbeiter,* p. 98.

10. "Das Frankfurter Maiwaldfest der Partei," *Volksstimme,* no. 102, May 2, 1908, clipping in Staatsarchiv Wiesbaden, Abt. 407/Nr. 67.

11. Cited in Klöcker, *Die Sozialdemokratie im Regierungsbezirk Aachen,* pp. 364–65.

12. Clipping from *Hamburger Echo,* May 8, 1898, Staatsarchiv Hamburg, Politische Polizei, S5416, Bd. 2.

13. Clippings from *Hamburger Echo,* February 2, 1910, and January 22, 1911, Staatsarchiv Hamburg, Politische Polizei, S16940.

14. Cf. the descriptions of the festivals of the Deutscher Sängerbund (founded in 1862), in Kötzschke, *Geschichte des deutschen Männergesanges,* pp. 153–83, and Mosse's chapter on "Public Festivals," in *The Nationalization of the Masses,* pp. 73–99.

15. Alex Hall, "By other Means: The Legal Struggle against the SPD in Wilhelmine Germany, 1890–1900," *The Historical Journal* 17, no. 2 (1974):369; and reports in the *Liedergemeinschaft,* no. 5 (1902), pp. 5–8.

16. Rüden, *Arbeitertheater,* pp. 95–97, cites three more instances in Chemnitz, two in Leipzig, and one each in Zwickau, Zittau, Friedrichshagen, and Munich in which police prohibited either part or all of programs that included dramatic presentations.

17. "Der Gau Kurhessen-Waldeck-Südhannover," *Arbeiter-Sängerzeitung,* no. 28, August 15, 1909 (hereafter cited as *ASZ*); Noack, *Arbeitersängerbund* (1931), pp. 52–53.

18. "Das westfälische Sängerfest," *Der wahre Jacob,* no. 215 (1894), p. 1798; Kaden, *Arbeitersängerbewegung im Gau Chemnitz,* pp. 83–88, 284–288.

19. *Bericht über die Tätigkeit des Agitationskomitees der Sozialdemokratischen Partei Leipzigs für das Jahr 1908–09* (Leipzig, 1909), p. 13; and *Berichte über die gemeinschaftlichen Einrichtungen von der Sozialdemokratischen Partei und den Gewerkschaften in Leipzig 1910* (Leipzig, 1910), pp. 15–16.

20. Clipping from the *Kleine Presse,* no. 103, May 3, 1893, Staatsarchiv Wiesbaden, Abt. 407/Nr. 67.

21. Otto Buchwitz, *50 Jahre Funktionär der deutschen Arbeiterbewegung* (Berlin, 1949), p. 26.

22. Hall, *Scandal, Sensation and Social Democracy,* pp. 7, 52–55, 60, 88, stresses that German authorities did not significantly relax their pressure against Social Democrats in the years between 1890 and 1914.

23. Cf. Nolan, "The Socialist Movement in Düsseldorf," chap. 6, p. 43; and Adelheid von Saldern concluded that the "police in Göttingen 'rewarded' [*honorierte*] the [Social Democratic] rejection of work-stoppages on May First by avoiding chicanery during the celebrations." *Vom Einwohner zum Bürger. Zur Emanzipation der städtischen Unterschicht Göttingens 1890–1920* (Berlin, 1973), p. 147.

24. "Arbeiter-Sängerbund für die Pfalz," *ASZ,* no. 19, December 1907, p. 4; Botho Frank, "VIII. Bayerisches Arbeitersängerfest," *ASZ,* no. 33, June 15, 1910, p. 3; "Gau Württemberg," *ASZ,* no. 40, August 15, 1911, p. 12; clipping from *Hamburger Fremdenblatt,* April 2, 1914, Staatsarchiv Hamburg, Politische Polizei, S2338, Bd. 2; and Sängerfest program, Görlitz (1907), Appendix A.

25. *Festbuch zu dem am Sonntag, 16. Juli 1899 zu Ohligs stattfindenden 8. Bundes-Stiftungsfeste in sämmtlichen Räumen der 'Schutzenburg' nebst Ausstellungshalle* (Krefeld, 1899).

26. For a festival (July 1913) of the third district of the Workers' Gymnastic Federation (including Hamburg, Lübeck, Schleswig-Holstein, Mecklenburg, Lauenburg, and East-Hanover), the festival book, consisting of 104 pages, included the following: About one-half was devoted to the *Kommers* program, a schedule of gymnastic events, several short essays on the local society, the city of Lübeck, and female gymnasts. The remainder was given to advertisements. *Fest-Schrift zum X. Kreisturnfest in Lübeck* (Lübeck, 1913). For a festival of the regional federation of workers' gymnasts in July 1907, 48 pages were given to gymnastic schedules, the concert program, a seven-page biographical sketch of "Turnvater" Jahn, and numerous short pieces on historical, social, and technical aspects of gymnastics. Another large portion of the book carried advertisements. *Festbuch zum III. Kreisturnfest des IX. Kreises des Arbeiter-Turner-Bundes am 6., 7. und 8. Juli 1907* (Frankfurt am Main, 1907).

27. These have now been reprinted in Udo Achten (ed.), *Zum Lichte Empor. Mai-Festzeitungen der Sozialdemokratie 1891–1914* (Berlin/Bonn, 1980).

28. These sample figures are taken from Noack, *Arbeiter-Sängerbund* (1931), pp. 80–82.

29. B. Strzelewicz, *35 Jahre Künstler Fahrten unter deutscher Monarchie und Republik* (Dresden, n. d.), p. 5. Several pieces by Strzelewicz are reprinted in Friedrich Knilli and Ursula Münchow (eds.), *Frühes deutsches Arbeitertheater 1847–1918* (Munich, 1970), pp. 319–34. For an evaluation of Strzelewicz's endeavors, see Rüden, *Arbeitertheater,* pp. 100–106.

30. See the following festival programs in Appendix A: Sängerfest, Limbach (1907); Turnerfest, Hanau (1907); and Turnerfest, Lübeck (1913).

31. Police report, July 28, 1899, Staatsarchiv Düsseldorf, Landesamt Solingen, no. 525.

32. See Appendix A, Turnfest, Langendiebach (1910).

33. Report in the *Liedergemeinschaft,* no. 7, November 1903, pp. 5, 7.

34. Police report, July 9, 1906, Staatsarchiv Düsseldorf, Reg. Düsseldorf, Präsidialbüro, Nr. 863.

35. At a festival of singers in Ohligs in 1899, 160 cyclists led the procession of 3,000 people; at least one policeman also marched at the head of each segment of the procession, and the police report stressed that the crowd had been well behaved, from which the veterans' associations (*Kriegervereine*) could take a lesson. In 1900, at a Summer Festival of the local Social Democratic party organization of the Solingen district, cyclists led the procession, and were followed in order by the fire department band from Gräfrath, members of the Social Democratic political organization of Wald (the host town), and the workers' singing societies from Solingen, Gräfrath, and Ohligs. The police estimated that between 4,000 and 5,000, including women and

children, took part in the procession. Clipping from the *Berg. Arbeiterstimme,* July 18, 1899, and a police report of August 6, 1900, both in Staatsarchiv Düsseldorf, Landesamt Solingen, no. 525.

36. Cited in Rüden, *Arbeitertheater,* p. 135.
37. Klöcker, *Die Sozialdemokratie im Regierungsbezirk Aachen,* pp. 364–65. See the discussion of the relationship between traditional miners' festivals and the new forms introduced by the Social Democratic labor movement in Klaus Tenfelde, "Mining Festivals in the Nineteenth Century," *Journal of Contemporary History* 13 (1978):402–3.
38. "Zweites Sängerfest des Gaues Osterland," *Reussische Tribune,* no. 187, August 12, 1913 (Beilage) clipping in Arbeiterliedarchiv, Sektion Musik, Deutsche Akademie der Künste, Berlin (DDR).
39. "Die freie Vogtländische Sänger-Vereinigung," *ASZ,* no. 22, August 15, 1908, p. 8; "Gau Württemberg," *ASZ,* no. 40, August 15, 1911, p. 12.
40. Kaden, *Arbeitersängerbewegung im Gau Chemnitz,* pp. 137–42.
41. At a workers' gymnastic festival in Stuttgart in 1907, the Schwäbische Liedergruppe from Württemberg's Royal Theater, directed by Herr Krohmer, presented several traditional Swabian songs. The program at a festival sponsored by the workers' sport cartel in Brunswick featured pieces by two local, nonsocialist composers, "Die Spinnerin" by Gustav Baldamus, and "Ewig liebe Heimat" by Fritz Heyland. In Hamburg the singers' festivals in 1892, 1897, 1898, 1904, and 1905 included numerous pieces by Oskar Fétras, a local composer of popular light music. A potpourri of his waltzes, "Moonlit Night on the Alster," enjoyed great popularity in Hamburg generally and at workers' festivals (programs in Appendix A). On the composers, see Franz Josef Ewens, *Lexikon des Chorwesens,* 2nd ed. (Mönchengladbach, 1960), pp. 16, 69, 111.
42. "Bayerisches Arbeitersängerfest," *ASZ,* no. 33, June 15, 1910, p. 4.
43. Clipping from *Hamburger Echo,* August 8, 1905, Staatsarchiv Hamburg, Politische Polizei, S2338, Bd. 1.
44. Elben, *Der volksthümliche deutsche Männergesang,* pp. 390–468; Kötzschke, *Geschichte des deutschen Männergesanges,* pp. 153–83.
45. Cf. Inge Lammel, *Das deutsche Arbeiterlied* (Leipzig/Jena/Berlin, 1962), p. 23; Margarete Nespital, *Das deutsche Proletariat in seinem Lied* (Rostock, 1932), pp. 58–59.
46. On several occasions Hermann Duncker criticized the new choral music for its lack of ideological fervor. He valued musical quality but argued that "all genuine art is committed art [*Tendenzkunst*]" and that therefore socialist composers should always give precedence to ideology and propaganda over virtuosity and aesthetic considerations. These arguments were presented with special force in two articles in the *Liedergemeinschaft:* "Was sollen wir singen?" no. 2 (October 1900), and "Unsere Lieder," no. 6 (May 1903).

47. Noack, *Arbeitersängerbund* (1911), pp. 15–17.
48. With the exception of Uthmann, little is known about most of these early socialist composers. See Nespital, *Das deutsche Proletariat in seinem Lied,* pp. 58–59; Inge Lammel, "Das Lied der deutschen Arbeiterbewegung. Von seinen Anfängen bis nach 1890 (II. Teil)," *Musik und Gesellschaft,* no. 10 (1954):356; and Kaden, *Arbeitersängerbewegung im Gau Chemnitz,* pp. 91, 142–82.
49. *Protokoll der 3. Generalversammlung des Deutschen Arbeiter-Sängerbundes. Abgehalten zu Leipzig am 14. und 15. Juni 1914* (Berlin, 1914), p. 47. Bothe identified Richard Trunk, Emil Burgstaller, and Ernst G. Elsässer as the composers associated with the workers' singing societies who also had achieved considerable recognition. On these three, see Ewens, *Lexikon des Chorwesens,* pp. 38, 62, 288.
50. These songs all appear on programs of the festivals of workers' singing societies as listed in Appendix A. The texts can be found in the *Liederbuch,* 7th ed. (Berlin, 1912), published under the auspices of the Berlin district of the Deutscher Arbeiter-Sängerbund.
51. "Die Schmiede im Walde" also appeared on the program of the singing society in Chemnitz in 1904. The text is reprinted in Kaden, *Arbeitersängerbewegung im Gau Chemnitz,* p. 306. Kaden reports that one J. Stauffacher wrote the lyrics, while the music was composed by Th. Michaelis. Festivals in Hamburg featured it in 1896, 1898, 1899, 1900, 1902, 1904, and 1905 (Appendix A).
52. Music by these composers appears on nearly all of the festival programs listed in Appendix A. But May Day and Lassalle festivals included less music by prominent classical composers than did the programs of other labor movement associations.
53. Above festival programs listed in Appendix A. Other programs that presented Wagnerian music included festivals of workers' singers at Giebichenstein bei Halle (1896) and Chemnitz (1910), a workers' gymnastic festival in Stuttgart (1907), and a Founders' Day Festival in Leipzig (1904).
54. Dieter Dowe, "The Workingmen's Choral Movement in Germany before the First World War," *Journal of Contemporary History* 13 (1978):285.
55. See the report of the Central Educational Commission as summarized in chapter 7. On Steiner's lecture, *Freie Volksbühne* 8 (1903):52; and on the "Wagner-Feier," in *Freie Volksbühne* 12 (1908):115.
56. Hermann Duncker, "Künstlerische Kultur," *Liedergemeinschaft,* no. 8 (May 1904); Clara Zetkin, *Kunst und Proletariat* (Stuttgart, 1911), pp. 9–10; Friedrich Caro, "Parsifal," *ASZ,* no. 56, February 15, 1914, p. 1. On Duncker's decisive move to the radical left during the first years of the twentieth century, see Günter Griep, Alfred Först, and Heinz Siegel, *Hermann Duncker—Lehrer dreier Generationen* (Berlin, DDR, 1974), pp. 20–31.

57. The sequence of dances (*Tanz-Ordnung*) is given with the program for the Twenty-fifth Founder's Day Festival of the Leipzig Workers' Educational Society, and there is a detailed fireworks listing with the program of the singers' festival in Hamburg in 1906 (Appendix A).
58. Karl Grünberg, *Episoden* (Berlin, DDR, 1960), cited in Rüden, *Arbeitertheater*, p. 89.
59. Giovanoli, *Die Maifeierbewegung,* pp. 93–95; Saldern, *Vom Einwohner zum Bürger,* pp. 145–47. Nolan notes a gradual but uneven tendency from militancy to moderation in May Day activities in Düsseldorf, so that by the early twentieth century the "festive element" outweighed the political dimensions. "The Socialist Movement in Düsseldorf," chap. 6, pp. 38–43.
60. Report by Police Commissioner Koch, July 9, 1906, Staatsarchiv Düsseldorf, Reg. Düsseldorf, Präsidialbüro, no. 863.

CHAPTER 5

1. Cf. Gert Hagelweide, *Das publizistische Erscheinungsbild des Menschen im kommunistischen Lied. Eine Untersuchung der Liedpublizistik der KPD (1919–1933) und der SED (1945–1960)* (Bremen, 1968); Margarete Nespital, *Das deutsche Proletariat in seinem Lied* (Rostock, 1932); Inge Lammel, *Das deutsche Arbeiterlied* (Leipzig/Jena/Berlin, 1962); Wolfgang Friedrich (ed.), *Im Klassenkampf. Deutsche revolutionäre Lieder und Gedichte aus der zweiten Hälfte des 19. Jahrhunderts* (Halle, 1962); Vernon L. Lidtke, "Songs and Politics: An Exploratory Essay on Arbeiterlieder in the Weimar Republic," *Archiv für Sozialgeschichte* 14 (1974):253–73.
2. Folklorists (*Volkskundler*) and music historians in the German Democratic Republic are an exception; especially valuable are the following works by Wolfgang Steinitz: *Deutsche Volkslieder demokratischen Charakters aus sechs Jahrhunderten,* 2 vols. (Berlin, 1954, 1962); "Das Leunalied. Zu Geschichte und Wesen des Arbeitervolksliedes," *Deutsches Jahrbuch für Volkskunde* 4 (1958):3–52; "Das Lied von Robert Blum," *Deutsches Jahrbuch für Volkskunde,* 7 (1961):9–40; "Arbeiterlied und Arbeiterkultur," *Beiträge zur Musikwissenschaft* 6 (1964):277–88; "Arbeiterlied und Volkslied," *Deutsches Jahrbuch für Volkskunde* 12 (1966):1–14. Also, Klaus Völkerling, "Der Crimmitschauer Textilarbeiterstreik von 1903/04 in der frühen sozialistischen Literatur und im revolutionären Arbeitervolkslied," *Weimarer Beiträge* 8 (1962):614–40; and Inge Lammel, "Politisches Lied und Volkslied in der Gesangpraxis der Arbeiterklasse," in *Arbeiterklasse und Musik. Theoretische Positionen in der deutschen Arbeiterklasse zur Musikkultur vor 1945,* ed. by the Akademie der Künste, Arbeitsheft 15 (Berlin, 1974), pp. 26–51.
3. Cf. Alan P. Merriam, *The Anthropology of Music* (Evanston, Ill.,

1964); Elie Siegmeister, *Music and Society* (New York, 1938, 1974). On the social functions of *Volkslieder*, the work by Ernst Klusen, *Volkslied. Fund und Erfindung* (Cologne, 1969), is most valuable. On a broader dimension, but with sections on European countries, Bruno Nettl, *Folk and Traditional Music of the Western Continents*, 2nd ed. (Englewood Cliffs, N. J., 1973).

4. Leo Stern (ed.), *Der Kampf der deutschen Sozialdemokratie in der Zeit des Sozialistengesetzes 1878–1890* (Berlin, 1956), vol. 1, pp. 11, 527–28, 537, 538, 540; Otto Atzrott, *Sozialdemokratische Druckschriften und Vereine verboten auf Grund des Reichsgesetzes gegen die gemeingefährlichen Bestrebungen der Sozialdemokratie vom 21. Oktober 1878* (Berlin, 1886), pp. 35–37.

5. *Kleine Press,* May 3, 1893. Clipping in Staatsarchiv Wiesbaden, Abt. 407, no. 151[1].

6. *Hamburger Echo,* April 18, 1903.

7. Buchwitz, *50 Jahre Funktionär der deutschen Arbeiterbewegung,* p. 26.

8. Schuchardt, *Sechs Monate Arbeitshaus,* p. 8.

9. Inge Lammel, "Zur Rolle und Bedeutung des Arbeiterliedes," *Beiträge zur Geschichte der deutschen Arbeiterbewegung* 4 (1962):730. Cf. also the article, "Arbeiterliederbücher," *Lexikon sozialistischer deutscher Literatur* (The Hague, 1973), pp. 64–70.

10. An overview of the *Liederbücher* is possible because of the systematic catalog prepared by Inge Lammel (ed.), *Bibliographie der deutschen Arbeiterliederbücher 1833–1945* (Leipzig, 1971). Also, Nespital, *Das deutsche Proletariat in seinem Lied,* passim, who discusses particular *Liederbücher.*

11. In the judgment of Nespital, *Das deutsche Proletariat in seinem Lied,* p. 50, Kegel's publication was the official Social Democratic party songbook. For titles, see n. 16, below.

12. Cf. the following: *Liederbuch,* ed. by the Deutscher Arbeiter-Sängerbund. Gau Berlin u. Umgegend, 7th ed. (Berlin, 1912); *Jugend-Liederbuch,* ed. by the Zentralstelle für die arbeitende Jugend Deutschlands (Berlin [1907]). Other *Vereinsliederbücher* included Konrad Beisswanger (ed.), *Kampflieder aus den Anfängen der freireligiösen Bewegung* (Nuremberg, 1907); *Liederbuch der Athletik treibenden Arbeiterschaft,* ed. by the Arbeiter-Athletenbund Deutschlands (Magdeburg, 1913); *Liederbuch für Naturfreunde,* ed. by the Deutscher Arbeiter-Wanderbund, Die Naturfreunde (Berlin, 1913); *Liederbuch für Arbeiter-Abstinenten* (Berlin, n. d., but before 1914).

13. *Der Freie Turner,* 9th ed. (Leipzig, 1907), pp. 3–59; *Liederbuch für Deutsche Turner,* 87th ed. (Braunschweig, [ca. 1890]; first published 1849).

14. *Liederbuch für Deutsche Turner,* p. 10; *Der freie Turner,* p. 30.

15. *Liederbuch für Deutsche Turner,* p. 17; *Der freie Turner,* p. 31.

16. In chronological order of publication, the six are: Johann Most (ed.), *Neuestes Proletarier-Liederbuch*, 4th ed. (Chemnitz, 1873); Max Kegel (ed.), *Sozialdemokratisches Liederbuch* (Stuttgart, 1891); *Lieder für Arbeiterradfahrer-Vereine* (Stuttgart, 1897); *Singe mit! Eine Sammlung politischer und gewerkschaftlicher Kampfeslieder*, 2nd ed. (Leipzig, 1904); *Der freie Turner*, 9th ed. (Leipzig, 1907); *Arbeiter-Liederbuch für Massen-Gesang* (Dortmund, 1911). To avoid a distortion, this survey includes from *Der freie Turner* only the section on "Arbeiter-Lieder," pp. 60–93.

17. Franz Magnus Böhme, *Volksthümliche Lieder der Deutschen im 18. und 19. Jahrhundert* (Leipzig, 1895), p. 225.

18. Most, *Neuestes Proletarier-Liederbuch*, pp. 70–71; *Lieder für Arbeiterradfahrer-Vereine*, p. 16.

19. Kegel, *Sozialdemokratisches Liederbuch*, p. 100; *Singe mit!*, p. 43.

20. Kegel, *Sozialdemokratisches Liederbuch*, p. 35; Böhme, *Volksthümliche Lieder*, p. 39.

21. Kegel, *Sozialdemokratisches Liederbuch*, p. 4.

22. The refrain that omits references to Lassalle is included in Most, *Neuestes Proletarier-Liederbuch*, pp. 52–55, and is identical with the refrain in Freiligrath's "Reveille," written in 1848–49 and, like Audorf's lyrics, sung to the melody of the "Marseillaise." The refrain by Freiligrath is as follows:

> :: Die neue Rebellion!
> Die ganze Rebellion!
> Marsch! Marsch!
> Marsch! Marsch!
> Marsch! Wär's zum Tod!
> Und unsre Fahn' ist rot!

In: Inge Lammel, *Das Arbeiterlied* (Leipzig, 1970), p. 97.

23. Kegel, *Sozialdemokratisches Liederbuch*, p. 5.

24. Ibid.

25. It was first sung in 1864 at the memorial service for Lassalle. The party congresses concluded by singing the "Arbeiter-Marseillaise" (normally the first stanza) in 1875, 1880, 1883, and at all others between 1890 and 1914, with the exception of 1907, when the assembled delegates sang the "Sozialistenmarsch" (text by Max Kegel, music by Carl Gramm).

26. *Der freie Turner*, p. 65. This is the original English text of "Is there for honest poverty" by Burns, from *The Complete Poems of Robert Burns* (Boston and New York, 1926), vol. 5, p. 185.

27. Most, *Neuestes Proletarier-Liederbuch*, p. 30. This translation is from a collection entitled *Socialist Songs* (no place, publisher, or date, but probably published in London), pp. 13–14.

28. Most, *Neuestes Proletarier-Liederbuch*, pp. 47–50.
29. Ibid., p. 3.
30. Kegel, *Sozialdemokratisches Liederbuch*, pp. 20–21, 48–49, 95–96.
31. Ibid., pp. 20–21.
32. *Singe mit!*, pp. 4–5.
33. Most, *Neuestes Proletarier-Liederbuch*, p. 76.
34. Kegel, *Sozialdemokratisches Liederbuch*, p. 39; Nespital, *Das deutsche Proletariat in seinem Lied*, p. 48. On the Petroleuses, Edward S. Mason, *The Paris Commune* (New York, 1930), p. 281.
35. Kegel, *Sozialdemokratisches Liederbuch*, p. 96.
36. Nespital, *Das deutsche Proletariat in seinem Lied*, pp. 58–59; Lammel, *Das Arbeiterlied*, pp. 64–65, 113. On Josef Scheu, see also Herbert Steiner, *Die Gebrüder Scheu. Eine Biographie* (Vienna, 1968); and Reinhard Kannonier, *Zwischen Beethoven und Eisler. Zur Arbeitermusikbewegung in Österreich* (Vienna, 1981).
37. Note, however, that the early Lassallean movement used much religious imagery, as discussed by Heiner Grote, *Sozialdemokratie und Religion* (Tübingen, 1968), pp. 8–25.
38. Thus Wilhelm Liebknecht testified at his trial for high treason in 1872 that "after 1863 the workers' song 'Pray and Work' ['Bet' und Arbeit'] circulated unhampered in thousands of copies and from that time was sung in the presence of policemen without the imposition of any kind of prosecution." Karl-Heinz Leidigkeit (ed.), *Der Leipziger Hochverratsprozess vom Jahre 1872 (Berlin, DDR, 1960), p. 239.*
39. Most, *Neuestes Proletarier-Liederbuch*, p. 64.
40. Ibid., pp. 28–29.
41. *Freiheits- und Vaterlandslieder* (freedom and patriotic songs) were often grouped together in German songbooks, even many years after 1871, as in the case of the book of the German Gymnastic League: *Liederbuch für deutsche Turner*, p. 53.
42. I have stressed the liberationist aspect more than Werner Conze and Dieter Groh, but there is a parallel argument in their book, *Die Arbeiterbewegung in der nationalen Bewegung* (Stuttgart, 1966), pp. 44–45, 114–26.
43. Lammel, *Das Arbeiterlied*, p. 221.
44. Although no other group, especially after 1870, incorporated the "Marseillaise" melody into its repertoire, there is one instance that I have found in which the melody was used for a "Festival Hymn" ("Festgesang") for some of the German gymnastic groups in the 1860s; in Fr. Erk and M. Schauenburg (eds.), *Allgemeines Deutsches Turnerliederbuch* (Lahr, [ca. 1860]), pp. 62–64. The lyrics show that it is a liberationist song of German patriotism. It is noteworthy that the "Marseillaise" does not appear as one of the parodied melodies in two extensive investigations by Heinrich Schwab, "Das Vereinslied des 19. Jahrhunderts," in Rolf W. Brednich et al., *Handbuch des*

Volksliedes (Munich, 1973), vol. 1, pp. 863–98; and "Das Lied der Berufsvereine," *Zeitschrift für Volkskunde* 63 (1967):1–15. Paul Nettl *National Anthems,* 2nd ed. (New York, 1967), p. 77, reports on how the "Marseillaise" was "defamed" in Imperial Germany.

45. Hermann Wendel, *Die Marseillaise* (Zurich, 1936), pp. 116–21, discusses the "Marseillaise" in Germany through the 1860s. Cf. also Nettl, *National Anthems,* pp. 70–71.

46. Lammel, "Politisches Lied und Volkslied in der Gesangspraxis der Arbeiterklasse," pp. 40–44.

47. The list is compiled from Steinitz, *Deutsche Volkslieder,* vol. 1, pp. 286–88; vol. 2, pp. 281–317. This does not exhaust all of the strikers' songs discovered and discussed by Steinitz. No. II on the list also appears in one of the six songbooks surveyed above, *Arbeiterliederbuch für Massengesang,* pp. 25–27.

48. Steinitz, *Deutsche Volkslieder,* vol. 1, pp. 286–87.

49. Ibid. On Kämpchen's poetry, see Karl Ecks, *Die Arbeiterdichtung im rheinisch-westfälischen Industriegebiet* (Borna-Leipzig, 1925), pp. viii, 25–26; and H.S., "Bergmannslieder," *Die neue Zeit* 23, part 1 (1904–5):562–66. Many of Kämpchen's poems were collected in Heinrich Kämpchen, *Aus der Tiefe. Gedichte und Lieder eines Bergmanns,* ed. by Wilhelm Helf (Bochum, 1931).

50. Steinitz, *Deutsche Volkslieder,* vol. 2, p. 288. The valuable research on the strikers' songs in Crimmitschau is in Klaus Völkerling, "Der Crimmitschauer Textilarbeiterstreik von 1903/04 in der frühen sozialistischen Literatur und im revolutionären Arbeitervolkslied," *Weimarer Beiträge* 8 (1962):614–40.

51. Steinitz, *Deutsche Volkslieder,* vol. 2, p. 284.

52. Ibid., pp. 281–82.

53. Ibid., p. 303.

CHAPTER 6

1. Socialist prose is touched on only in passing in this study, primarily because the focus is on those arts that were regularly a part of group activities in the labor movement. See Wolfgang Friedrich, "Die sozialistische deutsche Literatur in der Zeit des Aufschwungs der Arbeiterbewegung während der sechziger Jahre des 19. Jahrhunderts bis zum Erlass des Sozialistengesetzes," 2 vols. (Habilitationsschrift typescript, Univ. of Halle-Wittenberg, 1964); Gerald Stieg and Bernd Witte, *Abriss einer Geschichte der deutschen Arbeiterliteratur* (Stuttgart, 1973); Dirk Hoffmann, "Sozialismus und Literatur. Literatur als Mittel politisierender Beeinflussung im Literaturbetrieb der sozialistisch organisierten Arbeiterklasse des Deutschen Kaissereiches 1876–1918" (diss., Univ. of Münster, 1975); Walter Reese, *Zur Geschichte der sozialistischen Heine-Rezeption in Deutschland* (Frankfurt

am Main/Bern, 1979). In addition there are several anthologies of socialist prose: Cäcilia Friedrich (ed.), *Aus dem Schaffen früher sozialistischer Schriftstellerinnen* (Berlin, DDR, 1966); and Robert Schweichel, *Erzählungen*, ed. by Erika Pick (Berlin, DDR, 1964).

2. Rüden, *Arbeitertheater*, pp. 84, 177; Knilli and Münchow (eds.), *Frühes deutsches Arbeitertheater*, p. 436.

3. Heinrich Lange, "Aus einer alten Handwerksburschen-Mappe," cited in Knilli and Münchow (eds.), *Frühes deutsches Arbeitertheater*, pp. 176–77.

4. Rüden, *Arbeitertheater*, pp. 28–29. Social Democratic reverence for Schiller is interpreted as part of the concrete development of the party and trade unions by Wolfgang Hagen, *Die Schillerverehrung in der Sozialdemokratie. Zur ideologischen Formation proletarischer Kulturpolitik vor 1914* (Stuttgart, 1977), who also argues that the labor movement created its own image of Schiller, one that little resembled historical reality.

5. Engels' manuscript draft from 1840 of a play about Cola di Rienzi has been published under the auspices of the Friedrich-Engels-Haus in Wuppertal and the Karl-Marx-Haus in Trier: Michael Knieriem (ed.), *Friedrich Engels: Cola di Rienzi. Ein unbekannter dramatischer Entwurf* (Trier, 1974).

6. Ferdinand Lassalle, "Franz von Sickingen," in Lassalle, *Gesammelte Reden und Schriften*, ed. by Eduard Bernstein (Berlin, 1919), vol. 1, pp. 149–345; Knilli and Münchow (eds.), *Frühes Deutsches Arbeitertheater*, pp. 62–65.

7. Jean Baptiste von Schweitzer, "Eine Gans. Dramatisches Gespräch über die 'Erweiterung des weiblichen Arbeitsmarktes.' " in Knilli and Münchow (eds.), *Frühes Deutsches Arbeitertheater, pp. 106–40.*

8. Schweitzer, "Ein Schlingel. Eine nationalökonomisch-soziale Humoreske in einem Akt," in Ursula Münchow (ed.), *Aus den Anfängen der sozialistischen Dramatik I* (Berlin, DDR, 1964), pp. 1–32; Knilli and Münchow (eds.), *Frühes Deutsches Arbeitertheater*, pp. 102–5.

9. Friedrich Wilhelm Fritzsche, *Blut-Rosen. Sozialpolitische Gedichte*, 2nd ed. (Baltimore, 1890); Wilhelm Hasenclever, *Liebe, Leben, Kampf. Gedichte* (Hamburg, 1976); August Geib, *Gedichte, 2nd ed. (Leipzig, 1876).*

10. Karl Frohme, *Ein Immortellenkranz* (Bremen, 1872); *Feierstunden* (Frankfurt am Main, 1876); *Freikugeln* (Bockenheim, 1876); *Empor! Lieder und Gedichte* (Hamburg, 1910).

11. Wolfgang Friedrich (ed.), *August Otto-Walster. Leben und Werk. Eine Auswahl mit unveröffentlichten Briefen an Karl Marx* (Berlin, DDR, 1966), esp. Friedrich's introduction, pp. 3–34.

12. Reprinted in part in Knilli and Münchow (eds.), *Frühes Deutsches Arbeitertheater*, pp. 141–57. Also, Rüden, *Arbeitertheater*, pp. 40–42.

13. Robert Schweichel, *Erzählungen;* Wilhelm Blos, *Die Geächteten. So-*

zialpolitischer Roman aus der Zeit des Sozialistengesetzes (Frankfurt am Main, 1907).

14. Ursula Münchow (ed.), *Aus den Anfängen der sozialistischen Dramatik III* (Berlin, DDR, 1972), pp. xiii–xvi; and the text of "Kater Lampe," pp. 107–236. *Lexikon Sozialistischer Deutscher Literatur*, pp. 415–17; Kurt Eisner, "Emil Rosenow," *Freie Volksbühne* 16 (1911–12):6–10; and Franz Osterroth, *Biographisches Lexikon des Sozialismus* (Hanover, 1960), vol. 1, pp. 251–52.

15. Dietmar Trempenau, *Frühe sozialdemokratische und sozialistische Arbeiterdramatik (1890–1914)* (Stuttgart, 1979), pp. 115–17, 156, 166, 168, 169.

16. Cf. Fricke, *Die deutsche Arbeiterbewegung 1869 bis 1914*, pp. 363–477; Hall, *Scandal, Sensation and Social Democracy*, pp. 24–40; Kurt Koszyk, *Anfänge und frühe Entwicklung der sozialdemokratischen Presse im Ruhrgebiet 1875–1908* (Dortmund, 1953).

17. *Lexikon Sozialistischer Deutscher Literatur*, pp. 380–82; Brigitte Emig, *Die Veredelung des Arbeiters. Sozialdemokratie als Kulturbewegung* (Frankfurt am Main and New York, 1980), pp. 244–48, 261–65.

18. *Lexikon Sozialistischer Deutscher Literatur*, pp. 280–82. On the humor magazine, also Knut Hickethier, "Karikatur, Allegorie und Bilderfolge. Zur Bildpublizistik im Dienste der Arbeiterbewegung," in Peter von Rüden (ed.), *Beiträge zur Kulturgeschichte der deutschen Arbeiterbewegung 1848–1918* (Frankfurt am Main, Vienna, Zurich, 1979), pp. 79–165, esp. pp. 99–128. It is striking, from a reading of *Der wahre Jacob* for 1892–1902, that it ran the gamut of humor: from satire, mockery, and ridicule, to harmless jokes aimed at political leaders, Junkers and the Agrarian League, militarism, anti-Semitism, orthodox Christianity, and many other subjects. It combined humor with serious articles on literature, the international labor movement, and biographical sketches of figures endorsed by Social Democracy (for example, Freiligrath, Heine, Börne, Pestalozzi, and Georg Büchner).

19. Osterroth, *Biographisches Lexikon des Sozialismus*, pp. 62, 289; Münchow (ed.), *Aus den Anfängen der sozialistischen Dramatik I*, pp. 199–200; Knilli and Münchow (eds.), *Frühes Deutsches Arbeitertheater*, p. 390.

20. On Lavant, Hans Uhlig (ed.), *Rudolf Lavant. Gedichte* (Berlin, DDR, 1965), pp. vii–xxiv.

21. Paul Ernst, "Die Zukunft und die Kunst," *Die neue Zeit* 10, part 1 (1891–92):658–60, which is an answer to Gustav Landauer, "Die Zukunft und die Kunst," *Die neue Zeit* 10, part 1 (1891–92):532–35.

22. Georg Fülberth, *Proletarische Partei und bürgerliche Literatur* (Neuwied and Berlin, 1972), p. 62.

23. Rudolf Franz, *Theater und Volk* (Munich, [ca. 1912]), p. 13.

24. Fülberth, *Proletarische Partei und bürgerliche Literatur,* p. 63.
25. Ibid., pp. 42–45.
26. Ibid., pp. 49–50.
27. Franz Mehring, "Kunst und Proletariat," *Die neue Zeit* 15, part 1 (1896–97):129–33, as cited in Franz Mehring, *Aufsätze zur deutschen Literatur von Hebbel bis Schweichel* (Berlin, DDR, 1961), pp. 134–40.
28. Cf. Herbert Scherer, *Bürgerlich-oppositionelle Literaten und sozialdemokratische Arbeiterbewegung nach 1890. Die 'Friedrichshagener' und ihr Einfluss auf die sozialdemodratische Kulturpolitik* (Stuttgart, 1974), pp. 110–11.
29. Otto Krille, "Die Kunstphrase und die Arbeiterfeste," *Die neue Zeit* 23, part 1 (1904–5):459–60.
30. Emanuel Wurm, "Tendenzlieder," *Deutsche Arbeitersänger-Zeitung,* vol. 1, no. 17 (1907), pp. 1–2, and Hermann Duncker, "So, Mann der Arbeit, sollst du Feste feiern!" *Lieder-Gemeinschaft* 5 (November 1902), both reprinted in *Arbeiterklasse und Musik. Theoretische Positionen in der deutschen Arbeiterklasse zur Musikkultur vor 1945* (Berlin, DDR, 1974), pp. 110–13.
31. The whole debate is covered in detail in Fülberth, *Proletarische Partei und bürgerliche Literatur,* pp. 127–47.
32. *Vorwärts! Eine Sammlung von Gedichten für das arbeitende Volk* (Zurich, 1886; 1st printing, 1884), p. iii. Lavant's name does not appear on the publication, but a number of sources confirm that he edited the volume: Hans Uhlig (ed.), *Rudolf Lavant. Gedichte,* p. xx; *Lexikon Sozialistischer Deutscher Literatur,* pp. 317–19, 511–13.
33. *Deutsche Arbeiter-Dichtung. Eine Auswahl Lieder und Gedichte deutscher Proletarier* (Stuttgart, 1893), vol. 1: *Gedichte von W. Hasenclever, K. E. Frohme und Adolph Lepp;* Vol. 2: *Gedichte von Jakob Audorf;* Vol. 3: *In Reih und Glied. Gedichte von einem Namenlosen* [Rudolf Lavant]; Vol. 4: *Gedichte von Max Kegel;* Vol. 5: *Gedichte von Andreas Scheu.*
34. See chapter 7.
35. Karl Henckell (ed.), *Buch der Freiheit* (Berlin, 1893), pp. v–vii. Henckell believed in 1890 that socialism, as a "Weltanschauung" rather than as a party, was nonpartisan in matters of the arts. Henckell, "Literatur und Sozialismus. Ein Notsignal," in his *Gesammelte Werke* (Munich, 1923), vol. 5, pp. 363–64.
36. M. G. Conrad, *Die Sozialdemokratie und die Moderne* (Munich, 1893). This attack first appeared in 1891 in two parts in *Die Gesellschaft* 7 (1891):583–92, 719–41.
37. Subsequent anthologies of poetry published in association with the Social Democratic party may have been more suitable and effective than Henckell's, although this conclusion is not at all certain. In 1911 Franz Diederich edited a two-volume collection of "freedom" poetry,

entitled *Von unten auf. Ein neues Buch der Freiheit* (Berlin, 1911),
also based on broad literary principles, but less committed to naturalism than Henckell. Dietger Pforte has used *Von unten auf* as his
single sample for a case study to investigate the question of the extent
to which members of the labor movement comprehended and absorbed literature of a comparatively high quality. However, he had to
rely on published reviews by socialist writers in the press of the labor
movement to find evidence on how the anthology was received, evidence that does not necessarily reflect the views of the rank and file.
He also pays little attention to the ideological thrust of Diederich's
collection. Dietger Pforte, *Von unten auf. Studie zur Literarischen
Bildungsarbeit der frühen deutschen Sozialdemokratie und zum
Verhältnis von Literatur und Arbeiterklasse* (Giessen, 1979).

38. Rüden, *Arbeitertheater*, pp. 91–92; Nestriepke, *Geschichte der
Volksbühne in Berlin*, pp. 152–54; Albert Brodbeck, *Handbuch der
deutschen Volksbühnenbewegung* (Berlin, 1930), pp. 33, 253, 256–59,
280–81, 318; Carl Severing, *Mein Lebensweg. Bd. I: Vom Schlosser
zum Minister* (Cologne, 1950), pp. 86–88 (on Bielefeld). Paul Löbe,
"Volksbildungsversuche durch Arbeitervereine in Schlesien," *Sozialistische Monatshefte* 6, part 2 (1902):796–99, reports on how the
workers' educational organization in Breslau sponsored drama productions by professionals for workers. In Leipzig much the same was
true, particularly after 1907, when the Workers' Educational Institute
(Arbeiterbildungs-Institut) sponsored a theater program that resembled in every important respect what the Freie Volksbühne did in
Berlin and other cities; cf. Schäfers, *Zur sozialistischen Arbeiterbildung in Leipzig*, pp. 160–62.
39. Heinz Selo, *Die "Freie Volksbühne" in Berlin: Geschichte ihrer Entstehung und ihre Entwicklung bis zur Auflösung im Jahre 1896* (Berlin, [1930]), pp. 45–52, 56–60, 157–65; Conrad Schmidt, "Die freie
Volksbühne in der Zeit ihres Alleinwirkens (1913)," in Julius Bab
(ed.), *Wesen und Weg der Berliner Volksbühnenbewegung* (Berlin,
1919), pp. 8–11.
40. Friedrich Stampfer, *Erfahrungen und Erkenntnisse* (Cologne, 1957),
p. 97.
41. Bab (ed.), *Wesen und Weg*, pp. 34–35; Trempenau, *Frühe sozialdemokratische und sozialistische Arbeiterdramatik*, p. 264, n. 28.
42. Ursula Münchow (ed.), *Aus den Anfängen der sozialistischen Dramatik II* (Berlin, DDR, 1965), pp. 199–200; *Lexikon Sozialistischer
Deutscher Literatur*, pp. 405–7.
43. Ernst Preczang, "Im Hinterhause," reprinted in Münchow (ed.), *Aus
den Anfängen der sozialistischen Dramatik III*, pp. 1–105.
44. Ibid., p. 95.
45. Many of Mehring's commentaries are reprinted in Mehring, *Aufsätze*

zur deutschen Literatur von Hebbel bis Schweichel, passim; Scherer, *Bürgerlich-oppositionelle Literaten und sozialdemokratische Arbeiterbewegung nach 1890,* pp. 107–8.

46. Nonetheless, Rüden insists that the role of the amateur workers' theater could have been much greater if the party leaders had been more sympathetic. Rüden, *Arbeitertheater,* pp. 211–14.

47. Ibid., pp. 83–84.

48. Trempenau, *Frühe sozialdemokratische und sozialistische Arbeiterdramatik,* pp. 275–78.

49. Ibid., passim.

50. Ibid., pp. 211–12; Rüden, *Arbeitertheater,* pp. 100–106.

51. Anon., "Demos und Libertas oder: Der entlarvte Betrüger. Ein Liebesdrama in zwei Akten," reprinted in Münchow (ed.), *Aus den Anfängen der sozialistischen Dramatik I,* pp. 79–117.

52. Ibid., pp. 116–17.

53. C. M. Scävola, *12 Jahre der Verbannung oder Des Ausgewiesenen Heimkehr. Episch-dramatische Dichtung in 12 lebenden Bildern* (Berlin, 1893). Unfortunately, this text does not include descriptions of how the tableaux vivants were to be presented. Knilli and Münchow (eds.), *Frühes deutsches Arbeitertheater,* pp. 286–90; they reprint another "epic-drama poem" by Scävola, "Die französische Revolution," also with tableaux vivants, pp. 290–302.

54. Information on the festival performances in the programs in Appendix A, and Rüden, *Arbeitertheater,* p. 88.

55. Ibid., pp. 131, 134–35. Tableaux vivants were also special attractions at May Day in Solingen (1893) and Wald (1895), the Lassalle Festival in Ohligs (1895)—it featured the Goddess of Freedom as well—and the Sports Festival in Brunswick (1914). See Appendix A.

56. *Lexikon Sozialistischer Deutscher Literatur,* pp. 107–8; Münchow (ed.), *Aus den Anfängen der sozialistischen Dramatik I,* pp. 201–2; and Gustav Schröder (ed.), *Frühes Leipziger Arbeitertheater. Friedrich Bosse* (Berlin, DDR, 1972), pp. ix–xiv.

57. Especially his play, *Die Arbeiter und die Kunst,* in which he represents in dramatic form the debate on literature and naturalism that erupted in the middle 1890s and reached its apex at the Social Democratic party congress at Gotha in 1896; the play is reprinted in Münchow (ed.), *Aus den Anfängen der sozialistischen Dramatik I,* pp. 153–93.

58. Bosse, "Die Alten und die Neuen," in Schröder (ed.), *Frühes Leipziger Arbeitertheater,* p. 18.

59. Bosse, "Der erste Mai," in ibid., pp. 125–40. Cf. Trempenau, *Frühe sozialdemokratische und sozialistische Arbeiterdramatik,* pp. 171–73.

60. Bosse, "Im Kampf," in Schröder (ed.), *Frühes Leipziger Arbeitertheater,* pp. 141–248.

61. Rüden, *Arbeitertheater,* p. 96, and Appendix A for the program of the Stiftungs-Fest, Leipzig (1904) on which Bosse's play, *Das Volk erwacht!* is listed.

62. Trempenau, *Frühe sozialdemokratische und sozialistische Arbeiterdramatik,* pp. 148–50.

63. Excerpts from Kegel, "Press-Prozesse oder die Tochter des Staatsanwaltes," in Knilli and Münchow (eds.), *Frühes deutsches Arbeitertheater,* pp. 158–66. At the Grosses-Stiftungsfest of the workers' cycling clubs in Hamburg in 1908, the program featured another piece by Bosse, *Die Sozialdemokraten kommen*—it promoted moderate socialist ideas—a comedy by Ewald Nebe, *The Raven Innkeeper* (*Der Rabenwirt*), and a "dramatic prelude," entitled *Charge of the Red Cavalry* (*Aufbruch der roten Kavallerie*). Clipping from the *Hamburger Echo,* late October 1908, Staatsarchiv Hamburg, Politische Polizei, S4316, Bd. 1.

CHAPTER 7

1. Reinhard Buchwald, "Die deutsche Volksbildungsarbeit im Zeitalter des Liberalismus," *Bücherei und Bildungspflege* 12, no. 1/2; Emil Rossmässler, *Ein Wort an die deutschen Arbeiter* (Berlin, 1863), pp. 7, 10, 11; idem., "Rede des Hr. Prof. Rossmässler bei dem Einweihungsfest des Vereins 'Vorwärts' am 30. Nov.," *Mitteldeutsche Volkszeitung,* no. 283, December 6, 1862; and Friedrich Wilhelm Schlimper, *Was wollen die deutschen Arbeiter-Bildungsvereine? Zwei Reden gehalten am 1. und 2. Stiftungsfeste des Dresdener Arbeiterbildungsvereins* (Coburg, 1863), p. 17.

2. Ingeborg Heufer, "Deutsche Arbeiterbildungsvereine im 19. Jahrhundert" (diploma thesis, Univ. of Frankfurt, 1959), pp. 75–76, Table 9; Karl Birker, *Die deutschen Arbeiterbildungsvereine 1840–1870* (Berlin, 1973), pp. 149–59, 172–75.

3. A case in point is the Verband Süddeutscher Arbeiter-Bildungs-Vereine, an amalgamation of educational societies that remained true to the principle of "self-help" as represented by the liberal Schulze-Delitsch. The Executive Committee members of the Augsburg affiliate were all master artisans, while the list of honorary members included seven manufacturers, four factory directors, three wholesalers, and four commercial managers (*Kommerzienräte*). In *Festbericht zur Jubelfeier des 25jährigen Bestehens des Arbeiter-Fortbildungsvereins Augsburg* (Augsburg, 1887), pp. 8, 13, 21–22. A similar case was the society in Karlsruhe, which, although still called a "Workers' Educational Society," had a heavily middle-class social composition. In *Tätigkeits-Bericht des Arbeiter-Bildungs-Vereins Karlsruhe. Eingetragener Verein—Gegründet 1862 für das Vereinsjahr 1907/08* (Karlsruhe, 1908), pp. 2, 14–18.

4. The mixture of ideas in Liebknecht's educational conception has been treated critically by a number of scholars: Emig, *Die Veredelung des Arbeiters*, pp. 128–239; Hans-Wolf Butterhof, *Wissen und Macht. Widersprüche sozialdemokratischer Bildungspolitik bei Harkort, Liebknecht, Schulz* (Munich, 1978); and Ulrich Bendele, *Sozialdemokratische Schulpolitik und Pädagogik im wilhelminischen Deutschland* (Frankfurt am Main, New York, 1979), pp. 24–30. The most thorough treatment is by Werner Wendorff, *Schule und Bildung in der Politik von Wilhelm Liebknecht* (Berlin, 1978), who recognizes Liebknecht's eclecticism and theoretical weaknesses, but also argues that much of his conceptualization fit well into the overall development of the labor movement.

5. Wilhelm Liebknecht, "Wissen ist Macht—Macht ist Wissen. Festrede, gehalten zum Stiftungsfest des Dresdener Bildungsvereins am 5. Februar 1872," in Wilhelm Liebknecht, *Wissen ist Macht—Macht ist Wissen und andere bildungspolitisch-pädagogische Äusserungen*, ed. by Hans Brumme (Berlin, DDR, 1968), pp. 60, 70, 75.

6. Ibid., pp. 89, 93, 94. Italics in original.

7. Reprinted in ibid., pp. 192–94.

8. Eduard Bernstein, *Geschichte der Berliner Arbeiterbewegung*, 3 vols. (Berlin, 1907), vol. 3, pp. 390–92; Simon Katzenstein, "Geistige Bewegung," *Sozialistische Monatshefte* 8, part 1 (1904):91–92.

9. Report on the activities of the Arbeiter-Bildungsschule for 1898–99 [1899], p. 2 (title page missing from this copy).

10. Arbeiter-Bildungsschule Berlin, *Jahres-Bericht über die Tätigkeit vom 1. April 1907 bis 30. September 1908* (Berlin, 1908), pp. 4–11; and *Jahres-Bericht über die Tätigkeit vom 1. Oktober 1909 bis 30. September 1910* (Berlin, 1910), pp. 3–10.

11. *Protokoll über die Verhandlungen des Parteitages der Sozialdemokratischen Partei Deutschlands. Abgehalten zu Mannheim vom 23. bis 29. September 1906* (Berlin, 1906), pp. 134–37. Hereafter, proceedings of the party congresses cited as *Protokoll . . .* with place and date in parenthesis. Heinrich Schulz, *Politik und Bildung. Hundert Jahre Arbeiterbildung* (Berlin, 1931), pp. 95–96; Karl Christ, *Sozialdemokratie und Volkserziehung. Die Bedeutung des Mannheimer Parteitages der SPD in 1906 für die Entwicklung der Bildungspolitik und Pädagogik der deutschen Arbeiterbewegung vor dem Ersten Weltkrieg* (Bern and Frankfurt am Main, 1975), pp. 118–23.

12. "Protokoll über die erste Sitzung des Bildungsausschusses am 13. Dezember 1906 im Bureau, Lindenstrasse 3." Typescript carbon copy, Vollmar Archive, no. 240, p. 3. International Institute for Social History, Amsterdam (hereafter IISH). The records of the sessions of the Central Educational Commission are very full paraphrases and summaries but not actually stenographic reports.

13. Ibid., p. 4.

14. "Protokoll über die zweite Sitzung des Bildungsausschusses am 24. Juni 1907 in der Wohnung des Vorsitzenden Ulmenstr. 6." Mimeographed copy, p. 5. Vollmar Archive, no. 3494, IISH.

15. Ibid., p. 5.

16. Ibid., pp. 5–6. David continued his attack on Schulz's views, elaborating on the argument that knowledge is neither "bourgeois" nor "proletarian." Eduard David, "Volkserziehung und Sozialdemokratie," *Die neue Gesellschaft* 2 (September 26, 1906):461.

17. Heinrich Schulz, *Arbeiterbildung und Bildungsarbeit* (Berlin, 1913), p. 6.

18. Reported on in *Protokoll . . . Essen* (1907), pp. 95–102.

19. A summary of the survey appears as part of the report of the Central Educational Commission to the 1907 party congress; in ibid., pp. 96–100. However, the mimeographed report "Das Ergebnis der Umfrage," in the Vollmar Archive, no. 240, IISH, is more detailed.

20. "Das Ergebnis der Umfrage," p. 1.

21. Ibid., pp. 4, 5, 7, 8–9, 11. For educational and artistic programs sponsored by the local Educational Commission in Cologne immediately prior to the First World War, see the documentation in Günter Bers (ed.), *Die Kölner Sozialdemokratie im Jahre 1914* (Wentorf bei Hamburg, 1974), pp. 45–46.

22. *Protokoll . . . Essen* (1907), pp. 90–91; J. P. Nettl, *Rosa Luxemburg*, 2 vols. (London, 1966), vol. 1, p. 389.

23. Statements by Mauernbrecher, Mehring, and Knauf, as cited in Dieter Fricke, "Die sozialdemokratische Parteischule," *Zeitschrift für Geschichtswissenschaft* 5 (1957):235–36.

24. Max Mauernbrecher, "Die bürgerliche Wissenschaft," *Die neue Gesellschaft* 3 (October 31, 1906):54–56; Franz Laufkötter-Hamburg, "Parteischule und proletarische Bildungsbestrebungen," *Die neue Gesellschaft* 5 (September 18, 1907):353–58. Eduard Bernstein continued criticism of the Party School, in "Theorie in der Partei," *Sozialistische Monatshefte* 13, part 2 (December 2, 1909):1531–37, to which Mehring replied with great polemical skill, in *Die neue Zeit* 28, part 1 (December 10, 1909):364–67.

25. *Protokoll . . . Nürnberg* (1908), pp. 227–42.

26. Fritz Gumpert, *Die Bildungsbestrebungen der freien Gewerkschaften* (Jena, 1923), pp. 16–18.

27. Chr. Tischendörfer, "Unterrichtskurse," *Correspondenzblatt* 14, no. 36 (September 10, 1904):592.

28. Ibid., p. 593.

29. See the three unsigned articles, all entitled "Zur Frage der gewerkschaftlichen Unterrichtskurse" (not printed, however, as separate installments of a single article), in the *Correspondenzblatt* 15, no. 8 (February 25, 1905):120–22; no. 11 (March 18, 1905):171; and no. 18 (May 6, 1905):277–78. Also, Gumpert, *Die Bildungsbestrebungen,*

pp. 85–89. The practical goals of the trade union educational programs are also stressed by Peter Krug, *Gewerkschaften und Arbeiterbildung: gewerkschaftliche Bildungsarbeit von ihren Anfängen bis zur
Weimarer Republik* (Cologne, 1980). Unfortunately, I had access to
Krug's study too late to incorporate his findings in this chapter.

30. On the practices of the Party School, see M. Schneider, "Die Partei-
    schule. Gedanken über eine Reorganisation der Schule," *Die neue
    Zeit* 27, part 2 (August 13, 1909):694; *Protokoll . . . Leipzig* (1909),
    pp. 48–49; *Protokoll . . . Chemnitz* (1912), pp. 45–46; and *Proto-
    koll . . . Jena* (1913), pp. 34–35. On the practices of the Trade Union
    School, see Gumpert, *Die Bildungsbestrebungen*, pp. 18–23; the reso-
    lution that regulated the procedures of the Trade Union School, in
    *Protokoll der Konferenz der Vertreter der Vorstände der Zentral-
    verbände, Abgehalten im Berlin Gewerkschaftshaus vom 19. bis 23.
    Februar 1906* (Berlin, 1906), pp. 94–95; and Johannes Heiden, "Aus-
    bildungskurse der Gewerkschaften und der Partei," *Sozialistische
    Monatshefte* 16, part 2 (1910):756–62.
31. Heinrich Schulz, "Fünf Jahre Parteischule," *Die neue Zeit* 29, part 2
    (September 8, 1911):806–8.
32. Cited in Fricke, "Die sozialdemokratische Parteischule," p. 246.
33. Nicholas Jacobs, "The German Social Democratic Party School in
    Berlin 1906–1914," *History Workshop* 5 (Spring 1978):186.
34. Ibid., pp. 230, 234, 246. Also, Josef Schleifstein, "Bemerkungen zur
    sozialdemokratischen Parteischule (1906–1914)," *Zeitschrift für Ge-
    schichtswissenschaft* 5, no. 6 (1957):1292–93. In his memoir Kaisen
    expressed admiration for Luxemburg's great "pedagogical talent,"
    stressed the influence the Party School exercised on him, but also
    made it clear that Marxist theory itself had been unconvincing. On
    completing the course of study (1912–13), he returned to Hamburg
    once again as a stucco worker and began to write for the *Hamburger
    Echo*. Wilhelm Kaisen, *Meine Arbeit, mein Leben* (Munich, 1967),
    pp. 48–54.
35. *Protokoll der Konferenz der Vertreter der Vorstände der Zentralver-
    bände* (1906), p. 35.
36. Gumpert, *Die Bildungsbestrebungen*, pp. 19–20.
37. "Das Ergebnis der Umfrage," pp. 5, 7, 9, 11.
38. Wilhelm Bölsche described the atmosphere in a locale during a Social
    Democratic "Heine Celebration" (*Heine-Feier*): The air was heavy
    with tobacco smoke, the smell of beer was everywhere, and all
    around there were "harsh, worn faces." *Hinter der Weltstadt* (Jena
    and Leipzig, 1904), p. 56. Wilhelm Kaisen attended a workers' educa-
    tional club in Barmbek (near Hamburg)—it met in the "spacious club
    room" of a large restaurant—despite the fact that he had to walk to
    the sessions after a full day's labor. He managed, he says, to stay
    awake. Kaisen, *Meine Arbeit, mein Leben*, p. 33.

39. *Protokoll . . . Chemnitz* (1912), p. 48.

40. Socialist women thus developed a number of courses more directly suited to their problems and interests, as explained by Quataert, *Reluctant Feminists,* pp. 189–200.

41. *Protokoll . . . Nürnberg* (1908), pp. 89–91; *Protokoll . . . Leipzig* (1909), pp. 50–51; *Protokoll . . . Magdeburg* (1910), pp. 53–56; *Protokoll . . . Jena* (1911), pp. 51–53; *Protokoll . . . Chemnitz* (1912), pp. 50–53.

42. Cf. the following, published by the Zentralbildungsausschuss: *Ratschläge und Winke für ein Winter-Programm 1907/08* (Berlin, 1907); and *Winke und Ratschläge. Winterprogramm 1912/13* (Berlin, 1912).

43. A. H. Th. Pfannkuche, *Was liest der deutsche Arbeiter?* (Tübingen and Leipzig, 1900), pp. 19, 30.

44. "Was liest der deutsche Arbeiter?" *Correspondenzblatt* 10, no. 50 (December 17, 1900):9–10. By 1900 there were, at a minimum, several hundred individual workers' libraries in Germany. In Berlin alone, by 1894, there were fifty-one trade unions with their own libraries; in Munich thirty-nine trade unions had twenty-seven libraries with holdings totaling 3,241 volumes as of 1898. Dieter Langewiesche and Klaus Schönhoven, "Arbeiterbibliotheken und Arbeiterlektüre im Wilhelminischen Deutschland," *Archiv für Sozialgeschichte* 16 (1976):155–56.

45. "Die deutschen Arbeiterbibliotheken," *Der Bibliothekar* 6 (July 1914):758; Langewiesche and Schönhoven, "Arbeiterbibliotheken," p. 159. In 1901, out of 365 trade union cartels in Germany, 116 had central libraries, 8 with reading rooms. By 1908 trade union cartels in 242 localities had centralized libraries. Reported in "Eine Versammlung der Bibliothekare," *Der Bibliothekar* 1 (October 1909):63. Also, Gustav Hennig, "Allgemeine Bibliotheksstatistik," *Der Bibliothekar* 3 (July 1911):296. The larger libraries in particular printed catalogs, some of which were quite substantial. A new edition in 1912 of the catalog of the Central Workers' Library of Barmen-Elberfeld had 169 pages; the catalog for the library in Frankfurt am Main (same year) had 171 pages. "Bibliotheksberichte," *Der Bibliothekar* 5, no. 10 (October 1913):653, 655, (Beilage).

46. Gustav Hennig, *Zehn Jahre Bibliothekarbeit. Geschichte einer Arbeiterbibliothek. Ein Wegweiser für Bibliothekverwaltungen* (Leipzig, 1908), pp. 1–2.

47. Albert Südekam launched the first extension library by sending books from his own personal library to local organizations with very limited resources. Subsequently, the party executive and other Social Democrats contributed books to the central pool. By 1907 it consisted of 240 volumes, packaged into 16 sets of between 9 and 16 volumes each. Between October 1906 and May 1907 80 sets had been mailed

to 71 different places. Albert Südekam, "Wanderbibliotheken. Eine Anregung zur Arbeiterbildung," *Sozialistische Monatshefte* 11, part 2 (1907):770–74, and the short notice in *Sozialistische Monatshefte* 11, part 1 (1907):80.

48. "Bibliotheksberichte," *Der Bibliothekar* 4 (August 1912):481, 484 (Beilage); "Bibliotheksberichte," *Der Bibliothekar* 5, no. 10 (October 1913):654 (Beilage). The Workers' Central Library in Magdeburg acquired substantial quarters by 1914, with a reading room (no hours given), and 8,881 volumes, while its counterpart in Bielefeld kept its reading room open about two hours daily. "Bibliotheksberichte," *Der Bibliothekar* 6, no. 1 (January 1914):692, and no. 3 (March 1914):715.

49. One librarian actually received a salary of 7,500 marks annually! Ten received between 2,000 and 5,000 marks; 5 between 1,000 and 2,000; 7 between 500 and 1,000; 10 between 200 and 500; 23 between 100 and 200; 75 between 50 and 100; and 235 received 50 marks annually or less. "Die deutschen Arbeiterbibliotheken," *Der Bibliothekar* 6, no. 7 (July 1914):759.

50. The lecturers and their topics were: Dr. Gustav Eckstein on socialism and economics; Rudolph Wissel on trade unions and social-political literature; Emil Eichhorn on periodicals and historical literature; Dr. Conrad Schmidt on philosophy; Richard Woldt on technical subjects; Dr. M. H. Baege on natural science; Ernst Däumig on literary histories; and two lecturers covered cataloging and other technical matters of librarianship. Franz Petrich, "Ein Unterrichtskursus für Arbeiterbibliothekare," *Literatur-Beilage des Correspondenzblatt*, no. 7, July 25, 1914, p. 49.

51. Heinrich Schulz, "Vorbemerkung," in *Muster-Kataloge für Arbeiter-Bibliotheken* (Berlin, 1908), p. 5. The same sentiments expressed by Fr[anz] Petrich, "Bibliotheksfragen," *Literatur-Beilage des Correspondenzblatt*, no. 9, October 4, 1913, p. 70.

52. Ernst Mehlich, "Statistisches zur Bibliotheksarbeit," *Literatur-Beilage des Correspondenzblatt*, no. 5, May 24, 1913, p. 37.

53. "Was liest der deutsche Arbeiter?" *Correspondenzblatt* 10, no. 50 (December 17, 1900):10.

54. J. S. and E. F., "Was lesen die organisierten Arbeiter in Deutschland?" *Die neue Zeit* 13, part 2 (1894–95):154–55; Advocatus, "Was liest der deutsche Arbeiter?" *Die neue Zeit* 13, part 2 (1894–95):814–17; Advocatus, "Ein weiterer Beitrag zur Frage: 'Was liest der deutsche Arbeiter?'" *Die neue Zeit* 14, part 1 (1895–96):631–35. The preference for belletristic writing became even more apparent in the report by Konrad Haenisch, "Was lesen die Arbeiter?" *Die neue Zeit* 18, part 2 (1899–1900):692–93. The same conclusions were implicit in the tables compiled by Pfannkuche, *Was liest der deutsche Arbeiter?*, printed at the end of the volume (unpaginated). The data from these

early reports have been used both by Hans-Josef Steinberg, *Sozialismus und Deutsche Sozialdemokratie* (Hanover, 1967), pp. 129–32, and Langewiesche and Schönhoven, "Arbeiterbibliotheken."

55. For example, Paul Lensch, *Sozialistische Literatur. Zwei Vorträge* (Leipzig, 1907).

56. Hennig, *Zehn Jahre Bibliothekarbeit*, p. 33.

57. Ibid., p. 4.

58. *VIII. Jahres-Bericht für das Jahr 1907*, pub. by the Arbeiter-Sekretariat Mannheim (Mannheim, n. d. [1908]), p. 78; Pfannkuche, *Was liest der deutsche Arbeiter?*, pp. 64–65.

59. Rolf Engelsing, *Massenpublikum und Journalistentum im 19. Jahrhundert in Nordwestdeutschland* (Berlin, 1966), p. 78.

60. Ernst Mehlich, "Die Arbeiterbibliotheken," *Der Bibliothekar* 4, no. 6 (June 1912):438. Pfannkuche, on the other hand, was particularly critical of the one-sided nature of the holdings in the workers' libraries, in *Was liest der deutsche Arbeiter?*, pp. 73–74.

61. *Muster-Kataloge für Arbeiter-Bibliotheken*, pp. 9–29. The lowest-cost library, for ten marks, included the following: Bebel, *Die Frau;* Ad. Braun, *Zeitungs-Fremdwörter und politische Schlagworte;* Engels, *Die Entwicklung des Sozialismus von der Utopie zur Wissenschaft;* Kautsky and Schönlank, *Erläuterung zum Erfurter Programm;* Lassalle, *Arbeiterprogramm, Offenes Antwortschreiben,* and *Über Verfassungswesen;* Liebknecht, *Wissen ist Macht—Macht ist Wissen;* Marx and Engels, *Das Kommunistische Manifest;* and Marx, *Lohnarbeit und Kapital.*

62. Hennig, *Zehn Jahre Bibliothekarbeit*, pp. 38–39.

63. Ernst Mehlich, "Einige Grundfragen des Bibliothekbetriebs," *Der Zeitgeist* 5, no. 8 (August 1912):364.

64. In Dresden (1902), for every twenty-four skilled workers using the library, there were ten unskilled; in Göttingen (1904) the ratio was seventy-eight skilled to ten unskilled. Between 1909 and 1914 in Kiel, the unions with the highest percentage of readers were printers, bookbinders, lithographers, and paperhangers, followed by woodworkers, metalworkers, and bakers. Langewiesche and Schönhoven, "Arbeiterbibliotheken," pp. 173, 175, 178–79.

65. Ibid., pp. 167, 202. The discrepancy between the extensive holdings in social-scientific literature and the low rate at which they were borrowed was pointed out statistically by Ernst Mehlich, "Statistisches zur Bibliotheksarbeit," *Literatur-Beilage des Correspondenzblatt* no. 5 (May 24, 1913):37–38.

66. Hertha Siemering, *Arbeiterbildungswesen in Wien und Berlin* (Karlsruhe, 1911), p. 133.

67. Josef Kliche, "Arbeiterlektüre," *Sozialistische Monatshefte* 15, part 1 (1911):318; Pfannkuche, *Was liest der deutsche Arbeiter?*, p. 59.

68. Kliche, "Arbeiterlektüre," p. 317; Pfannkuche, *Was liest der deutsche Arbeiter?*, pp. 57–59; *Der Bibliothekar* 2, no. 8 (August 1910):168.

69. Pfannkuche, "Tabelle der am meisten gelesenen Bücher," in *Was liest der deutsche Arbeiter?;* Hennig, *Zehn Jahre Bibliothekarbeit,* pp. 6–7; Advocatus, "Was liest der deutsche Arbeiter?" *Die neue Zeit* 13, part 2 (1894–95):815.

70. Langewiesche and Schönhoven, "Arbeiterbibliotheken," p. 189; Adelheid Popp, *The Autobiography of a Working Woman,* trans. by F. C. Harvey (London, 1912), pp. 36–37; Heinrich Holek, *Unterwegs,* pp. 83, 86, 161–62; Moritz Bromme, *Lebensgeschichte eines modernen Fabrikarbeiters,* ed. by Paul Göhre (Jena and Leipzig, 1905), p. 117; and Georg Heinrich Dikreiter, *Vom Waisenhaus zur Fabrik. Geschichte einer Proletarierjugend* (Berlin, [1914]), p. 170.

71. E. Decker, "Zur Frage der Gewerkschafts-Bibliotheken," *Correspondenzblatt* 11, no. 4 (January 28, 1901):64.

72. In the library managed by Gustav Hennig in Lindenau (near Leipzig), 25 percent of the holdings were in the social sciences in 1898; by 1907 that had dropped to 8.1 percent. Langewiesche and Schönhoven, "Arbeiterbibliotheken," pp. 169–71.

73. Pfannkuche, *Was liest der deutsche Arbeiter?,* pp. 9, 38; Engelsing, *Massenpublikum,* pp. 117–18.

74. Comparative data from Langewiesche and Schönhoven, "Arbeiterbibliotheken," pp. 182, 184, 185, 187, 193.

75. Cited in Adolf Levenstein (ed.), *Aus der Tiefe. Arbeiterbriefe,* 2nd ed. (Berlin, 1909), p. 121.

76. Buchwitz, *50 Jahre Funktionär,* p. 37. Wilhelm Kaisen, *Meine Arbeit, mein Leben,* p. 34, comments on the difficulty he had trying to comprehend Marx's theories of surplus value and immiserization when he attended the Worker's School in Barmbek as a young man.

77. Pfannkuche, *Was liest der deutsche Arbeiter?,* p. 69; Dikreiter, *Vom Waisenhaus zur Fabrik,* p. 170; Popp, *Autobiography,* pp. 35–36; Heinrich Holek, "Wie ich mich emporlas," *Der Bibliothekar* 3, no. 12 (December 1912):357–61.

78. Engelsing, *Massenpublikum,* pp. 86–87.

79. Buchwitz, *50 Jahre Funktionär,* p. 43.

80. That the Social Democrats overestimated the influence of the printed word has been argued very persuasively by Jochen Loreck. On the basis of an extensive use of workers' memoirs and other evidence, he shows that personal contact, attending meetings, and listening to speeches were more effective as means of communication and persuasion. Loreck, *Wie man früher Sozialdemokrat wurde,* pp. 27–30, 103–58, 247–54.

CHAPTER 8

1. Adolf Levenstein edited the following: *Arbeiter-Philosophen und Dichter* (Berlin, 1909); *Proletariers Jugendjahre* (Berlin, 1909); *Friedrich Nietzsche im Urteil der Arbeiterklasse,* 2nd ed. (Leipzig, 1919),

1st ed. (Berlin, 1914); and *Aus der Tiefe. Arbeiterbriefe,* 2nd ed. (Berlin, 1909). He published the results of his survey in *Die Arbeiterfrage* (Munich, 1912). Levenstein also sponsored an exhibition of paintings and lithographs by workers, on which, unfortunately, little evidence can be found. It was reviewed briefly by Lisbeth Stern, in the *Sozialistische Monatshefte* 15, part 3 (1909):1730.

2. Zetkin, *Kunst und Proletariat* (Stuttgart, 1911), pp. 6–7.

3. Ibid., p. 14.

4. Schulz, *Arbeiterbildung und Bildungsarbeit,* pp. 8–9.

5. Arbeiter-Sekretariat Jena, report for 1900 (title page missing), p. 77; Arbeiter-Sekretariat Bremen, *Vierter Jahresbericht. Geschäftsjahr 1903* (Bremen, 1904), pp. 65, 66; Karl-Ernst Moring, *Die Sozialdemokratische Partei in Bremen 1890–1914* (Hanover, 1968), pp. 77–80, 93.

Bibliography

ARCHIVAL MATERIALS

Many of the archives in the Federal Republic of Germany have unpublished material related to the Social Democratic labor movement, and a limited amount bears directly on the themes of this book. Numerous divisions of the government kept records on the party, free trade unions, and auxiliary organizations. The written reports of policemen are often brief and superficial, but many of the same files also contain a variety of printed documents (e.g., local festival programs) that are otherwise difficult to locate. For this kind of printed material, as well as for some unpublished sources, the most fruitful archives were the following: Staatsarchiv Hamburg, Staatsarchiv Düsseldorf, and Staatsarchiv Wiesbaden. Materials from these archives are cited in the notes and in the appendixes on festival programs. In addition, the Vollmar Archive in the Internationaal Instituut voor Sociale Geschiedenis, Amsterdam, contains unpublished minutes for several sessions of the Central Educational Commission of the Social Democratic party. Other printed sources in the Internationaal Instituut have been used extensively. An important part of the documentation in this book also comes from two archives with some rare and valuable holdings: the Arbeiterliedarchiv, a division of the Akademie der Künste zu Berlin, DDR; and the Archiv der sozialen Demokratie, Bonn, especially the collection on the Arbeiter Turn- und Sportbewegung (ATUS).

PROTOCOLS AND ORGANIZATIONAL DOCUMENTS

Arbeiter-Bildungsschule Berlin. *Jahres-Bericht über die Thätigkeit vom 1. April 1901 bis 31. März 1902.* Berlin, 1902.

————. *Jahres-Bericht über die Thätigkeit vom 1. April 1903 bis 31. März 1904.* Berlin, 1904.

————. *Jahres-Bericht über die Tätigkeit vom 1. April bis 30. September 1908.* Berlin, 1908.

————. *Jahres-Bericht über die Tätigkeit vom 1. Oktober 1909 bis 30. September 1910.* Berlin, 1910. Also: *Jahres-Bericht* for 1898–99, but without title page.

Arbeiter-Radfahrer-Verein "Vorwärts." *Mitgliedsbuch.* Hamburg, [ca. 1890].

Arbeiterstenographenbund. *Protokoll des Achten Bundestag. Vom 6. bis 8. Juni 1908 in Elberfeld.* Karlsruhe, 1908.

————. *Protokoll des 10. Bundestages vom 5. bis 8. April 1912 in Berlin (Gewerkschaftshaus).* Freiburg i. Br., 1912.

Bericht über die gemeinschaftlichen Einrichtungen von der Sozialdemokratischen Partei und den Gewerkschaften in Leipzig 1910. Leipzig, 1910.

Bericht über die Tätigkeit des Agitationskomitees der Sozialdemokratischen Partei Leipzigs für das Jahr 1908–09 nebst Bericht über die Tätigkeit des Allgemeinen Arbeiterbildungs-Instituts für Leipzig: in der Zeit vom 11. Juli 1908 bis 30. Juni 1909. Leipzig, 1909.

Bildungsausschuss der Sozialdemokratischen Partei Deutschlands. *Muster-Kataloge für Arbeiter-Bibliotheken.* Berlin, 1908.

Deutscher Arbeiter-Sängerbund. *Protokoll der 3. Generalversammlung des Deutschen Arbeiter-Sängerbundes. Abgehalten zu Leipzig am 14. und 15. 1914.* Berlin, 1914.

Festbericht zur Jubelfeier des 25jährigen Bestehens des Arbeiter-Fortbildungsvereins Augsburg. Augsburg, 1887.

Freie Gewerkschaften Deutschlands. *Protokoll der Konferenz der Vertreter der Vorstände der Zentralverbände. Abgehalten im Berlin Gewerkschaftshaus vom 19. bis 23. Februar 1906.* Berlin, 1906.

————. *Protokoll der Konferenz der Vorstände der Zentralverbände. Abgehalten im Berlin Gewerkschaftshaus am Montag den 26. und Dienstag den 27. November 1906.* Berlin, 1906.

————. *Protokoll der Konferenz von Vertretern der Zentralverbands-Vorstände. Abgehalten im Berliner Gewerkschaftshaus am Montag, den 16. und Dienstag, den 17. Dezember 1907.* Berlin, 1907.

Freie Turnerschaft Hammerbrook-Rotenburgsort. *Mitgliedsbuch.* Hamburg, n.d.

Leidigkeit, Karl-Heinz, ed. *Der Leipziger Hochverratsprozess vom Jahre 1872.* Berlin-DDR, 1960.

Protokoll vom Kreisturntag des 4. Turnkreises (Sachsen) des Arbeiter-Turnerbundes Deutschland, abgehalten am 14. und 15. Mai 1894 in Hohenstein-Ernstthal (Gasthaus "Zur Zeche"). Dresden, 1894.

Sozialdemokratische Partei Deutschlands. *Protokoll über die Verhandlungen des Parteitages der Sozialdemokratischen Partei Deutschlands.* Berlin, 1890–1913, especially 1905 onwards.

Statistischer Bericht über den Mitgliederbestand und den Turnbetrieb innerhalb des Arbeiter-Turnerbundes vom 1. Januar bis 31. Dezember 1910. Leipzig, [1911].

Statut der "Freien Turnerschaft" in Fechenheim a. M. Mitglied des Arbeiter-Turnerbundes Deutschlands 1904. N. p., n. d.

Statut des Zentral-Verbandes der proletarischen Freidenker Deutschlands. Nuremberg, n. d.

Statuten der Freien Turnerschaft an der Kieler Förde (Mitglied des Arbeiter-Turnerbundes). Kiel, 1904.

Stern, Leo, ed. *Der Kampf der deutschen Sozialdemokratie in der Zeit des Sozialistengesetzes. Die Tätigkeit der Reichs-Commission.* 2 vols. Berlin-DDR, 1956.

Tätigkeits-Bericht des Arbeiter-Bildungs-Vereins Karlsruhe. Eingetragener Verein—Gegründet 1862 für das Vereinsjahr 1907/08. Karlsruhe, 1908.

Zentralbildungsausschuss der Sozialdemokratischen Partei Deutschlands. *Ratschläge und Winke für ein Winter-Programm 1907/08.* Berlin, 1907.

———. *Winke und Ratschläge. Winterprogramm 1912/13.* Berlin, 1912.

Zentralkommission für das Arbeiterbildungswesen von Hamburg-Altona und Umgegend. *Geschäftsbericht für das Jahr 1911/12.* Hamburg, [1912].

———. *Geschäftsbericht für das Jahr 1912/13.* Hamburg, [1913].

———. *Geschäftsbericht für das Jahr 1913/14.* Hamburg, [1914].

NEWSPAPERS AND PERIODICALS

Arbeiter-Jugend. Berlin, 1909–14.

Arbeiter-Sänger-Zeitung. Berlin, 1907–14.

Arbeiter-Schwimmerzeitung. Organ für die Interessen der volkstümlichen Schwimmerei. Berlin, 1912–14. Began publication ca. 1899.

Arbeiter-Turn-Zeitung. Organ für die Interessen der volkstümlichen Turnerei. Leipzig, 1893–1914.

Der Atheist. Illustrierte Wochenschrift für Volksaufklärung. Nuremberg/ Leipzig, 1905–14.

Der Bibliothekar. Monatsschrift für Arbeiterbibliotheken. Leipzig, 1909– 14.

Correspondenzblatt der Generalkommission der Gewerkschaften Deutschlands. Hamburg/Berlin, 1891–1914.

Literatur-Beilage des Correspondenzblatt, 1909–14.

Deutsche Arbeiter-Schachzeitung. Monatsschrift zur Förderung der Schachspielkunst in Arbeiterkreisen. Munich, 1909–14.

Freie Volksbühne. Berlin, 1903–14, incomplete. Began publication 1897.

Liedergemeinschaft der Arbeiter-Sängervereinigungen Deutschlands. Berlin, 1899–1906.

Die neue Gesellschaft. Sozialistische Wochenschrift. Berlin-Wilmersdorf, 1905–7.

Die neue Welt. Illustriertes Unterhaltungsblatt für das Volk. Leipzig, 1876–83; Stuttgart, 1883–1914.

Die neue Zeit. Stuttgart, 1883–1914.

Sozialistische Monatshefte. Internationale Revue des Sozialismus. Berlin, 1897–1914.

Der wahre Jacob. Illustrietes humoristisch-satirisches Monatsblatt. Stuttgart, 1892–1902. Began publication 1884.

Der Zeitgeist. Monatliches Bildungsorgan des Deutschen Metallarbeiter-Verbandes. Stuttgart, 1908–14.

SONGS, DRAMA, POETRY, PROSE

Arbeiter-Liederbuch für Massen-Gesang. Dortmund, 1911.

Beisswanger, Konrad, ed. *Kampflieder aus den Anfängen der frei-religiösen Bewegung.* Nuremberg, 1907.

————, ed. *Stimmen der Freiheit. Blüthenlese der hervorragendsten Schöpfungen unserer Arbeiter- u. Volksdichter.* Nuremberg, 1900.

Blos, Wilhelm. *Die Geächteten. Sozialpolitischer Roman aus der Zeit des Sozialistengesetzes.* Frankfurt am Main, 1907.

Böhme, Franz Magnus, ed. *Volksthümliche Lieder der Deutschen im 18. und 19. Jahrhundert.* Leipzig, 1895.

Deutsche Arbeiter-Dichtung. Eine Auswahl Lieder und Gedichte deutscher Proletarier. Stuttgart, 1893. Vol. 1: *Gedichte von W. Hasenclever, K. E. Frohme und Adolf Lepp.* Vol. 2: *Gedichte von Jakob Audorf.* Vol. 3: *In Reih und Glied. Gedichte von einem Namenlosen* [Rudolf Lavant]. Vol. 4: *Gedichte von Max Kegel.* Vol. 5: *Gedichte von Andreas Scheu.*

Diederich, Franz, ed. *Von unten auf. Ein neues Buch der Freiheit.* 2 vols. Berlin, 1911.

Erk, Fr., and M. Schauenburg, eds. *Allgemeines Deutsches Turnerlieder-buch.* Lahr, [ca. 1860].

Franz, J. ed. *Gedichte und Lieder freisinniger und besonders sozialdemo-kratischer Tendenz.* Zurich, 1872.

Der freie Turner. 2nd ed. Leipzig, 1896; 9th ed. Leipzig, 1907.

Friedrich, Cäcilia, ed. *Aus dem Schaffen früher sozialistischer Schriftstel-lerinnen.* Berlin-DDR, 1966.

Friedrich, Wolfgang, ed. *August Otto-Walster. Leben und Werk. Eine Auswahl mit unveröffentlichten Briefen an Karl Marx.* Berlin-DDR, 1966.

————, ed. *Im Klassenkampf. Deutsche revolutionäre Lieder und Ge-dichte aus der zweiten Hälfte des 19. Jahrhunderts.* Halle, 1962.

Fritzsche, F. W. *Blut-Rosen. Sozial-politische Gedichte.* 2nd ed. Baltimore, 1890.

Frohme, Karl. *Empor! Lieder und Gedichte.* Hamburg, 1910.

———. *Feierstunden.* Frankfurt am Main, 1876.

———. *Ein Immortellenkranz.* Bremen, 1872.

Geib, August. *Gedichte.* 2nd ed. Leipzig, 1876.

Häckel, Manfred, ed. *Gedichte über Marx und Engels.* Berlin-DDR, 1963.

Hasenclever, Wilhelm. *Liebe, Leben, Kampf. Gedichte.* Hamburg, 1876.

Henckell, Karl, ed. *Buch der Freiheit.* Berlin, 1893.

Jugend-Liederbuch. Edited by the Zentralstelle für die arbeitende Jugend Deutschlands. Berlin, [1907].

Kämpchen, Heinrich. *Aus der Tiefe. Gedichte und Lieder eines Bergmanns.* Edited by Wilhelm Helf. Bochum, 1931.

Kegel, Max, ed. *Sozialdemokratisches Liederbuch.* Stuttgart, 1891; 8th ed. Stuttgart, 1897.

Knieriem, Michael, ed. *Friedrich Engels: Cola di Rienzi. Ein unbekannter dramatischer Entwurf.* Trier, 1974.

Knilli, Friedrich, and Ursula Münchow, eds. *Frühes deutsches Arbeitertheater 1847–1918. Eine Dokumentation.* Munich, 1970.

Lassalle, Ferdinand. *Gesammelte Reden und Schriften.* Edited by Eduard Bernstein. Vol. 1: *Der Italienische Krieg. Franz von Sickingen.* Berlin, 1919.

Lavant, Rudolf [Richard Cramer]. *Gedichte.* Edited by Hans Uhlig. Berlin-DDR, 1965.

Lessen, Ludwig. *Fackeln der Zeit. Gedichte.* Berlin 1904.

Lieder für Arbeiterradfahrer-Vereine. Edited by the Bundesvorstand des Arbeiterradfahrerbundes Solidarität. Stuttgart, 1897.

Liederbuch. Edited by the Deutscher Arbeiter-Sängerbund, Gau Berlin u. Umgegend. 7th ed. Berlin, 1912.

Liederbuch der Athletik treibenden Arbeiterschaft. Edited by the Arbeiter-Athletenbund Deutschlands. Magdeburg, 1913.

Liederbuch für Arbeiter-Abstinenten. Berlin, n.d.

Liederbuch für Deutsche Turner. 87th ed. Brunswick, [ca. 1890].

Liederbuch für Naturfreunde. Edited by the Deutscher Arbeiter-Wanderbund, Die Naturfreunde. Berlin, 1913.

Most, Johann, ed. *Neuestes Proletarier-Liederbuch von verschiedenen Arbeiterdichtern.* 4th ed. Chemnitz, 1873.

Most's Proletarier-Liederbuch. Edited by Gustav Geilhof. 5th ed. Chemnitz, 1875.

Münchow, Ursula, ed. *Aus den Anfängen der sozialistischen Dramatik I.* Berlin-DDR, 1964.

———. *Aus den Anfängen der sozialistischen Dramatik II.* Berlin-DDR, 1965.

———. *Aus den Anfängen der sozialistischen Dramatik III.* Berlin-DDR, 1972.

Scävola, C. M. *12 Jahre der Verbannung oder Des Ausgewiesenen Heim-*

kehr. Episch-dramatische Dichtung in 12 lebenden Bildern. Berlin, 1893.

Schröder, Gustav, ed. *Frühes Leipziger Arbeitertheater. Friedrich Bosse.* Berlin-DDR, 1972.

Schweichel, Robert. *Erzählungen.* Edited by Erika Pick. Berlin-DDR, 1964.

Seifert, C. E. ed. *Sammlung sozialdemokratischer Lieder. 2nd Heft.* Leipzig, 1871.

Singe mit! Eine Sammlung politischer und gewerkschaftlicher Kampfeslieder. 2nd ed. Leipzig, 1904.

Der sozialdemokratische Deklamator. Sammlung von ernsten und heitern Gedichten. Hottingen-Zurich, 1897.

Sozialdemokratische Lieder und Deklamationen. 5th ed. Zurich, 1878.

Vorwärts! Eine Sammlung von Gedichten für das arbeitende Volk. Zurich, 1886. 1st printing 1884.

Wittich, Manfred. *Gelegenheitsgedichte und Prologe für Arbeiterfeste.* Munich, 1892. 2nd ed. Munich, 1894.

Memoirs and Other Contemporary Sources

Achten, Udo, ed. *Zum Lichte empor. Mai-Festzeitungen der Sozialdemokratie 1891–1914.* Berlin/Bonn, 1980.

Atzrott, Otto. *Sozialdemokratische Druckschriften und Vereine verboten auf Grund des Reichsgesetzes gegen die gemeingefährlichen Bestrebungen der Sozialdemokratie vom 21. Oktober 1878.* Berlin, 1886.

Bölsche, Wilhelm. *Hinter der Weltstadt.* Jena/Leipzig, 1904.

Bromme, Moritz W. T. *Lebensgeschichte eines modernen Fabrikarbeiters.* Edited by Paul Göhre. Jena/Leipzig, 1905.

Buchwitz, Otto. *50 Jahre Funktionär der deutschen Arbeiterbewegung.* Berlin, 1949.

Conrad, Michael Georg. *Die Sozialdemokratie und die Moderne. Münchener Flugschrift.* Munich, 1893.

Dikreiter, Heinrich. *Vom Waisenhaus zur Fabrik. Geschichte einer Proletarierjugend.* Berlin, [1914].

Franz, Rudolf. *Theater und Volk.* Munich, [1912].

Göhre, Paul. *Drei Monate Fabrikarbeiter und Handwerksbursche. Eine praktische Studie.* Leipzig, 1891.

Hennig, Gustav. *Zehn Jahre Bibliothekarbeit. Geschichte einer Arbeiterbibliothek. Ein Wegweiser für Bibliothekverwaltung.* Leipzig, 1908.

Holek, Heinrich. *Unterwegs. Eine Selbstbiographie.* Vienna, 1927.

Kaisen, Wilhelm. *Meine Arbeit, mein Leben.* Munich, 1967.

Lensch, Paul. *Sozialistische Literatur. Zwei Vorträge.* Leipzig, 1907.

Levenstein, Adolf. *Die Arbeiterfrage.* Munich, 1912.

———. *Arbeiter-Philosophen und -Dichter.* Berlin, 1909.

————. *Aus der Tiefe. Arbeiterbriefe. Beiträge zur Seelen-Analyse moderner Arbeiter.* 3rd ed. Berlin, 1909.

————. *Friedrich Nietzsche im Urteil der Arbeiterklasse.* 2nd ed. Leipzig, 1919.

Liebknecht, Wilhelm. *Wissen ist Macht—Macht ist Wissen, und andere bildungspolitische-pädagogische Äusserungen.* Edited by Hans Brumme. Berlin-DDR, 1968.

Mehring, Franz. *Gesammelte Schriften.* Edited by Thomas Höhle, Hans Koch, and Josef Schleifstein. Vol. 11: *Aufsätze zur deutschen Literatur von Hebbel bis Schweichel.* Berlin-DDR, 1961.

Pfannkuche, A. H. Th. *Was liest der deutsche Arbeiter?* Tübingen/Leipzig, 1900.

Popp, Adelheid. *The Autobiography of a Working Woman.* Translated by F. C. Harvey. London, 1912.

Rossmässler, E[mil] A[dolph]. *Ein Wort an die deutschen Arbeiter.* Berlin, 1863.

Schlimper, Friedrich Wilhelm. *Was wollen die deutschen Arbeiter-Bildungsvereine? Zwei Reden gehalten am 1. und 2. Stiftungsfeste des Dresdener Arbeiterbildungsvereine.* Coburg, 1863.

Schuchardt, Ernst. *Sechs Monate Arbeitshaus. Erlebnisse eines wandernden Arbeiters.* 2nd ed. Berlin, n.d. Original preface 1907.

Schulz, Heinrich. *Arbeiterbildung und Bildungsarbeit!* Berlin, 1913.

————. *Politik und Bildung. Hundert Jahre Arbeiterbildung.* Berlin, 1931.

Severing, Carl. *Mein Lebensweg.* Vol. 1: *Vom Schlosser zum Minister.* Cologne, 1950.

Stampfer, Friedrich. *Erfahrungen und Erkenntnisse. Aufzeichnungen aus meinem Leben.* Cologne, 1957.

Strzelewicz, B[oleslav]. *35 Jahre Künstlerfahrten unter deutscher Monarchie und Republik.* Dresden, n.d.

Wildung, Fritz, ed. *Handbuch des Arbeiter-Turnerbundes.* Leipzig, 1911.

Zetkin, Clara. *Kunst und Proletariat.* Stuttgart, 1911.

SECONDARY LITERATURE

Bab, Julius. *Wesen und Weg der Berliner Volksbühnenbewegung.* Berlin, 1919.

Baker, William J. "The Making of a Working-Class Football Culture in Victorian England." *Journal of Social History* 13 (1979), 241–51.

Beisswanger, Konrad. *50 Jahre Freidenkertum. Der Aufstieg einer Kulturbewegung.* Nuremberg, [ca. 1930].

Bendele, Ulrich. *Sozialdemokratische Schulpolitik und Pädagogik in Wilhelminischen Deutschland 1890–1914.* Frankfurt am Main/New York, 1979.

Bernays, Marie. "Berufswahl und Berufsschicksal des modernen Industriearbeiters." *Archiv für Sozialwissenschaft und Sozialpolitik* 35 (1912), 123–76; 36 (1913), 884–915.

Bernstein, Eduard. *Geschichte der Berliner Arbeiterbewegung*. 3 vols. Berlin, 1907–10.

Bers, Günter. *Die Kölner Sozialdemokratie im Jahre 1914*. Wentorf bei Hamburg, 1974.

———, and Michael Klöcker. *Die sozialdemokratische Arbeiterbewegung im Kölner Raum 1890–1895*. Wentorf bei Hamburg, 1976.

Birker, Karl. *Die deutschen Arbeiterbildungsvereine 1840–1870*. Berlin, 1973.

Blackbourn, David. "The Problem of Democratisation: German Catholics and the Role of the Centre Party." In Richard J. Evans, ed. *Society and Politics in Wilhelmine Germany*. London, 1978.

Bocock, Robert. *Ritual in Industrial Society. A Sociological Analysis of Ritualism in Modern England*. London, 1974.

Breunig, Willi. *Soziale Verhältnisse der Arbeiterschaft und sozialistische Arbeiterbewegung in Ludwigshafen am Rhein 1869–1919*. Ludwigshafen am Rhein, 1976.

Brodbeck, Albert. *Handbuch der deutschen Volksbühnenbewegung*. Berlin, 1930.

Buchwald, Reinhard. "Die deutsche Volksbildungsarbeit im Zeitalter des Liberalismus." Reprinted in: *Bücherei und Bildungspflege* 12, nos. 1/2 (1932).

Butterhof, Hans-Wolf. *Wissen und Macht. Widersprüche sozialdemokratischer Bildungspolitik bei Harkort, Liebknecht, Schulz*. Munich, 1978.

Christ, Karl. *Sozialdemokratie und Volkserziehung. Die Bedeutung des Mannheimer Parteitags der SPD in 1906 für die Entwicklung der Bildungspolitik und Pädagogik der deutschen Arbeiterbewegung vor dem Ersten Weltkrieg*. Frankfurt am Main/Bern, 1875.

Clarke, John, et al. *Working-Class Culture. Studies in History and Theory*. London, 1979.

Conze, Werner, and Dieter Groh. *Die Arbeiterbewegung in der nationalen Bewegung*. Stuttgart, 1966.

Dahrendorf, Ralf. *Class and Class Conflict in Industrial Society*. Stanford, Calif., 1959.

———. *Society and Democracy in Germany*. Garden City, N.Y., 1967.

Dowe, Dieter. "The Workingmen's Choral Movement in Germany before the First World War." *Journal of Contemporary History* 13 (1978), 269–96.

Ecks, Karl. *Die Arbeiterdichtung im rheinisch-westfälischen Industriegebiet*. Borna-Leipzig, 1925.

Elben, Otto. *Der volksthümliche deutsche Männergesang. Geschichte und Stellung im Leben der Nation; der deutsche Sängerbund und seine Glieder*. 2nd ed. Tübingen, 1887.

Eley, Geoff. *Reshaping the German Right: Radical Nationalism and Political Change after Bismarck.* New Haven/London, 1980.

Emig, Brigitte. *Die Veredelung des Arbeiters: Sozialdemokratie als Kulturbewegung.* Frankfurt am Main/New York 1980.

Engelsing, Rolf. *Analphabetentum und Lektüre. Zur Sozialgeschichte des Lesens in Deutschland zwischen feudaler und industrieller Gesellschaft.* Stuttgart, 1973.

————. *Massenpublikum und Journalistentum im 19. Jahrhundert in Nordwestdeutschland.* Berlin, 1966.

Evans, Richard J. "Introduction: The Sociological Interpretation of German Labour History." In Richard J. Evans, ed. *The German Working Class 1888–1933. The Politics of Everyday Life.* London/Totowa, N.J., 1982.

Ewens, Franz Josef. *Lexikon des Chorwesens.* 2nd ed. Mönchengladbach, 1960.

Fillies, Walter. "Die Arbeitersängerbewegung. Ein Beitrag zur Klassengeschichte der Arbeiterschaft." Dissertation, University of Rostock, 1932.

Freudenthal, Herbert. *Vereine in Hamburg, Ein Beitrag zur Geschichte und Volkskunde der Geselligkeit.* Hamburg, 1968.

Fricke, Dieter. *Die deutsche Arbeiterbewegung 1869 bis 1914. Ein Handbuch über ihre Organisation und Tätigkeit im Klassenkampf.* Berlin-DDR, 1976.

————. "Die sozialdemokratische Parteischule (1906 bis 1914)." *Zeitschrift für Geschichtswissenschaft* 5 (1957), 229–47.

Friedrich, Wolfgang. "Die sozialistische deutsche Literatur in der Zeit des Aufschwungs der Arbeiterbewegung während der sechziger Jahre des 19. Jahrhunderts bis zum Erlass des Sozialistengesetzes." 2 vols. Habilitationsschrift, Typescript. University of Halle-Wittenberg, 1964.

Fülberth, Georg. *Proletarische Partei und bürgerliche Literatur. Auseinandersetzungen in der deutschen Sozialdemokratie der II. Internationale über Möglichkeiten und Grenzen einer sozialistischen Literaturpolitik.* Neuweid/Berlin, 1972.

Gallagher, Orvoell R. "Voluntary Associations in France." *Social Forces* 36 (December 1957), 153–60.

Giovanoli, Friedrich. *Die Maifeierbewegung. Ihre wirtschaftlichen und soziologischen Ursprünge und Wirkungen.* Karlsruhe, 1925.

Gordon, C. Wayne, and Nicholas Babchuk. "A Typology of Voluntary Associations." *American Sociological Review* 24 (1959), 22–29.

Griep, Günter, Alfred Förster, and Heinz Siegel. *Hermann Duncker—Lehrer dreier Generationen. Ein Lebensbild.* Berlin-DDR, 1974.

Groh, Dieter. *Negative Integration und revolutionärer Attentismus. Die deutschen Sozialdemokratie am Vorabend des Ersten Weltkrieges.* Frankfurt am Main/Berlin/Vienna, 1973.

Grote, Heiner. *Sozialdemokratie und Religion. Eine Dokumentation für die Jahre 1863 bis 1875*. Tübingen, 1968.

Grüttner, Michael. "Working-Class Crime and the Labour Movement: Pilfering in the Hamburg Docks 1888–1923." In Richard J. Evans, ed. *The German Working Class 1888–1933*. London/Totowa, N.J., 1982.

Gumpert, Fritz. *Die Bildungsbestrebungen der freien Gewerkschaften*. Jena, 1923.

Guttsman, W. L. *The German Social Democratic Party 1875–1933. From Ghetto to Government*. London/Boston/Sydney, 1981.

Hagelweide, Gert. *Das publizistische Erscheinungsbild des Menschen im kommunistischen Lied. Eine Untersuchung der Liedpublizistik der KPD (1919–1933) und der SED (1945–1960)*. Bremen, 1968.

Hagen, Wolfgang. *Die Schillerverehrung in der Sozialdemokratie. Zur ideologischen Formation proletarischer Kulturpolitik vor 1914*. Stuttgart, 1977.

Hall, Alex. "By Other Means: The Legal Struggle against the SPD in Wilhelmine Germany 1890–1900." *The Historical Journal* 17 (1974), 365–86.

———. *Scandal, Sensation, and Social Democracy: The SPD Press and Wilhelmine Germany 1890–1914*. Cambridge/London/New York/Melbourne, 1977.

Heine, Fritz. "Die Arbeitersportbewegung." Typescript manuscript in the Archiv der sozialen Demokratie, Bonn–Bad Godesberg.

Heufer, Ingeborg. "Deutsche Arbeiterbildungsvereine im 19. Jahrhundert." Diploma Thesis, University of Frankfurt, 1959.

Hickethier, Knut. "Karikatur, Allegorie und Bilderfolge. Zur Bildpublizistik im Dienste der Arbeiterbewegung." In Peter von Rüden, *Beiträge zur Kulturgeschichte der deutschen Arbeiterbewegung 1848–1918*. Frankfurt am Main/Vienna/Zurich, 1979.

Hoffmann, Dirk. "Sozialismus und Literatur. Literatur als Mittel politisierender Beeinflussung im Literaturbetrieb der sozialistisch organisierten Arbeiterklasse des Deutschen Kaiserreichs 1876–1918." Dissertation, University of Münster, 1975; photoduplicated printing, 1978.

Hommer, Otto. *Die Entwicklung und Tätigkeit des Deutschen Metallarbeiterverbandes*. Berlin, 1912.

Huck, Gerhard, ed. *Sozialgeschichte der Freizeit. Untersuchungen zum Wandel der Alltagskultur in Deutschland*. Wuppertal, 1980.

Husmann, Heinrich. "Lebensform und ihr Wandel beim Arbeiter in Hamborn." *Rheinisch-Westfälische Zeitschrift für Volkskunde* 4 (1957), 1–39, 133–214.

Ilgenstein, W. *Die Gedankenwelt der modernen Arbeiterjugend*. 4th ed. Berlin, 1913.

Jacobs, Nicholas. "The German Social Democratic Party School in Berlin 1906–1914." *History Workshop*, no. 5 (Spring 1978), 179–87.

Jacoby, Arthur P., and Nicholas Babchuk. "Instrumental and Expressive Voluntary Associations." *Sociology and Social Research* 47 (July 1963), 461–71.

Kaden, Werner. *Die Entwicklung der Arbeitersängerbewegung im Gau Chemnitz des Deutschen Arbeitersängerbundes von den Anfängen bis 1933.* Zwickau, 1966.

Kaiser, Jochen-Christoph. *Arbeiterbewegung und organisierte Religions-kritik. Proletarische Freidenkerverbände in Kaiserreich und Weimarer Republik.* Stuttgart, 1981.

Kannonier, Reinhard. *Zwischen Beethoven und Eisler. Zur Arbeitermu-sikbewegung in Österreich.* Vienna, 1981.

Kapp, Arno. *Vom Gesang der Handwerksgesellen zum ersten deutschen Arbeitergesangverein unter Bebel.* Halle (Saale), n.d.

———. "Die politische Funktion der Arbeitersänger unter dem Soziali-stengesetz (Ausnahmegesetz der Jahre 1878–1890)." Typescript in Arbeiterliedarchiv, Deutsche Akademie der Künste zu Berlin (DDR).

Klessmann, Christoph. *Polnische Bergarbeiter im Ruhrgebiet 1870–1945. Soziale Integration und nationale Subkultur einer Minderheit in der deutschen Industriegesellschaft.* Göttingen, 1978.

Klöcker, Michael. *Die Sozialdemokratie im Regierungsbezirk Aachen vor dem I. Weltkrieg.* Wentorf bei Hamburg, 1977.

Klusen, Ernst. *Volkslied. Fund und Erfindung.* Cologne, 1969.

Kötzschke, Richard. *Geschichte des deutschen Männergesanges, haupt-sächlich des Vereinswesens.* Dresden, [1926].

Korff, Gottfried. "Volkskultur und Arbeiterkultur. Überlegungen am Beispiel der sozialistischen Maifesttradition." *Geschichte und Gesell-schaft* 5 (1979), 83–102.

Koszyk, Kurt. *Anfänge und frühe Entwicklung der sozialdemokratischen Presse im Ruhrgebiet 1875–1908.* Dortmund, 1953.

———. "Die sozialdemokratische Arbeiterbewegung 1890 bis 1914." In Jürgen Reulecke, ed. *Arbeiterbewegung an Rhein und Ruhr.* Wup-pertal, 1974.

Krug, Peter. *Gewerkschaften und Arbeiterbildung: gewerkschaftliche Bil-dungsarbeit von ihren Anfängen bis zur Weimarer Republik.* Co-logne, 1980.

Kuczynski, Jürgen. *Geschichte des Alltags des Deutschen Volkes. Studien.* 5 vols. Berlin-DDR, 1980–82. Vol. 4: *Studien 4, 1871–1918.*

Labisch, Alfons. "The Workingmen's Samaritan Federation (Arbeiter-Samariter-Bund) 1888–1933." *Journal of Contemporary History* 13 (1978), 297–322.

Lammel, Inge. *Das Arbeiterlied.* Leipzig, 1970.

———. ed. *Bibliographie der deutschen Arbeiterliederbücher 1833–1945.* Leipzig, 1973.

———. *Das deutsche Arbeiterlied.* Leipzig/Jena/Berlin, 1962.

————. "Das Lied der deutschen Arbeiterbewegung. Von seinen Anfängen bis nach 1890." *Musik und Gesellschaft,* no. 9 (1954), 310–16; no. 10 (1954), 353–57.

————. "Politisches Lied und Volkslied in der Gesangspraxis der Arbeiterklasse." In Akademie der Künste, ed. *Arbeiterklasse und Musik. Theoretische Positionen in der deutschen Arbeiterklasse zur Musikkultur vor 1945.* Arbeitsheft 15. Berlin, 1974.

————. "Zur Rolle und Bedeutung des Arbeiterliedes." *Beiträge zur Geschichte der deutschen Arbeiterbewegung* 4 (1962), 726–42.

Landecker, Werner S. "Types of Integration and Their Measurement." *American Journal of Sociology* 56 (January 1951), 332–40.

Langer, Erich. "Das Vereinswesen." In Franz Josef Ewens, ed. *Deutsches Lied und Deutscher Sang.* Karlsruhe/Dortmund, 1930.

Langewiesche, Dieter. "Arbeiterkultur in Österreich: Aspekte, Tendenzen und Thesen." In Gerhard A. Ritter, ed. *Arbeiterkultur.* Königstein/Ts., 1979.

————. *Zur Freizeit des Arbeiters. Bildungsbestrebungen und Freizeitgestaltung österreichischer Arbeiter im Kaiserreich und in der Ersten Republik.* Stuttgart, 1979.

————, and Klaus Schönhoven. "Arbeiterbibliotheken und Arbeiterlektüre im Wilhelminischen Deutschland." *Archiv für Sozialgeschichte* 16 (1976), 135–204.

Lepenies, Wolf. "Arbeiterkultur. Wissenschaftssoziologische Anmerkungen zur Konjunktur eines Begriffs." *Geschichte und Gesellschaft* 5 (1979), 125–36.

Lepsius, M. Rainer. "Parteiensystem und Sozialstruktur: zum Problem der Demokratisierung der deutschen Gesellschaft." In Wilhelm Abel et al., eds. *Wirtschaft, Geschichte und Wirtschaftsgeschichte: Festschrift zum 65. Geburtstag von Friedrich Lütge.* Stuttgart, 1966.

Levine, Donald, and Robert Cooley Angell. "Integration." In *International Encyclopedia of the Social Sciences* (1968), 7, 372–86.

Lexikon Sozialistischer Deutscher Literatur. Von den Anfängen bis 1945. Monographisch-Biographische Darstellungen. The Hague, 1973.

Lidtke, Vernon L. "August Bebel and German Social Democracy's Relation to the Christian Churches." *Journal of the History of Ideas,* 27 (April–June 1966), 245–64.

————. *The Outlawed Party. Social Democracy in Germany, 1878–1890.* Princeton, N.J., 1966.

————. "Social Class and Secularisation in Imperial Germany. The Working Classes." *Yearbook of the Leo Baeck Institute* 25 (1980), 21–40.

————. "Socialism and Naturalism in Germany." *American Historical Review* 79 (February 1974), 14–37.

————. "Songs and Politics. An Exploratory Essay on Arbeiterlieder in the Weimar Republic." *Archiv für Sozialgeschichte* 14 (1974), 253–73.

Loreck, Jochen. *Wie man früher Sozialdemokrat wurde. Das Kommunikationsverhalten in der deutschen Arbeiterbewegung und die Konzeption der sozialistischen Parteipublizistik durch August Bebel.* Bonn–Bad Godesberg, 1977.

Lüdtke, Alf. "Rekonstruktion von Alltagswirklichkeit—Entpolitisierung der Sozialgeschichte?" In Robert Berdahl et al. *Klassen und Kultur. Sozialanthropologische Perspektiven in der Geschichtsschreibung.* Frankfurt am Main, 1982.

———. "Alltagswirklichkeit, Lebensweise und Bedürfnisartikulation. Ein Arbeitsprogramm zu den Bedingungen 'proletarischen Bewusstseins' in der Entfaltung der Fabrikindustrie." *Gesellschaft. Beiträge zur Marxschen Theorie,* no. 11 (1978), 311–50.

Mason, Edward S. *The Paris Commune.* New York, 1930.

Merriam, Alan P. *The Anthropology of Music.* Evanston, Ill., 1964.

Meyer, Wolfgang. *Das Vereinswesen der Stadt Nürnberg im 19.Jahrhundert.* Nuremberg, 1970.

Moore, Sally F., and Barbara G. Myerhoff. "Introduction: Secular Ritual: Forms and Meanings." In Moore and Myerhoff, eds. *Secular Ritual.* Assen/Amsterdam, 1977.

Moring, Karl-Ernst. *Die Sozialdemokratische Partei in Bremen 1890–1914. Reformismus und Radikalismus in der Sozialdemokratischen Partei Bremens.* Hanover, 1968.

Mosse, George L. *The Nationalization of the Masses.* New York, 1975.

Nespital, Margarete. *Das deutsche Proletariat in seinem Lied.* Rostock, 1932.

Nestriepke, Siegfried. *Geschichte der Volksbühne in Berlin.* Berlin, 1930.

Nettl, Bruno. *Folk and Traditional Music of the Western Continents.* 2nd ed. Englewood Cliffs, N.J., 1973.

Nettl, J. P. *Rosa Luxemburg.* 2 vols. London/New York/Toronto, 1966.

Nettl, Paul. *National Anthems.* Translated by Alexander Gode. 2nd ed. New York, [1967].

Nipperdey, Thomas. "Verein als soziale Struktur in Deutschland im späten 18. und frühen 19.Jahrhundert." In Hartmut Boockmann et al. *Geschichtswissenschaft und Vereinswesen im 19. Jahrhundert.* Göttingen, 1972.

Noack, Victor. *Der Deutsche Arbeiter-Sängerbund. Eine Materialsammlung des Bundes-Vorstandes.* Berlin, 1911.

———. *Deutscher Arbeiter-Sängerbund. Entstehung, Kampf und Aufstieg.* Berlin, [1931]. A revision of the 1911 edition, in page proofs but not published. In Arbeiterliedarchiv, Deutsche Akademie der Künste zu Berlin (DDR).

Nolan, Mary. *Social Democracy and Society. Working-class Radicalism in Düsseldorf, 1890–1920.* Cambridge/London/New York, 1981.

———. "The Socialist Movement in Düsseldorf, 1890–1914." Dissertation, Columbia University, 1975.

Osterroth, Franz. *Biographisches Lexikon des Sozialismus.* Vol. 1. Hanover, 1960.

Pahncke, Wolfgang. "Traditionen der Rostocker Arbeiter-Turn- und Sportbewegung. Ein Beitrag zur Geschichte der örtlichen Arbeiterbewegung." *Wissenschaftliche Zeitschrift der Universität Rostock, Gesellschafts- und Sprachwissenschaftliche Reihe* 13, nos. 2/3 (1964), 285–338.

Pforte, Dietger. *Von unten auf. Studie zur literarischen Bildungsarbeit der frühen deutschen Sozialdemokratie und zum Verhältnis von Literatur und Arbeiterklasse.* Giessen, 1979.

Pollard, Sidney. "Englische Arbeiterkultur im Zeitalter der Industrialisierung." *Geschichte und Gesellschaft* 5 (1979), 150–66.

Quataert, Jean H. *Reluctant Feminists in German Social Democracy, 1885–1917.* Princeton, N.J., 1979.

Reck, Siegfried. *Arbeiter nach der Arbeit. Sozialhistorische Studie zu den Wandlungen des Arbeiteralltags.* Lahn-Giessen, 1977.

Reese, Walter. *Zur Geschichte der sozialistischen Heine-Rezeption in Deutschland.* Frankfurt am Main/Bern, 1979.

Reulecke, Jürgen, and Wolfhard Weber, eds. *Fabrik. Familie. Feierabend. Beiträge zur Sozialgeschichte des Alltags im Industriezeitalter.* Wuppertal, 1978.

Ritter, Gerhard A. *Die Arbeiterbewegung im Wilhelminischen Reich.* Berlin-Dahlem, 1959.

———. "Workers' Culture in Imperial Germany: Problems and Points of Departure for Research." *Journal of Contemporary History* 13 (1978), 165–89.

———, ed. *Arbeiterkultur.* Königstein/Ts., 1979.

Ritter, Gerhard A., and Klaus Tenfelde, "Der Durchbruch der Freien Gewerkschaften Deutschlands zur Massenbewegung im letzten Viertel des 19. Jahrhunderts." In Heinz Oskar Vetter, ed. *Vom Sozialistengesetz zur Mitbestimmung.* Cologne, 1975.

Roberts, James S. "Wirtshaus und Politik in der deutschen Arbeiterbewegung." In Gerhard Huck, ed. *Sozialgeschichte der Freizeit.* Wuppertal, 1980.

Rose, Arnold. "Voluntary Associations in France." In Arnold Rose, *Theory and Method in the Social Sciences.* Minneapolis, Minn., 1954.

Roth, Guenther. *The Social Democrats in Imperial Germany. A Study in Working-Class Isolation and National Integration.* Totowa, N.J., 1963.

Rüden, Peter von, ed. *Beiträge zur Kulturgeschichte der deutschen Arbeiterbewegung 1848–1918.* Frankfurt am Main/Vienna/Zurich, 1979.

———. *Sozialdemokratisches Arbeitertheater (1848–1914). Ein Beitrag zur Geschichte des politischen Theaters.* Frankfurt am Main, 1973.

Saldern, Adelheid von. *Vom Einwohner zum Bürger. Zur Emanzipation der städtischen Unterschicht Göttingens 1890–1920.* Berlin, 1973.

————. "Wilhelminischen Gesellschaft und Arbeiterklasse: Emanzipations- und Integrationsprozesse im kulturellen und sozialen Bereich." *Internationale wissenschaftliche Korrespondenz* 13 (December 1977), 469–505.

Saul, Klaus. "Der Kampf um die Jugend zwischen Volksschule und Kaserne: Ein Beitrag zur 'Jugendpflege' im Wilhelminischen Reich 1890–1914." *Militärgeschichtliche Mitteilungen,* no. 1 (1971), 97–143.

————. *Staat, Industrie, Arbeiterbewegung im Kaiserreich. Zur Innen- und Sozialpolitik des wilhelminischen Deutschlands 1903–1914.* Düsseldorf, 1974.

————. "Zwischen Repression und Integration. Staat, Gewerkschaften und Arbeitskampf im kaiserlichen Deutschland 1884 bis 1914." In Klaus Tenfelde and Heinrich Volkmann, eds. *Streik. Zur Geschichte des Arbeitskampfes in Deutschland während der Industrialisierung.* Munich, 1981.

Schäfers, Hans-Joachim. *Zur sozialistischen Arbeiterbildung in Leipzig 1890 bis 1914.* Leipzig, 1961.

Scherer, Herbert. *Bürgerlich-oppositionelle Literaten und sozialdemokratische Arbeiterbewegung nach 1890.* Stuttgart, 1974.

Scheu, Josef. *Die Arbeiter-Gesangvereine und ihre Bedeutung für die sozialdemokratische Partei.* Dresden, n.d.

Schleifstein, Josef. "Bemerkungen zur sozialdemokratischen Parteischule (1906–1914)." *Zeitschrift für Geschichtswissenschaft* 5 (1957), 1291–93.

Schmierer, Wolfgang. *Von der Arbeiterbildung zur Arbeiterpolitik. Die Anfänge der Arbeiterbewegung in Württemberg 1862/63–1878.* Hanover, 1970.

Schmitt, Heinz. *Das Vereinswesen der Stadt Weinheim an der Bergstrasse. Volkskundliche Untersuchung zum kulturellen Leben einer Mittelstadt.* Weinheim an der Bergstrasse, 1963.

Schorske, Carl E. *German Social Democracy, 1905–1917. The Development of the Great Schism.* Cambridge, Mass., 1955.

Schult, Johannes. *Die Hamburger Arbeiterbewegung als Kulturfaktor.* Hamburg-Bahrenfeld, 1954.

Schuster, Hans. *Arbeiterturner im Kampf um die Jugend. Zur Geschichte des revolutionären Arbeitersports 1893–1914.* Berlin-DDR, 1962.

Schwab, Heinrich W. "Das Lied der Berufsvereine. Ihr Beitrag zur 'Volkskunst' im 19. Jahrhundert." *Zeitschrift für Volkskunde* 63 (1967), 1–15.

————. "Das Vereinslied des 19. Jahrhunderts." In Rolf Wilhelm Brednich et al., eds. *Handbuch des Volksliedes.* Vol. 1: *Die Gattungen des Volksliedes.* Munich, 1973.

Schwartze, Herbert. "Zur Geschichte des Arbeiter-Samariter-Bundes." In Kurt Kühn, ed. *Ärzte an der Seite der Arbeiterklasse. Beiträge zur*

Geschichte des Bundnisses der deutschen Arbeiterklasse mit der me-dizinischen Intelligenz. Berlin-DDR, 1973.

Selo, Heinz. *Die 'Freie Volksbühne' in Berlin. Geschichte ihrer Entste-hung und ihre Entwicklung bis zur Auflösung im Jahre 1896.* Berlin, 1930.

Siegmeister, Elie. *Music and Society.* New York, 1938; reprinted New York, 1974.

Siemering, Hertha. *Arbeiterbildungswesen in Wien und Berlin. Eine kri-tische Untersuchung. Freiburger Volkswirtschaftliche Abhandlungen,* 1. Band, 3. Ergänzungsheft. Karlsruhe, 1911.

Staudinger, Hans. *Individuum und Gesellschaft in der Kulturorganisation des Vereins.* Jena, 1913.

Stearns, Peter N. "The Effort at Continuity in Working-Class Culture." *Journal of Modern History* 52 (December 1980), 625–55.

Steenson, Gary P. *"Not One Man! Not One Penny!" German Social Democracy, 1863–1914.* Pittsburgh, Pa., 1981.

Steinberg, Hans-Josef. *Sozialismus und deutsche Sozialdemokratie. Zur Ideologie der Partei vor dem I. Weltkrieg.* Hanover, 1967.

Steiner, Herbert. *Die Gebrüder Scheu. Eine Biographie.* Vienna, 1968.

Steinitz, Wolfgang. "Arbeiterlied und Arbeiterkultur." *Beiträge zur Mu-sikwissenschft* 6 (1964), 279–88.

———. "Arbeiterlied und Volkslied." *Deutsches Jahrbuch für Volks-kunde* 12 (1966), 1–14.

———. *Deutsche Volkslieder demokratischen Charakters aus sechs Jahr-hunderten.* 2 vols. Berlin-DDR, 1954, 1962.

———. "Das Leunalied. Zu Geschichte und Wesen des Arbeitervolks-liedes." *Deutsches Jahrbuch für Volkskunde* 4, Teil 1 (1958), 3–52.

———. "Das Lied von Robert Blum." *Deutsches Jahrbuch für Volks-kunde* 7 (1961), 9–40.

Stern, Fritz. "The Political Consequences of the Unpolitical German." In Fritz Stern, *The Failure of Illiberalism. Essays on the Political Culture of Modern Germany.* New York, 1972.

Stieg, Gerald, and Bernd Witte. *Abriss einer Geschichte der deutschen Arbeiterliteratur.* Stuttgart, 1973.

Tenfelde, Klaus. "Anmerkungen zur Arbeiterkultur." In Wolfgang Rup-pert, ed. *Erinnerungsblatt. Geschichte und demokratische Identität in Deutschland.* Opladen, 1982.

———. "Bergarbeiterkultur in Deutschland. Ein Überblick." *Geschichte und Gesellschaft* 5 (1979), 12–53.

———. "Mining Festivals in the Nineteenth Century." *Journal of Con-temporary History* 13 (1978), 377–412.

Thomas, Kurt. *Arbeitergesang—Arbeitermusik. Traditionen der Arbeiter-chöre und der Arbeitermusik im Bezirk Erfurt.* Weimar, 1974.

Timmermann, Heinz. "Geschichte und Struktur der Arbeitersportbewegung 1893–1933." Dissertation, University of Marburg, 1969. Published under same title: Ahrensburg, 1973.

Trempenau, Dietmar. *Frühe sozialdemokratische und sozialistische Arbeiterdramatik (1890–1914). Entstehungsbedingungen—Entwicklungslinien—Ziele—Funktion.* Stuttgart, 1979.

Troeltsch, W., and P. Hirschfeld. *Die deutschen Sozialdemokratischen Gewerkschaften.* Berlin, 1905.

25 Jahre Arbeiter-Samariter-Bund E. V. Kolonne Hamburg 1907–1932. [Hamburg, 1932].

Ueberhorst, Horst. *Frisch, frei, stark und treu. Die Arbeitersportbewegung in Deutschland 1893–1933.* Düsseldorf, 1973.

Völkerling, Klaus. "Der Crimmitschauer Textilarbeiterstreik von 1903/04 in der frühen sozialistischen Literatur und im revolutionären Arbeitervolkslied." *Weimarer Beiträge. Zeitschrift für deutsche Literaturgeschichte* 8 (1962), 614–40.

Warriner, Charles K., and Jane Emery Prather. "Four Types of Voluntary Associations." *Sociological Enquiry* 35 (Spring 1965), 138–48.

Wendel, Hermann. *Die Marseillaise.* Zurich, 1936.

Wendorff, Werner. *Schule und Bildung in der Politik von Wilhelm Liebknecht.* Berlin, 1978.

Wuerth, Dieter. "The Politics and Sociology of Organized Labor in a Middle-Sized German Town: Göppingen 1910–1919." Dissertation, University of Wisconsin, 1974.

Wunderer, Hartmann. *Arbeitervereine und Arbeiterparteien. Kultur- und Massenorganisationen in der Arbeiterbewegung (1890–1933).* Frankfurt am Main/New York, 1980.

———. "Der Touristenverein 'Die Naturfreunde'—Eine sozialdemokratische Arbeiterkulturorganisation (1895–1933)," *Internationale wissenschaftliche Korrespondenz* 13 (December 1977), 506–20.

Index